Frommer's®

S0-CEX-291

Niagara Region
4th Edition

by Barbara Ramsay Orr

WILEY

John Wiley & Sons, Inc.

Published by:
JOHN WILEY & SONS, INC.
111 River St.
Hoboken, NJ 07030-5774

ISBN 978-1-118-10026-4 (paper); 978-1-118-10125-4 (ebk); 978-1-118-10129-2 (ebk); 978-1-118-10131-5 (ebk)

Editor: Gene Shannon
Production Editor: Lindsay Conner
Cartographer: Guy Ruggiero
Photo Editor: Richard Fox
Production by Wiley Indianapolis Composition Services

Front cover photo: Niagara Falls © Raimund Koch / Photonica / Getty Images
Back cover photo: Tasting room of Cave Springs Cellars Winery © Kevin Argue / Cephas Picture Library / Alamy Images

For information on our other products and services or to obtain technical support, please contact our Customer Care Department within the U.S. at 877/762-2974, outside the U.S. at 317/572-3993 or fax 317/572-4002.

Wiley also publishes its books in a variety of electronic formats. Some content that appears in print may not be available in electronic formats.

Manufactured in the United States of America

5 4 3 2 1

CONTENTS

4 WHERE TO STAY 45

5 WHERE TO EAT 69

6 WHAT TO SEE & DO IN THE NIAGARA REGION 97

LIST OF MAPS

ABOUT THE AUTHOR

Barbara Ramsay Orr has been writing about world travel, food, wine, and culture for over 20 years and is still awed by the beauty of her home turf. Her work has appeared in most of the major publications in Canada, in international publications, and online. She maintains a trio of blogs that document her encounters with food, with the world, and with the local scene in Niagara and has won awards for both her writing and her travel photography. While she appreciates the pleasures of a good hike or an energetic bike ride, they are still, basically, just good ways to work up an appetite.

ACKNOWLEDGMENTS

To Niagara, a place that virtually writes its own story; to Betsy and John who showed me the insider's view; to my patient husband, to Sylvia, my frequent sidekick on food adventures; and to my editor, Gene, who ruled with a light hand.

HOW TO CONTACT US

In researching this book, we discovered many wonderful places—hotels, restaurants, shops, and more. We're sure you'll find others. Please tell us about them, so we can share the information with your fellow travelers in upcoming editions. If you were disappointed with a recommendation, we'd love to know that, too. Please write to:

Frommer's Niagara Region, 4th Edition
John Wiley & Sons, Inc. • 111 River St. • Hoboken, NJ 07030-5774
frommersfeedback@wiley.com

ADVISORY & DISCLAIMER

Travel information can change quickly and unexpectedly, and we strongly advise you to confirm important details locally before traveling, including information on visas, health and safety, traffic and transport, accommodations, shopping, and eating out. We also encourage you to stay alert while traveling and to remain aware of your surroundings. Avoid civil disturbances, and keep a close eye on cameras, purses, wallets, and other valuables.

While we have endeavored to ensure that the information contained within this guide is accurate and up-to-date at the time of publication, we make no representations or warranties with respect to the accuracy or completeness of the contents of this work and specifically disclaim all warranties, including without limitation warranties of fitness for a particular purpose. We accept no responsibility or liability for any inaccuracy or errors or omissions, or for any inconvenience, loss, damage, costs, or expenses of any nature whatsoever incurred or suffered by anyone as a result of any advice or information contained in this guide.

The inclusion of a company, organization, or website in this guide as a service provider and/or potential source of further information does not mean that we endorse them or the information they provide. Be aware that information provided through some websites may be unreliable and can change without notice. Neither the publisher nor author shall be liable for any damages arising herefrom.

FROMMER'S STAR RATINGS, ICONS & ABBREVIATIONS

Every hotel, restaurant, and attraction listing in this guide has been ranked for quality, value, service, amenities, and special features using a **star-rating system.** In country, state, and regional guides, we also rate towns and regions to help you narrow down your choices and budget your time accordingly. Hotels and restaurants are rated on a scale of zero (recommended) to three stars (exceptional). Attractions, shopping, nightlife, towns, and regions are rated according to the following scale: zero stars (recommended), one star (highly recommended), two stars (very highly recommended), and three stars (must-see).

In addition to the star-rating system, we also use **seven feature icons** that point you to the great deals, in-the-know advice, and unique experiences that separate travelers from tourists. Throughout the book, look for:

special finds—those places only insiders know about

fun facts—details that make travelers more informed and their trips more fun

kids—best bets for kids and advice for the whole family

special moments—those experiences that memories are made of

overrated—places or experiences not worth your time or money

insider tips—great ways to save time and money

great values—where to get the best deals

The following abbreviations are used for credit cards:

AE	American Express	DISC	Discover	V	Visa
DC	Diners Club	MC	MasterCard		

TRAVEL RESOURCES AT FROMMERS.COM

Frommer's travel resources don't end with this guide. **Frommers.com** has travel information on more than 4,000 destinations. We update features regularly, giving you access to the most current trip-planning information and the best airfare, lodging, and car-rental bargains. You can also listen to podcasts, connect with other Frommers.com members through our active-reader forums, share your travel photos, read blogs from guidebook editors and fellow travelers, and much more.

THE BEST OF THE NIAGARA REGION

One of the world's natural wonders, Niagara Falls, rests beside bucolic vineyards, manicured gardens, and important museums that preserve the history of this often fought-over land. Bordered by the Niagara River that channels water over Niagara Falls from Lake Erie to Lake Ontario, this protected area is a culinary destination, a wine lover's delight and a historian's dream. Whether you are biking the Niagara Trail, sipping wine in one of 80 vineyards, or enjoying a play in the theaters of Niagara-on-the-Lake, the region's draw is irresistible.

THINGS TO DO   The mighty **Niagara Falls** has kept visitors in thrall since the first traveler stood at its edge. Today you can stand on the top deck of the *Maid of the Mist* ferry, visit in winter when the falling water is lit with colored lights, or even take a helicopter flight to admire the natural wonder. Beyond the Falls, stop at a roadside fruit stand for fresh cherries or homemade preserves, linger in **Niagara-on-the-Lake** to experience the world-renowned **Shaw Festival,** or shop along the town's elegant main street.

ACTIVE PURSUITS   The **Niagara Circle Route** takes cyclists on a tour of the region, including the challenging ascent alongside the historic locks of the **Welland Canal.** Ride on horseback along the white beaches of **Lake Erie** at sunset, or hike the **Niagara** portion of the **Bruce Trail** along the escarpment to experience the paths worn by the feet of early First Nation's people and the first settlers. For hardy winter visitors, there's the possibility of helping with the **Icewine harvest.**

EATING AND DRINKING   **Niagara wine country,** with its explosion of restaurants and wineries, is a favored culinary destination for tutored tastings and locally themed dining alongside the vines. Some of Canada's best chefs, whether in wine château dining rooms or casual bistros, are celebrating what's fresh and local—like verjuice vinaigrette on organic greens, chicken Veronique, fresh peach tarts, and artisanal cheeses. The region is renowned for its Riesling and Icewines, but wineries like **Le Clos Jordan** are making prize-winning reds, too.

HISTORY   The British, French, and Americans fought for control of Niagara, and the remnants of those struggles make for fascinating history in **Old Fort George, Fort Niagara,** or in the many museums like the **Laura Secord Homestead.** The 200-year anniversary of the **War of 1812** is being celebrated through 2014 with military re-enactments and festivals, while the **Niagara Falls History Museum** has been renovated and expanded to preserve the story of the battles that raged on its doorstep.

THE most UNFORGETTABLE NIAGARA REGION EXPERIENCES

○ **Visiting the Falls:** It's the jewel in the crown and the unmistakable center of attention for visitors. You haven't done the Falls justice if you've seen them only once. To see them in bright sunshine, with a "sunbow" in the mist, is one kind of thrill, but seeing the Falls illuminated at night is a different kind of beauty. My favorite views are the winter ones, when nearby trees turn into ice sculptures from the spray, and, in particularly cold winters, an ice bridge forms. You can walk behind the Falls, gaze at them from below on the *Maid of the Mist,* or fly over them by helicopter. See p. 98 in chapter 6.

○ **Dining in Wine Country:** With more than 80 wineries, Niagara has an embarrassment of great wines. The area also offers some of the best dining in the country. A casual lunch on a patio terrace, with views of the vineyards and the lake—perhaps accompanied by a chilled glass of the Riesling that Niagara does so well—is an ideal way to spend a summer afternoon. See chapter 7.

○ **Walking Through the Spring Blossoms:** Blossom Sunday is traditionally celebrated on the Sunday before Mother's Day, when the orchards are alive with color—ivory, white, and pink from apple, cherry, pear, apricot, and peach blossoms. Formal gardens, like Queen Victoria Park near the Falls, are ablaze with tulips, daffodils, foxglove, and muscari in the spring, and continue with vibrant colors right through to first frost. See chapter 6.

○ **Immersing Yourself in History:** Fort Niagara, Fort George, Old Fort Erie, and Fort Mississauga are testaments to the War of 1812. A visit to one of these forts will take you back in time. The 200th anniversary of the war will bring these historic properties to life with authentic re-enactments, and unique culinary events. Lundy's Lane Historical Museum, in its newly renovated facility that will open officially in July 2012, contains artifacts from that period, as well as a significant collection of items from the early days of the Falls. See chapter 6.

○ **Immersing Yourself in Culture:** In addition to the celebrated Shaw Theatre Festival in Niagara-on-the-Lake, which celebrated its 50th year in 2011, a variety of niche museums abound, ranging from a dollhouse collection to a printing museum, as well as artists' galleries, like the Angie Strauss Gallery in Niagara-on-the-Lake. See chapter 6.

○ **Niagara Wine Festival and the Harvest Experience:** Niagara's Food & Wine Expo, in May, is a festival of local growers and wineries that celebrates the best the area has to offer. There are more than 100 events, including tastings, tours, concerts, artisan shows, and family entertainment as the area celebrates the grape harvest in late September. Many of the wineries are eager to welcome the real aficionado to participate in the fall harvest—especially some of the smaller wineries where much of the work of harvesting and sorting the grapes is done by hand. See chapter 7.

o **Tour Niagara's Wine Country:** Touring through the small towns and larger villages along the Niagara Wine Route to visit the wineries is a pleasure not to be missed. You can do it by bike, in a limousine, on a bus tour, or on a drive-yourself visit. Whichever way you choose, you will be sure to discover wines that are delicious finds not available anywhere else but at the winery gate.

THE best SPLURGE HOTELS

o **Harbour House Hotel:** With its large, light-filled rooms in soft colors, Harbour House provides a homey respite for the visitor. Breakfast is served in the conservatory, with the hotel's famous homemade granola, and a complimentary tasting of local wines is served at 4pm in the library lobby. Harbour House is in easy walking distance to the theater, restaurants, or shopping, and is a stone's throw from the lake and the sailing boats. See p. 54.

o **Sheraton Fallsview Hotel & Conference Center:** For the ultimate sleepover that includes the Falls, check into a falls-view loft suite at the Sheraton Fallsview. Two-story-high windows capture the entire dramatic view. See p. 58.

o **Prince of Wales:** Once a bit too fussy for most tastes, the Prince of Wales Hotel has been carefully recalibrated; the result is an opulent hotel with rooms that are rich with natural light and uniquely designed bedrooms. There's a fresh rose on your pillow each night. The hotel's Churchill Bar is the watering hole of choice for actors and theater people. See p. 56.

o **The Sterling Inn & Spa:** This boutique inn spoils its visitors with large rooms, dark wood floors, and oversized showers with rain shower heads and body jets, as well as two-person Jacuzzis. **One** is the in-house spa, and the dining room, **AG,** serves some of the best food in the area. All the attractions of the Falls are a short walk away. See p. 41.

o **The Oban Inn:** The inn began life as a private home in 1824, and was extensively renovated in 2006. Rooms are decorated in an English Country style with contemporary accents. There are views of the lake and of the oldest golf course in Ontario. The **OSpa** is a soothing space that includes a lap pool and an outdoor hot spring and steam room. See p. 56.

o **The Riverbend Inn & Vineyard:** This property is under new management, and the dining room is on its way to being one of the best in the area. This romantic 21-room restored Georgian mansion is beautifully situated by the river, with a patio that looks out over the vineyards. Walking and biking trails are close by, as are all the charms of Niagara-on-the-Lake. See p. 57.

best MODERATELY PRICED HOTELS

o **Doubletree Fallsview Resort & Spa:** The public spaces of this hotel recall the designs of the Frank Lloyd Wright era, with the feel of a National Park Lodge. Ask for a king-bed room with Jacuzzi and a view of the American Falls. See p. 49.

o **Black Walnut Manor:** Nothing in the entire Niagara region compares with the Black Walnut. An old farmstead property in the country, it is equipped with the upscale urban amenities of a downtown boutique hotel. See p. 62.

- **Keefer Mansion Inn:** A perfect inn for booklovers. Bibliophiles take note: It's located near the largest book remaindering depot in North America. This carefully restored historic home has spacious rooms, each unique, and an excellent dining room and spa. See p. 65.

- **Moffat Inn:** More like a country cottage than a hotel, this inviting inn has recently been completely redone, with fresh carpets, linens, and bathrooms, but it still retains its personality. It's very British, with a pub that serves the largest number of beers on tap in the area, and a cozy spot by the fireplace for a romantic evening. See p. 60.

- **Old Bank House Historic Inn:** With such an abundance of intriguing and charming historical properties in Niagara-on-the-Lake, choosing one to highlight seems grossly unfair. However, the Old Bank is a fine example of the type of accommodations you can expect to find in the town. It has a prime location close to the theater, shops, and restaurants, yet it's on a quiet street steps away from Simcoe Park and Lake Ontario. Rooms are furnished in period decor, and a spacious veranda runs along the front of the house. The property's historical secret is that it was the site of the first branch of the Bank of Canada—the original vault is still in the house. See p. 59.

- **American Loyalist Peter Secord Inn:** For an affordable yet historic stay, book one of the two bedrooms in this authentic stone house that dates to 1782, the oldest home in Ontario. The sparkling-clean inn comes with coverlets on the four-poster beds so white they almost hurt your eyes, not to mention the polished original wide-planked floors. The inn is a short drive from both Niagara-on-the-Lake and the Falls. See p. 64.

- **Three Forty Gate Bed and Breakfast:** You certainly don't feel like you're sleeping in Aunt Martha's back bedroom when you stay here. Three Forty Gate is sleek and attractive, and within walking distance of the heart of town. See p. 59.

THE most UNFORGETTABLE DINING EXPERIENCES

- **De Luca's Wine Country Restaurant:** This cozy little bistro, with its long windows looking out to the vineyards, serves regional cuisine full of honest flavors. Each course comes with a suggested Niagara wine pairing. See p. 78.

- **AG:** Tucked inside the only boutique hotel in Niagara Falls is arguably the city's best restaurant. Chef Cory Linkson creates traditional French cuisine by harnessing the myriad flavors of local ingredients. An all-VQA wine list carries some exceptional offerings from regional vineyards. See p. 73.

- **Treadwell's Farm to Table Cuisine:** Voted one of the 10 best new restaurants in Canada the year it opened, Stephen Treadwell's Farm to Table Cuisine is an homage to locality. His elegant cooking style is married beautifully to his commitment to using the freshest local ingredients. See p. 80.

- **Elements on the Falls:** Chef Paul Pennock prepares inventive cuisine in a comfortable and relaxing dining room. But it's the view here that counts, as you won't find a better place to dine in style this close to the edge of the Falls. Even if you don't have dinner, sit at the bar for a martini and tapas at sunset and watch the colors change on the water. See p. 70.

- **Terroir La Cachette:** Although Terroir La Cachette's cuisine focuses on regional wines and ingredients, the French Provençal style that Quebecois chef Alain Levesque has perfected remains at the heart of the restaurant's dishes. It's a perfect partnership—French sensibilities and the best local ingredients. The dining room overlooks the vineyards. See p. 89.
- **Vineland Estates Winery Restaurant:** This was at one time the flagship winery dining room, the one that set the pace and style for many of the other wineries to follow. It is still one of the prettiest places to dine in the Peninsula, especially outside on the patio on a fine day. The menu is seasonal and local, and the views of the vineyards, especially at sunset, are enchanting. See p. 88.

THE most ROMANTIC NIAGARA MOMENTS

- **Awakening to a Perfect View of the Falls from Your Bed:** The high-rise hotels on Fallsview Avenue in Niagara Falls, Ontario, have spectacular views of the Falls from many of their rooms. Try the Tower Hotel, which has an angled floor-to-ceiling wall of windows and king-size beds, or the Marriott Gateway on the Falls, which has stunning loft suites with a two-story wall of windows. Order breakfast in bed, throw open the curtains, and luxuriate in the spectacular views. See p. 52 and 49.
- **A Horse-Drawn Carriage Ride in Niagara-on-the-Lake:** The historical streets are a picture-perfect setting for a romantic carriage ride in summer, when the gardens and hanging baskets are filled to overflowing with colorful blooms, or on a crisp, sunny winter day, bundled up under a blanket. The guides are knowledgeable and entertaining. See p. 40.
- **A Leisurely Meal on a Winery Patio, Overlooking the Vineyards:** There is no better way to dine than outdoors in the fresh air. A summer breeze, a glass of fine wine at your fingertips, and your amore—they all add up to a memorable experience. Try Peller Estates on a summer evening, where there are rosebushes at the end of each row of vines and the terrace twinkles with candlelight, or Vineland Estates on a warm June afternoon, with the rolling vineyards spread out before you. Some of the hotels and restaurants in wine country will provide you with a picnic lunch that you can enjoy in one of the many parks. See p. 160 and 161.
- **A Concert Under the Stars in the Vineyards at Jackson-Triggs:** Each year, the lineup of performers gets better. Sit in the amphitheater, sip a glass of wine, dine alfresco at the casual market grill, or just nibble some tapas, and enjoy the music of Canada's best—Chantal Kreviazuk, Rufus Wainright, Bruce Cockburn, the Canadian Tenors, Colin James, and Jesse Cook, to name a few who have performed here. See p. 196

THE best THINGS TO DO FOR FREE (OR ALMOST)

- **View the Falls from Both Sides of the Border:** The best views of the Falls are enjoyed in Niagara Falls, Ontario, but you are free to stroll up and down the sidewalks along the Niagara Gorge on both sides of the Niagara River to view both sets of the Falls. On Friday, Sunday, and holiday evenings at 10pm from May to September, spectacular fireworks light up the Falls. See p. 127.

- **Watch a Ship Go Through the Locks on the Welland Canal:** Lock 3 and Lock 7 are the best viewing locations. See p. 113.
- **Hike or Bike the Bruce Trail on the Niagara Escarpment:** The Bruce Trail is an 850km (528-mile) meandering path overlooking the Niagara River. The trail passes through countless orchards and wineries, yet feels secluded and wild. Hikers can experience fantastic views, waterfalls, steep inclines, and lush fauna and flora. The southern terminus of the Bruce Trail is located in Queenston Heights Park. Follow the white blazes as the trail winds along the Niagara Escarpment, a prominent ridge that cuts through the Niagara region from east to west. See p. 132.
- **Taste Wine at a Winery Tasting Room:** Some wineries charge a nominal fee for each sample but will wave the fee if you buy a bottle of wine, and a few ask for a donation to charity. Many, however, are free. Several of the small wineries have patios where you can sit outside to enjoy your wine. Some also have walking paths or are adjacent to the Bruce Trail. See p. 155.
- **Stroll Through the Niagara Parks Commission Botanical Gardens:** These gardens are open all year. The displays of flowers, shrubs, and trees are an inspiration to gardeners and a delight to everyone. See p. 126.

best ACTIVITIES FOR FAMILIES

- *Maid of the Mist* (www.maidofthemist.com): One of the oldest tourist attractions in North America, this is still the most popular activity for visitors to the Falls. Aim for one of the first sailings, which start at 9am in high season, to avoid long lines, or wait for a late-day sailing after 7pm, when the light is softer. Find a place on the upper deck if you want the best views and if you don't mind getting a bit wet. This is where you will really feel the power of the Falls. The big blue raincoats will keep you relatively dry. Tours start on both sides of the border. See p. 105.
- **Cave of the Winds:** A wooden boardwalk takes visitors to the base of the American Falls, where they get up close with the Falls. Souvenir non-slip sandals and lightweight recyclable rain ponchos are provided. Tour hours have been extended so visitors can see the fireworks displays from vantage points on the boardwalk. See p. 105.
- **Niagara's Fury:** Visit Table Rock for this new experience—the re-creation of the birth of Niagara, complete with the sights, sounds, and movements of glacial action, as glaciers calve and water rushes to create the Falls. You'll have a whole new appreciation for the Falls after you experience this 3-D sensory-surround experience. Don't miss the handmade chocolates at Pop & Lolly's. See p. 101.
- **Butterfly Conservatory:** The conservatory, on the Niagara Parkway in Ontario, is a bright and airy rainforest-like environment, with a multilevel pathway (stroller and wheelchair accessible) that winds its way through the lush foliage. Two thousand tropical butterflies, representing 50 different species, live freely in the conservatory. The trick is to walk slowly and pause often, because the most rewarding sights are usually found through quiet observation. Even boisterous kids will enjoy the soothing atmosphere of this magical jungle. See p. 102.
- **Carousel at Lakeside Park:** One of the largest and best-preserved examples of a Looff menagerie carousel, the carousel at Lakeside Park on Lake Ontario in Old

Port Dalhousie is a fantastic sight. Built in 1898, there are 69 carousel animals, arranged in four rings; and it costs only a nickel a ride! See p. 122.

- **Sheep at Featherstone Estate Winery:** If you are visiting wineries in July and early August, don't miss a visit to Featherstone. The vintners found a solution to thinning the grapevines. For 6 weeks, they send in dozens of contented sheep to munch on the lower grape leaves. Come watch and interact with the wooly workers, as well as try the winery's excellent Black Sheep Riesling. See p. 169.

- **Niagara Freefall Indoor Skydiving:** For an extreme adventure, consider flying without a plane. In this wind-tunnel experience, you can experience free-fall, do tumbling tricks, and float on a current of air. The staff will train you and supply the helmets and equipment. There's also Lazer Ball and a climbing wall. See p. 124.

- **Take a Ride on the Orchard Express:** Puddicombe Estate Farm invites kids to take a ride on a miniature train that tours the orchards, while the grown-ups visit the winery. There's also a petting zoo. See p. 172.

NIAGARA IN DEPTH

Consider this: One-fifth of all the fresh water in the world is found in the four upper great lakes—Michigan, Huron, Superior, and Erie—and all the overflow tumbles over the Falls at Niagara. That's an awesome amount of water, and it flows continuously, having been stopped only once by an ice jam in 1848, and then for only 30 hours. This unique geological formation is truly one of the wonders of the world, and as such it tends to be the feature that draws visitors. The Falls are high on the "must-see" list of every world traveler.

But while the Falls forms the heart of the area, there is far more to the Niagara region than this mighty natural phenomenon. Niagara is a place of distinct contrasts. There's the splendor of the Falls, but then, cheek-by-jowl, is the neon brightness of the Clifton Hill area, which offers a choice of adventures ranging from the drama of the casino to the zaniness of the Fun House to the breath-stopping action of free-fall skydiving. Wander a bit farther from the Falls, and you encounter picture-perfect parks, showcasing floral artistry and a tranquil butterfly conservatory.

Vying with the Falls for ascendancy is the sophistication of Niagara wine country, where internationally recognized vintages are being made, and where acclaimed chefs like Tony Deluca and Mark Picone are using the bounty of local produce to create innovative cuisine. While the architecture of the newest wineries evokes an edgy modernity, there's also a well preserved history around every corner. There's even a golf course fairway that was diverted to leave intact a field where a pivotal battle of the War of 1812 was fought. The United Empire Loyalists left their mark in the place names, the buildings, and the culture of Niagara.

And somehow, even in the hubbub of Clifton Hill, there's an inherent Canadian polish to everything.

NIAGARA TODAY

The Falls are the first things that come to mind when you mention Niagara. More than 430,000 people live in the region, but the population jumps up to millions more when you count the number of visitors. Within the region's 1,852 sq. km (715 sq. miles) is a rich mix of natural and cultural attractions.

Niagara became part of the governmental reform movement in 1970, when the provincial legislature enacted the Regional Municipality of

Niagara Act. On January 1, 1970, 12 area municipal governments and one regional government replaced the two counties and 26 municipal structures. The Niagara Regional Council is today comprised of a Chair, plus 30 Councilors representing five cities, five towns, and two townships. The 12 municipalities range from large urban, industrial, and service centers to rural locations. The area is very well placed for accessibility to major markets in North America and around the world.

Niagara is within a 1-day drive of approximately half of the population of Canada and the United States. Its major industrial sectors include tourism, manufacturing, telecommunications, agriculture and greenhouse production, and service industries. Locals and visitors alike enjoy a wealth of golf courses, wineries, parks, and marinas under a sun that shines more than 2,000 hours annually.

Niagara as a region has great potential for prosperity. The word "Niagara" has global brand recognition, and its diverse economic base ensures a degree of stability. Recent investments have been huge, from the multitude of new wineries and hotels to the C$1-billion Niagara Fallsview Casino Resort.

One momentous addition to the city is the C$100 million Scotiabank Convention Centre Niagara (SCCN), completed in April 2011. This state-of-the-art venue is home to the Niagara Food & Wine Expo, the Niagara Bridal Show, live theater, and international competitions and conventions. The SCCN is a "green" convention and meeting facility designed to foster environmental sustainability and community leadership.

There are basically four areas of interest to visitors. First are the Falls themselves and the vibrant entertainment area that has been part of the Falls experience practically since the first tourist. Second is the ever-expanding wine and culinary sector, which now is comprised of more than 80 wineries and includes many of the top restaurants in Ontario. Third is the parkland and recreational tourism sector, which includes a vast assortment of trails, golf courses, and gardens. And fourth is the historic and cultural richness of Niagara, which was one of the earliest parts of Canada to be settled, and is home to the unique Shaw Theatre Festival.

Despite economic uncertainty, the tourism and entertainment sector of the Falls continues to grow exponentially. Hilton Hotels has just completed a new C$200-million, 53-story wing, making the Hilton Hotel and Suites Fallsview the tallest hotel in Canada. Another phase of the Hilton expansion, a C$150-million 3,716-sq.-m (40,000-sq.-ft.) space, will be completed by spring 2012.

A Booming Wine Culture

The wineries of Niagara have never been more buoyant. While the early wines of the area were not stellar, a massive investment in infrastructure, and the arrival of knowledgeable winemakers and increasingly sophisticated viniculture practices have turned the region around. The wine world was shocked in spring 2009 when a prestigious wine tasting at the Montreal Restaurant La Colombe ended with an Ontario wine, Le Clos Jordanne's 2005 Claystone Terrace Chardonnay, winning top prize. The Ontario wine was a "pirate wine," in a tasting where the judges expected to only taste California and French wines.

It shouldn't have come as a surprise, though. Geographically, the Niagara region is perfect for winegrowing. Situated on the 42nd parallel—the same latitude as Bordeaux, France—Niagara also shares the cool climate, and the clay loam and limestone soil of the famous French wine-producing region. But it is Icewine, produced best here, that has brought the most fame to the area.

THE vqa APPELLATION

The **Vintners Quality Alliance (VQA)** is a provincial regulatory authority that administers Ontario's wine appellation system. Its primary functions are wine testing, audits, inspections, and compliance. It also acts as a resource for independent information about Ontario's appellations and wines of origin.

Every VQA wine meets the following standards:

○ Wine must be made from 100% fresh Ontario-grown grapes—no concentrates are permitted.

○ Grapes used must meet a quality standard for each variety (measured by natural sugar content in the ripe grapes).

○ No water can be added in the winemaking process.

○ Labels must be truthful and accurately represent the wine in the bottle.

○ All wines except for sparkling wines must be vintage dated and meet vintage requirements.

○ All wines must be packaged in glass bottles with cork, synthetic, or approved screw-cap closures.

○ All finished wines are evaluated by an expert taste panel and a laboratory analysis and must meet minimum quality standards before release.

The thriving Niagara wine industry had humble beginnings, with the first European settlers making use of the native labrusca grapes, which unfortunately did not produce palatable table wines. Modest success was achieved with Canadian hybrids, and the grape industry became established in Niagara during the early 1900s. By midcentury, six million vines were growing in the province, with the bulk of them in Niagara. French hybrids were becoming more popular, as consumer taste shifted toward dryer, lower-alcohol table wines and away from sweeter table and dessert wines.

By the 1970s, several enterprising growers had already begun planting *Vitis vinifera* vines, the so-called noble grape varietals that produce many of the world's finest wines, such as chardonnay, cabernet, gamay, and Riesling. Fertile, rich soils and a unique microclimate make Niagara a prime grape-growing region, and contrary to popular public opinion of the proposed outcome, the *vinifera* vines thrived.

The rise of Niagara wine country is the result of the drive of a handful of enterprising and visionary winemakers, like Donald Ziraldo and Karl Kaiser of Inniskillin, and John Howard, who turned Vineland Estates into a premier destination winery and restaurant. In 1974, Inniskillin received the first estate winery license since Prohibition. This was the beginning of a wine industry that would give Canada a real presence in the wine world.

The biggest contributor to the transformation of Ontario's wine industry was the introduction of international trade agreements in 1988. The loss of tariff and retail price protection put Ontario wines on par with imports from the world's most respected and well-established wine regions, and the industry was faced with surrendering its market share or reinventing itself as a worthy contender. Growers, wineries, and the provincial government decided to revitalize the wine industry, and together they rose to the challenge. Like similar appellation systems in France and Italy, in 1988, the Vintners Quality Alliance, or VQA, was formed, and helped to establish the reliability of quality of Ontario wines.

Today, Niagara has approximately 6,500 hectares (16,062 acres) under vine, in an area stretching from Niagara-on-the-Lake in the east to Grimsby in the west. More than 80 wineries now make their home in Niagara, many with fine restaurants and boutiques on-site. A large number offer wine-tasting and tours to the public. Niagara wines consistently bring home medals and awards from many of the world's most prestigious wine competitions. World attention has turned to the Niagara wine industry, not least because of the superb quality of its Icewine, a dessert wine produced from grapes that have been left on the vine after the fall harvest to freeze naturally. The frozen grapes are handpicked and immediately pressed to capture the thick, yellow-gold liquid, high in natural sugars and acidity.

Another important factor in the rise of Niagara wines was the initiative of the Ontario government, in the early 1980s, to subsidize the removal of the old Labrusca vines and the planting of European *vinifera* vines. Those vines are now 20 and 30 years old in some vineyards, and the wines being produced are exceptional.

While the area is best known for its whites, especially Riesling and chardonnay, reds are becoming just as important. Marynissen Estates, Stratus, Le Clos Jordanne, and Daniel Lenko are all names that are producing some of the finest red wines in the country.

With this boost in productivity and quality, Niagara has become a wine destination, and there is an energy and experimental zeal here that is reminiscent of the early days of Napa Valley. Now prominent Canadian celebrities are putting their names on Niagara wines. Dan Ackroyd, Wayne Gretzky, and Mike Weir all have their own labels. A new solar-powered winery, Hinterbrook Estate Winery, has begun operations, as well as Between The Lines Winery, operated by two winemakers who claim to be, at 23 and 26, the youngest in the area. In 2010, the Niagara Wine Festival attracted more than 500,000 visitors.

A Culinary Hot Spot

The culinary development of the area has developed in lockstep with the wineries. Because this is a unique agricultural area, the produce of its farms is exceptional and diverse, and an emphasis on organic and sustainable farming practices has added to the quality. In addition to orchards of peaches, pears, plums, apples, and cherries, there are unique crops like lavender, specialty greens, nuts, heritage berries, and, surprisingly, kiwis. For visitors who wish to experience the agricultural bounty, there's a culinary trail that will help you search out even the smallest niche producer.

The readily available supply of fresh and quality produce has lured restaurateurs and chefs to open top-end establishments, and most of the major wineries have excellent restaurants as a part of their developments. Visitors these days come with the expectation of a great meal when they visit the Peninsula and are seldom disappointed.

Checks & Balances

While this growth is obviously good economically, the rapid expansion of tourism highlights one of the region's primary concerns: How much growth is too much? There are days in July and August when the crowds make it almost impossible to see the Falls themselves. Parking is difficult to find, streets are choked with cars, and many of the attractions have long lines. Golf courses are beautiful, but they are also huge users of pesticides and chemicals. Wineries are too, although many of the wineries are moving toward organic or biodynamic production.

Thankfully, there were visionaries in power who could foresee the need to preserve and protect the area around the Falls. In a brilliant move in 1885, the Niagara Parks Commission was created to act as steward for the green spaces in Niagara Falls and the Niagara River corridor from Niagara Falls to Niagara-on-the-Lake. This area has been kept as parkland, and it is maintained primarily by students of the Niagara Parks School of Horticulture. As a result, the parkland and trails are green and lush, and the drive from the Falls to Niagara-on-the-Lake is one of the prettiest in Canada. You can also hike or bike it. The Niagara Peninsula is considered part of the Carolinian Life Zone, making up the northernmost edge of the deciduous forest region in eastern North America.

The work done by Niagara Parks was part of the reason that the Niagara Escarpment was declared a **World Biosphere Reserve** by the United Nations Educational, Scientific and Cultural Organization (UNESCO) on April 4, 1990. The wildlife of the Niagara Escarpment, with its wide diversity of birds, mammals, reptiles, and amphibians, including a number of rare or endangered species, was a contributing factor to the UNESCO decision.

The Niagara Gorge is home to 21 Red Mulberry trees, a rare native tree that is on the endangered species list. The Gorge is also the only place where the endangered Northern Dusky Salamander is found, living in a few coldwater seeps along the face of the gorge. Niagara Parks also operates the People Mover, a shuttle-bus system intended to aid transportation along the Niagara River and help reduce automobile crowding near the Falls. The buses are powered by propane and include a trailer unit during most popular hours. In the long term, the Commission is planning a fixed track transit system along the Niagara River Parkway.

But even the good care that Niagara Parks has taken has not totally stopped the effects of the human footprint. The Niagara Glen Nature Reserve inside the parkland, for example, contains one of the largest concentrations of species at risk anywhere in Canada. That's the result of too many visitors who wander off the hiking trails and endanger vulnerable habitats.

And the Niagara Parks Commission itself has had a rough time in the past few years. Doubts about its methods of awarding contracts, accusations of cronyism and elitism, and some questionable spending practices have led to a complete overhaul of the board. A new direction has emerged for the Commission, which will take their work toward preserving the heritage and the natural beauty of Niagara away from some of the less authentic ventures of the past.

Cultural Preservation

History and culture continue to be a strong drawing card for visitors to the area, and with the 200th anniversary of the War of 1812 on the horizon, the museums, historic forts, and monuments are getting face-lifts. The federal government has fully supported the bicentennial celebrations. About C$12 million has been allocated to sites associated with the War of 1812 in Ontario, Quebec, and New Brunswick.

One sign of this commitment is the restoration of the statue of General Brock on Queenston Heights. On April 5, 1929, during a heavy gale, the outstretched arm of the statue of General Brock broke off and fell to the ground, breaking into three pieces. The arm and the entire upper portion of the statue were replaced. Structural problems with the arm and the base, however, were detected in 2004, and the statue was closed to the public for 4 years as repairs were made. It was reopened in spring

2009, with a new schedule of tours and interpretive activities designed for this important historical venue.

The Laura Secord Homestead has been enlarged and improved, McFarland House has added a conservatory that will serve as a tearoom year-round (as well as improving existing facilities), and Old Fort Erie had undergone significant improvements. Close to C$10 million will ultimately be spent on heritage projects in Niagara before the 2012 festivities begin.

The internationally known Shaw Theatre Festival in Niagara-on-the-Lake has added a new performance space and continues to attract large audiences despite the economic downturn. The festival marked its 50th anniversary in 2011.

LOOKING BACK AT NIAGARA
From Hunting Ground to Battlefield

The history of the Niagara region stretches back 10,000 years, to the time when the glaciers of the last ice age retreated north. Vast herds of game roamed the boreal forests surrounding Lake Ontario and its environs, bringing tribes of hunters to the area. For several millennia, the first peoples of Niagara survived as hunters, fishers, gatherers, and eventually agriculturalists.

The first Europeans arrived in the mid-1600s, driven by the desire to expand the fur trade and led by French explorers and missionaries. Although several white men visited the Falls prior to Father Louis Hennepin, he was the first to record a description of the mighty wonder of nature following his visit in 1678. His account of the Falls was a dramatic exaggeration, leading to the production of a hand-tinted engraving that depicted the Falls much higher and narrower than in reality, with mountains rising in the distance. This misrepresentation became the standard pictorial representation for many decades to follow.

For the next hundred years or so, the Niagara area remained populated by various Native groups, although their numbers were increasingly depleted by European-borne diseases and clashes with warring tribes.

French and British troops fought for control of the continent during the first half of the 18th century. During this period, Fort Niagara was built by the French on the east bank of the Niagara River, at the point where it flows into Lake Ontario. At the end of the Seven Years War in 1763, all of New France was ceded to Great Britain, and the British established control of the Niagara River. Fort Erie was built in 1764 on the west side of the mouth of the Niagara River and Lake Erie.

The next wave of newcomers to the district was the United Empire Loyalists, who fled to Upper Canada seeking sanctuary from the fierce fighting of the American Revolution of 1775 to 1783. When the war ended, remaining Loyalists were expelled from American territory and many of them settled along the western shore of the Niagara River.

At the end of the American Revolution, Fort Niagara, on the eastern side of the Niagara River, was in the hands of the United States. To protect their interests in Upper Canada, the British constructed a fort on the opposite side of the river. In 1802, Fort George was completed and became the headquarters for the British army, local militia, and the Indian Department.

The War of 1812 was the last military confrontation between Canada and the U.S. Eager to expand the nation, the United States declared war on Britain in June 1812. By attacking on four fronts, one of which was Niagara, the Americans hoped to

Looking Back at Niagara

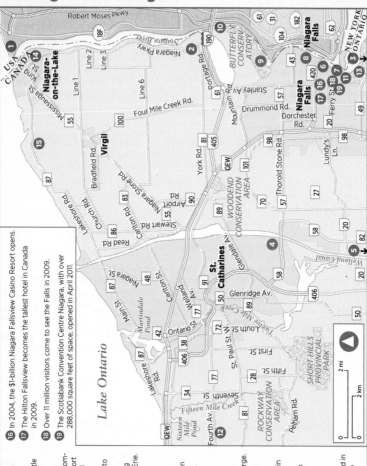

1 Fort Niagara is built by the French in 1726 on the east bank of the Niagara River.

2 British General Sir Isaac Brock is killed at the Battle of Queenston Heights in 1812, one of the largest battles of the War between America and Britain.

3 From the early to mid-1800s, thousands of freedom-seeking black slaves cross the Niagara River at Fort Erie, one of the main termini of the Underground Railroad.

4 Canadian heroine Laura Secord helps the British to victory at the Battle of Beaverdams in 1813.

5 First Welland Canal is completed in 1829, opening a shipping lane between Lake Ontario and Lake Erie.

6 The First *Maid of the Mist* is launched in 1846.

7 Niagara Falls stops running in 1848 due to an ice dam.

8 "The Great Blondin" crosses the Niagara Gorge on a tightrope in 1859.

9 Niagara Parks Commission is formed in 1885 to preserve the natural beauty of the Falls and the Niagara River Corridor.

10 The first large-scale hydro electric station in the world begins operation in 1895 in the Niagara Gorge.

11 In 1901, schoolteacher Annie Taylor becomes the first person to survive a plunge over the Falls.

12 Hybrid grape varieties are introduced to Ontario in 1940 and the wine industry is born.

13 In 1953, Marilyn Monroe puts the Falls on the map with her film, *Niagara*.

14 The Shaw Theatre Festival begins in 1962 in the Courthouse in Niagara-on-the-Lake.

15 The Vintners' Quality Alliance (VQA) is introduced in 1989 to ensure standards of excellence in Ontario winemaking.

16 In 2004, the $1-billion Niagara Fallsview Casino Resort opens.

17 The Hilton Fallsview becomes the tallest hotel in Canada in 2009.

18 Over 11 million visitors come to see the Falls in 2009.

19 The Scotiabank Convention Centre Niagara, with over 288,000 square feet of space, opened in April 2011.

achieve a swift victory. Several bloody battles ensued over the next 2 years, but the eventual outcome was a stalemate. The Treaty of Ghent, signed on Christmas Eve 1814, brought the hostilities to a close and the Niagara River was reestablished as the border between Upper Canada and the U.S. Throughout the region, historic forts, monuments, and memorials stand as reminders of the war.

Upper Canada became the first place in the British Empire to abolish slavery, when Governor General John Graves Simcoe introduced legislation in 1793. In the years that followed, the country became a haven for black men and women escaping from slavery in the American South. To enable the freedom seekers to reach safety, supporters of the abolition of slavery throughout America and Canada provided secret "safe houses," where escaping slaves were given food, shelter, and directions north. The routes that passed by the safe houses became known as the Underground Railroad. Niagara was one of the main termini for the freedom seekers. Fugitive men, women, and children were transported across the Niagara River at Fort Erie. Niagara Falls, Niagara-on-the-Lake, and St. Catharines became important settlement areas for refugee slaves. From the early to the mid-1800s, thousands of fugitive slaves made their way into Canada through Fort Erie.

The Birth of Tourism at the Falls

Tourists first began to visit the Falls in the 1820s. Official guides were available to take sightseers on a tour of the major points of interest in the area. By the time the first *Maid of the Mist* steamboat was launched on the American side of the Falls in 1846, with its accompanying water-powered Inclined Railway to take passengers down the face of the gorge to the boat dock, the Falls were welcoming 50,000 summer visitors a year. A mere decade later, following the completion of the world's first railway suspension bridge, which included a plank roadway for foot passengers and horse-drawn carriages on its underside, Niagara Falls became the best-known tourist destination in North America.

One of the main attractions in those early days of tourism was Table Rock, a large platform of dolostone at the edge of the Horseshoe Falls. Although the overhang

HISTORY OF NIAGARA

1678 Father Louis Hennepin is the first person to record a description of the Falls.

1721 A trading post is established by the French at Lewiston to protect the fur trade.

1726 The French build a sturdy stone fort on the east bank of the Niagara River at the point where it flows into Lake Ontario, called Fort Niagara.

1759 Fort Niagara is attacked by the British. Nineteen days later, the French surrender and withdraw from the Niagara Peninsula.

1764 Fort Erie is constructed by the British.

1792 John Graves Simcoe is appointed Governor of Upper Canada and the town of Newark (now known as Niagara-on-the-Lake) is established as the capital.

1793 The first Parliament of Upper Canada passes a bill that prevents further slavery in Upper Canada.

1812 The War of 1812 commences when the fledgling country America declares war on Britain, sending U.S. forces north into Canada. Because of its proximity to the

continues

dramatically collapsed in 1850, the landmass remains the most beloved vantage point on the Canadian side. Just over a century later, most of Prospect Point, the prime location to view the Falls on the American side, collapsed and 185,000 tons of rock crashed into the gorge below.

As the crowds grew, a rowdy strip of concession stands, hotels, and carnival booths sprung up, all eager to grab a piece of the tourist dollar. Despite the popularity of these attractions, many members of the public were concerned at the desecration of such a wonder of nature. Accordingly, in 1878, Lord Dufferin, then Governor General of Canada, proposed that a strategy be developed to preserve the natural beauty of Niagara Falls. Seven years later, the Niagara Parks Commission was founded. Its mandate was to preserve and enhance the natural beauty of the Falls and the Niagara River corridor. On the U.S. side of the border, the New York State Reservation at Niagara Falls was established in the same year. But the kitsch could not be suppressed, and to this day, Niagara audaciously exhibits both extremes of the tourist experience—the majesty and grandeur of the Falls, surrounded by beautifully groomed parks and pristine gardens, and the noise and clutter of the Clifton Hill district and Lundy's Lane, with its neon lights, fast food, carnival atmosphere, and motel strip.

Niagara's Other Industries: Shipping and Agriculture

The commercial growth at the Falls was not restricted to the tourist industry. Engineers and scientists of the 19th century eagerly contemplated the potential of the powerful rapids and waterfalls. Since the 1700s, mills had made use of the water to drive their machinery, but the full potential of Niagara to produce hydroelectric power could not be realized until the invention of the alternating-current system, the basis of the long-distance transmission of electricity. In 1891, Nikola Tesla, who had invented alternating-current dynamos, transformers, and motors, sold his patents to George Westinghouse. Together, they designed generators for the first large-scale hydroelectric plant in the world, the Adams Station. Since then, a number of power

	border, Niagara becomes the focus of a major offensive.		Table Rock marks the beginning of uncontrolled commercial development.
1813	The first wave of freedom-seeking black slaves arrives in the region via the Underground Railroad.	1829	The first Welland Canal is completed, opening a shipping lane between Lake Ontario and Lake Erie.
1814	The War of 1812 comes to an end upon the signing of the Treaty of Ghent. The Niagara River is reestablished as the border between Upper Canada and the United States.	1845	The second Welland Canal opens, with 27 locks of cut stone replacing the 40 original wooden locks.
1820	The Falls become a sightseeing attraction for the burgeoning tourist class.	1846	The first *Maid of the Mist,* a steamboat carrying passengers daringly close to the American and Horseshoe Falls, is launched.
1827	The establishment of a strip of hotels between Robinson Street and	1848	The Niagara River ceases its flow and the Falls stop for 30 long, silent hours when millions of tons of ice at the

stations have been constructed in Canada and the U.S., and in total, the Niagara River now generates approximately 4,400 megawatts of electricity. In order to protect the thunder of the Falls as a major tourist attraction, only half of the river's flow is available for power, mostly at night. But only the most perceptive of tourists can distinguish the difference in flow.

The Niagara Tunnel Project will add, with the building of a huge tunnel beneath the city of Niagara Falls, enough clean water power to generate an extra 1.6 billion kilowatt-hours of electricity annually—enough to meet the electricity needs of about 160,000 homes. The tunnel is 14.4m (47.3 ft.) high—as tall as a four-story building—and more than 10km (6.3 miles) long. It's so big you could easily drive a double-stacked container freight train through it. The structure was created by Big Becky, the largest hard rock boring machine in the world. The breakthrough ceremony was held on May 13, 2011, as Big Becky officially broke through to the surface, ending the mining portion of the project. The tunnel is slated to be finished in 2013.

The other major endeavor that boosted the area's economy was the construction of a shipping canal between Lake Erie and Lake Ontario. The St. Lawrence River and the Great Lakes form the largest inland waterway in the world, extending 3,700km (2,299 miles) from the Atlantic Ocean to the heart of North America, and a canal was needed to bypass the Niagara River corridor and establish a mighty commercial shipping route.

The first canal was completed in 1829. Consisting of 40 wooden locks, the canal served its purpose for only a few years before deterioration of the wood and the increasing size of ships required a second canal to be built. The Second Welland Canal had 27 cut stone locks and went into operation in 1845. In 1881, a third canal was built, following the same route as previous canals in the southern part of the region, but taking a new line in the north. The banks of the Third Welland Canal were kept free of industry by government decree. The fourth canal, known as the Welland Ship Canal, was completed in 1932. The number of locks was drastically reduced to eight and the canal adopted a direct north-south route over the Escarpment.

---

source of the river block the channel. The ice dam is eventually released by the forces of nature, and a solid wall of water crashes over the brink of the Falls.

1850 The Falls entertain 60,000 visitors a year.

1855 With the completion of the first railway suspension bridge across the gorge, and the arrival of the steam train in the town of Clifton, Niagara Falls becomes the best-known tourist destination in North America.

1859 Frenchman Jean Francois Gravelet, known as "The Great Blondin," is the first tightrope walker to cross the gorge of the Niagara River.

1881 The third Welland Canal is constructed. Part of the route is altered, and unlike the previous two canals, the banks are kept free of mills by government policy.

1885 The Niagara Parks Commission is founded. Its mandate is to preserve and enhance the natural beauty of the Falls and the Niagara River corridor.

1888 The Niagara Parks Commission opens Queen Victoria Park, a 62-hectare (153-acre) park adjacent to the Horseshoe Falls.

continues

Agricultural development of the region was aggressively pursued due to the unique combination of climate, physical geography, soil, and location. More than 50% of the Niagara land base is farmed, although increasing pressure for urban expansion and urban-type land use is a threat. Fruit trees dominate the agricultural landscape, although greenhouses and agri–food processing industries (including wineries) generate the most revenue in the agricultural sector of Niagara's economy.

NIAGARA IN POPULAR CULTURE: BOOKS, FILM & MUSIC.

Books

While the Falls and surrounding area have been scenic backdrops for films, they have also inspired writers to use Niagara as the setting, the catalyst, and sometimes the foils for their books. Early writers like Mark Twain and Nathaniel Hawthorne wrote travel stories about their visits to the Falls. Novels about the Falls include Tom Marshall's *Voices on the Brink: A Border Tale*; Joyce Carol Oates's *The Falls: A Novel*; *Niagara* by Robert Lewis Taylor; *Too Close to the Falls* by Catherine Gildiner; *Falling* by Anne Simpson; and *The Whirlpool* by Governor-General Award–winning author Jane Urquhart.

Music

As one would expect, the thunder of the Falls has inspired musicians and composers. Of the pieces by European visitors, *Niagara* (violin and piano ca. 1845), by the Norwegian violinist Ole Bull, is probably the earliest. Rimsky-Korsakov visited the Falls in 1863, Offenbach in 1876, and Tchaikovsky in 1891. Two years later, Dvořák stood in silence for several minutes, as though hypnotized, then exclaimed "Lord God, this will become a symphony in b minor." Ravel visited in 1928, but while these famous composers were undoubtedly moved by and perhaps unconsciously inspired by the

1895	The first large-scale hydroelectric station in the world begins operation in the Niagara Gorge, using alternating-current generators.		from crossing the frozen Niagara River during the winter.
1900	Irish-American Fenian sympathizers target Lock 24 of the Welland Canal in an unsuccessful bombing attack.	1914	More than one million tourists a year visit the Falls.
1901	Schoolteacher Annie Taylor is the first person to conquer the Falls, when she plunges over the Horseshoe Falls in a barrel. She survives, gaining fame but not the fortune she had eagerly sought.	1922	The Clock Tower, now a well-known landmark on Queen Street in Niagara-on-the-Lake, is erected as a memorial to the Niagara men who died in World War I.
1912	Three tourists lose their lives on the "ice bridge" when it suddenly breaks up, and from this point people are prohibited	1925	The Falls are illuminated for the first time, setting off a nightly event that has continued uninterrupted since that time, much to the delight of millions of visitors.

Falls, none of them actually named a piece after Niagara, although sketches for a Dvořák piece do exist. Works by U.S. composers include Anthony Philip Heinrich's *The War of the Elements and the Thundering of Niagara* (1845); George Bristow's *Niagara Symphony* for voices and orchestra (1898); Harvey Gaul's *The Masque of Niagara* (1934), which includes "Thunder of Waters" and "Indian River Song" sections; and Johan Franco's *Rainbow Bridge Nocturne* for the Rainbow Tower carillon.

EATING & DRINKING IN NIAGARA

There is little doubt that food is often the first access point through which visitors absorb local culture. Perhaps that's why travelers will frequently make their destination choices based on the unique culinary adventures they may experience there. Such travelers who visit the Niagara region will not be disappointed, as it is exceptionally blessed in its culinary richness. Not only is it a unique climate, but the area has also benefited from years of carefully planned growth and a farsighted objective of preserving this unique space from overdevelopment. In addition, the movement toward more organic growing practices, and toward celebrating local products, began here early. As a result, a broad spectrum of fresh produce abounds that will beguile any traveling foodie.

For the visitor intent on sampling the best local produce that Niagara has to offer, you can't find a better place to start than the **Niagara Culinary Trail Map.** The Culinary Trail has more than 65 member farmers and producers. The map is available at tourist offices and many businesses, or can be downloaded from www.niagara culinarytrail.com. There is a useful NCT Culinary Guide, also downloadable from that website, that provides behind the scenes information about local food, farmers, chefs, and markets.

There's also an excellent map to adjacent Norfolk County, the green basket of Ontario. For a free copy, call ☎ **800/699-9038,** or pick up a copy at any of Norfolk

1930s The government takes on a series of projects to boost tourism to Niagara, including the construction of the roadway now known as Queen Elizabeth Way and the reconstruction of Fort George, which had been destroyed in the War of 1812.	**1950** The Floral Clock, consisting of 15,000 plants, is constructed along the Niagara Parkway north of the Botanical Gardens.
	1953 Niagara Falls becomes the backdrop for the Marilyn Monroe film *Niagara.*
1932 The fourth Welland Canal, consisting of eight concrete locks in a direct north-south route over the Niagara Escarpment, opens.	**1954** Prospect Point, the most famous viewing point for the Falls on the American side, collapses into the gorge below.
1940s Hybrid grape varieties are introduced to Ontario and a fledgling wine industry is born.	**1960** A 7-year-old boy is swept over the Horseshoe Falls following a boating accident in the upper Niagara River, wearing only a lifejacket. He survives and is rescued by the *Maid of the Mist* tourist boat.

continues

ounty's tourist information centers in Port Dover, Simcoe, Delhi, Waterford, and Port Rowan.

Eating

When an area is this rich in produce, it's hard for the best chefs to resist. Rarely do visitors plan a trip to the Falls without a careful deliberation of the dining options. And they are many and they are superb. Some complain that the "gourmet" restaurants are overpriced, but I have not found that to be true. What needs to be remembered is that organic and locally produced, not to mention highly perishable, products like pea shoots, baby organic greens, and herb tendrils, are the result of often labor-intensive handwork, and that comes at a price. When the chef serves his own smoked ketchup, and the charcuterie comes from a local producer whose output is small, you need to expect the cost will reflect the effort required.

In spring, for example, area restaurants celebrate the wild onion—called ramps—in many dishes. There's Ontario Spring lamb on offer, its special flavor the result of the lamb perhaps having dined on the young grape leaves in the vineyards. Then local strawberries arrive, more flavorful than those raised in warmer climates, followed by our own tender asparagus. They hit restaurant menus as soon as the farmers can harvest them.

Soon after, cherries, plums, apricots, and the region's world-renowned peaches begin to show up. They appear in various guises that range from a dried cherry vinaigrette to a peach melba, from plum salsa to apricot gelato. Of course the grape figures prominently; its green juice pressed from young grapes is used in vinaigrette and chicken Veronique, with white wine, brie, and green seedless grapes.

There are also many affordable alternatives to the kind of culinary masterpieces you will find at the winery restaurants and fine dining rooms. There are pubs and little bistros frequented by locals where the quality is excellent and the prices moderate. There are also picnic options, provided by several of the wineries and some of the food stores, which will supply you with the makings of a memorable alfresco meal.

1962	The Shaw Theatre Festival stages its first two productions in the old courthouse in Niagara-on-the-Lake.
1969	The flow over the American Falls is stopped completely for several months while the feasibility of removing much of the loose rock from the base of the waterfall is investigated. It is decided that the expense would be prohibitive.
1970s	Local grape growers begin planting *viniferas*, the so-called noble grape varietals that produce many of the world's finest wines—cabernet, chardonnay, gamay, and Riesling.
1973	The purpose-built Shaw Festival Theatre opens in Niagara-on-the-Lake.
1975	Niagara-based Inniskillin Wines is granted the first new winery license in Ontario since 1929.
1979	Niagara Falls finds Hollywood fame once again when scenes from *Superman II* are filmed there.
1988	The introduction of international trade agreements induces the Niagara wine region to reinvent itself as a worthy world competitor in order to survive.
1989	The Vintners' Quality Alliance appellation system is introduced to

There are a full range of restaurants in Niagara Falls, particularly around Clifton Hill. Head down the Niagara Parkway and you will find six restaurants and several food outlets operated by the Niagara Parks Commission, and offering views of the Canadian Horseshoe Falls, the American Falls, the golf courses, the river, and the Niagara Gorge. Farther down, the wineries begin, many of them with excellent dining rooms that use local ingredients to complement the flavors of the Niagara wines.

Niagara-on-the-Lake is full of prime dining possibilities, often in historic settings.

The city of St. Catharines offers many variations on the dining experience, from the sophistication of the cuisine at Wellington Court to the casual take-away of the Bleu Turtle. In nearby Port Dalhousie, Stephen Treadwell's restaurant is a local gem, chosen as one of the 10 best new restaurants in Canada by *Enroute* magazine.

You will not go hungry in Niagara.

The Niagara Wine Experience

What makes Niagara wine country different from other wine regions is the *joie de vivre* that you find, almost without exception, at every winery. There is little pretension here. That energy translates into an experience that is relaxed and informal. And if you are a true connoisseur of wine, you'll find the winemakers are happy to answer questions and engage in conversation.

That energy also means that many of the wineries, especially the newer ones, are open to new ideas. Foreign Affair in Vineland is producing the area's first *amarone*-style Niagara wines, a result of the owner's sojourn in Tuscany. Daniel Lenko is trying a white cabernet, a peachy and delicious rose wine, while Southbrook recently brought out Canada's first certified Demeter Biodynamic wine. Pondview Estate Winery received its biodynamic certification in 2011.

John Howard's Megalomaniac Winery is perched atop the highest point on the Escarpment between Toronto and Niagara, but the winery is all underground. You can't even see the building until you swing around a curve in the road and encounter the main gate. If you stand at the top of the hill that disguises the winery, you can see, to the left, the CN tower in Toronto, and to the right, the mist from Niagara Falls.

ensure standards of excellence in Ontario winemaking.

1996   The 150th anniversary of the launch of the first *Maid of the Mist* is celebrated.

2004   The C$1-billion Niagara Fallsview Casino Resort opens.

2007   An astounding 10 million visitors a year pour into the Niagara region.

2010   Hilton Hotel and Suites Fallsview officially becomes the tallest hotel in Canada with the addition of its new 59-story wing.

2011   Scotiabank Convention Centre Niagara opens, providing a much needed modern venue for local, national, and international events and conferences.

MOVIES

When you are as spectacular as Niagara, you are bound to end up on film. Its star power has attracted the rich and famous for years, from Aaron Burr's daughter and Princess Diana, to Brad Pitt and his children, who took a cruise on the *Maid of the Mist* while mommy Angelina Jolie was filming her new action movie, *Salt*. Niagara Falls is also the birthplace of James Cameron, the director who filmed *Titanic* and *Avatar*.

Niagara (1953)   The Falls served as the co-star alongside Marilyn Monroe in this story of forbidden love, deception, and a failed marriage, with a murder plot thrown in. *Niagara*'s location shots were done in Niagara Falls, Ontario, while the rest of the movie was shot on a sound stage in Hollywood. While the movie was not a huge blockbuster, it showed the Falls in all their dramatic splendor. This is the only Marilyn Monroe movie in which her character dies.

Superman II (1980)   Fans and media clustered around the Falls to get a glimpse of the stars, Christopher Reeve and Margot Kidder, during filming. The Falls scenes were shot in some of the busy tourist areas, but the movie shooting went off without incident. While the Falls were obviously wonderful, they didn't measure up to Superman. As Lois Lane says in the movie, "Once a girl's seen Superman in action, Niagara Falls kind of leaves you cold. You know what I mean?"

Pirates of the Caribbean: At World's End (2006)   Most viewers thought that the scene that shows the ship going over a waterfall was computer-generated animation. In fact, that was Niagara Falls. The producers of the movie shot footage of the Falls from the American side, and then used that footage to create their world-ending waterfall in this blockbuster film starring Johnny Depp, Orlando Bloom, and Keira Knightley.

Canadian Bacon (1985)   Alan Alda, Rip Torn, and John Candy star in this comedy in which the United States decides to invade Canada. It is the only fictional film written, directed, and produced by Michael Moore. Many of the scenes were filmed in and around Niagara Falls.

The Dead Zone (1983)   This chilling story, adapted from the Stephen King novel, was filmed largely in the Niagara area. A David Cronenberg film, it starred Christopher Walken and Martin Sheen and tells the story of Johnny Smith, a New England schoolteacher who is left in a coma after a car accident. When he awakens, he discovers he has psychic powers. Various locations in and around Niagara-on-the-Lake seen in the movie include the Court House, Simcoe Park, St. Mark's Anglican Church, and the gazebo in Queen's Royal Park.

A large part of the thrill of visiting Megalomaniac is that you are invited in to where the action happens, the heart of the wine production area. And as at many of the smaller wineries, you can rarely buy these wines anywhere else. Production is limited, so when it's gone—it's gone! So if you taste one you like, make sure to snap up a bottle then and there.

There is also the varied and beautiful architecture of many of the wineries. Peninsula Ridge is a vision of Victorian dignity, Southbrook is a proud modern lavender statement by architects Diamond and Schmitt, and Jackson-Triggs is an architectural inspiration that combines the tradition of post-and-beam and stone with aluminum and glass, while Château des Charmes recalls the grandeur of a French manor house.

COOLER souvenirs

Never head out for a trip down the Peninsula without a cooler in the trunk. I long ago gave up bringing home T-shirts or trinkets from my trips. Now I bring home unique foods that I share with family and friends—jars of preserves, jams, sauces, cookbooks, cheeses, wines, and chocolates. I once returned from Niagara with a complete meal in the cooler, from an organic rack of lamb from Lake Land Meats to a perfect peach tart from the Pie Plate.

Visit Colaneri Estate Winery to see a work in progress—the Italian-Romanesque style winery will someday be the largest of the winery buildings, but it is developing in stages, with a completion date "sometime in the future." It is a unique place to see, and enjoyable to envision its ultimate conclusion.

Your tour of the wine country depends on the type of traveler you are. If you like to have precise instructions, a timetable, and a well-planned itinerary, you might want to consider using one of the many excellent tour companies that run wine route tours (see chapter 7 for some suggestions). Using VIA Rail, tour companies have put together packages that require you simply to board a train in Toronto; from here on in, every other detail is taken care of. First you are picked up at the station in either St. Catharines or Niagara Falls by limousine, then you spend the day touring a selection of wineries, enjoy a great lunch, and are delivered back to the station in time to return to Toronto. Other tours take you by trolley or by bus, or, for the adventurous, by bike, to a selection of vineyards. The character and scope of the tours is highly varied and comes at several price points.

For the more independent visitor, a self-driving tour of the vineyards is easy to plan. One of the most useful guides for touring the Niagara wine country is put out by the Wine Council of Ontario each spring. It lists all the members, with pictures, a brief description of the wines and the winemakers, and an excellent map to all the member properties. The vineyards are not too far apart, and the dining possibilities are endless.

For the free spirit, I recommend setting out with a map and an open mind. Most of the wineries have easily recognizable signs and they are open to the public 7 days a week during high season. But don't be afraid to visit some of the smaller, independent wineries that are not on the wine route map.

Planning a trip to Niagara is easy—this is, after all, one of the oldest tourist areas in Canada, and the infrastructure is well established. There are excellent tourism information centers throughout the region, informative websites, and well-trained staff who are happy to help or answer questions, as well as downloadable apps for your iPhone that will guide you around the region.

For additional help in planning your trip and for more on-the-ground resources in Niagara, see chapter 11, "Planning Your Trip to Niagara."

WHEN TO GO

Because the Niagara region is so diverse, high season varies according to what your primary interests are. If you are coming to just see the Falls, the busiest times are the

AN olympic WINE

In spring 2004, Inniskillin Winery created a special planting of Riesling grapes that was used specifically for a unique Icewine, harvested to coincide with the 2010 Winter Olympics in Vancouver. It was a great success and sold out quickly.

summer months, beginning in June, building to peak highs during July and August, and starting to slow in September. The same applies to visitors who come for the Shaw Theatre Festival and to see the historical venues. However, if wine country is the place you most want to explore, September and October are the busiest times, as the Niagara Wine Festival commences in mid-September, and all the harvest activities are in full swing. This is also one of the prettiest times to see the area, with trees turning color and the grapes and apples ripening.

Thus, hotel rooms fill up quickly during July and August, and also during major events such as Canada Day (July 1), Independence Day (July 4), and the Niagara Wine Festival (mid- to late Sept). If you plan to visit during these times, reserve accommodations several weeks or even months ahead. If you want to avoid the crowds but still maximize your chances of good weather, visit during the last week of August or first week of September. With the kids heading back to school and the Wine Festival not yet begun, this time of year is great for traveling to the Falls, to avoid lines and enjoy a little peace and quiet.

Note that several of the top Falls attractions, including the *Maid of the Mist* and the Cave of the Winds tours, operate only during the summer months. They open each year once the ice has melted in April or May, and end their season during the month of October.

Bear in mind that many activities abound in and around the Falls during the winter months. The Festival of Lights runs from November to early January, where the Falls and the surrounding parks are illuminated and there are winter fireworks. It's also a magical time to see the Falls. The spray freezes on the trees to create a very special scene. One of the truly "Only in Niagara" experiences, the Ice Wine Festival, and the Niagara equivalent to the Oscars, the Wine Cuvee, are special winter celebrations that draw visitors in large numbers.

The Climate

Spring in the Niagara region runs from late March to mid-May (although late snowfalls may surprise visitors in Apr, and frosts are not uncommon in May). **Summer** temperatures are usually enjoyed from mid- to late May to mid-September. June, July, and August are the hottest months, with average highs of 79°F (26°C) and lows of 59°F (15°C). It can be very hot in the summer, a surprise for many international visitors who think of Canada as a place that is always cold. The **fall** season runs from mid-September to mid-November, although even October can be quite brisk. **Winter** spans November to March, with temperatures varying between 16° and 39°F (–9° to 4°C). Snowfall is abundant, and winter temperatures have been known to plunge well below 16°F (–9°C) some years.

Keep in mind that the Great Lakes can adversely affect local weather conditions, ranging from high humidity and sudden thunderstorms in the summer to lake-effect snow squalls and freezing rain in the winter. Lake Erie and, in particular, Lake Ontario, are the main influences on the unique microclimate of the Niagara Peninsula, though, with a tendency to moderate summer heat and winter cold most years. The Niagara Escarpment also acts as a natural shelter against frost in the spring and fall. The weather can be somewhat unpredictable in this region, so I recommend packing some long-sleeved shirts for unexpectedly cool summer days and multiple layers to shed during a warm winter.

Visitors standing close to the Falls can get quite wet from the mist, especially if the wind is blowing in their direction. This can be welcome on a hot summer's day, but be prepared to don rain gear or even change into dry clothing. With the recent high-rise development around the Falls, the mist has actually increased in the area, and you don't need to be that close to the water to get wet.

Daily Average High Temperatures for Niagara

	JAN	FEB	MAR	APR	MAY	JUNE	JULY	AUG	SEPT	OCT	NOV	DEC
Temp (°F)	30	32	39	56	66	76	81	79	71	61	47	35
Temp (°C)	-1	0	4	13	19	24	27	26	22	16	8	2

Holidays

Ontario celebrates the following holidays: New Year's Day (Jan 1), Family Day (third Mon of Feb), Good Friday and Easter Monday (Mar or Apr), Victoria Day (Mon following the third weekend in May), Canada Day (July 1), Simcoe Day (first Mon in Aug), Labour Day (first Mon in Sept), Thanksgiving (second Mon in Oct), Remembrance Day (Nov 11), Christmas Day (Dec 25), and Boxing Day (Dec 26).

On Good Friday and Easter Monday, schools and government offices close; most corporations close on one or the other, and a few close on both. Only banks and government offices close on Remembrance Day (Nov 11).

Niagara Region Calendar of Events

The following list of events will help you to plan your visit to the Niagara region. Keep in mind that the largest, most successful events sometimes retire, some events are biennial, and dates may change from those listed here. In addition to the following events, numerous smaller community and cultural events take place throughout the year. Contact the relevant tourist information center (see "Visitor Information," p. 150) to confirm details if a particular event is a major reason for your vacation.

For an exhaustive list of events beyond those listed here, check http://events.frommers. com, where you'll find a searchable, up-to-the-minute roster of what's happening in cities all over the world.

 Nightly Illuminations

The American Falls and the Horseshoe Falls are illuminated nightly throughout the year. All times posted are approximate and subject to change according to light conditions. April lights go on at 8:30pm and shut down at 11pm. During the peak tourist season, May 1 to August 24, the Falls are flooded with light between 9pm and midnight. From August 24 to September 30, lights are on at 8:30pm (off at midnight); and during October, the Falls are lit at 7pm and the lights are switched off at midnight.

JANUARY

Niagara Icewine Festival. Winter is toasted at this festival with the delicious wine that made Niagara famous. There's a bar carved from ice on Queen Street in Niagara-on-the-Lake, Icewine samples, tours, tastings, and weekend hotel packages, as well as other winter activities. For more information, call ✆ **905/688-0212** or visit www. icewinefestival.com.

FEBRUARY

Niagara Wine Cuvee. The "who's who" of the wine world don black ties and ball gowns to attend this gala, where the awards for best wines are announced. There are winemakers' dinners, special weekend packages, and wine-tasting activities as well, all designed to celebrate the best of the grape harvest. For more info, call ✆ **905/684-8688** or visit www. cuvee.ca.

APRIL

Shaw Theatre Festival Season opens. The Shaw Theatre Festival exclusively produces the plays of George Bernard Shaw and his contemporaries, and plays set during Shaw's (very long) lifetime. The season runs from April to November, on four stages in Niagara-on-the-Lake. Call ✆ **800/511-7429** or visit www.shawfest. com.

Maple syrup season. When the daytime temperatures begin to climb above 32°F (0°C) in late winter, the maple sap begins to run. Local farms offer tours of the "sugar bush," pancake breakfasts, and maple syrup products for sale.

MAY

Niagara Folk Arts Festival. This annual event is billed as Canada's oldest heritage festival, spanning more than 2 weeks in mid- to late May. Multicultural music, theater, dance, food, and traditions are celebrated. Held at various sites throughout the Niagara region. Call ✆ **905/685-6589** or visit www.folk-arts.ca.

Niagara-on-the-Lake: Wine and Herb Festival. Every weekend throughout May, the wineries of Niagara-on-the Lake feature a different herb-themed food pairing matched to a premium VQA wine selected to highlight the flavor and aroma of the herb. Visit www.wineriesofniagara onthelake.com.

Shaw Guild Spring Garden Tour. A tour of up to 10 local gardens in Niagara-on-the-Lake. Call ✆ **905/468-2172** or visit www. shawguild.ca.

JUNE

Welland Rose Festival. Early June smells sweet as a variety of events lead up to the display and judging of the fairest roses in the land. Call ✆ **905/732-7673** or visit www.wellandrosefestival.on.ca.

Niagara New Vintage Festival. Dozens of Niagara wineries present the first taste of the season of their award-winning wines. Events are held in Jordan, St. Catharines, and other sites throughout the region. Call ✆ **905/688-0212** or visit www.niagara winefestival.ca.

Beamsville Strawberry Festival. This festival features strawberry treats, live entertainment, crafters, a car show, and more. Call ✆ **905/563-7274** or visit www. strawberryfest.ca. Third weekend in June.

Illuminaqua. The Welland Recreational Waterway is transformed into an interactive production of fire and music on water, while street performers and vendors entertain on land. There's a concert series set on a floating stage and pods of fire illuminating the old Welland Canal. The events take place on various dates from June to September. Call ✆ **905/735-1700** or visit www.illuminaqua.com.

Flavors of Niagara. Located at the Knoll Lakeview Park, this festival celebrates the ethnic and cultural diversity in Niagara through folk arts, international cuisine, wine, beer, dance, and jazz. Visit www. portcolborne.ca.

Vine Dining. A strolling picnic through the vineyards at Vineland Estates Winery, where wine and food are provided by the best chefs and wineries in the area. Call ✆ **800/465-7529 or visit www. theatreaquarius.org**.

JULY

Friendship Festival. This is a celebration of shared history and culture and friendship between Canada and the U.S. Events are held in Fort Erie, Ontario, and Buffalo, New York. Call ✆ 888/333-1987 or visit www.friendshipfestival.com.

Canada Day. Each July 1, Canadians gather in communities across the country to celebrate the nation's birthday. In the Niagara region, celebrations take place at the Falls and surrounding towns, including Port Dalhousie, Welland, St. Catharines, and Port Colborne.

Dragon Boat Festival. Teams from Niagara and across the globe compete and raise funds for the St. Catharines Museum and the United Way. Held on Martindale Pond, home of the Royal Canadian Henley Regatta in historical Port Dalhousie. Call ✆ 905/984-8880 or visit www.stcatharinesdragonboat.org. Late July.

Niagara Motorcycle Rally, Niagara Falls, New York. Bike enthusiasts can speak with custom bike builders, listen to live bands, compete in the chili cook-off, and buy swag from bike companies. Visit www.buffalothrills.com/events/ev-festivals events/niagaramotorcycle.htm.

AUGUST

Canal Days Marine Heritage Festival. On the Civic Holiday weekend (incorporating the first Mon in Aug), Port Colborne hosts this waterfront festival celebrating the community's marine heritage. Call ✆ 888/ PORT-FUN (767-8386) or visit www.canaldays.ca.

Royal Canadian Henley Regatta. This annual rowing regatta draws more than 3,500 international competitors. Held on Martindale Pond, Port Dalhousie. Call ✆ 905/937-1117 or visit www.henleyregatta.ca.

Winona Peach Festival. Everything from arts and crafts, entertainment, amusement rides, and of course peaches—pies, ice cream sundaes, jams, and preserves. Held at Winona Park. Call ✆ 905/643-2084 or visit www.winonapeach.com. End of August.

SEPTEMBER

Niagara Wine Festival. More than 100 events including winery tours and tastings, concerts, Niagara cuisine, artisan shows, wine seminars, live entertainment, and one of Canada's largest street parades. Call ✆ 905/688-0212 or visit www.niagarawinefestival.com.

NOVEMBER

Winter Festival of Lights. This is Canada's largest lights festival with nearly two million lights and over 100 animated lighting displays, as well as concerts, theater, and spectacular fireworks. Call ✆ 905/374-1616 or visit www.wfol.com. Early November to January.

THE LAY OF THE LAND

The Niagara region is a peninsula bordered by Lake Ontario to the north, the Niagara River to the east, and Lake Erie to the south. A ridge of land known as the Niagara Escarpment, characterized by a steep face on one side and a gentle slope on the other, rises from Queenston on the Niagara River and runs east to west through the region. The other major physical structure in the landscape is the Welland Canal, which connects Lake Ontario with Lake Erie via a series of eight locks, and roughly divides the region in half. At the head of the Canal sits the port city of St. Catharines.

The Falls are situated midway along the Niagara River, which connects Lake Ontario and Lake Erie. They consist of two main waterfalls. The American Falls (which are, appropriately, located on U.S. soil) dramatically cascade onto tons of fallen rock that lie at the base of the waterfall. The Horseshoe Falls, located across the border in Canada, send clouds of mist into the air from their concave center. Afternoon sunlight creates a rainbow in the swirling droplets of water.

Fauna & Flora

The Niagara region is home to a large variety of wildlife, including more than 300 species of birds, 53 mammals, and 36 different species of reptiles and amphibians.

The more common bird species that inhabit the area are cardinals, robins, woodpeckers, blue jays, herons, wrens, finches, thrushes, gulls, Canada geese, and chickadees. The region is also home to many birds of prey, including turkey vultures, red-tailed hawks, sparrow hawks, and several species of owls. There are also more than 25 species of water fowl in the area, including many species of ducks and the great blue heron.

Mammals that live in the Escarpment include squirrels, skunks, and raccoons. You may encounter white-tailed deer, red foxes, weasels, rabbits, and muskrats while exploring the Escarpment and the surrounding area.

The Niagara region has one of the largest populations of reptiles and amphibians in the country. Several varieties of snakes can be found in the area, as well as many species of frogs, painted turtles, and snapping turtles.

Niagara is a fertile area, blessed with excellent soil and moderate temperatures. The region is known for its large variety of tender fruits, including grapes. The Niagara region has more than 70 species of trees, including evergreen pines, spruce, cedar, and hemlock trees, but the woods are dominated by deciduous species such as oak, maple, and beech trees.

Because the area is part of the Carolinian region, its forests include rare tulip trees, sassafras, black cherry, papaw, and blue ash trees, which are scattered amongst more common species such as sugar maples. This region is one of the most biologically diverse in Canada, with 40% of rare plants occurring only in this area.

RESPONSIBLE TRAVEL

Ontario is a very progressive and proactive province when it comes to ecotourism. From a province-wide ban on herbicides to subsidies for environmentally friendly tourism initiatives, the province tries to make respect for the environment a priority.

In Niagara, many of the farms and vineyards are moving toward organic or biodynamic production methods. Most hotels have policies to reduce laundry, and recycling has become a daily habit for everyone.

Niagara Parks features environmentally friendly products at Table Rock, including:

- Organic cotton textiles and clothing products like bamboo T-shirts and recycled cotton tote bags
- Recycled and biodegradable plastics and paper products like postcards and calendars
- All plastic and paper retail bags used at Niagara Parks are recyclable or biodegradable.
- All green products are clearly labeled with a Green Products logo that reads "Niagara Parks Green Product."

In addition to the Green retail line, Niagara Parks implements several Project Green initiatives that focus on preservation and general enhancement of existing natural features, and has developed a commendable record of land stewardship and leadership based on conservation, education, environmental management, innovation, preservation, and restoration. Other "greening" projects include recyclable and biodegradable raincoats at the Journey Behind the Falls attraction, which is visited by nearly one million visitors each year.

THE NIAGARA escarpment

The Niagara Escarpment forms the backbone of the Niagara Peninsula. The unique natural features of the Escarpment and its ecological importance have been recognized by the United Nations Education, Scientific and Cultural Organization (UNESCO), and the Escarpment has been duly designated as a Man and the Biosphere Reserve. The designation has elevated the Escarpment's significance, joining the growing ranks of Biosphere Reserves that include the Galápagos Islands, the Serengeti National Park, and the Florida Everglades.

The Niagara Escarpment is a 1,050km (652-mile), crescent-shaped *cuesta*—a ridge formed by inclined rock strata, with a gentle slope on one side and a steep slope on the other. Its origin lies in New York State, south of Rochester. The ridge extends into Canada, running through Queenston on the Niagara River, bisecting the Niagara region from east to west, and then traveling north before plunging into Lake Huron. It eventually ends at the Door Peninsula in Wisconsin, in the Midwestern United States.

The southern part of the Escarpment, which contains the section that is found in Niagara, is located in Canada's warmest region, the Carolinian Canada Zone. It is a fragile ecosystem containing roughly one-quarter of the country's population and half of the endangered species—in an area that represents less than one-quarter of 1% of Canada's total landmass. This region is one of the most threatened of all Ontario's natural areas, and numerous organizations are involved in the preservation and conservation of the Niagara Escarpment's natural and cultural heritage.

The Bruce Trail follows the Niagara Escarpment through Ontario from Queenston Heights in the south to Tobermory at the northern tip of the Bruce Peninsula. The trail, which is marked by white blazes painted on trees, fence posts, and rocks, links parks and conservation areas along the route. The path is steep and rocky in places, but its rugged beauty, accented by waterfalls tumbling over the dolostone cliffs, is worth the effort. The trail offers a welcome escape from the urban landscape and agricultural development that cover much of the Niagara region.

The People Mover, another green initiative, uses propane-powered vehicles with a goal of reducing traffic along the Parkway.

To get a comprehensive appreciation of the land in Niagara, **Niagara Nature Tours** (www.niagaranaturetours.ca) offers tours that delve into the geology and even the soil—known for producing high-quality *vinifera* grapes—of the Niagara region. Open since 1996, environmentalist and agriculture/horticulture expert Carla Carlson leads visitors through an informative and healthy tour of the area. Starting and ending in Toronto, **Something's Afoot** (© **416/695-1838**) offers adventure ecotours through the Niagara region that include accommodations for 2- to 5-night stays on specific dates only.

Although one could argue that any vacation that includes an airplane flight can't be truly "green," you can go on holiday and still contribute positively to the environment. You can offset carbon emissions from your flight in other ways. Choose forward-looking companies that embrace responsible development practices, helping preserve destinations for the future by working alongside local people. An increasing number of sustainable tourism initiatives can help you plan a family trip and leave as small a "footprint" as possible on the places you visit.

GENERAL RESOURCES FOR green TRAVEL

In addition to the resources for Niagara listed above, the following websites provide valuable wide-ranging information on sustainable travel. For a list of even more sustainable resources, as well as tips and explanations on how to travel greener, visit www.frommers.com/planning.

○ **Responsible Travel** (www.responsibletravel.com) is a great source of sustainable travel ideas; the site is run by a spokesperson for ethical tourism in the travel industry. **Sustainable Travel International** (www.sustainabletravelinternational.org) promotes ethical tourism practices, and manages an extensive directory of sustainable properties and tour operators around the world.

○ In the U.K., **Tourism Concern** (www.tourismconcern.org.uk) works to reduce social and environmental problems connected to tourism. The **Association of Independent Tour Operators (AITO)** (www.aito.co.uk) is a group of specialist operators leading the field in making holidays sustainable.

○ In Canada, **www.greenlivingonline.com** offers extensive content on how to travel sustainably, including a travel and transport section and profiles of the best green shops and services in Toronto, Vancouver, and Calgary.

○ In Australia, the national body that sets guidelines and standards for ecotourism is **Ecotourism Australia** (www.ecotourism.org.au). **The Green Directory** (www.thegreendirectory.com.au), **Green Pages** (www.thegreen

pages.com.au), and **Eco Directory** (www.ecodirectory.com.au) offer sustainable travel tips and directories of green businesses.

○ **Carbonfund** (www.carbonfund.org), **TerraPass** (www.terrapass.org), and **Carbon Neutral** (www.carbonneutral.org) provide info on "carbon offsetting," or offsetting the greenhouse gases emitted during flights.

○ **Greenhotels** (www.greenhotels.com) recommends green-rated member hotels around the world that fulfill the company's stringent environmental requirements. **Environmentally Friendly Hotels** (www.environmentallyfriendlyhotels.com) offers more green accommodations ratings. The **Hotel Association of Canada** (www.hacgreenhotels.com) has a Green Key Eco-Rating Program, which audits the environmental performance of Canadian hotels, motels, and resorts.

○ **Sustain Lane** (www.sustainlane.com) lists sustainable eating and drinking choices around the U.S.; also visit **www.eatwellguide.org** for tips on eating sustainably in the U.S. and Canada.

○ For information on animal-friendly issues throughout the world, visit **Tread Lightly** (www.treadlightly.org).

○ **Volunteer International** (www.volunteerinternational.org) has a list of questions to help you determine the intentions and the nature of a volunteer program. For general info on volunteer travel, visit **www.volunteerabroad.org** and **www.idealist.org**.

You can find eco-friendly travel tips, statistics, and touring companies and associations—listed by destination under "Travel Choice"—at the **International Ecotourism Society** website, www.ecotourism.org. Also check out **Conservation International** (www.conservation.org), which, with *National Geographic Traveler*, annually presents **World Legacy Awards** (www.nationalgeographic.com/traveler/worldlegacy_winners.html) to those travel tour operators, businesses, organizations, and places that have made a significant contribution to sustainable tourism. **Ecotravel.com** is part online magazine and part eco-directory that lets you search for touring companies in several categories (water-based, land-based, spiritually oriented, and so on).

TOURS

Academic Trips

For an in-depth look at the history of Niagara, follow the Niagara Heritage Trail, a historic and scenic route running the entire 56km (35-mile) Canadian coastline of the Niagara River from Fort Erie northward to Niagara-on-the-Lake. The trail has been designed as a self-guided tour by Niagara Parks (www.niagaraparks.com/heritage).

Along the route, visitors can access many of the important historical sites, like Old Fort Erie, site of a major battle in July 1814 between British troops and American troops, and the Laura Secord Homestead, historical home of the woman who set out on a historical walk from Queenston, Ontario, to the village of Beaverdams, warning British soldiers of an impending American attack in 1814.

The trail starts in Queen Victoria Park near the main tourist area, and passes by attractions such as the Whirlpool Golf Course, Niagara Botanical Gardens, the Butterfly Conservatory, and the Floral Clock. See p. 106 for details.

Bike Trips

One of the most popular and environmentally friendly ways to see Niagara is by bike. There are several companies that offer guided bike tours of the Niagara Parkway and the wine country. Walking tours, particularly of the famous Bruce Trail, are also a good way to get familiar with the terrain. Many of the tours feature a stop at a winery. See p. 132 for details.

Food & Wine Trips

Probably the fastest growing activity in Niagara is culinary tourism. Many companies are offering wine and food tours of the region, many combining a stay in a historic hotel or inn, wine tastings, cooking classes, and gourmet dining. **Jewel of Niagara,** for example, offers guided winery tours and luncheons, country market tours, and wine pairing tours (www.jewelofniagara.com). **Niagara Vintage Wine Tours** provides similar excursions through the wineries and restaurants of the region, (www.niagaravintagewinetours.com). **Wine Country Tours** runs three different culinary tours in conjunction with the Niagara Culinary Trail during July, August, and September (www.winecountrytours.ca). See chapter 7 for more companies that provide wine and dine tours.

For the visitor intent on sampling the best local produce that Niagara has to offer, you can't find a better place to start than the Niagara Culinary Trail Map. The Culinary Trail has more than 65 member farmers and producers. The map includes restaurants, retail stores, cafes, bakeries, bed-and-breakfasts, and wineries, which all offer Niagara-grown produce. It lists all the producers, from cheese makers to the grower of heritage strawberries, with descriptions and contact information. The map is available in hardcopy at tourist offices and many businesses, or can be downloaded from www.niagaraculinarytrail.com.

The Wine Council of Ontario publishes an excellent map of their participating wineries. It can help you plan a self-guided tour. The main routes in wine country are well marked, including signs to wineries not on the Wine Council map.

Escorted General Interest Tours

For more information on escorted general interest tours, including questions to ask before booking your trip, see www.frommers.com/planning.

SUGGESTED ITINERARIES FOR THE NIAGARA REGION

E very guest I have ever had has always asked to visit the Falls, the first item on their list of things they must see while visiting. And none of them has ever been disappointed, except maybe my Norwegian friend who visited in October and was chilled to the bone by a cold wind and the spray from the Falls. But he was awed by the Falls and vowed to come back in summer.

But just as Napa Valley surprised Californians by surpassing Disneyland as a tourism draw, the wine-country experience is fast becoming another reason that visitors come here. Add to that Niagara-on-the-Lake, an elegant, small Ontario town with exquisite accommodations, excellent shopping and dining, and the renowned Shaw Festival Theatre, and you have multiple reasons for an extended visit.

The historic locks of the Welland Canal, small farming villages, bicycle trails, and nature preserves add variety to your schedule and allow you to discover delights of the Niagara region you might never have realized were on the doorstep of the world's best-known waterfalls.

Note: These itineraries have been set up for visitors who come to Niagara during the prime tourist season between April and October. Many, but not all, of the attractions are open in the winter months, and Niagara under snow can be a magical winter wonder. However, please call ahead (or check chapter 6) if you are planning to visit outside the main tourist season and there are specific attractions or itineraries you wish to include.

THE REGION IN BRIEF

NIAGARA FALLS, ONTARIO, CANADA The Niagara Falls area is the hub of the region. This is where you will find the mighty "thundering waters" of the powerful American Falls and the spectacular Canadian Horseshoe. A protected strip of land lies between the Falls and the commercial mayhem of the city of Niagara Falls. The Niagara Parks Commission is the steward of this oasis, which provides a mix of immaculately groomed lawns and flowerbeds along the edge of the Falls and the Niagara Gorge. Traveling north along the western bank of the Niagara River, the scenic Niagara Parkway links Niagara Falls and Niagara-on-the-Lake by road, passing by the Niagara Parks Botanical Gardens, Butterfly Conservatory, Niagara Glen Nature Area, Floral Clock, McFarland House, Queenston Heights, Sir Adam Beck 2 Generating Station, and other places of interest.

NIAGARA FALLS, NEW YORK, U.S.   You can take in the view of the Falls from the American side and also see the pre-falls rapids. The district includes the Niagara Falls State Park, the oldest state park in the United States. There are a number of other tourist attractions on the American side, including the *Maid of the Mist* (which launched here in 1846), Cave of the Winds, a boardwalk constructed next to the American Falls, and an observation tower. The infrastructure for tourists is not as well developed in Niagara Falls, New York, as it is in Niagara Falls, Ontario, however, so if you start your Niagara visit on the U.S. side of the border, it's well worth crossing to Canada.

NIAGARA-ON-THE-LAKE   Only a 1½-hour drive from Toronto, Canada's largest city, lies one of North America's prettiest and best-preserved 19th-century villages. The streets of Niagara-on-the-Lake are lined with mature trees. Dozens of immaculately restored and maintained historical brick and clapboard homes grace the town. The town center is home to the Shaw Theatre Festival, boutique shopping, B&Bs, inns, and a choice of fine restaurants. On the edges of the town you'll find a number of wineries, as well as Fort George National Historic Site. If you like elegance and don't mind the bustle of tourists stepping out of packed tour buses during the busy summer months, base yourself in Niagara-on-the-Lake and tour the region from here.

WINE ROUTE   The Niagara Peninsula is home to more than 80 wineries and is the largest designated viticultural area in Canada. The region is divided into three areas, each of which offers a variety of accommodations, primarily in B&Bs and inns, and restaurants ranging from exquisite winery cuisine to cozy tea shops and delicious ethnic fare.

   Grimsby and **Beamsville** are the farthest west. This plateau of fertile land, which lies between the Escarpment ridge and Lake Ontario, runs from Grimsby to just west of St. Catharines.

   Jordan and Vineland is the next region you will meet as you travel east. This area offers art galleries, unique shopping in quaint villages, and follows the Bruce Trail, which at 850km (528 miles) is Ontario's longest footpath. The Bruce Trail can be accessed from several wineries that back onto the Niagara Escarpment. (Grimsby, Beamsville, Jordan, and Vineland are all part of an area known as "The Bench.")

   Niagara-on-the-Lake is the third viticultural area in Niagara (see above).

WELLAND CANAL CORRIDOR & FORT ERIE   **St. Catharines** is the largest city in the Niagara region. The city has two main heritage districts—downtown St. Catharines (encompassing Queen St. Heritage District and Yates St. District, which feature fine examples of historical residential architecture) and the lakeside village of Port Dalhousie. St. Catharines is known as the "Garden City," due to its surrounding vineyards, gardens, nurseries, and farmland. The Welland Canals Centre is located at Lock 3 along the Welland Canal.

   Thorold, south of St. Catharines, offers another visitor-friendly viewing point, the Lock 7 Viewing Complex. The Twinned Flight Locks, which raise and lower ships up and down the Niagara Escarpment (42m/138 ft.), are also located in Thorold. A revitalization plan has resulted in new stores and the restoration of the Keefer Mansion Inn, overlooking the town, and the town, once an ugly duckling, is on its way to becoming a swan.

Welland is the next city along the canal. Canada's Rose city, Welland hosts a Rose Festival each summer. Recreational trails run alongside the canal here. Merritt Island, a haven for outdoor enthusiasts, is a highlight of the area.

Port Colborne is the community situated at the mouth of the Welland Canal and Lake Erie. The city's signature event is the Canal Days Marine Heritage Festival.

Fort Erie lies on the banks of the Niagara River, overlooking Buffalo and just a few minutes from the Peace Bridge. Attractions include Historic Fort Erie, Fort Erie Historical Museum, Ridgeway Battlefield Site, Fort Erie Railroad Museum, Mahoney Dolls' House Gallery, the Slave Quarters, and Fort Erie Racetrack.

THE BEST OF NIAGARA IN 1 DAY

If all you have is 1 day, then you must see Niagara Falls and as much of the surrounding attractions as possible. That will require an early start and a clearly defined schedule, but it's quite doable. Start on the Canadian side, since it is on this side of the river that you get the gorgeous panorama of both the American and Horseshoe falls. First, park your car in an all-day parking lot, and then buy one of the tourist passes. The large lot on the Niagara Parkway, south of the Horseshoe Falls in Canada, is a convenient place to park, but if you don't mind a short walk, park up by Robinson Street and Fallsview Boulevard. There'll be more spaces and it's less expensive. In fact, the best buy for parking in Niagara Falls is in the IMAX parking lot just off Fallsview Boulevard. You don't need to attend a movie there, and the price, C$2 for the day, Monday to Thursday, C$4 for the day from Friday to Sunday, is the best you will find. The drawback is that the lot is small, holding about 50 cars, and fills up quickly. If you are planning an early start, try this parking lot first. You can purchase your Niagara Falls **Adventure Pass** (adults, C$45, children 6-12, C$33, children 5 and under free) at the kiosk at the bottom of Murray Street, enjoy the Falls at your leisure, and then take the People Mover (unlimited transport for the day is included with the pass) to the other Niagara Parks attractions. *Suggestion:* Buy your Adventure Pass tickets ahead of time at www.niagaraparks.com. You can pay by credit card, customize your pass, and print out your ticket. You can also arrange for an MP3 player with an audio tour, or you can download free, with your pass, the audio tour for your own MP3 device. *Start: The Fabulous Falls.*

1 The Mighty Voice of Thunder

Try to arrive at Niagara Falls shortly after 8am and head straight for the Falls. You'll have a perfect vantage point to see them early in the morning. By mid-morning in high season, the crowds make it difficult to gain a prime place by the wall overlooking the Falls, and it's tricky to take a good picture with all those people moving around. Besides, you will want a picture of you and your family with the Falls behind you!

Park up by Fallsview Boulevard and walk toward the Falls down Murray Street, and suddenly there they are—the Falls! Be prepared to be awed. Walk south along the edge of the Niagara River to Table Rock Point, which is where you will be closest to the Falls. Now is the time to drink in the views and marvel at the thundering waters of Niagara.

2 The *Maid of the Mist*

Don't spend too much time staring at the Falls. There's more to come. Head straight for the *Maid of the Mist* and try to catch one of the first sailings. The dock is just a short walk from Table Rock. The first boat leaves at 9am for most of the high season. There's a reason why celebrities and royalty have included a trip on the *Maid* as part of their visit—it is a dramatic and thrilling way to get up close and personal with one of the world's most famous landmarks. From the vantage of railside, you can truly appreciate the size and power of both the Canadian and the American Falls. Grab a spot on the starboard side of the boat (that's the right-hand side, for you landlubbers)—you'll get closer to the Horseshoe Falls and will still have great views of the American Falls on your return to the dock. See p. 98 and 105.

3 Niagara's Fury

Now that you've seen the Falls, it is time to find out how they were created and to learn a bit of the history. Niagara's Fury is located in Table Rock and is a multi-sensory experience of the glacial events that formed the Falls and the gorge 10,000 years ago. The experience starts with an 8-minute animated pre-show, where cartoon woodland characters explain how the Ice Age formed Niagara Falls. Then, in a specially designed, 360-degree theater, you can witness the creation of the Falls in a 6-minute, multi-sensory presentation where the floor moves, mist rises, and the temperatures plummet. See p. 101

4 Pop & Lolly's 🥤

Take a truly decadent break at Pop & Lolly's (6650 Niagara Pkwy., Niagara Falls, ON; ☎ **905/354-3631) in the Table Rock Centre. In this sweets' paradise, a confectionary chef makes hand-crafted chocolates at a chocolate station, while staff dip fresh fruit or candy into a chocolate fountain. Take your treats outside and order a coffee or soft drink on the patio, with a great view of the Falls. There are also several excellent souvenir shops in Table Rock if you have time.**

5 Journey Behind the Falls

Now it's time to plunge down into the gorge on foot. Use your Niagara Falls Adventure Pass in Canada and enter Table Rock House to take the Journey Behind the Falls tour. Walk through tunnels bored into the rock behind the Horseshoe Falls and emerge onto the lower balcony at the northern edge. This is where you will feel the power of the Horseshoe Falls at its mightiest. See p. 100.

6 The Thrill of Clifton Hill

Sure it's a bit tacky and corny, but it has been part of the Falls experience practically since the first tourist visited. Children and teens will love it, and there's a lot here for adults too. It's an easy walk from Table Rock. Try out some of the attractions—the **Haunted House** is actually scary, and **Ripley's Believe It or Not** has some incredible things, from authentic shrunken heads to the Chippendale chair that belonged to the world's tallest man. See p. 118.

7 Niagara SkyWheel

While you are in the area, take a ride on the SkyWheel. Don't worry about getting dizzy; it's quite stable, and you can get some of the best photographs of the Falls

Niagara in 1 Day

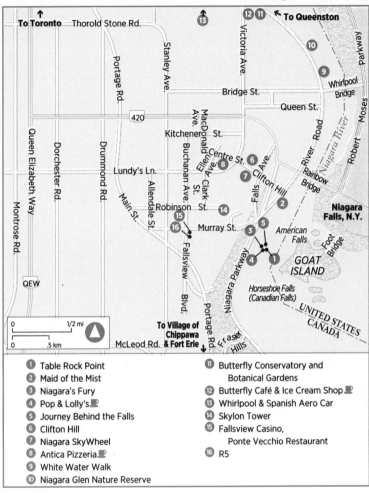

1. Table Rock Point
2. Maid of the Mist
3. Niagara's Fury
4. Pop & Lolly's
5. Journey Behind the Falls
6. Clifton Hill
7. Niagara SkyWheel
8. Antica Pizzeria
9. White Water Walk
10. Niagara Glen Nature Reserve
11. Butterfly Conservatory and Botanical Gardens
12. Butterfly Café & Ice Cream Shop
13. Whirlpool & Spanish Aero Car
14. Skylon Tower
15. Fallsview Casino, Ponte Vecchio Restaurant
16. R5

from up here. For a mere C$10, ride this giant Ferris wheel, which is heated in the winter and cooled in the summer. The ride gives you outlooks over the Falls and into New York. The 7-minute ride does three loops in all. See p. 119.

8 Antica Pizzeria

Stay for a family-friendly lunch at Antica Pizzeria (5785 Victoria Ave., Niagara Falls, ON; 905/356-3844), at the top of Clifton Hill, on Victoria Avenue. In keeping with the area, this little Italian pizza parlor, with an authentic wood-burning pizza oven, is casual and busy. If the weather is nice, sit outside on the patio, order a thin-crust pizza, and watch the action. If there's a group of you, they'll serve your spaghetti and gnocchi family style on big platters. See p. 74.

9 White Water Walk

Now it's time to enjoy the Niagara River and its surrounding parks and attractions, all of which are included in your Adventure Pass. Walk back down to the parkway and jump on the People Mover, which will take you to all the Niagara Parks attractions. First stop is the **White Water Walk.** Don't worry about having to negotiate stairs—the elevator takes you right to the walk at the bottom of the Niagara Gorge. A boardwalk along the edge of the base of the gorge brings you face-to-face with one of the world's wildest stretches of white water. See p. 104.

10 Niagara Glen Nature Reserve

On the east side of the Niagara Parkway, a short drive north of the whirlpool, you'll find the Niagara Glen Nature Reserve, which features a series of seven linked trails, ranging in length from .4km (.25 mile) to 3.3km (2.1 miles). These are excellent walks through some of the most biodiverse woodlands in Canada. Note that each of the paths, or access to them, is steep in places—River Path is the flattest, but you need to descend the cliff to reach it. See p. 136.

11 Butterfly Conservatory

Take the People Mover to the Butterfly Conservatory, a delightful place to visit for an hour or so. The Conservatory doubles as the display greenhouse for the Niagara Parks Botanical Gardens and is blessed with an abundance of natural light. The butterflies spend a considerable amount of time resting, so it's a great place to bring your camera. Afterwards, stroll through the adjacent botanical gardens to view the famous rose gardens, with more than 2,400 different kinds of roses and a maze and aviary. See p. 102.

12 Butterfly Café and Ice Cream Shop ☕

These gardens are too beautiful to leave! Rest for a while in the pretty Butterfly Café and Ice Cream Shop while enjoying the surroundings of the botanical gardens.

13 Whirlpool Aero Car

The next stop is the aero car, a vintage metal carriage, suspended on cables above the whirlpool phenomenon in the Niagara Gorge. The ride takes passengers on a 1km (⅔-mile) round-trip overlooking the whirlpool. See p. 103.

14 Skylon Tower

Take the People Mover back to the Falls to the Incline Railway, situated opposite Table Rock House terminus. If you have an Adventure Pass, the trip is free; otherwise you will have to pay a small fee to ride up the cliff. Once at the top, walk farther up the hill to Fallsview Boulevard, and turn right (north) for the **Skylon Tower.** The aerial view of the Falls offers a unique and panoramic perspective. You'll feel as if you are on top of the Falls. (p. 101.).

15 Ponte Vecchio ☕

You have plenty of dining options to choose from in the Falls area. Even if you are not a gambler, the Fallsview Casino is worth a visit, and there are some stunning restaurants inside. I recommend Ponte Vecchio (6380 Fallsview Blvd., Niagara Falls, ON; ℰ 888/325-5788), an upscale restaurant with an extensive wine list. Don't miss the roasted fig and walnut gelato with wild berries. See p. 72.

16 The Falls by Night

After sunset, both Falls are magically illuminated with rainbow colors. I guarantee that one of the most romantic moments of your life will happen at **R5,** an intimate little cocktail bar on the fifth floor of the **Fallsview Casino** (p. 51). Order a signature drink like the Eden's Ember, sit on one of the grey suede sofas, and watch the colors change on the Falls through the floor-to-ceiling windows. Or step out on the balcony for a closer look.

THE BEST OF THE NIAGARA REGION IN 2 DAYS

Head north on the Niagara Parkway by car or the Niagara-on-the-Lake Shuttle (p. 227). Take time to enjoy this beautiful and historic drive. The route, built in 1912, is a two-lane arterial road with a 60kmph (37 mph) speed limit for most of the way. Several small but significant museums are worth a stop, and the homes along the parkway are some of the oldest in the country. Visit historic Queenston Heights Park, scene of one of the most famous battles of the War of 1812. Explore Niagara-on-the-Lake, including the quaint shops and restaurants along Queen Street. *Start: Niagara Parkway, alongside Victoria Park.*

1 ## Helicopter Ride

A short drive from Niagara Falls brings you to **Niagara Helicopters,** on your left just past the Great Wolf Lodge. At C$132 per person, it's expensive but a real, authentic thrill. It is not possible to really understand the topography of the Falls and the surrounding area until you see it this way. It's smooth and safe, and an audio tour is delivered through headphones. Flights depart daily from 9am until sunset. Starting near the gorge, the 12-minute ride swoops over the gorge, over the Falls, down the Welland Canal, and back. See p. 120.

2 ## Queenston Heights Park

Queenston Heights Park has a variety of facilities and attractions for visitors. View Brock's Monument, where many events are planned for the 2012 celebration of the War of 1812. Take a 45-minute self-guided walking tour of the battleground of the War of 1812's Battle of Queenston Heights, or enjoy the mature shade trees and grassy open spaces of the park, perfect for ballgames and family fun. See p. 126

3 ### Queenston Heights Restaurant ☕

If you're looking for an early lunch, Queenston Heights Restaurant (14184 Niagara Pkwy., Queenston; ℓ 905/262-4274), located right in the park, enjoys beautiful open vistas looking north along the Niagara River toward Lake Ontario. Lunch, afternoon tea, and dinner are served, and a children's menu is available. See p. 74. If you have a picnic basket with you, enjoy lunch on one of the many picnic tables throughout the park.

4 ## The Museums of Queenston

Just before you reach Niagara-on-the-Lake is the small but historically rich town of Queenston. A cluster of interesting museums here are worth visiting. Mackenzie Heritage Printery Museum, housed in the restored home of rebel publisher William Lyon Mackenzie, reveals 500 years of printing technology in an authentic period print shop. Rarest is the Louis Roy Press, oldest in Canada and one of the few original wooden presses remaining in the world. Also here is the Laura Secord Homestead, home of Canada's most famous heroines. The homestead has undergone an exciting rejuvenation with new visitor facilities, museum displays, and the addition of the historic 1842 Queenston Baptist Church. During the War of 1812, Laura Secord is credited with helping to secure victory for the British when she set out on a perilous journey in the service of her country. The homestead is carefully restored and interpreted by authentically costumed guides. A bit closer to Niagara-on-the-Lake is MacFarlane House, built in 1800 by John McFarland and his sons, on land granted to him by King George III. See p. 108.

5 Fort George

Just before you reach the town of Niagara-on-the-Lake, stop for a visit at **Old Fort George,** a reconstructed British fort that played a key role in the War of 1812. Highlights of the fort include the reconstructed guardhouse, officers' quarters, flag bastion, blockhouses, and Brock's bastion, the fort's most strategic artillery battery (p. 108).

6 Queen Street Shopping

The best boutique shopping in Niagara can be found along Queen Street in Niagara-on-the-Lake. There's a variety of boutiques here, ranging from a Christmas store to one of the best hat stores I have ever been in. The shop often supplies hats for actors at the Shaw Theatre Festival. The street gets crowded in the summer months, but the shops are quaint, unique, and entertaining. See chapter 8.

7 Prince of Wales Hotel ☕

An experience not to be missed—high tea at the Prince of Wales Hotel (6 Picton St., Niagara-on-the-Lake; ☎ 888/669-5566). With tiered plates with little sandwiches, cakes, pastries, and a pot of tea, you'll feel like royalty. See p. 56.

8 The Leafy Side Streets—by Foot or Horse & Carriage

Walk off the pastries with a tour of the graceful and pleasant streets of Niagara-on-the-Lake's Heritage District—the "Old Town." The streets are laid out in a grid fashion, making it simple to find your way around. Just head down any side street off the main shopping district on Queen Street and you will find quaint streets lined with impressively restored historic homes. You can pick up a map of the town at the Niagara-on-the-Lake Visitor & Convention Bureau, at 26 Queen St. Sentinel Carriages will take you around town in a horse-drawn carriage, passing by places of historic interest on the way.

9 Charles Inn ☕

If you have tickets for an evening Shaw performance, then make a reservation for an early dinner for around 5:30pm, which will allow you time to walk to the theater afterward without having to rush. If you *aren't* going to the theater, then wait until around 7pm, when the pre-theater crowds have thinned out; you will enjoy a more peaceful and relaxed meal. Try the Charles Inn (209 Queen St.; ☎ 905/468-4588) for a continuation of that historic feel you have been experiencing all day. The Charles is right on the main street, and it's an easy walk to the theaters. See p. 54.

10 Shaw Theatre Festival Evening Performance

I recommend booking tickets in advance if you wish to see a performance at the world-renowned Shaw Theatre Festival. The Shaw has four performance spaces in Niagara-on-the-Lake, and presents plays written by George Bernard Shaw and his contemporaries, along with plays set during the period of Shaw's lifetime. The theatre celebrated its 50th anniversary in 2011. See p. 194.

① Niagara Helicopters
② Queenston Heights Park
③ Queenston Heights Restaurant 🍵
④a MacKenzie Heritage Printery Museum
④b Laura Secord Homestead
④c McFarland House
⑤ Old Fort George

⑥ Queen Street Shopping Area
⑦ Prince of Wales Hotel 🍵
⑧ Heritage District
⑨ Charles Inn 🍵
⑩ Festival Theatre
⑪ Churchill Lounge, Prince of Wales Hotel 🍵

11 Churchill Lounge 🍵

If you are looking for a quiet place for an after-theater drink, try the Churchill Lounge in the Prince of Wales Hotel (6 Picton St., Niagara-on-the-Lake; ✆ 905/468-3246). Theater people often drop in here after the performance.

THE BEST OF THE NIAGARA REGION IN 3 DAYS

On the third day, you can really get to the heart of Niagara. Today you'll discover the riches of the wine country, the charm of small agricultural-based towns, and the special appeal of Jordan Village, a shopper's paradise. The Welland Canal is well worth a visit, but only if you have your own vehicle to drive to one of the two main viewing locations *and* a ship will be entering or leaving the lock you choose to view at a convenient time. See chapter 7 for how to find the shipping traffic schedule for the day of your visit. **Start:** *Niagara-on-the-Lake, at Peller Estates Winery or Inniskillen Winery.*

1 The Niagara Peninsula Wine Route

Start your wine-country tour early, before the crowds arrive. The samples are only 30ml (1 oz.), and you can always spit the wine out after tasting, so it's quite acceptable to try the wine before noon. Most wineries open at 10am and you are likely to have the tasting bar staff all to yourself, which means you can take time to savor the flavors, ask questions, and perhaps purchase a bottle of the one that you like best. You probably won't manage more than five, perhaps six, wineries in a day trip. Check out chapter 7 for more details.

2 Charming St. Davids

Head toward the small town of St. Davids along Route 81, stopping at Château des Charmes, a French-style château. Don't miss the chance to try out their sauvignon Icewine, a lovely nectar with aromas of marmalade, mandarin, lemon, and sponge toffee. Then head to Ravine Vineyard. Here you can tour the beautifully restored 1830s home that has been in the owner's family for many years and has a great story to go with it. See p. 89.

3 Ravine Bistro 🍷

Stop for lunch at Ravine Bistro (✆ 905/262-8463), an authentic French-style bistro and deli next to Ravine's tasting room. There's a wide veranda where you can sit at rustic tables and enjoy artisanal cheeses, classic bistro dishes, homemade clay-oven breads and pizzas, local charcuterie, and of course, Ravine Estate's wine. See p. 172.

4 Welland Canal Lock 3 or Lock 7

Stay on York Road (Rte. 81) parallel to the QEW, cross the lift bridge, then turn left onto Welland Canal Parkway. The Welland Canal Centre is located at Lock 3, which is also home to the St. Catharines Museum. If you want to see more of this fascinating corner of marine history, continue south to Thorold. At Thorold Lock 7 Viewing Complex, you can watch the "salties" (ocean-going ships) and "lakers" (those ships that sail the Great Lakes) climb up and down the Escarpment through a series of three twinned locks. There is a tourist information center and small cafe at this location (p. 112).

5 Jordan Village and the Twenty Valley

Head back down to the QEW and continue west until exit 55 to Jordan. Enjoy a walk through the leafy town of Jordan, where shopping opportunities are plentiful. If you are still up for wine, stop for a tasting at Cave Spring Cellars. Also here is Jordan Historical Museum, which contains a collection of well-preserved artifacts from the United Empire Loyalist and Pennsylvania German Mennonite roots in the area.

6 Toute Sweet Ice Cream & Chocolate Shop 🍷

Have a mid-afternoon break at the Toute Sweet Ice Cream & Chocolate Shop (771 19th St., Jordan; ✆ 905/562-9666), where you can experience frozen granite slab ice cream.

Niagara in 3 Days

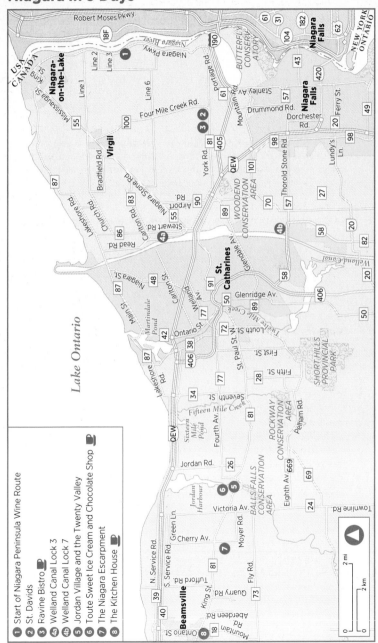

1 Start of Niagara Peninsula Wine Route
2 St. Davids
3 Ravine Bistro
4a Welland Canal Lock 3
4b Welland Canal Lock 7
5 Jordan Village and the Twenty Valley
6 Toute Sweet Ice Cream and Chocolate Shop
7 The Niagara Escarpment
8 The Kitchen House

Create your own ice-cream blend using ice creams and sorbets, fresh Niagara fruits and wines, chocolate, nuts, and candies. Enjoy your treats on the garden patio. See p. 188.

7 The Niagara Escarpment

From Jordan, head west along Regional Road 81, the former Hwy. 8, and one of the oldest highways in the province. It follows the pathways that were established by the aboriginal peoples and early settlers, and winds through valleys and farmlands that hug the Escarpment. There are more than 40 wineries in this protected area, called "The Bench," many of them not on the wine map, but well worth a visit.

8 The Kitchen House ☕

As the perfect end to a day in wine country, experience the perfect marriage of fine cuisine and good wine in the very place it was produced. If you manage to get as far as Beamsville, The Kitchen House (5600 King St. W., Beamsville; ☎ 905/563-0900) at Peninsula Ridge Winery is a fine-dining choice. It's located in the William D. Kitchen house, a red-brick Victorian manor that was meticulously restored in 2000. Built in 1885 in the Queen Anne style by Grimsby architect Frank Hill, the house was recently declared as a historic site under the Ontario Heritage Act for its historical and architectural significance. See p. 86.

WHERE TO STAY

Niagara Falls has been welcoming tourists and honeymooners for hundreds of years, so it is no surprise that the area is rich in possibilities for places to stay. The choices range from iconic hotel properties like the historic Crowne Plaza to the humble comfort of family-run B&Bs. Many of the properties listed in this chapter are clustered around the Falls themselves, or in the beautiful, serene setting of Niagara-on-the-Lake. Wine-country choices abound, with everything from luxurious inns to cozy cottages for two. If you are looking for somewhere off the beaten tourist path, head for Port Dalhousie, the white sand beaches of Lake Erie, or alongside Welland Canal.

best NIAGARA HOTEL BETS

○ **Best Historic Hotel:** For one of the best views of the Falls, and for a connection with history, stay at the **Crowne Plaza**. It is the oldest hotel in the city of Niagara Falls and was originally called the General Brock Hotel. Marilyn Monroe stayed in Suite 801 in 1952 when she was in town to film *Niagara*. See p. 47.

○ **Best for Business Travelers:** The **Hilton Niagara Falls Fallsview** has all the up-to-date business facilities that a busy traveler may need, including videoconferencing capabilities and a multi-lingual staff. But when the workday is done, there's a glassed-in walkway to the Casino, several in-hotel restaurants, and the Falls are just a short walk away. See p. 48.

○ **Best for a Romantic Getaway:** Romantic for me means small and intimate, and the best bet for that kind of experience is the **Charles Inn** in Niagara-on-the-Lake. Each room is one of a kind, the views of the lake and golf course are engaging, and the Shaw Festival Theatre is down the street. A twilight dinner on the veranda is a patented recipe for romance. See p. 54.

○ **Best Service:** Call me silly, but when someone arranges breakfast to be served on my hotel room veranda, and helps me get theater tickets and arrange a wine tour, all with a warm smile, I feel I've been well served. You'll find that at the **Riverbend Inn** in Niagara-on-the-Lake. See p. 57.

○ **Best Splurge:** For old-world elegance, reserve a suite at the **Prince of Wales** in Niagara-on-the-Lake. There'll be a rose on your pillow at

PRICE CATEGORIES

Very Expensive	Moderate
C$275 and up	C$100–C$200
Expensive	Inexpensive
C$200–C$275	Under C$100

turndown, a bowl of oranges by your bed, and complimentary bottled water. The bathroom is big, with a deep bath for soaking, and you will be just a short elevator ride away from high tea in the Drawing Room. See p. 56.

o **Most Relaxing Hotel:** Nothing makes me feel more relaxed and pampered than breakfast in bed, and that is standard practice for the **Sterling Inn & Spa.** Continental breakfast is delivered each morning as part of the rate. There's also a lovely spa and showers with sauna-like steam jets. See p. 51.

o **Best Location in Niagara Falls**: Just 100 yards from the Falls, the **Marriott Niagara Falls Fallsview Hotel & Spa** is the most conveniently located place to stay for touring. Just steps outside the door, you can feel the spray on your face. The hotel is right next to the Fallsview Casino and a stone's throw from most attractions and restaurants. See p. 49.

o **Best for Families:** The **Great Wolf Lodge** is family paradise, with an activity-packed indoor and outdoor water park and lots of special events for children. A large group may want to consider the Loft Fireplace Suite, with three queen beds, one in the upstairs loft. There's also a kids' club and in-hotel babysitting services. See p. 50.

o **Best Budget Hotel:** The **Lion's Head B&B** is close to everything, the beds are dressed in goose down duvets, and the individually designed and artistically themed rooms are ideal for couples who like a little history and some personal attention when they travel. Rates start at $125 and include a sumptuous breakfast. See p. 53

o **Best Views:** Hands down, the hotel with the best view is the **Tower Hotel.** Make sure you reserve one of the newly renovated rooms with a Falls view and you will find yourself in a small jewel box, where one complete wall is window, and that window is filled with awesome views of the Falls in all their glory. The perfect place for watching the sunset, or the sunrise, over the Falls. See p. 52.

NIAGARA FALLS, ONTARIO & NEW YORK

With 11 million visitors to the Falls every year, you would expect the vicinity to be awash in hotels and motels—and you'd be right, at least on the Canadian side. There are fewer choices on U.S. soil.

Best For: Families and couples, since all the major hotels on the Canadian side woo both groups with honeymooner and family packages.

Drawbacks: Almost all the hotels are in busy areas so you will be surrounded by activity, especially in high season.

Niagara Falls Hotels

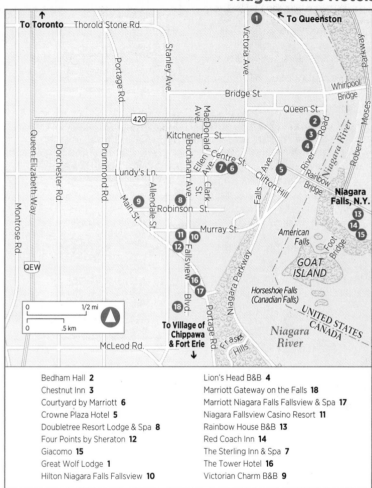

Bedham Hall **2**	Lion's Head B&B **4**
Chestnut Inn **3**	Marriott Gateway on the Falls **18**
Courtyard by Marriott **6**	Marriott Niagara Falls Fallsview & Spa **17**
Crowne Plaza Hotel **5**	Niagara Fallsview Casino Resort **11**
Doubletree Resort Lodge & Spa **8**	Rainbow House B&B **13**
Four Points by Sheraton **12**	Red Coach Inn **14**
Giacomo **15**	The Sterling Inn & Spa **7**
Great Wolf Lodge **1**	The Tower Hotel **16**
Hilton Niagara Falls Fallsview **10**	Victorian Charm B&B **9**

Very Expensive

Crowne Plaza Hotel   Built in the late 1920s, the hotel has been extensively and recently remodeled but still retains the large public rooms and elegant style of a grand old hotel. It is rumored that the customs officials in the Rainbow Bridge offices just across the street brought their binoculars to work each day while Marilyn Monroe stayed here. John Lennon and Yoko Ono also stayed here on their honeymoon. The big new innovation is celebrated Chef Massimo Capra, who has given his name to the menu of The Rainbow Room located on the 10th floor. The hotel is directly connected by an enclosed walkway to Casino Niagara and the Fallsview Waterpark.

WHAT YOU'LL really PAY

The prices quoted here are for hotels' rack rate, the maximum that they charge; it is, however, unlikely that you'll end up paying that rate. You can typically find discounts of up to 20% for rooms when booking through websites such as hotels.com or Expedia. Sometimes the best rates can be obtained from the hotel website as the properties often offer a lower rate for online bookings or for customers who are part of their loyalty programs. The best rates can be found in off season, for a room without a Falls view, when it is not unheard of to get a good room in an upscale property in the C$100 range. Rack rates at the Niagara Hilton in November start at C$119 but you can get the same room for C$99 on hotel. com. If you're the gambling type, you can bid for a room on Priceline. *Note:* Quoted discount rates almost never include breakfast, hotel tax, or any applicable resort fees. Wi-Fi fees are paid separately and are independent of the hotel rate.

5685 Falls Ave., Niagara Falls, ON L2E 6W7. www.niagarafallscrowneplazahotel.com. © **800/263-7135** or 905/374-4447. 234 units. C$89–C$499 standard double; children 18 and under stay free in parent's room. AE, DC, DISC, MC, V. Self-parking C$19; valet parking C$30. **Amenities:** Restaurant; shopping concourse bar; concierge; indoor pool; room service; sauna & whirlpool. *In room:* A/C, TV w/pay movies, hair dryer, Wi-Fi (paid).

The Giacomo ★★ The only boutique hotel in Niagara Falls, NY, this new hotel is situated in a renovated Art Deco office building near the Niagara Falls State Park, complete with Mayan-style reliefs. The rooms are large, with platform beds, hardwood floors, high ceilings, and many have fireplaces and Jacuzzi baths. The upper floor rooms have fine views of the Falls and the river. This is a very elegant property and really the only upscale hotel on the American side of the river.

222 First St., Niagara Falls, NY 14303. www.thegiacomo.com. © **716/299-0200.** 38 units. C$164–C$338 double,. Suites C$251–C$349. Prices include breakfast. Packages available, complimentary valet parking, shuttle service. AE, DC, MC, V. **Amenities:** 2 lounges; fitness center; room service. *In room:* A/C, flatscreen TV, fridge, hair dryer, Wi-Fi (free).

Hilton Niagara Falls Fallsview ★★ ☺ This hotel is officially the tallest in Canada because of its new 53-story tower addition. Family focused, this large 1,000-room hotel has an Adventure Pool with a water slide and cascading waterfall. Above the pool, parents can work out in a fitness area. Kids can also play in the neighboring arcade and waterpark. Rooms are generously proportioned. Guests can choose from city views, or more expensive rooms with views of the Falls. The new tower has all-suite rooms with fireplaces and sitting rooms. In addition to the fine-dining Watermark restaurant, there's the first Romano's Macaroni Grill in Ontario and the Brasa Brazilian Steakhouse and Wine Bar. This is a busy hotel whose lobby is often crowded in high season, and there can be long waits for elevators and valet parking. For a blowout stay experience, try the Presidential Suite on the 50th floor of the new tower.

6361 Fallsview Blvd., Niagara Falls, ON L2G 3V9. www.niagarafallshilton.com. © **888/370-0325** or 905/354-7887. Fax 905/374-6707. 1,000 units. C$119–C$199 double; suites from C$199. Special packages available. AE, DC, MC, V. Valet and self-parking C$25. **Amenities:** Restaurant; bar; coffee shop; babysitting; concierge; golf nearby; exercise room; Jacuzzi; pool; limited room service; sauna; spa. *In room:* A/C, TV w/pay movies, hair dryer, Wi-Fi (paid).

Marriott Gateway On the Falls ★   At the far end of Fallsview Boulevard, away from the hustle of the casino area, lies the Marriott Gateway (formerly the Sheraton Fallsview Hotel & Conference Centre). The hotel has undergone extensive renovations, so the lobby and rooms are fresh and the staff at the front desk is friendly and efficient. Rooms on the upper floors have the best views of the Falls, with floor-to-ceiling windows, but you'll pay extra for these rooms. And it's family-friendly: There are a number of packages available, including ones geared to romance, family, and sightseeing.

6755 Fallsview Blvd., Niagara Falls, ON L2G 3W7. www.niagarafallsgateway.com. ✆ **905/374-1077.** 402 units. C$129–C$179 standard double; C$169–C$499 suite. Children 18 and under stay free in parent's room. AE, DC, DISC, MC, V. Self-parking C$20; valet parking C$25. **Amenities:** 3 restaurants; bar; concierge; golf course nearby; exercise room; hot tub; indoor pool; limited room service; sauna. *In room:* A/C, TV w/pay movies, hair dryer, Wi-Fi (paid).

Marriott Niagara Falls Fallsview & Spa ★★ ☺   Families traveling with children will love the entertainment possibilities—a pool, a PlayStation in the rooms, a game room, and a clear view of the Falls from the rooms (including the fireworks display held on summer weekends). Holiday packages for families may include popcorn and movie night, complimentary tickets to one or more local attractions, and a magician's workshop. There are family shows in the on-site live theater and a kids' club to keep the little darlings busy. The hotel is only 90m (295 ft.) from the Falls and built in a curving design that allows virtually every room an unobstructed view. Even the standard rooms are generously sized with large bathrooms; upgraded rooms let you take a whirlpool bath with the Falls just a glance away. This is a busy hotel, but the staff members are friendly and customer oriented. The only negative is the fake, and often dusty, flowers in every corner.

6740 Fallsview Blvd., Niagara Falls, ON L2G 3W6. www.niagarafallsmarriott.com. ✆ **888/501-8916** or 905/357-7300. Fax 905/357-0490. 427 units. C$120–C$190 double; from C$170 suite. Packages available. AE, DC, DISC, MC, V. Valet parking C$20. **Amenities:** Restaurant; lounge; babysitting; children's programs; concierge; executive-level rooms; exercise room; 2 Jacuzzis; large indoor pool; limited room service; sauna; spa. *In room:* A/C, TV w/pay movies, hair dryer, minibar, Wi-Fi (paid).

Expensive

Courtyard by Marriott ☺   A great place to sleep but not necessarily linger. The standard rooms are similar to those at many chain hotels: They're clean and large but are slightly generic without any frills. But there's loads of space in these rooms and a variety of options to upgrade—presidential suites offer a Jacuzzi and fireplace, and king-size suites include a whirlpool bath for two in the room. The entire family can stay in a two-room family suite that sleeps up to six. This newer hotel is great for families; there are many amenities, such as an indoor pool with whirlpool and outdoor pool with slide, and the large Keg Restaurant. There's an excellent new package available, called Kids Love Niagara, which includes attractions, meals, and accommodations. It's a great location: next to all the attractions of the Falls, without being too immersed in the mayhem of Clifton Hill.

5950 Victoria Ave., Niagara Falls, ON L2G 3L7. www.nfcourtyard.com. ✆ **800/321-2211** or 905/358-3083. Fax 905/358-8720. 258 units. June–Aug from C$99 double, from C$140 suite; Sept–May from C$80 double, from C$120 suite. Packages available. AE, DC, MC, V. Self-parking June–Aug C$10, other times free. **Amenities:** Large restaurant; children's programs; small exercise room; Jacuzzi; indoor/outdoor pool; limited room service; sauna. *In room:* A/C, TV w/pay movies, hair dryer, Wi-Fi (paid).

Doubletree Resort Lodge & Spa Fallsview Niagara Falls ★★   The foyer of this hotel has an Arts and Crafts feel—spacious, with high ceilings decorated with wooden beams and an abundance of fieldstone. The opulent feeling continues at the Five Lakes Spa AVEDA. Beyond these elegant touches, the rooms are spacious and warmly decorated in cherry and burgundy wood furniture. One touch that I appreciated was the little wire grill on the windows that can be opened to allow fresh air into the room. Free Wi-Fi in the rooms and in the lobby is also a bonus. And despite its big-hotel feel, each room is decorated with local art and black-and-white photos of Ontario from days gone by. There's an outside hot tub in the summer surrounded by trees from Ontario's Algonquin Park. A new art gallery, called the Ochre Gallery, features beautiful Canadian landscape art and totem poles from British Columbia. The staff is particularly welcoming and helpful, even offering warm chocolate chip cookies at check-in.

6039 Fallsview Blvd., Niagara Falls, ON L2G 3V6. www.niagarafallsdoubletree.com. © **800/730-8609** or 905/358-3817. Fax 905/358-3680. 224 units. C$99–C$189 double; suites from C$129. Children 18 and under stay free in parent's room. Weekend packages available. AE, DC, MC, V. Self-parking C$12. **Amenities:** Restaurant; pub; coffee shop; babysitting; concierge; golf nearby; exercise room; seasonal hot tub; indoor pool; limited room service; sauna; spa. *In room:* A/C, TV w/pay movies, hair dryer, Wi-Fi (free).

Four Points by Sheraton ★

Bright reds and yellows liven up this large hotel (formerly the Renaissance Fallsview), which is a good bet for families. Adjoining rooms mean parents can have some peace and quiet, while kids can talk all night. Rooms are very spacious, particularly the Executive Fallsview, with two doubles (or a king-size) in one room adjoined to a room with another two queen-size beds—not to mention a great view of the Horseshoe Falls. Or for the adults, choose from a spacious deluxe room with Jacuzzi (heart-shaped tubs are optional) and king-size bed. Kids 12 and under receive half-price meals and age 5 and under eat free. Cribs and rollaway beds are complimentary. Squash and racquetball are available beside the small gym, which is in need of better ventilation. Located in the heart of Niagara Falls, there is a convenient catwalk attached to the casino, which is loaded with more restaurants, shops, and spa services. East Side Marios and IHOP are located right in the hotel.

6455 Fallsview Blvd., Niagara Falls, ON L2G 3V9. www.fallsviewplaza.com. © **888/238-9190** or 905/357-5200. Fax 905/357-7487. 262 units. From C$89 double; suites from C$189. Children 18 and under stay free in parent's room. Weekend packages available. AE, DC, MC, V. Valet parking C$20. **Amenities:** 2 restaurants; lounge; babysitting; children's programs; seasonal concierge; executive floor; golf nearby; exercise room; Jacuzzi; pool; limited room service; sauna. *In room:* A/C, TV w/pay movies, fridge available (C$10), hair dryer, Wi-Fi (free on 9th floor and in lobby).

Great Wolf Lodge ★★ ☺

"Can we stay longer?" is a refrain I often overheard kids asking their parents at this kid-inspired lodge. The main attraction is over 9,300 sq. m (100,104 sq. ft.) of water slides and pools, with roller coaster–style water slides, and the wicked Vortex. Activities are available for the wee ones also. The kid-focused rooms, some featuring a segregated sleeping area with bunk beds, allow families to double or triple up. For more luxury, there's the Loft Fireplace Suite, with three queen beds, one in the upstairs loft. Rooms are kid-proofed with no loose figurines and no sharp table edges. Although the rooms are big, the bathrooms might be a squeeze for two or more.

There's a spa and a tranquil room with a waterfall. Three hours of babysitting costs C$20 at the Cub Club, where kids can make crafts, play video games, or watch movies. There are seven eateries but beware: It's not healthy food and it is expensive. Wristbands, which act as room keys, can also be loaded up with money for kids to spend at will. Rates include water-park passes and parking.

3950 Victoria Ave., Niagara Falls, ON L2E 7M8. www.greatwolflodge.com. © **800/605-WOLF** (9653) or 905/354-4888. 406 units. C$199–C$799. C$20 extra person. Packages available. AE, DC, MC, V. Self-parking free. **Amenities:** 2 restaurants; 3 snack bars (one seasonal); pizza takeout; 2 coffee shops; bar; babysitting; children's center; concierge; 18-hole minigolf; health club; hot tub; adults-only Jacuzzi; pools (indoor/outdoor); spa. *In room:* A/C, TV w/pay movies, fridge, hair dryer, Wi-Fi (paid).

Niagara Fallsview Casino Resort ★★ If you want to be pampered, try this upscale Canadian version of Las Vegas. This casino is a self-contained biosphere of hedonism. The rooms, although nicely decorated in burgundy and green earth tones, are standard hotel fare. The standard Diplomat rooms are quite small, and I recommend upgrading to the more spacious Deluxe. Jacuzzis are found in all suites. The falls-view rooms boast great views.

The real fun is outside the rooms, however: The bright, white-tiled pool area, with large tropical plants and glass windows, feels like an exotic spa. To get the full spa treatment, walk down the hall from the pool for pedicures and therapeutic massages. Next door is an impressive workout room—all-new machines face four large flatscreen TVs. Staff members come by frequently with fresh towels for guests. Jacuzzis are located in all suites, as well as in the spa and pool areas. Everything feels new and flashy throughout the resort.

6380 Fallsview Blvd., Niagara Falls, ON L2G 7X5. www.fallsviewcasinoresort.com. © **888/FALLSVU** (325-5788) or 905/358-3255. 374 units. C$149–C$349 double. AE, DC, MC, V. Valet Parking from C$20, Self-parking from C$5, or free with Fallsview Players Advantage Club membership (membership free). **Amenities:** 10 restaurants; 4 bars; babysitting; bike rental; concierge; executive floor; golf nearby; exercise room; Jacuzzi; pool; room service; sauna, casino. *In room:* A/C, TV w/pay movies, hair dryer, Internet (paid).

Red Coach Inn ★★ This 1920s-era Tudor-style hotel with its distinctive gabled roof is the most historic property on the American side of the Falls by a nautical mile, and its individuality is worth crossing the border for. The prices are set at a reasonable level for the high standard of service and room amenities, and the restaurant is worth eating in. Located just across the street from the Niagara River rapids, you're at the gateway of Niagara Falls State Park's attractions. The standard rooms are rather small and basic; I'd recommend staying in one of the suites, which are more like apartments, with full kitchens, dining tables, and comfortable furniture. Suites also enjoy a view of the rapids, a separate bedroom, and spacious bathrooms. The feel of the place is like an English country house.

2 Buffalo Ave., Niagara Falls, NY 14303-1133. www.redcoach.com. © **800/282-1459** or 716/282-1459. 19 units. C$125–C$183 double; C$193–C$280 suite. Packages available. AE, DISC, MC, V. **Amenities:** Restaurant; lounge. *In room:* A/C, TV/VCR, fridge, hair dryer, Wi-Fi (free).

The Sterling Inn & Spa ★★★ If you're looking for something other than a chain hotel or a B&B, the Sterling is the perfect fit. This is Niagara Falls's only boutique hotel, and while the surrounding neighborhood is a bit run-down, the Falls are only a short walk away and the Greg Frewin Dinner Theatre is just across the parking lot. The exterior of the building is a bit odd—it used to be a dairy at one time, and the concrete milk bottle has been retained. But the surprise is the interior, with its modern foyer, perhaps a bit too stark, and large, contemporary rooms that are appointed with large glassed-in rainforest showers, fireplaces, and four-poster beds. A great reason to stay here is the dining room. AG (clever—the chemical symbol for silver) is the best restaurant in Niagara Falls. An in-house spa delivers a range of treatments, there's free Wi-Fi in all the rooms, and—the clincher for me—complimentary breakfast is delivered to your room in the morning.

5195 Magdalen St., Niagara Falls, ON L2G 3S6. www.sterlingniagara.com. ℂ **289/292-0000** or 877/783-7772. 41 units. C$125–C$150 double including breakfast. Packages available. AE, DC, MC, V. Complimentary parking. **Amenities:** Restaurant; bar/lounge; concierge; room service; spa; Falls shuttle available. *In room:* A/C, TV w/pay movies, hair dryer, Wi-Fi (free).

Moderate

Bedham Hall ★   Old-country decor meets relaxing amenities of the 21st century. Mature guests will appreciate fireplaces and Jacuzzis (except in the Buckingham Room) added to spacious rooms, with sizable bathrooms that feature Ghilcrest & Soames products. Flowery wallpaper and dainty touches abound. The Windsor Room, on the third floor, is decked out with a four-poster bed and a separate living area overlooking the gorge. The Buckingham Room is the smallest but most charming, with a sitting room located in the turret of the house, opposite stairs leading from the sitting room directly to the bedroom. In the yellow and blue (feels like royalty) breakfast area downstairs, guests can eat at the communal table or at a table for two near the window overlooking the gorge. The host is an informative concierge and will whip up eggs, any style, for breakfast.

4835 River Rd., Niagara Falls, ON L2E 3G4. www.bedhamhall.com. ℂ **877/374-8515** or 905/374-8515. Fax 905/374-9189. 4 units. C$115–C$150 double. Packages available. Rates include breakfast. MC, V. Free parking. **Amenities:** Spa services arranged. *In room:* A/C, TV/DVD, fridge, hair dryer, no phone, Wi-Fi (free).

Chestnut Inn   No frills and plain decor but good value with some good add-ons. Parents will appreciate the Grey Room—no one above or underneath to hear the pitter-patter of little feet. Every room except the loft has a single bed built into the curved windows—perfect for wee ones. Likewise, a large front lawn with gazebo and a pool in the back allow kids to be kids, or adults to linger. There are private patios for every room; all rooms are also equipped with electric fireplaces. A communal room has tea and coffee, as well as a hair dryer and iron. There's plenty of common space in the living and sun rooms, full of wicker chairs, with decks of cards and books. Breakfast is continental—shreddies and corn flakes—but also features apple cinnamon French toast—the house specialty.

4983 River Rd., Niagara Falls, ON L2E 3G6. www.chestnutinnbb.com. ℂ **905/374-4616.** 4 units. C$100–C$120 double. C$35 extra person. Rates include breakfast. MC, V. Free parking. **Amenities:** Outdoor pool. *In room:* A/C, TV, no phone.

The Tower Hotel ★★ 🌿   A landmark of Ontario's Niagara Falls skyline for decades and now under new ownership, the newly remodeled and renamed Tower Hotel (formerly the Ramada Plaza Fallsview Hotel) features a mere 42 guest rooms, in a pod at the top of the Konica Minolta Tower Centre. This gives the property a distinctive boutique hotel feel. Most of the rooms have been updated to a funky almost Art Deco style, with upholstered headboards, flatscreen TVs, and mirrored side tables—not to mention the fabulous views of the Falls. Ask for a renovated room—the old rooms can be dingy and unattractive—and insist on a Falls view. The hotel feels young and edgy—a great place for a weekend getaway. Guests have free access to the observation deck, which has arguably the best view of the Falls in the city.

6732 Fallsview Blvd., Niagara Falls, ON L2G 3W6. www.niagaratower.com. ℂ **866/325-5784** or 905/356-1501. Fax 905/356-8245. 42 units. Queen or king C$79–C$169 double. AE, DC, MC, V. Valet parking C$15. **Amenities:** Restaurant; bar; golf course nearby; limited room service. *In room:* A/C, TV, fridge, hair dryer, Wi-Fi (free).

Victorian Charm B&B 🍴 ☺ Starched embroidered linens, a piano in the foyer, and a turret combine to make the name appropriate. The Garden Room—my favorite—has a terrace overlooking the garden, a remote-controlled fireplace, and an air-jet therapeutic tub. Decorated with white wicker furniture and yellow walls, it's an airy and fresh room. The Grande Room has a mini–living space with sofa and bathtub in the room, while the bathroom is located immediately outside the door. Owner Anne Marie, the mother of five children, is happy to cater to the little ones—there is a brand-new crib, and a carriage and stroller are ready to go for a jaunt through the quiet residential area, only a short walk from the casino and Falls. For breakfast, the Belgian waffles with fruit from Anne Marie's organic garden (or preserves in the winter) are tasty, as are the crepes with whipped cream and maple syrup. *Note:* This establishment is entirely nonsmoking.

6039 Culp St., Niagara Falls, ON L2G 2B7. www.victoriancharmbb.com. ⓒ **877/794-6758** or 905/357-4221. Fax 905/357-9115. 5 units. C$120–C$170 double. Rates include breakfast. Weekly rates offer 1 day free. AE, MC, V. Free parking. **Amenities:** Free train station pickup/drop-off; babysitting; golf nearby; Jacuzzi; spa services available in room; rooms for those w/limited mobility. *In room:* A/C, TV/VCR, fridge, hair dryer, no phone, Wi-Fi (free).

Inexpensive

Lion's Head B&B ★ This bed-and-breakfast hasn't changed structurally since 1910. Overlooking the gorge, it's a cozy retreat from the bright lights of downtown Niagara Falls, only a 10-minute walk away. Each room is decorated in keeping with its artist namesake—the coral pink walls and dark wood furniture in the Georgia O'Keeffe Room are decidedly bohemian, while the luminescent yellows of the van Gogh are as bright as a sunflower. The third-floor French Quarter room offers privacy for a couple with its own entrance, while friends can be accommodated in an adjacent room.

The eclectic, funky decor throughout the home reflects owner Helena Harrington's effervescent personality and world travels, as does her breakfast menu, which is constantly changing; recent dishes include stuffed tomatoes with asiago cheese and her signature poached pears with orange spice glaze and yogurt topping. More added touches in the rooms include goose-down bedding and Italian ceramic tiles. The B&B is entirely nonsmoking.

5239 River Rd., Niagara Falls, ON L2E 3G9. www.lionsheadbb.com. ⓒ **905/374-1681.** 5 units. C$125–C$185 double, Suite C$165–C$225. Rates include breakfast. AE, MC, V. Free parking. **Amenities:** Golf nearby. *In room:* A/C, hair dryer.

Rainbow House B&B This historic Victorian home has wrought-iron beds, embroidered doilies, stained-glass windows, and heaps of charming clutter. Think whitewashed wicker furniture and lots of collectables. A bit fussy for my tastes, but owner Laura Lee takes pride in her cozy home and has made it extremely cheery and welcoming. Standard rooms offer better value than the suite. If you get the urge to get hitched in the honeymoon capital of the world, there is a wedding chapel conveniently located on the premises. This property is best suited to adults and older children; no smoking is allowed.

423 Rainbow Blvd. S., Niagara Falls, NY 14303. www.rainbowhousebb.com. ⓒ **800/724-3536** or 716/282-1135. Fax 716/292-1135. 4 units. $85–$160 double. Packages available. Rates include breakfast. MC, V. Free parking. *In room:* A/C, hair dryer.

4

Where can you take the kids and have fun at the same time? You'll find a warm welcome at **Victorian Charm B&B,** 6039 Culp St., Niagara Falls, ON L2G 2B7 (✆ **877/794-6758**). Crib, carriage, and stroller are waiting for your little one. Crepes and Belgian waffles will put a smile on sleepy faces. If your kids like nonstop entertainment, head for the **Marriott Niagara Falls Fallsview & Spa,** 6740 Fallsview Blvd., Niagara Falls, ON L2G 3W6 (✆ **888/501-8916**). With a pool, game room, kids' club, live family theater, PlayStation, and movie and popcorn nights, your children will play hard and sleep well. For a country vacation, experience the charm of the farm at **Feast of Fields Organic Vineyard B&B Cottage,** 3403 Eleventh St., Jordan, ON L2R 6P7 (✆ **905/562-0151**). This self-contained two-bedroom cottage with full kitchen is part of a restored farmhouse (ca. 1835). The surrounding paddocks are inhabited not only by horses and cows, but also by llamas and a peacock or two.

NIAGARA-ON-THE-LAKE

Niagara-on-the-Lake, with its historical streets, fine choice of restaurants, and boutique shopping, is an attractive place to spend a night or two. Adult vacationers without children in tow will find the town to be a welcome contrast to the razzmatazz of Niagara Falls.

Best for: Those interested in culture and history, and those who love higher-end shopping.

Drawbacks: The area is very busy and expensive from May to October, and the nightlife is on the sedate side.

Very Expensive

Charles Inn ★★★   Built in 1832, the historic Charles Inn is the perfect antidote to cookie-cutter chain hotels. The pleasing symmetry of the Georgian architecture and sweeping verandas make you want to sink into a wicker chair, order a cup of tea, and absorb the feeling of a gentler time. The Charles stands on a quiet part of the main street in town, far enough away from the action yet close enough to walk to the theater or shopping. Reserve the Verandah Room, once the kitchen, which still has its original fireplace and a screened-in porch that looks out to the garden, the nearby golf course, and the river. Bed linens are 300-thread-count Egyptian cotton, while the duvets and pillows are down-filled. Creaking floors and wooden antique furniture throughout the property add to the experience. The restaurant is very pretty, the food is good, and later you can enjoy a drink in the oak bar.

209 Queen St., Niagara-on-the-Lake, ON L0S 1J0. www.charlesinn.ca. ✆ **866/556-8883** or 905/468-4588. 12 units. C$210–C$335 double. Rates include breakfast. Weekend packages available. AE, MC, V. Free parking. **Amenities:** Restaurant; lounge; enclosed veranda dining year-round; babysitting; golf course next door; limited room service. *In room:* A/C, hair dryer, Internet (paid), no phone.

Harbour House Hotel ★★   Harbour House is a perfect base for exploring the pleasures of Niagara, instantly making you feel welcomed. The lobby is a warm shade of Tuscan yellow, with a cozy fireplace and overstuffed sofas and chairs. In the rooms, there are Frette robes in the closet, and the king-size beds have fluffy goose-down

Niagara-on-the-Lake Hotels

Niagara River

Niagara Parkway

To Queenston →

Queen's Parade

Niagara River

To Niagara-on-the-Lake ←

To Queenston

Queenston St.

Queenston

Niagara

York Rd.

Niagara Pkwy.

To Niagara Falls ↗

405

Portage Rd.

1/4 Mi

25 km

Melville St.

Ball St.

Delatre St.

Ricardo St.

Wellington St.

Byron St.

Picton St.

Davy St.

Platoff St.

Gage St.

Castlereagh St.

Nelles St.

Christopher Ct.

Weatherstone Ct.

Pafford St.

Park Ct.

King St.

Regent St.

Victoria St.

Front St.

Prideaux St.

Queen St.

Johnson St.

Centre St.

Gate St.

Karsam Ct

Anne St.

John St.

Simcoe St.

Mississauga St.

William St.

Mary St.

Balmoral Dr.

To QEW →

Butler St.

Dorchester St.

Nassau St.

Butler's Ln.

Lakeshore Rd.

Palatine Pl.

Niagara Blvd.

Lake Ontario

1/4 mi

25 km

Birdsong Chalet **22**
Brockamour Manor Inn and B&B **18**
Charles Inn **3**
Clover Field House Bed and Breakfast **16**
The Doctor's House **4**
Everheart Country Manor **20**
Gate House Hotel **5**
Grand Victorian B&B **14**
Greaves Sweet Escapes **6**
Harbour House Hotel **10**
Lakewinds Country Manor **1**
The Moffatt Inn **8**
Oban Inn **2**
The Old Bank House **9**
Orchid Inn **17**
Pillar and Post **19**
Prince of Wales **7**
Queens Landing **11**
Riverbend Inn & Vineyard **13**
Shaw Club **12**
Three Forty Gate Bed and Breakfast **15**
White Oaks Conference Resort & Spa **21**

duvets, with 300-thread-count Egyptian cotton sheets, and Mount Orford feather beds. There are Judith Jackson toiletries and soft throws to cuddle up in next to the fire. The Conservatory, where breakfast is served, is large and cheery, and breakfast is a selection of warm and cold dishes. In summer, guests can take their coffee out to the patio. At 4pm each day, there is a wine tasting, featuring a different area winery. The Harbour House guests can arrange to have lunch or dinner at the Charles Inn or Zee's (p. 78 and 83), using the complimentary shuttle.

85 Melville St., Niagara-on-the-Lake, ON L0S 1J0. www.harbourhousehotel.ca. ✆ **866/277-6677** or 905/468-4683. Fax 905/468-0366. 31 units. C$199–C$395 double; C$425 and up suite. Packages available. Rates include breakfast. AE, MC, V. Free parking. Pets allowed in two specific guest rooms, C$25 per day. **Amenities:** Babysitting; bike rentals; concierge; limited room service. *In room:* A/C, TV, hair dryer, Wi-Fi (free).

Oban Inn ★★   If you have stayed at the Oban Inn in years past, you won't recognize it in its new incarnation. The hotel has undergone a complete renovation. It's now a sleek interpretation of the hedonistic inn-cum-spa. The rooms, which were rather ornately Victorian, are now smartly modern, with spare, clean lines and all the most modern comforts. O Spa, its in-hotel wellness retreat, has a state-of-the-art exercise facility, lap pool, outdoor hot spring, and steam room. The dining room, Kir, serves classic dishes, like beef tenderloin with king crab remoulade. The gardens are lovely, as is the view of the lake and Fort Niagara. The Oban is just a short walk from the center of NOTL, but the trees, green lawns, and quiet streets make it seem discretely removed from the bustle of the town.

160 Front St., Niagara-on-the-Lake, ON L0S 1J0. www.obaninn.ca. ✆ **866/359-6226** or 905/468-2165. 26 units. C$150–C$320 double; C$250–C$420 suite. AE, MC, V. Packages available. Rates include breakfast. AE, MC, V. Free parking. **Amenities:** Restaurant; bar; concierge; health club; pool; spa. *In room:* TV.

Pillar and Post ★   The Pillar and Post has rustic charm, with its post-and-beam structure, and original windows, which have been preserved where possible. The inn's rooms are laid out in a U-shape around a central courtyard with lovely gardens. Guest-room decor has been updated to feel more contemporary: Black-and-white photographs, plasma TVs, and fresh white bedspreads contrast with the dark furniture. Deluxe rooms have fireplaces, while premium rooms have fireplaces and jetted tubs. Rooms can feel cramped and rooms in some wings have larger bathrooms than others; request a more spacious one if that's important to you. The real highlight of this inn is the spa—the 100 Fountain Spa; for the height of romance, soak with your partner in the outdoor hot pool. It is particularly sybaritic in the winter, when it's snowing. The dining room is heavy on wood; the food and service are more than satisfactory (p. 81).

48 John St., Niagara-on-the-Lake, ON L0S 1J0. www.vintage-hotels.com. ✆ **888/669-5566** or 905/468-2123. Fax 905/468-3551. 122 units. From C$225 double; from C$425 suite. AE, DC, DISC, MC, V. Free parking. **Amenities:** Restaurant; bar; babysitting; bike rental; concierge; Jacuzzi; indoor and outdoor pools; sauna; spa. *In room:* A/C, TV w/pay movies, hair dryer, minibar, Wi-Fi (paid).

Prince of Wales ★★   As the flagship property in the old town of Niagara-on-the-Lake, standing in prime position at the southeast corner of Picton and King streets, the Prince of Wales is less Victorian than it used to be. The decor has been decluttered, and the dining room is now more Tuscan than British. That being said, afternoon tea in the Drawing Room is a beautifully realized exercise in good taste and good food. Rooms are individually decorated, drawing their inspiration from days gone by, with an abundance of floral fabrics and antiques, complemented by reproductions and 21st-century amenities. Rooms have recently been refurbished and are bright and cheerful, while suites are elegant, with spacious bathrooms and a separate living area. A nightly turndown service includes a fresh rose on your pillow and the in-house spa offers a nice choice of treatments to relax you after the theater.

6 Picton St., Niagara-on-the-Lake, ON L0S 1J0. www.vintage-hotels.com. © **888/669-5566** or 905/468-3246. Fax 905/468-5521. 110 units. C$169–C$315 double. Packages available. AE, DC, DISC, MC, V. Valet parking C$5; self-parking free. Pets accepted (C$35). **Amenities:** Restaurant; cafe; bar; lounge; babysitting; bike rental; concierge; health club; Jacuzzi; indoor pool; room service; spa. *In room:* A/C, TV w/pay movies, hair dryer, minibar, Wi-Fi (paid, or free in the business center).

Queens Landing ★★
Poised above the meeting point of the Niagara River and Lake Ontario, this elegant hotel is large but has the feel of a boutique hotel. It is a lovely property, with a high-ceilinged lobby and beautifully designed public spaces. A short walk from all the NOTL attractions, this Georgian-style hotel has an excellent restaurant, Tiara, that proudly serves regionally inspired cuisine. Rooms are contemporary in style, with clean lines, and fireplaces in deluxe and premium rooms.

155 Byron St., Niagara-on-the-Lake, ON L0S 1J0. www.vintage-hotels.com. © **888/669-5566** or 905/468-2195. 142 units. C$159-C$415 double; C$300-C$465 suite. AE, MC, V. Complimentary valet parking. **Amenities:** Restaurant; Jacuzzi; indoor pool; room service; sauna; spa; rooms for those w/ limited mobility. *In room:* TV w/pay movies, hair dryer, Wi-Fi (paid).

Riverbend Inn & Vineyard ★
This restored Georgian property with its own vineyards, and its own wine, bottled for the Riverbend by nearby Reif Estate Winery, is the quintessential NOTL hotel. The inn has been completely renovated by new owners. Rooms that were a bit dark and Victorian are now bright and light. All 21 rooms are large and have fireplaces. Corner rooms have several windows, offering different views over the vineyards and gardens, some with private balconies. A large fireplace accents the Belle Epoque style saloon bar, and the dining room is one of the prettiest in town. The food is exceptional, with Chef William Brunyansky producing delectable locally inspired dishes that look like edible art. Open for breakfast, lunch, and dinner for nonresidents as well as guests, this dining room, with its outdoor patio with views over the surrounding vineyards and its gifted chef, is one of the best places to stay and dine in the area.

16104 Niagara River Pkwy., Niagara-on-the-Lake, ON L0S 1J0. www.riverbendinn.ca. © **905/468-8866.** Fax 905/468-8829. 21 units. C$185–C$280 double; C$300–C$390 suite. Kids 10 and under stay free in parent's room. C$25 per extra person 11 years and over in room. AE, MC, V. Free parking. **Amenities:** Restaurant; bar; babysitting; bike rental; limited room service. *In room:* A/C, TV, hair dryer, Wi-Fi (paid).

White Oaks Conference Resort & Spa ★
Don't be put off by the exterior of this hotel—it's decidedly industrial in appearance, and it's located beside a busy highway. Inside, the spaces are elegantly stylish, and there is even a nice garden tucked in behind. Striving to be the ultimate in a combined resort/spa/ conference center, White Oaks has a list of facilities, amenities, and activities as long as your arm. Their spa offers skin-care treatments, massage, hydrotherapy, and a variety of retreat packages. Fitness nuts will lap up private sessions with personal trainers and Pilates instructors. Rooms are spacious, swathed in muted earth tones, and all have either a sunrise or sunset view. Ask for a room facing the gardens rather than the parking lot. Also, lower-priced superior rooms are quite a bit smaller than the tower rooms (35 sq. m/377 sq. ft. vs. 51 sq. m/549 sq. ft.). The property has an artsy "athletic club" feel.

253 Taylor Rd., Niagara-on-the-Lake, ON L0S 1J0. www.whiteoaksresort.com. ☎ **800/263-5766** or 905/688-2550. 220 units. From C$149 double; C$229–C$599 suite. Children 12 and under stay free in parent's room. AE, MC, V. Free parking. **Amenities:** 2 restaurants; babysitting; bike rental; concierge; executive rooms; golf course; health club; hot tub; indoor pool; spa; indoor tennis courts. *In room:* A/C, TV w/pay movies, hair dryer, minibar, Wi-Fi (paid).

Expensive

Brockamour Manor Inn and B&B ★★   Romance and history combine in this 1809 country inn, where Sir Isaac Brock wooed Lady Sophia Shaw, to whom he was secretly betrothed and where they last met on the eve of the War of 1812. He was later killed at the Battle of Queenston Heights. All rooms feature period furnishings and decor, fireplaces, central air-conditioning, en suite baths, and Jacuzzi-style tubs. You can sit on the veranda and enjoy the flower gardens or take a short walk to the theater and shopping district.

433 King St., Box 402, Niagara-on-the-Lake, ON L0S 1J0. www.brockamour.com. ☎ **905/468-5527.** 6 units. C$169–C$250 double. Rates include breakfast. AE, DISC, MC, V. No pets. **Amenities:** Billiard table. *In room:* A/C, TV, fireplace, hair dryer, Wi-Fi (free).

Grand Victorian B&B ★   This mansion on the Niagara Parkway was built in the Victorian era in the Queen Anne Revival style as a rebellion against the boxy, crowded Victorian architectural fashion of the day. Evidence of Quaker influences can be seen throughout the property. Each room is individually decorated and appointed; all are charming. A pretty sunroom/conservatory was added in 1899 and now serves as a breakfast nook for guests. The interior has a very open, airy feel, with high ceilings and an open floor plan allowing flow through the main-floor rooms. The property is popular for weddings; it's also a great place to stay for lovers of historical homes and antiques. The owner has acquired a considerable collection of antique furniture from Europe and North America over the years, in addition to a number of items from her grandmother's seaside homes in England, including draperies and china. The property is TV- and smoke-free.

15618 Niagara Pkwy., Niagara-on-the-Lake, ON L0S 1J0. www.grandvictorian.ca. ☎ **905/468-0997.** Fax 905/468-1551. 6 units. C$170–C$225 room; C$225 suite. MC, V. Free parking. **Amenities:** Bike rental; outdoor tennis court. *In room:* A/C, no phone.

Lakewinds Country Manor ★★★   This lovely house was built in 1880–81 and became the summer home for Gustav Fleischmann, a wealthy distiller from Buffalo, New York, and member of the famous Fleischmann's yeast family. Originally named "Clarette" (in tribute to his two oldest daughters, Clara and Thornetta), the house stood on the entire 1.6-hectare (4-acre) block, with gardens and stables at the rear.

Staff cottages and a guesthouse can still be found on properties adjacent to the original manor. Today, the home has been carefully renovated as a sumptuous inn. Each room is individually decorated, in styles that range from Victorian elegance to French country, and each has its own fireplace. Extras include a large heated pool with loungers, four guest bicycles, a pool table in the game room, a solarium, and secluded spots to sit and enjoy the views of North America's oldest golf course, the Niagara-on-the-Lake Golf Course, where play started in 1875. Breakfasts, using herbs and produce from the garden, are served in the grand dining room, or you may have a continental breakfast delivered to your room.

328 Queen St., Niagara-on-the-Lake, ON L0S 1J0. www.lakewinds.ca. ✆ **905/468-1888.** 6 units. C$165–C$245. Rates include breakfast. DISC, MC, V. No pets. **Amenities:** Pool. *In room:* A/C, Wi-Fi (free).

The Old Bank House ★   This two-story Georgian home, built around 1817, has an eclectic collection of artifacts from around the world, as well as a direct view of old Fort Niagara across the river. It was originally the first branch of the Bank of Canada. In 1902, the Prince and Princess of Wales stayed here. The comfortable sitting room features a cozy fireplace and three separate dining areas. Upstairs, the Arbour Room features French-style flowered wallpaper and a big oval mirror with red velvet chairs. The Pine Room has French doors leading out to a shared patio, while the high-ceilinged Cedar Room—open to bright sunlight—has a private patio. Walking through the uneven, creaky hardwood floors to the front entrance, you'll find a guest book under the nose of the house mascot—a stuffed eland (mooselike animal) from South Africa named Master Ted. He is the guardian of this quiet, contemplative place and a friend of the owners, Judy and Michael, who are gracious and warm.

10 Front St., Niagara-on-the-Lake, ON L0S 1J0. www.oldbankhouse.com. ✆ **877/468-7136** or 905/468-7136. 9 units. C$109–C$159 double. Rates include breakfast. AE, MC, V. Free parking. **Amenities:** Jacuzzi. *In room:* A/C, no phone.

Three Forty Gate Bed and Breakfast ★★★   This beautifully designed B&B is within easy walking distance of the theater and shopping district. Unlike the usual folksy style that many B&Bs adopt, Three Forty Gate is sleek and classic in design. It has the feel of a fine inn and, even if you don't normally like to go the B&B route, this one may delight you. All three rooms (there is one more small bedroom that can be rented if a group needs an extra bedroom) are on the top floor and have excellent views of the creek and gardens. All the small details have been taken care of, including MP3 docking stations in each room and premium-quality coffee and teas. Pre-breakfast coffee and the daily newspaper arrive each morning, with a full hot breakfast to follow at 9am.

340 Gate St. (P.O. Box 1238), Niagara-on-the-Lake, ON L0S 1J0. www.threefortygate.com. ✆ **905/468-9043.** 3 units. C$175–C$225 double. Rates include breakfast. Free parking. **Amenities:** TV. *In room:* A/C, hair dryer, Wi-Fi (free).

Moderate

Everheart Country Manor ★   Guests appreciate the seclusion of this manor in the sleepy town of Queenston at the foot of the Brock monument. Guests are able to chat with others on the wraparound patio, or they can find a secluded table out in the sunken gardens. There's an indoor pool, Jacuzzis, a fireplace in every room, and plenty of living space. The French doors of the Riverview Suite open to reveal the Niagara River, letting in lots of natural light, while the Garden View Suite, decorated in burgundy, feels like a gentlemen's club. The Turret Room is great for couples, with two chairs and a dining table in the turret. There's a small communal kitchen area—a separate room—that has a fridge for the day's food shopping. Choose your own breakfast the night before—you can eat in the dining room or in one of the many areas outside. Former Torontonians Doug and Joyce are wonderful conversationalists, but also respect guests' desire for privacy.

137 Queenston St., Queenston, ON L0S 1L0. www.everheart.ca. ✆ **866/284-0544** or 905/262-5444. 3 units. C$145–C$175 double. C$30 extra person. MC, V. Free parking. **Amenities:** Golf nearby; indoor pool. *In room:* A/C, TV/VCR (2 w/DVD), hair dryer, no phone, Wi-Fi (free).

Gate House Hotel   Located right in the heart of the action, the Gate House is a good choice, particularly if you make use of their very nice outdoor patio that gives you a front-row seat for people-watching. The hotel has been operating here for 20 years. The rooms are basic, contemporary in design, and clean, with flatscreen TVs.

42 Queen St., Niagara-on-the-Lake, ON L0S 1J0. www.gatehouse-niagara.com. ✆ **905/468-3263.** 10 units. C$130–C$215. Rates include continental breakfast. MC, V. **Amenities:** Restaurant, outdoor patio. *In room:* A/C, TV.

Greaves Sweet Escapes ✦   This two-bedroom, two-bath loft is perfectly located in the center of town, above the historic Greaves Jam & Marmalade store. Dating from 1845, the loft bedrooms are completely renovated, classically comfortable, and a bargain for two couples who want to be central to the action (or three couples, if they're willing to sleep on the pull-out couch). There is a large living space including a fully equipped kitchen with large bar island, stainless steel appliances and dishwasher, comfortable living room with gas fireplace and pull-out sofa bed and dining area. This would be a fine place to stay as the base camp for a wine-country exploration tour or for a Shaw Festival extravaganza, and when shared with friends, a real bargain.

55 Queen St., Niagara-on-the-Lake, ON L0S 1J0. www.greavesjams.com/sweetescape. ✆ **800/515-9939.** 1 unit. C$340 high season, 2-night minimum. AE, MC, V. **Amenities:** Kitchen; parking, fireplace, plasma TV. *In room:* A/C, Wi-Fi (free).

The Moffatt Inn ✦   This is a cozy hotel with an old English cottage feel to it that has been freshly renovated but remains an affordable bargain in this popular theater town. Rooms are cheery, the location is perfect, and the Coach & Horses English pub in-house serves bistro fare and becomes a comfy place for drinks after dark. Guests can use the fitness room and access the spa next door at the Prince of Wales.

60 Picton St. (at the corner of Davy St.), Niagara-on-the-Lake, ON L0S 1J0. www.vintage-hotels.com. ✆ **888/669-5566** or 905/468-4116. 24 units. From C$144 double. Packages available. AE, DC, MC, V. Free parking. **Amenities:** Restaurant; pub; babysitting arranged; concierge; golf nearby; room service. *In room:* A/C, TV, hair dryer, Wi-Fi (paid).

Shaw Club ★   The decor is sleek and minimalist: chic black furniture, bamboo plants, and steel accents. But it also has a home-away-from-home feel: DVDs and Italian coffees (espressos and cappuccinos) are complimentary in the lobby. Goldfish in the rooms also add a colorful touch. Rooms are quite cramped, but they're full of cool gadgets: an MP3 docking station, plasma TV, another TV in the bathroom, and a DVD/CD player. Other touches include 300-count Egyptian cotton linens, down pillows and duvet, and a gigantic shower head. The king suite with fireplace has its own balcony, wet bar, double soaker tub, and living room. Downstairs features Zee's Patio and Grill, which includes an outdoor wraparound patio to see theater-goers heading to the Shaw Theatre across the street.

92 Picton St., Niagara-on-the-Lake, ON L0S 1J0. www.shawclub.com. © **800/511-7070** or 905/468-5711. Fax 905/468-4988. 30 units. C$99–C$230 double. Packages available. Breakfast included. AE, DC, MC, V. Free parking. Pet accepted for C$25 per night. **Amenities:** Restaurant; lounge; babysitting arranged; concierge; golf nearby; exercise room; limited room service; spa. *In room:* A/C, TV/DVD w/ pay movies (free DVD library), fridge, hair dryer, Wi-Fi (paid).

Inexpensive

Birdsong Chalet 🎁 Crickets chirp at night and the rooster crows in the morning at this Swiss chalet hidden in wine country. Centrally located 10 minutes from downtown Niagara-on-the-Lake, and minutes from several wineries, this place feels like an island. Inside, the rooms remind me of my grandmother's cottage—small, tacky, and flowery, but cozy. Bathrooms are a squeeze: The Morning Glory Room has only a shower, while the Wisteria Room has a tub/shower. The upstairs breakfast area is full of knickknacks, figurines, and plants. Guests can also picnic on the banks of the man-made pond and garden. Breakfast includes fresh seasonal produce from the garden (frozen for winter visitors). A common area includes a kitchenette with fridge and coffeemaker, as well as a hair dryer and an iron.

982 Line 6, Niagara-on-the-Lake, ON L0S 1J0. www.birdsongchaletniagara.com. © **905/262-5080.** 2 units. C$89–C$125 double. Rates include breakfast. **Amenities:** Golf course nearby. *In room:* A/C, TV/DVD (Morning Glory only), no phone.

Clover Field House Bed & Breakfast Down the road from the epicenter of Niagara-on-the-Lake is this home, decorated with pictures of ski trips and family on the wall that add personality. Out back is a dense garden full of sitting areas and vines. Inside, rooms are also quite cramped, with queen beds and table and chairs in every room. Vine-covered patios for every room offer private retreats. The deluxe suite has the most room with a separate living room, private entrance, and private courtyard outside. Whirlpool tubs are also in every room. Breakfasts are a high point and include fresh fruit, yogurt, and a hot dish. Guests are invited to bring furry dog friends to play with the owners' two sheep dogs. This establishment is entirely nonsmoking.

1879 Lakeshore Rd., Niagara-on-the-Lake, ON L0S 1J0. www.cloverfieldhouse.com. © **905/468-7377.** Fax 905/468-0293. 3 units. C$145–C$175. Discounts for multiple nights. **Amenities:** Free bike use. *In room:* A/C, stereo, fridge, hair dryer.

The Doctor's House Located on Queen Street in the heart of the old town, this historic house is just steps from shopping, dining, and the Shaw theaters. The inn has a wraparound covered veranda, gazebo, landscaped gardens, library, and comfortable guest rooms. Breakfast is served in the formal dining room. For a family or for those who want more space for an extended stay, there are the Stone Cottage and the Courtside Cottage.

154 Queen St. (Box 304), Niagara-on-the-Lake, ON L0S 1J0. www.doctorshousebb.ca. © **905/468-5413.** 2 units. C$99 double. Cottages, May 1–October 15, $225 per night; October 16–April 30, $175 per night. MC, V. Free parking. **Amenities:** TV, Wi-Fi (free).

Orchid Inn 🌿 One of this inn's main selling points is its location, set back from the throngs of tourists on the main street in Niagara-on-the-Lake. Industrial carpet and officelike hallways contribute to a generic feeling; the rooms are also basic but bright and clean, decorated in lemony yellows with bamboo accents and dark furniture. Bathrooms are exceptionally spacious, with whirlpool tubs. Afternoon tea is offered from May to October.

390 Mary St., Niagara-on-the-Lake, ON L0S 1J0. www.orchidinn.ca. © **905/468-3871.** 9 units. C$140–C$210 double. Packages available. Rates include breakfast for 2. AE, MC, V. Free parking. **Amenities:** Restaurant; golf nearby; limited spa. *In room:* A/C, TV, hair dryer, no phone, Wi-Fi (free).

WINE COUNTRY

The choice of accommodations in wine country is as diverse as the wineries themselves. Each has a distinctive personality and ambience. The list below is a representative sample of the best of the region, although there are many more lovely properties nestled among the vines.

Best For: Wine lovers, theater devotees, and foodies. This is an area of Canada that is devoted to the vine and culinary excellence.

Drawbacks: This is adult country. There are few activities for children, although there are many opportunities for hiking, biking, and picnicking.

Very Expensive

Inn on the Twenty ★★★   This upscale inn in Jordan features a variety of guest room and suite styles in a converted sugar warehouse and nearby buildings, including two small adjoining cottages and a historical home with three rustic suites. All the main-inn suites have gas fireplaces, comfortable seating areas, and Jacuzzi tubs. Some suites have private gardens. The room decor is an artistic blend of antiques and contemporary accessories. Bathrooms are spacious and luxuriously appointed. The inn is located in the center of the compact, fashionable commercial area in Jordan Village, with gift shops, art galleries, designer clothing stores, and antiques retailers only steps away. Breakfast is served in the renowned On the Twenty Restaurant on the other side of the street from the guest accommodations. Please note that the reception desk is on the second floor of the main inn building. If you require assistance with your luggage, you'll need to climb the stairs to the lobby to alert the staff. The property is nonsmoking.

3845 Main St., Jordan, ON L0S 1J0. www.innonthetwenty.com. © **800/701-8074** or 905/562-5336. Fax 905/562-0009. 29 units. C$159–C$289 and up regular suite; C$239–C$359 and up deluxe and cottage suites. Rates include breakfast. Children 11 and under stay free in parent's room. C$40 per rollaway bed per night. AE, DC, MC, V. Free parking. **Amenities:** Restaurant; bar; babysitting; bike rental; limited room service; spa. *In room:* A/C, TV/VCR, hair dryer, Wi-Fi (free).

Expensive

Black Walnut Manor ★★   Black Walnut Manor has a sophisticated atmosphere with three spacious en suite guest rooms decorated in cool, modern, ultrachic style, yet the property is a historical homestead set in the rolling hills near the village of Vineland. The rooms are named to evoke a feeling of tranquillity and restfulness—"Retreat," "Return," and "Relax." Two rooms have private rooftop terraces. The most luxurious and romantic room (also the most expensive) is "Retreat," with its king-size bed, an air-jet tub, and a large shower. The proprietor's distinctive personality touches everything in the house, from her dog (trained to stay at paw's length from the guests) to the black-and-white photographs shot on a trip to Paris. Thoughtful touches include amenities bags filled with essential toiletries to replace those forgotten-at-home items, fluffy bathrobes, and wineglasses and corkscrews in the rooms. There is a wine fridge in the common room that guests can use to chill their winery purchases.

Niagara Region Hotels

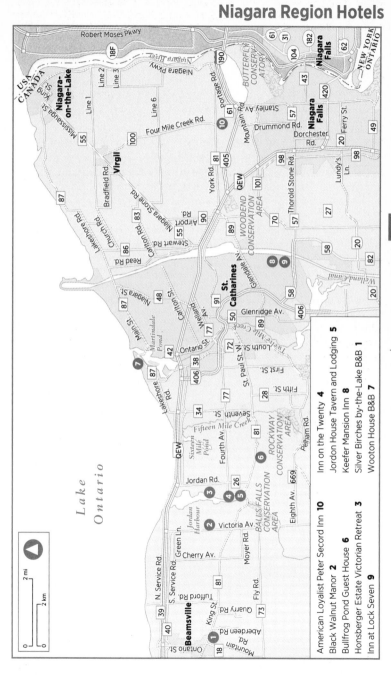

American Loyalist Peter Secord Inn **10**
Black Walnut Manor **2**
Bullfrog Pond Guest House **6**
Honsberger Estate Victorian Retreat **3**
Inn at Lock Seven **9**

Inn on the Twenty **4**
Jordon House Tavern and Lodging **5**
Keefer Mansion Inn **8**
Silver Birches by-the-Lake B&B **1**
Wooton House B&B **7**

4255 Victoria Ave., Vineland, ON L0R 2E0. www.blackwalnutmanor.com. © **800/859-4786** or 905/562-8675. 3 units. C$165–C$210 double. Children ages 3 and up in parent's room C$25 per night. AE, MC, V. Free parking. **Amenities:** Bikes available for use free of charge. *In room:* A/C, TV/VCR, hair dryer, no phone.

Honsberger Estate Victorian Retreat ★

This Victorian country house is one of the finest examples of its type in the Niagara region. The Honsberger Estate is located on a 16-hectare (40-acre) working farm, with orchards gracing the fields leading up the sweeping drive to the home. The bedrooms are arranged in two separate wings on the second floor; booking the entire property is quite commonplace, but bookings are also accepted for a minimum of eight guests (a full house is 12 guests). Breakfast is included with the rates, and for an extra cost the proprietor will arrange for a chef to prepare dinner, which is served in the formal dining room. The grounds of the estate are peaceful and relaxing, with plenty of mature shade trees and even an old-fashioned wooden-seated swing. If you've ever wanted to play the part of a country squire and gentrified family, this is the place for you.

4060 Jordan Rd., Jordan Station, ON L0S 1J0. www.honsbergerestate.com. © **905/562-6789.** Fax 905/227-4663. 6 units. C$150–C$200 double. MC, V. **Amenities:** Massage. *In room:* A/C, Internet (free), no phone.

Moderate

Jordan House Tavern and Lodging ★ 🍴

This refurbished industrial building is an inexpensive alternative to some of the high-priced inns in the area. All rooms have queen beds and a flatscreen television. Studio rooms are tight for space; for more room there are three executive rooms with an electric fireplace, pull-out sofa, full tub, and a small desk. Rooms facing west have a nice sunset view. While the rest of the town shuts down after 6pm, there's free live music every Friday night at the tavern downstairs.

3751 Main St., Jordan, ON L0R 1S0. www.jordanhouse.ca. © **800/701-8074** or 905/562-9591. 14 units. C$99–C$179 double. Packages available. AE, DC, MC, V. Self-parking free. **Amenities:** Restaurant; concierge; golf nearby; limited room service. *In room:* A/C, TV, hair dryer, Wi-Fi (paid).

Silver Birches by-the-Lake Bed & Breakfast

Silver Birches is much more than a B&B. Its level of comfort and amenities puts it more in the league of a country house or inn. With its large outdoor swimming pool, luxury indoor hot tub, tennis court, and 1.2 hectares (3 acres) of parklike gardens, you will feel relaxed and pampered. You can extend the pleasure by pre-booking a four-course gourmet dinner prepared by owners and hosts Paul and Leah Padfield (a minimum of four guests is required). Or take advantage of one of their many packages, put together in partnership with local wineries, restaurants, and theaters. Families can book the two-bedroom suite, which sleeps up to seven and has a private bathroom. Three other bedrooms, each with en suite and individual decor, are located on the second floor. Gorgeous sunrises flood the sky above Lake Ontario and can be seen from the front porch—if you're awake early enough to enjoy them.

4902 Mountain View Rd., Beamsville, ON L0R 1B3. www.silverbirchesbythelake.com. © **905/563-9479.** 5 units. C$130 double; suite from C$240 based on 4 sharing. AE, MC, V. Free parking. Inquire about children. **Amenities:** Bikes available free of charge; indoor hot tub; outdoor pool; outdoor tennis. *In room:* Hair dryer, Internet (free).

Inexpensive

American Loyalist Peter Secord Inn ★

If you crave a real date with history, you can sleep in this Inn, the oldest home in Ontario. It has been in the present owner's family for more than 100 years, but was originally built in 1782 at the side of what was once an Indian trail. There are two immaculately clean, spacious bedrooms at the top of the stairs. The sitting room dates from 1805 and has the original fireplace, windows, and floors. Collette serves a full hot breakfast. The Inn is close to Ravine Winery.

15 Creek Rd., Niagara-on-the-Lake, St. Davids, ON L0S 1P0. www.petersecordinn.ca. ✆ **905/262-1030.** 2 units. From C$145 double. MC, V. Free parking. *In room:* A/C, TV.

Bullfrog Pond Guest House If you like walking, whether it's a stroll to one of the nearby wineries or hiking the Bruce Trail, this is a good place to base yourself. The proprietors will cheerfully pack a picnic basket if you're heading out on an adventure. The guest accommodations are accessed at the rear of the house and are on ground level, so there are no steps to climb up and down. There is a common room with limited kitchen facilities and a cozy sitting area, and a hallway leading to the comfortable en suite bedrooms, both with fireplaces. Rooms feature Mennonite furniture, homemade quilts, and simple decor—it feels like Grandma's house. Guests are welcome to enjoy the .4-hectare (1-acre) sweep of lawns and flower gardens and the outdoor patio. You might luck out and arrive on a day when the proprietor has just baked a batch of her delicious chocolate chip cookies.

3801 Cherry Ave., Vineland, ON L0R 2C0. www.bullfrogpond.com. ✆ **905/562-1232.** 3 units. C$130–C$145 double. C$25 for extra person. MC, V. Free parking. **Amenities:** Bikes available at no charge. *In room:* A/C, TV/VCR, hair dryer, no phone.

WELLAND CANAL CORRIDOR

The village of Port Dalhousie has a handful of bed-and-breakfast properties if you'd like to stay over and enjoy an evening at the community theater, or if you just want to stroll along the lakeshore and relax.

Best for: Those who like a quiet country environment.

Drawbacks: Visitors are a bit removed from the central attractions of Niagara.

Inexpensive

Inn at Lock Seven For the real boat/lock aficionado, this is the place to stay. It's a very basic motel with concrete walls, and the biggest draws are the view of the Locks, the quiet neighborhood, and the price. You can watch international ocean freighters and tankers from your outdoor balcony. The Welland Canal water route—a link between the St. Lawrence and the Great Lakes—has seen more than 2 billion tons of cargo pass through since opening in 1959. Guests receive "The ABCs of the Seaway" and quickly become boat nerds, say owners Ed Kuiper and Patty Szoldra.

24 Chapel St. S., Thorold, ON L2V 2C6. www.innatlock7.com. ✆ **877/INN-LOCK7** (465-6257). 24 units. C$73–C$125 double. Rates include breakfast. AE, DC, MC, V. Free parking. *In room:* A/C, TV, no phone, Wi-Fi (free).

Keefer Mansion Inn ★★🍴 Overlooking the town of Thorold, the Keefer Mansion is one of the finest inns in the Niagara region for its amenities and wonderful history. Slated for demolition a few years ago, the impeccably restored 1886 inn is now a symbol of what can happen when residents believe in their heritage. The grand curving staircase is the showcase, with dining rooms on both the left and right; there also are wooden fireplaces on both sides and a bar with stools on the right. Upstairs, all rooms are named after homeowners of the Keefer Mansion and town icons. Rooms facing the Welland Canal have the best views: On the third floor, rooms have fantastic bird's-eye views of the town or canal. The most cozy and unique room is the Hugh Keefer, which has half-stone walls and angled ceilings. There are also two rooms dedicated to a spa for massages and a fine-dining restaurant below.

14 St. Davids St. W., Thorold, ON L2V 2K9. www.keefermansion.com. ✆ **905/680-9581.** 9 units. C$119–C$149 double. Packages available. Rates include breakfast. AE, MC, V. Free parking. **Amenities:** Restaurant; babysitting arranged; concierge; golf nearby; limited room service; spa. *In room:* A/C, TV/DVD, hair dryer, Wi-Fi (free).

Wooton House Bed & Breakfast   The pubs, lake marina, shops, and live theater of historical Port Dalhousie are all within walking distance of this charming home built in 1885. Watch world-class rowing on Martindale Pond from the lawn as you eat your Wooton House waffles with fresh-fruit topping. The "View with a Room" room has a balcony overlooking Lake Ontario. Ideal for a long stay, this unit has its own kitchen and dining area, complete with microwave and en suite bathroom with Jacuzzi. Discounts are available for longer stays. If you're the bookish type, you'll appreciate the library room, with its skylight and built-in shelves full of classics. All rooms offer cable TV and are accessed through a private entrance. All beds are queen-size four-posters. Niagara-on-the-Lake and Niagara Falls are only a 15-minute drive away. The cozy corner room has an adjacent private bathroom.

2 Elgin St., St. Catharines, ON L2N 5G3. www.wootonhouse.com. ✆ **905/937-4696.** 3 units. C$90–C$150 double. Rates include breakfast. AE, MC, V. Free parking. **Amenities:** Fully equipped galley kitchen. *In room:* TV, no phone.

PRACTICAL INFORMATION
The Big Picture

Today, with millions of visitors a year, the Niagara region offers a wide range of accommodations options. The area offers every kind of accommodation, from loft suites with views of the Falls to historic inns and family-friendly B&Bs.

You can choose from options ranging from huge chains to quaint B&Bs to roadside motels. In general, hotels are much nicer on the Canadian side. In Niagara Falls, New York, your best bet is to pamper yourself at the Red Coach Inn or the Giacomo. More moderate accommodations on the American side can be found along Niagara Falls Boulevard (Hwy. 62), where there are a number of chain hotels, like the **Super 8,** or the **Econolodge.**

Falls-view hotels fill up quickly in high season so if you have your heart set on sleeping beside the Falls, reserve your room well in advance. If you are planning to get married by the Falls, or to spend your honeymoon there, many of the large hotels have special packages that include flowers, champagne, and even the iconic heart-shaped tub. Hotel rooms, particularly those overlooking the Falls, are more expensive during the high season, but if you are willing to stay in a property that is back from the Falls, you can get more moderate rates.

Away from the Falls, wine country offers a selection of historic hotels, like the Riverbend Inn or the Charles Inn in Niagara-on-the-Lake. For a more rural experience, guesthouses and B&Bs, like the Bullfrog Pond Guest House or Black Walnut Manor, allow you to enjoy the countryside and place you close to the vineyards for which the area is famous.

The Niagara region, in particular Niagara-on-the-Lake and the River Road district in the city of Niagara Falls, has an abundance of gracious, older homes which have been transformed into charming B&Bs. For the most part, B&Bs are located in quiet residential neighborhoods with tree-lined streets. If you're traveling solo or as a couple, then a B&B presents an economical alternative to a hotel room, but families will usually need to rent two rooms to secure enough sleeping area, and that must be taken into account when estimating costs. Also, be aware that B&Bs and inns are usually geared to adult visitors. Many homes have expensive antiques on display and guests are expecting a quiet, restful stay. If you have children with you and they're young, boisterous, or both, then you're better off in a family-oriented property.

During the busy summer season, some B&Bs require a 2-night minimum stay. If one is full, hosts are more than happy to suggest another in the area; most of them know each other and are pleased to recommend one nearby.

Happily, many of the properties in the Niagara region are entirely or almost entirely nonsmoking, partly due to a reduced demand for smoking rooms and partly due to the increasing trend toward smoking bylaws that prohibit smoking in public places. However, never assume that you'll get a smoke-free room if you don't specifically request one.

All rooms have private bathrooms unless otherwise noted. Many hotels provide complimentary Wi-Fi in either part or all of their facilities, although this continues to be a work in progress for some properties. Ask about the most current Internet options when reserving a room. Rates vary from C$10–C$15 for a 24-hour period.

Alternative Accommodations

If history is your thing, consider staying in one of the heritage properties, like the small but perfect Peter Secord Inn in St. Davids, situated in one of the oldest hostelries in Ontario.

For those traveling with children, I strongly recommend staying in a one- or two-bedroom suite with kitchenette facilities if your budget will allow, or hunt down a self-contained cottage in Niagara-on-the-Lake or along the shores of Lake Ontario. In return for your investment, you'll get a comfortable base with space for everyone to spread out, a place to make meals on your own schedule, and usually more than one TV. You may even get some private time once the kids are asleep, when you can enjoy a glass of wine with your spouse.

Couples looking for a more romantic getaway will do well to base themselves at an inn or B&B in Niagara-on-the-Lake, like the romantic Prince of Wales, or in the wine country.

Getting the Best Deal

The prices quoted in this chapter generally range from the cheapest low-season rate up to corporate or rack rates (rack rates are the highest posted rates, although rooms are rarely sold at the full rack rate). In each listing, the prices include accommodations for two adults sharing. Discounts can result in a dramatic drop in the rate, typically anywhere from 10% to 50%.

Almost every hotelier I spoke with mentioned that weekend specials or family packages are available at various times throughout the year. Note also that the 5% accommodations tax and 13% HST (Harmonized Sales Tax) are required by law to be added to your bill.

If you have a vehicle with you, remember to factor in parking charges when estimating the cost of your accommodations if you plan to stay at one of the larger properties close to the Falls. Hotel parking rates at these locations vary from C$5 to C$20 per night.

Always ask for a deal. Corporate discounts, club memberships (CAA, AAA, and others), and discounts linked to credit cards are just a few of the ways you can get a lower price. Often the best rates are offered only online, so be sure to check the website of a hotel before you book. Rates between June and August are decidedly higher than the rest of the year and fluctuate wildly depending on the particular week; if any events are scheduled that increase the rates, try the following week. A standard double room at the Crowne Plaza, for example, varied from C$89 to an astronomical C$499 for the same room during periods of high demand. Weekend rates and getaway packages for couples and families are often available. Packages may include golf, spa treatments, attraction tickets or discounts, restaurant coupons, or other money-saving deals.

Reservation Services

Most hotels don't ask for deposits but require that you pay the whole fee upfront, and usually won't reserve your room until your credit card transaction goes through successfully. Most of the larger hotels allow you to cancel rooms, but do check in advance how many days you have to receive all your money back.

Check-out time is usually around 11am, but can normally be extended to noon or 1pm if requested. Similarly, check-in time is routinely after 3pm.

In addition to sites like Expedia and Hotel.com, consider contacting Niagara Tourism (www.tourismniagara.com), which maintains a database of hotels and B&Bs.

WHERE TO EAT

Niagara's evolution into a culinary destination was a natural one. Not only is the cuisine supported by numerous farms and orchards producing locally grown, often organic, fruits and vegetables, but it also is inspired by the many wineries that make their homes in the Peninsula. And with wine comes food, thus a continuous influx of great restaurants, helmed by some of the best chefs in the country: Michael Olson, Tony De Luca, Stephen Treadwell, Mark Picone, William Brunyansky, and several others have opened restaurants dedicated to celebrating the products of this unique microclimate. Uber-popular Canadian chefs like Massimo Capra have also taken the helm of major dining rooms at the Falls.

best EATING BETS

- **Best Historic Dining:** The dining room at the **Riverbend Inn & Vineyard** is located in an elegantly restored Georgian mansion with a long history. The cuisine is historically good too. And just around the corner is Old Fort George and the well preserved charms of Niagara-on-the-Lake. See p. 80.

- **Best for Business Travelers:** If you are doing business, you want to dine without interruption and without too much lingering. The **Tiara Restaurant** in the Queen's Landing Hotel in Niagara-on-the-Lake has tables far enough apart for privacy, and extra-fast service if requested. The view and the food are good too, and there are conference and meeting rooms you can retire to for serious discussions. See p. 80.

- **Best for a Romantic Dinner:** Romantic for me means small and intimate, and the best bet for that kind of experience is **De Luca's Wine Country Restaurant** in Niagara-on-the-Lake. The space is small, the service is smooth, the lights are low, and the food is stellar. No one will intrude on your conversation. See p. 78.

5

PRICE CATEGORIES

Very Expensive	C$35 and up
Expensive	C$25–C$35
Moderate	C$15–C$25
Inexpensive	Under C$20

- **Best Regional Cuisine:** When I dine in a new area, I always want to eat like a local—but a local gourmet. **AG at the Sterling** is a place where local produce and dishes are not just celebrated, they are elevated to high art. Dining here is an experience that you will remember for a long time, and it will be an immersion course in Niagara's culinary soul. See p. 73.
- **Best Splurge:** Make like you've won big at the tables and head for **17 Noir,** the sexy and sophisticated restaurant high up in the Niagara Fallsview Casino. You might be sharing space with one of the big stars from the show in the Avalon Ballroom. It is flamboyant and fun, but bring a well-stocked wallet. See p. 72.
- **Most Relaxing Dining: August Restaurant** in Beamsville has become a hangout for local vintners, who may show up with their muddy boots. The food is also relaxed, but inventive too. See p. 89.
- **Best Location for Dining in Niagara Falls:** Try **Elements on the Falls** if you want to get up close and personal with a world icon for dinner. Just feet from the Falls, you can dine and drink in the awesomeness of the water, especially when the Falls are illuminated or when there are fireworks. Floor-to-ceiling windows allow for perfect viewing. See p. 70.
- **Best for Family Dining:** My kids love pizza, but it has to be good and it has to be fast and fun. **Antica Pizzeria** delivers on all counts, with really good brick-oven pizzas, friendly staff, and family platters for a group. It can be very busy in high season, but the staff are used to dealing with crowds. Prices are very affordable. See p. 74.
- **Best Budget Dining: Betty's Restaurant** is down-home good, serving homemade pies and all the family-style food you crave, at good prices and in large quantities. See p. 74.
- **Best Views:** The views of the Falls from **The Rainbow Room by Massimo Capra** in the Crown Plaza Hotel are superb—you can see both the American and Canadian Falls through the large windows on the 10th floor. The cuisine is complex, market fresh, and elegant. This is a grown-up place, and maybe a spot for a proposal? See p. 72.

NIAGARA FALLS, ONTARIO & NEW YORK

There's a restaurant wherever you look in Niagara Falls. To meet the needs of the massive numbers of tourists who visit, fast-food places and inexpensive family-style restaurants abound. But there are some real food gems, too. Niagara Falls has a large Italian population, so almost any Italian restaurant is a good choice. There are also some excellent hotel restaurants. Be wary, though, of the Falls-side restaurants—you will pay extra for the great view with your meal, and you won't be guaranteed it will be good.

Most of the tourist amenities, including restaurants, are concentrated on the Canadian side of the Falls.

Very Expensive

Elements on the Falls REGIONAL/CANADIAN   Recently renovated, this dining room is devoted to Canadian cuisine, but the best part about dining here is the view. The restaurant is located on the upper level of Table Rock, next to Horseshoe

Niagara Falls Dining

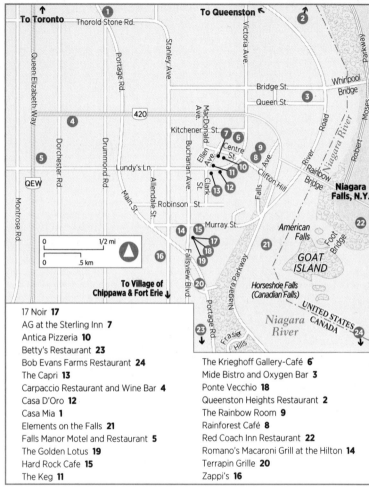

To Toronto
To Queenston
Thorold Stone Rd.
To Queenston
Bridge St.
Queen St.
Kitchener St.
Centre St.
Lundy's Ln.
Robinson St.
Murray St.
American Falls
Niagara Falls, N.Y.
GOAT ISLAND
Horseshoe Falls (Canadian Falls)
To Village of Chippawa & Fort Erie
UNITED STATES / CANADA
Niagara River

17 Noir **17**
AG at the Sterling Inn **7**
Antica Pizzeria **10**
Betty's Restaurant **23**
Bob Evans Farms Restaurant **24**
The Capri **13**
Carpaccio Restaurant and Wine Bar **4**
Casa D'Oro **12**
Casa Mia **1**
Elements on the Falls **21**
Falls Manor Motel and Restaurant **5**
The Golden Lotus **19**
Hard Rock Cafe **15**
The Keg **11**

The Krieghoff Gallery-Café **6**
Mide Bistro and Oxygen Bar **3**
Ponte Vecchio **18**
Queenston Heights Restaurant **2**
The Rainbow Room **9**
Rainforest Café **8**
Red Coach Inn Restaurant **22**
Romano's Macaroni Grill at the Hilton **14**
Terrapin Grille **20**
Zappi's **16**

Falls and the viewing gallery. Nowhere else can you get a good meal this close to the Falls. The main courses are heavy on protein—steaks, pork, and salmon—but there is usually a pasta dish available. Salads are fresh and generous. While you can have a very enjoyable meal here, it's not inexpensive, but there is compensation in knowing that all profits go to the Niagara Parks Commission. I'd do lunch here, indulge in the tapas, or opt for a salad and soup, and just enjoy the view. It's also a great place for a sunset cocktail.

6650 Niagara Pkwy., Niagara Falls, ON. © **905/354-3631.** www.niagaraparks.com. Reservations recommended. Main courses C$30–C$50. AE, MC, V. Daily 11:30am–10pm.

Ponte Vecchio ★★ ITALIAN   The newest dining room in the Fallsview Casino, this restaurant is devoted to all things Tuscan. It's a very pretty space, with Merano glass vases and chandeliers, and a sepia-toned mural of Florence along one wall. The wine list highlights mostly Italian wines, although there are some Canadian. The Frito Misto starter is excellent, created with scallops, lake perch calamari, and shrimp on a bed of frisée with lemon vinaigrette, though pricey at C$22. Grilled halibut with capers, tomatoes, olives, and couscous is a hit, but the restaurant makes its mark with the old Italian standby—spaghetti, enhanced with porcini meatballs. Desserts are exceptional: Try the roasted fig and walnut gelato with fresh berries in a tuile or the blue plum crostado with Bailey's gelato. As you would hope in a good Italian place, the espresso is exceptional.

6380 Fallsview Blvd., Niagara Falls, ON. ✆ **888/325-5788.** www.fallsviewcasinoresort.com. Main courses C$22-C$59. Reservations recommended. AE, MC, V. Tues-Sat 5-11pm.

The Rainbow Room by Massimo Capra ★ REGIONAL/CANADIAN   The famous Italian chef from Toronto has put his imprint on the Crowne Plaza's 10th-floor restaurant. Notable guests in the past have included King George VI and Queen Elizabeth, the King and Queen of Nepal, Bruce Willis, Matthew Perry, and the Jonas Brothers. Maybe more will come to try out the new fresh market style menu, which includes maple glazed pork chops and Sterling salmon. The view is amazing, especially when the fireworks are on.

5685 Falls Ave., Niagara Falls, ON. ✆ **905-374-4447,** ext. 4134. www.niagarafallscrowneplazahotel.com. Reservations recommended. Main Courses C$29-C$48. AE, DC, MC, V. Daily 7am-10pm.

17 Noir ★★ CONTEMPORARY   It only makes sense that the Fallsview Casino has a restaurant that pays homage to gambling and the good life. Decorated in reds and blacks to mimic a roulette table, the room has fuzzy felt chairs and round tables. You'll feel like a high roller here. The best six tables in Niagara Falls are on the "dance floor" by the windows, with a fabulous view of the Falls. There are three private chef's tables, usually reserved for visiting stars who may be performing in the Avalon Ballroom Theatre, like Kevin Costner or Michael Bolton. The menu is strong on steaks and seafood—try the Iced Seafood Tower for a dramatic dish, or a Kobe beef steak, or for complete decadence, the lobster poutine. Downstairs from the dining room, have a seat at the sushi and noodle bar, which is open late. Watch the Japanese master sushi chefs (two on staff) prepare delicacies right in front of your eyes.

6380 Fallsview Blvd., Niagara Falls, ON. ✆ **888/WINFALL** (946-3255). www.fallsviewcasinoresort.com. Reservations recommended. Dining room C$32-C$48. AE, MC, V. Dining room daily 5-11pm; sushi and noodle bar daily 11am-4am.

Terrapin Grille ★ AMERICAN   While it does not boast the boldest of menus, some ordinary fare gets a nice touch-up: The filet mignon is topped with béarnaise sauce, and sea bass with an Asian herb rub is served with a raspberry reduction. Main entrees are well prepared, but the side dishes are a bit dull. The extensive wine list features Niagara wines. The view from your chair is one of the best in the city: With a wall of windows facing the panorama, every diner gets a piece of the action. Booths facing the Falls are cozy for couples, while calming music plays in the background. With its high-class atmosphere, this restaurant is a good choice for falls-view dining.

6740 Fallsview Blvd., Niagara Falls, ON. ✆ **905/357-7300.** Reservations recommended. Main courses C$34-C$69. AE, DC, MC, V. Mon-Thurs 6:30-11am and 11:30am-11pm; Fri 6:30-11am and 12:30-11pm; Sat-Sun 6:30am-11pm.

Expensive

AG at the Sterling Inn ★★★ REGIONAL/CANADIAN   This is, without a doubt, the best restaurant in Niagara Falls, and possibly in the Peninsula. Dining here is a hedonistic pleasure, and the young but gifted chef, Cory Linkson, never makes a wrong move. Put yourself in his hands for a tasting menu paired with VQA wines and you will have a culinary experience you will not soon forget. He's totally devoted to local—on the menu you will find Fifth Town artisanal cheeses, Cro Farm Quail, Pinque prosciutto, Lakeland Farm duck, Simcoe asparagus, and Effingham greens. Wine sommelier Darren pairs each course perfectly. When you reserve, ask for the semicircular banquette in the corner, with side curtains, that makes this a very private place to enjoy the meal. Maroon and cream leather, sparkly hanging lights, and the sophisticated bar make you forget you are actually in a basement room.

5195 Magdalen St., Niagara Falls, ON. © **877/783-7772** or 289/292-0000. www.sterlingniagara.com. Reservations recommended. Main courses C$23–C$35; 5-course tasting menu C$110 with wine pairing. AE, DISC, MC, V. Tues–Sun 5:30–11pm.

Carpaccio Restaurant and Wine Bar ★ ITALIAN   This place is consistently good. The rich, earthy tones of the decor make the dining space welcoming and comfortable. There's not much to find fault with here. I highly recommend the thin-crust brick-oven pizzas, especially the *Quattro stagioni,* which features tomatoes, mozzarella, artichokes, black olives, mushrooms, and prosciutto. This place offers an extensive selection of Italian fare. There are several main-course chicken and veal dishes to choose from, and the tiramisu is very good. If you are a wine aficionado, hang out in the wine bar and let someone else drive—Carpaccio has more than 300 wines on its list, with 3-ounce tasting glasses available for a handful of selections.

6840 Lundy's Lane, Niagara Falls, ON. © **905/371-2063.** www.carpacciorestaurant.com. Reservations recommended Sat. Main courses C$16–C$35. AE, DC, MC, V. Summer Mon–Fri 11:30am–11pm, Sat–Sun 4pm–midnight; winter Mon–Fri 11:30am–10pm, Sat–Sun 4–11pm.

The Keg ★ STEAKHOUSE   Dark ambience complemented by a stone fireplace—this chain restaurant will pleasantly surprise you. Steak comes cooked just the way you like it—it's their specialty. Choose from steak combinations with ribs and seafood, or try steak cuts such as sirloin, New York, and prime rib. But don't hold back. Try other items such as the baked garlic shrimp or the crab, Parmesan, and spinach dip. Baked goat cheese is warm and smooth, while steak and lobster—even though it's Atlantic frozen—is quite good. Yes, it's a steakhouse, but you'll leave

---

Try a Tasting Menu

A tasting menu is an adventure for the senses as well as the imagination. Carefully created by the *chef de cuisine,* a tasting menu will incorporate local seasonal produce in a presentation of a series of small-portion courses, often matched with wines. In some restaurants, the menu is set; in others, you can choose among dishes. Advance notice is required at some establishments. If you are eager to experience a tasting menu, ask about availability when you call to make your reservation.

impressed because whether you ask for well done or rare, it's done exactly how you want it.

5950 Victoria Ave., Niagara Falls, ON. ✆ **905/353-4022.** Main courses C$18–C$44. AE, DC, MC, V. Summer noon–1am daily; winter Sun–Thurs noon–midnight, Fri–Sat noon–1am.

Queenston Heights Restaurant ★ REGIONAL/CANADIAN   Perched above the Niagara River, the dining room of this restaurant is in the heart of Queenston Heights Park. Ask for a table by the window, to the right of the room, overlooking the river. The a la carte menu offers good solid fare from a variety of cuisines but no surprises. The sauces on many dishes are locally inspired, like the late-harvest vidal gastrique that accompanies the duck. One good option for lunch is the signature sandwich with summer greens and the soup of the day, good value at C$19. The potato-leek soup is perfect—smooth, creamy, and not oversalted. Salads are fresh and the sandwich generous. The white tablecloths, giant painting of the Falls hanging over the stone fireplace, and the panoramic windows make this place feel like a dining room at a well-heeled country club. Service is pleasant. Check for special historic dinners planned to celebrate the anniversary of the War of 1812.

14184 Niagara Pkwy., Queenston. ✆ **905/262-4274.** www.niagaraparks.com. Reservations recommended. Main courses C$28–C$36. AE, DC, MC, V. May 1–Oct 11 11am–9pm, closed Mon.

Moderate

Antica Pizzeria ★ ITALIAN   For many regular visitors to the Falls, Antica is a regular stop. The busy and cheerful pizza place has a genuine Napolitano brick oven, and the pizzas are tasty. You may end up waiting in line for a table during the busy season, but it will be worth it. The staff is young and the restaurant is family run, with family photos and pictures of the Amalfi Coast on the walls. Get a table outside if the weather is fine. And if you sit outside, you get a ring-side seat to watch all the action at the top of Clifton Hill. If you have a large group, they will serve family-style platters.

5785 Victoria Ave., Niagara Falls, ON. ✆ **905/356-3844.** www.anticapizzeria.ca. Main courses C$9–C$15. AE, MC, V. Daily noon–12:30am.

Betty's Restaurant DINER   The decor is simple, the prices reasonable, and the food is freshly made and very good. Locals come here regularly for Betty's famous fish and chips (C$12) and for the homemade pies (C$3.30 for a generous slice). Kids are made to feel very welcome.

8921 Sodom Rd., Niagara Falls, ON. ✆ **905/295-4436.** www.bettysrestaurant.com. Main courses $8–$14. AE, MC, V. Daily 8am–9pm (seasonally adjusted).

Bob Evans Farms Restaurant DINER   Yes, it is a chain, but it's a darn good, reliable one. Their all-day breakfast dishes range from C$4 to C$10. Main courses are generous in portion size and are likely to evoke happy but long-forgotten memories of hot gravy, mashed potatoes, and meatloaf in older folk. Service is fast and friendly. If you phone ahead, you can order entire home-style meals to go and whole pies.

6543 Niagara Falls Blvd. (southeast corner of Hwy. 62 and I-90), Niagara Falls, NY. ✆ **716/283-2965.** Main courses C$8–C$12. AE, DISC, MC, V. Daily 6am–9pm.

Casa D'Oro ITALIAN   For 35 years, this über-Italianate *osteria* has been producing Italian favorites—veal parmigiana, stuffed peppers, rigatoni, pasta, and pizzas, as well as steaks and seafood. Not gourmet fare, but generous portions keep appetites satisfied. During high season, the restaurant can get very busy.

5875 Victoria Ave., Niagara Falls, ON. © **905/356-5646.** www.thecasadoro.com. Main courses C$15–C$40. AE, MC, V. Sun–Fri 11:30am–9pm; Sat 4–9pm.

Casa Mia ITALIAN   A family-owned, sophisticated, yet affordable trattoria for more than 25 years, Casa Mia is just far enough away from the tourist fray to be relaxing. Pasta, veal, chicken, and seafood dishes, as well as fresh salads and pizzas, are all good bets. On weekends, you can hear live jazz.

3518 Portage Rd., Niagara Falls, ON. © **905/356-5410.** www.casamiaristorante.com. Main courses C$9–C$52. AE, MC, V. Mon–Fri 11:30am–2:30pm, 5–10pm; Sat–Sun 5–10pm.

Falls Manor Motel and Restaurant ★ DINER   Drive down Lundy's Lane until you see the big chicken. The Falls Manor Motel and Restaurant has been family owned and operated since 1953—that's a lot of roasted chicken. Falls Manor serves comfort food—kettle-cooked barbecue ribs, pepper steak with mashed potatoes and gravy, toasted club sandwiches, hot corned beef, and grilled cheese. A bottomless mug of coffee is just C$1.60. The Hungry Jack breakfast is an amazing value at C$7.50—two each of eggs, bacon, and sausage, plus a slice of Canadian peameal bacon, potatoes, and toast. The Belgian waffles are crisp, sweet, and filling. Seniors' portions are available for those over age 60—you get a little less on your plate and a little less on your check. The front section of the restaurant is cozy, but if the tables are full, there are plenty more in the back room and on an outdoor terrace at the rear.

7104 Lundy's Lane, Niagara Falls, ON. © **888/693-9357** or 905/358-3211. Main courses C$8–C$17. AE, DC, MC, V. Summer Sun–Thurs 6am–9pm, Fri–Sat 6am–10pm; winter Sun–Thurs 6am–8pm, Fri–Sat 6am–9pm.

The Golden Lotus ★★ ASIAN   This is the closest I've been to China without crossing continents. Here you'll find food for the adventurous eater: homemade noodles swimming in spicy beef soup, seafood dumpling with shark's fin soup (who would have guessed that shark tastes like mushrooms?), and my new Chinese favorite, chicken and roasted duck in congee, which looks like oatmeal but is rice boiled in a savory broth. More than 200 menu items include North American–style food for the delicate eater. There's a buffet during lunch hour. With bright violet tablecloths and Easter-colored circular lamps, it feels very contemporary; located inside a glass dome in part of the Fallsview Casino, one side of the restaurant follows the circular shape overlooking a fountain and the Falls in the background. Word to the wise: Drinking Chinese tea will undercut the spicy foods.

6380 Fallsview Blvd., Niagara Falls, ON. © **888/698-3888.** www.fallsviewcasinoresort.com. Reservations recommended for dinner. Main dishes C$12–C$15. AE, MC, V. Mon–Fri 11am–2am; Sat–Sun 10am–2am.

Hard Rock Cafe ☺ AMERICAN   Situated at the main entrance to Casino Niagara, this upbeat, rockin' restaurant is full of music memorabilia and filling food. The menu is enormous and features barbecue favorites, such as a hickory barbecue bacon burger, and entrees such as New York strip steak or blackened chicken pasta. Top it all off with a good old-fashioned hot fudge sundae. If you're a night owl, the restaurant is open until 2am. The food is average, but the scenery is cool and energy high.

6705 Fallsview Ave., Niagara Falls, ON. © **905/356-7625.** Main courses C$14–C$30. AE, DC, MC, V. Daily 11am–2am. U.S. location: 33 Prospect St., Niagara Falls, NY. © **716/282-0007.** Sun–Thurs 11am–11pm; Fri–Sat 11am–midnight.

The Krieghoff Gallery-Café BISTRO/CAFE   I recommend this place more for its atmosphere than its food (it serves platters, light fare, and dessert brought in from a local pastry shop). Dubbed a cultural cafe, it's a change from nearby Clifton Hill. Inside, crisp white tablecloths and bench-back seating is refined. The wine list is extensive. On the menu are bite-sized pastries (cream puffs filled with amaretto custard, chocolate shortbread) and platters for sharing, including smoked salmon with crackers, bread and crème fraîche, or the Niagara charcuterie plate with a selection of salami, prosciutto, and dry cured meat with sweet onions and a baguette. The menu also has a few sandwiches. There's also an artisanal cheese plate to have with your local wine. Named after artist Cornelius Krieghoff (1815–72), the in-house gallery features paintings of early Canadian settlers and North American Natives. Free educational tours through the gallery are offered in six languages.

5470 Victoria Ave., Niagara Falls, ON. ✆ **905/358-9700.** www.krieghoff.ca. Platters C$13–C$17. AE, MC, V. Daily 9am–11pm.

Mide Bistro and Oxygen Bar BISTRO   Tucked in at one end of the newly reinvigorated Queen Street area, this bistro has a pleasant patio. There are several vegetarian and vegan offerings, and many of the ingredients are organic. The menu includes several pastas, meats, and chicken dishes, along with a small selection of tapas. If you need to clear your head, try the oxygen bar. There's live entertainment on weekends. While you're here, take some time to explore the new Queen Street. It's still a work in progress, but galleries and interesting little shops are opening and the area is fast becoming an authentic grassroots community, with art shows, music, and street events.

4337 Queen St., Niagara Falls, ON. ✆ **289/296-5632.** www.midebistro.com. Main courses C$12–C$29. AE, MC, V. Mon–Thurs 11am–8pm; Fri–Sat 11am–9pm; Sun11am–6pm.

Rainforest Café ☺ AMERICAN   This place is the epicenter of chaos on Clifton Hill—leave the overpriced rides and kitsch for an equally overpriced restaurant. But the kids will appreciate the tropical setting: Thunderstorms and animatronic gorillas, snakes, and elephants entertain with their antics at regular intervals. Perhaps the theatrics are trying to mask the food? Bruschetta comes out cold, fries are not fresh, and burgers are more bun than beef. The best option is the tropical smoothies, which are nutritious and come in a variety of flavors such as coconut with strawberry. The Niagara Falls Rainforest Café features a live shark exhibit (free) and promises daily encounters with live animals. Get your wallet ready for more than the check; the Rainforest Café shop has mountains of brightly colored rainforest-themed merchandise, including an extensive line of private-label Rainforest Café clothing and toys.

5785 Falls Ave., Niagara Falls, ON. ✆ **905/374-2233.** Main courses C$12–C$26. AE, DC, MC, V. Sun–Thurs 11am–10pm; Fri–Sat 11am–midnight.

Red Coach Inn Restaurant ★ AMERICAN   The decor is all deep, dark wood and subdued tapestry, with fine views of the Niagara River rapids. Dine on the veranda in warm weather. The restaurant is traditional and formal, while the food is predictable but good. Menu highlights include Black Angus steak (several cuts), scallops, Australian lobster tail, and swordfish. Choose from dozens of toppers and sides, including fruit salsa, mushroom and Marsala wine sauce, smoked tomato coulis, chive cream cheese, or roasted red pepper. The service is genuine and personable—they'll remember your name at the end of the meal. There's a limited wine list.

falls-view DINING

To enjoy a meal with one of the world's most impressive natural wonders at your tableside is a special experience. And for a view of the tons of cascading waters, several restaurants can provide you with a fabulous falls-view dining experience. But be prepared to pay more for your "meal with a view."

Elements on the Falls (℡ **905/354-3631;** p. 70) is one of the Niagara Parks Commission's restaurants. The second-floor dining room features indoor and outdoor dining. Or try the **Terrapin Grille,** the Niagara Falls Marriott Fallsview's restaurant (p. 72). The two observation towers each have a falls-view dining room. The Konica Minolta Tower Centre (6732 Fallsview Blvd.; ℡ **905/356-1501**), which houses the Tower Hotel, has the **Pinnacle Restaurant,** which has a great view, but I wouldn't recommend eating here. You'll find this structure tucked between recently constructed high-rise blocks, but don't be fooled—the views from the restaurant are the best in the city. Try to book a table that looks right out onto the American Falls if you are going to watch the fireworks. They explode right

at eye-level. The distinctive **Skylon Tower** (5200 Robinson St.; ℡ **905/356-2651**) has a revolving restaurant that completes each revolution in 1 hour, giving you a view of the Falls for approximately half that time. **The Golden Lotus** and **17 Noir** in the Fallsview Casino also have great dining rooms with Falls views. Massimo Capra's Rainbow Room in the Crowne Plaza (p. 72) has lovely views from the tenth floor, as well as market fresh dishes.

Of these offerings, the better food is probably found at Terrapin Grille, but expect to pay dearly for it. Reservations are recommended at all of these locations to avoid disappointment. Check the time of the illuminations before booking if you want them to be an integral part of your dinner.

For a special treat, try the **Marriott Gateway on the Falls** (see chapter 4). The hotel ramps up the romance factor for its guests. Book a room or loft suite with a glassed-in alcove overlooking the Falls, and ask the hotel to set you up a table for two in the alcove for one of their special in-room dinners.

2 Buffalo Ave., Niagara Falls, NY. ℡ **800/282-1459** or 716/282-1459. www.redcoach.com. Reservations recommended. Main courses C$15–C$39. AE, MC, V. Nov 1–Apr 30 Mon–Thurs 11:30am–2:30pm and 5–9pm; Fri–Sat 11:30am–10pm; Sun noon–9pm. May 1–Oct 31 Mon–Thurs 11:30am–9:30pm; Fri–Sat 11:30am–10:30pm; Sun noon–9:30pm.

Romano's Macaroni Grill at the Hilton ITALIAN   This American chain restaurant has a pretty successful formula for creating cheery and approachable Italian dining. The usual fare—wood-oven pizzas, pastas, and seafood—is served by a wait-staff who may occasionally break out in an opera aria. There are high ceilings, woven wicker paddle fans, and dining space on two levels. Service is prompt and cheerful, but the music can be a bit loud to enjoy a conversation over the meal. Try the wild mushroom soup with a tomato base or the Four Season Pizza, which is generous enough to serve two. You get a great view of the casino and the fountain across the street.

6361 Fallsview Blvd., Niagara Falls, ON. ℡ **905/354-7887.** www.niagarafallshilton.com. Main courses C$13–C$25. AE, MC, V. Daily 11am–11pm.

Zappi's ☺ PIZZA   Families will appreciate this pizzeria, around since 1971, with red-and-white-checked tablecloths, that gets a little rowdy at suppertime—just like at home. There's also more than just pizza: Salads run the gamut from Caesar to Greek, and traditional Italian dishes include lasagna, calzone, and pasta primavera. Pizzas come in a huge variety, including the Diavolo for meat lovers topped with bacon, ham, and pepperoni. The White Greek includes feta and olives, while the Four Cheeses is topped with provolone, mozzarella, Romano, and Parmesan cheeses.

6663 Stanley Ave., Niagara Falls, ON. ℂ **905/357-7100.** www.zappis.com. Main dishes C$9–C$15. AE, MC, V. Mon-Sat 11am–midnight; Sun 3–10pm.

NIAGARA-ON-THE-LAKE

The town of Niagara-on-the-Lake has an eclectic and highly regarded culinary scene. Whether you are looking for an Old-English-style pub, elegant French service gourmet dining in a Victorian dining room, a casual outdoor patio, or a small-town diner, you'll find it here. If you're torn between choices of where to eat, ask for opinions from your B&B host or hotel staff—they are knowledgeable about local restaurants and will be eager to share their recommendations with you. Some of the hotels and inns in town will provide a shuttle service to and from restaurants in the evening upon request, saving you from hunting for an unfamiliar address and allowing you the indulgence of a glass or two of local wine.

Very Expensive

Charles Inn Restaurant ★★★ CONTEMPORARY   Set in an 1832 Georgian-style house, this restaurant is a throwback to gracious service and an elegant romantic dining experience; expect to linger for a few hours. If the weather is fine, ask for table 64 on the veranda and enjoy views of the river and the golf course, and perhaps a perfect sunset. New chef Steve Sperling worked with former chef William Brunyan-sky for eight years and carries on in the same culinary style. Starters like seared Quebec *foie gras* with ginger, orange and honey scented pain perdu, poached rhubarb, balsamic vinegar and honey syrup are consistent favorites. The elegant menu is a match with the decor: calm persimmon-colored walls, two large fireplaces, white crown molding, and replica chandeliers from the old apothecary. In the summer, have afternoon tea with scones and preserves on the veranda; in the winter, a glass of port in front of the lounge's fireplace.

209 Queen St., Niagara-on-the-Lake. ℂ **866/556-8883** or 905/468-4588. www.charlesinn.ca. Reservations recommended, especially in summer. Main courses C$23–C$35. Tasting menu with wine, C$110. AE, DC, MC, V. Summer daily 7:30–10am, 11am–4pm, and 5–9pm; winter Wed–Sun 5–9pm.

De Luca's Wine Country Restaurant ★★★ BISTRO/REGIONAL   Tony de Luca is one of the architects of Niagara wine-country cuisine. His intimate bistro is small but perfectly designed to make guests feel comfortable. Reclaimed wood floors, high ceilings, and burnt orange and olive tones make this the kind of restaurant where you want to linger. The food is superb, even down to the smallest details, like the fresh bread accompanied by fresh pressed canola oil from Manitoba and balsamic vinegar from British Columbia. Asparagus soup is a silky smooth pleasure, topped with shaved asparagus and a few drops of olive oil. The chocolate tart is not to be missed. Servers are smartly dressed in striped ties, white shirts, and olive/grey vests with white aprons. On the menu, the chef suggests wine pairings to match each

Niagara-on-the-Lake Dining

Niagara Parkway

To Queenston →

Niagara River

Melville St.

Ball St. Wellington St.

Delatre St.

Ricardo St.

Byron St.

Picton St. Davy St.

Platoff St.

Gage St. Castlereagh St.

Nelles St.

Queen's Parade

Christopher Ct.

Weatherstone Ct.

Pafford St.

Park Ct.

King St.

Regent St.

Victoria St.

Gate St.

Karsam Ct

Anne St.

Lake Ontario

Front St.

Prideaux St.

Queen St.

Johnson St.

Centre St.

Simcoe St.

Mississauga St.

Butler St.

Dorchester St.

Nassau St.

William St.

Mary St.

John St.

Balmoral Dr.

↓ To QEW

Butler's Ln.

Lakeshore Rd.

Niagara Blvd.

Palatine Pl.

5

WHERE TO EAT | Niagara-on-the-Lake

1/4 mi

25 km

course. He only serves VQA wines, many available by the glass. There's also a patio with views of the nearby wineries and vineyards.

111C Garrison Village Dr. (across from Jackson-Triggs Winery and Stratus), Niagara-on-the-Lake. ✆ **905/468-7900.** www.tonydeluca.ca. Reservations recommended. Main courses C$18–C$32. AE, MC, V. Daily 11:30am–9pm. Call for winter hours.

LIV Restaurant ★★ INTERNATIONAL   Sink back in the tall black chairs as waiters bring hot towels and an amuse-bouche. There are fresh flowers on the table, gauze-wrapped hanging lights, and a pretty view of the gardens through tall windows. A Southeast Asian influence highlights both the decor and the menu. This is a very attractive dining room, but the cuisine can be hit-or-miss. The red duck curry and the crab cakes are both divine, but the jumbo prawns and the rack of lamb are predictable. The breakfast menu, however, may just be the healthiest and tastiest in the area, featuring organic quinoa with dates, dried cherries, and soy milk; egg-white omelet with feta, tomato, and onion; toasted gluten-free bread and local preserves. The wine list is impressive, with an emphasis on locally produced wines, and there are 25 wines available by the glass, ranging in price from C$9 to C$22.

253 Taylor Rd. (inside White Oaks Conference Resort & Spa), Niagara-on-the-Lake. ✆ **800/263-5766** or 905/688-2550. Reservations required in summer, recommended in winter. Main courses C$25–C$46. AE, DC, MC, V. Summer daily 7am–2pm and 5–10pm; winter Sun–Thurs 7am–2pm, Fri–Sat 7am–2pm and 5–10pm.

Riverbend Inn & Vineyard ★★★ REGIONAL/CANADIAN   There are few lovelier places to dine than the patio at Riverbend. The new management of the Inn has hired one of the best chefs in the area to lead their kitchen. Chef William Brunyansky, formerly of the Charles, has brought his fine local food sensibilities to the Riverbend and given them a slightly Tuscan flavor. The cream-and-yellow dining room is the perfect backdrop for his superb dishes—Tuscan risotto with caramelized scallops and wild mushrooms with truffle oil drizzle, perfect grilled calamari with olive tapenade on a bed of baby greens, and a totally decadent chocolate passion fruit cake. Reserve a table in the gazebo, watch the sunset over the vineyards, and savor a memorable meal. The Inn has its own vineyards, and Reif Winery makes the wines for the restaurant, but there are a range of other wines on the menu too.

16104 Niagara River Pkwy., Niagara-on-the-Lake. ✆ **905/468-8866** or 888/955-5553. www.riverbend inn.ca. Reservations recommendedC$25–C$38. . AE, DC, MV, V. Daily 11am–11pm.

Tiara Restaurant ★★ CANADIAN   The elegant dining room at Queen's Landing Inn has an elegant menu to match. The food here is often locally sourced and mainly traditional, but some dishes challenge the palate, like edgy *sous-vide* entrees. A dessert plate that includes Belgian chocolate pavé, a cherry cheese sphere with caramel sauce, raspberry gelée/foam, and a white chocolate shell filled with strawberry sorbet is a knockout. There are claims that the iconic Icewine martini, the signature drink of Niagara, was invented here. Tiara is filled with light that streams in through a bank of windows overlooking the historic Niagara-on-the-Lake harbor. Waitstaff are warm, and an in-house wine expert will impart an encyclopedia of wine facts to ensure the perfect meal accompaniment. You'll be well cared for.

155 Byron St., Niagara-on-the-Lake. ✆ **888/669-5566.** Reservations recommended. Main courses C$32–C$42. AE, MC, V. Daily 7–10:30am, 11am–2pm, and 5–9pm.

Treadwell's Farm to Table Cuisine ★★ REGIONAL/CANADIAN   Like the decor, Stephen Treadwell's plates are elegant and pure, lacking any superfluous

HIGH tea

Take a step back in time to a gentler moment, when people had time to linger over afternoon tea and conversation. The **Drawing Room at the Prince of Wales** (6 Picton St., Niagara-on-the-Lake; ℂ **905/468-3246;** www.vintage_hotels. com) is a lovely space, and the high tea served is totally indulgent. There are fresh flowers and comfy chairs, tables in corners all around the room, and tiered plates full of wonderful finger foods. The bottom tier held the savories: little sandwiches, spinach and prosciutto rolls, cheese and mango chutney, and egg salad. The next layer was warm English scones with jam and clotted cream and little vol-ou-vents. The top held Chai crème brûlée and lemon meringue tarts. I highly recommend the high tea

ceremony. Afternoon tea is served daily from noon to 6pm, and costs from C$32.

Housed in a renovated rural barn, the **Berry Patch Tea Room** (398 Canboro Rd., Ridgeville; ℂ **905/892-4209**) serves a full lunch menu, but most people come for the afternoon tea and the massive slices of homemade pie. Afternoon tea includes a platter of tea sandwiches, vegetables and dip, fresh scones with jam and clotted cream, fruit, homemade squares and cookies, and tea of your choice—at C$18. It is situated on a little country road, but despite its isolation, it is often completely booked, so a reservation is a good idea. The tearoom is open June to September daily from 11:30am to 4pm.

touches. He tells me he will take us on a "serious exploration of Niagara cuisine," and that is precisely what a meal here is. That involves exploring the flavors of locally caught fish, freshly picked greens, ripe local fruit, and also the marriage of the food with wine. The pork on the menu for a main course is a complete indulgence—bacon-wrapped pork tenderloin with pork belly, goat cheese, and chive crushed potatoes with lemon gastrique. His son James is an accomplished sommelier and runs the wine program at the restaurant. Chef Stephen also has a chef's table right in his kitchen, where you can watch him and his staff cook, ask questions, and be part of the action. For a more casual meal, book a table in the wine bar restaurant called "Snob," where many of the same dishes from the main restaurant are served, but in a less formal way and for a lesser price.

61 Lakeport Rd., Port Dalhousie. ℂ **905/934-9797.** www.treadwellcuisine.com. Reservations recommended. Main courses C$32–C$45; 6-course tasting menu with wine pairing C$80–C$130. AE, MC, V. Daily noon–3pm and 5–9pm; Snob daily 5–11pm.

Expensive

Cannery Restaurant at the Pillar and Post CONTEMPORARY Cannery Restaurant has a relaxed, informal atmosphere and a large menu of perennial favorites. Try the crab cakes created by chef Randy Dupuis, served with pineapple salsa and smoked jalapeño aioli. An open-hearth oven is the heart of the restaurant, where thin-crust pizzas are created. Attention to freshness, cheerful service, and good variety make this a comfortable place to bring the family for dinner. The restaurant has won the CAA/AAA Four Diamond rating for 9 consecutive years.

48 John St., Niagara-on-the-Lake. ℂ **905/468-2123** or 888/669-5566. Main courses C$24–C$60. AE, MC, V. Mon–Sat 7am–2pm and 5–9pm; Sun 10:30am–2pm and 5–9pm.

The Epicurean Restaurant ★ INTERNATIONAL/BISTRO/CAFE This bistro eatery has two faces—a laid-back, come-on-up counter at the front entrance, with sandwiches and daily specials chalked on a blackboard for daytime diners, and a casual fine-dining section at the rear that opens onto a gorgeous shaded patio for evening patrons. Perfect for a hot summer day, the cold tomato soup (gazpacho) tastes like it was made from fruit picked straight off the vines, and the extra-large portion of quiche makes this a good spot to get a healthy meal. The Epicurean offers simple dishes in a less formal atmosphere than some of its neighbors. The dinner menu includes suggestions for wine matched to each course. Dessert is decadent, such as warm chocolate cake with crème anglaise and butterscotch sauce.

84 Queen St., Niagara-on-the-Lake. © **905/468-0288.** www.epicurian.ca. Reservations recommended. Main courses C$22–C$29. MC, V. Summer daily 9am–9pm; winter Wed–Sun 9am–9pm.

Restaurant at the Oban Inn ★ CANADIAN This is a very attractive property that has been renovated to a classic contemporary style. But it is still a formal place, with great views of the river and a quite traditional take on local cuisine. Ask for a room in the sunroom. Juniper-scented lamb, pan-seared scallops, Pacific black cod, and oven-roasted chicken with homemade pasta are some of the mains. It's a good place for a leisurely dinner, and afterwards, you can take a quiet stroll to the river and the golf course.

60 Front St., Niagara-on-the-Lake. © **866/359-6226** or 905/468-2165. www.obaninn.ca. Main courses C$15–C$40. AE, MC, V. Daily 11:30am–3pm and 5–9pm.

The Shaw Café & Wine Bar CANADIAN Although this cafe can be on the expensive side, it offers some good light-lunch options; if you want to people-watch, the patio looks on to the town's busiest street. The flower boxes and greenery make this a very pretty place to dine. Lunch choices include inventive salads and wraps, and a large assortment of cakes and pastries is also available. For those tired of wine tasting, a flight of locally brewed beers is offered. Dinner is also served here, with entrees including braised lamb and blackened catfish, but it's not the cafe's strong suit.

92 Queen St., Niagara-on-the-Lake. © **888/669-5566** or 905/468-4772. www.shawcafe.ca. Main courses C$16–C$25. AE, V, MC. Summer daily 10am–11:30pm; winter Mon–Fri 10am–6pm, Sat–Sun 10am–9pm.

Stone Road Grille ★★ 🏛 REGIONAL Located in a generic strip mall with a sign that reads REST (ask a server for the story), this place is anything but generic. Inside, waitresses sporting stylish black dresses and funky shoes attend to guests like it's a large dinner party—there's lots of talking and jazzy music in the background. Fresh ingredients are mainstays, as are fun combinations—an entree called Three Little Pigs features small portions of various pieces of pork jazzed up with innovative spices and tastes. Fun sides like crispy pork belly and roasted bone marrow make for an interesting pairing. The small take-out section beside the formal restaurant is still a favorite with the local crowd, as well as with visitors who want to do an informal meal. They offer great sandwiches—one will actually feed two people—like Thai chicken salad on a multigrain bun. They also do a wicked poutine and gourmet pizzas. And they deliver.

In the Garrison Plaza, corner of Mary and Mississauga sts., Niagara-on-the-Lake. © **905/468-3474.** www.stoneroadgrille.com. Main courses C$18–C$30. MC, V. Summer Tues–Fri 11:30am–2pm and 5–10pm, Sat–Sun 5–10pm; winter Tues–Thurs 11:30am–2pm and 5–9pm, Fri–Sat 5–10pm, Sun 5–9pm.

Zee's Patio & Grill ★★ REGIONAL   This is one of the busiest restaurants in town, primarily for the sake of convenience rather than the cuisine. Because the Festival Theatre is just a few steps away, it is the perfect choice for theater-goers. It's upscale casual, with a convivial and lighthearted approach to food. The lobster poutine is a good bet. The menu begins with appetizers such as a popcorn shrimp, crusted in coconut and touched up with a sweet soy, lime, and chili dipping sauce. Lobster bisque is tasty though light on the lobster flavor. There is usually a good selection of sandwiches and paninis on the lunch menu. Service is crisp and enthusiastic but can get a bit haphazard when the crowds are heavy. The cheese plate has a good selection of Canadian artisanal cheeses, which pair nicely with a glass of Niagara red.

92 Picton St., Niagara-on-the-Lake. © **905/468-5715.** www.zees.ca. Reservations recommended. Main courses C$26–C$33. AE, MC, V. Summer Tues–Sat 7:30am–midnight, Sun–Mon 7:30am–9pm; winter Mon–Wed 5–9pm, Thurs–Sun noon–9pm.

Moderate

Coach & Horses Pub PUB 🦐   This centrally located restaurant provides bistro style food on the main floor, but downstairs there's an English pub with a warming fireplace and an inviting bar. Pub favorites like fish and chips and shepherd's pie are available, as well as chicken Marsala and a signature burger. They also serve a selection of local wines and, of course, there are several beers on tap. They will do take-out meals as well.

60 Picton St. (at the corner of Davy St.), Niagara-on-the-Lake. © **905/468-4116** or 888/669-5566. www.vintage-hotels.com. Main courses C$12–C$19. AE, MC, V. Daily May–Oct 11am–midnight.

Ginger Restaurant ★ 🦐 ASIAN   Asian (Thai, Chinese, Malaysian) cuisine is presented in a North American style here. Favorites include a filet of salmon on top of soba noodles dressed with soy sesame glaze, chicken stir fry (bok choy, sweet peppers), teriyaki beef served with vegetables and steamed rice, or house-made Canton-style barbecued pork with Singapore noodles. It's a small one-room restaurant on the main floor of the Orchid Inn. Simple black-and-white photographs of Hong Kong and other cities line the walls. The service is gracious in this family-run restaurant. They also do takeout.

390 Mary St., Niagara-on-the-Lake. © **905/468-3871.** Main dishes C$20–C$25. AE, MC, V. Daily 5–9pm.

Little Red Rooster 🦐 DINER   This spacious down-home diner is filled with comfy upholstered banquettes and booths. Popular with locals, it's a perfect spot to drop in and relax. If you're looking for cheap eats, you've found the place. Homey menu items include pork chops with applesauce, liver and onions, toasted western sandwiches, and french fries with gravy. Home-baked pies, old-fashioned milkshakes, and ice-cream sundaes are all dependable desserts. All-day breakfast with two eggs and bacon, ham, or sausage is only C$4, and the kids' menu for 10 and under is just C$5 for a main course, small drink, and ice-cream sundae.

271 Mary St., Niagara-on-the-Lake. ✆ **905/468-3072.** Main courses C$4–C$13. MC, V. Daily 7am–8pm.

Niagara-on-the-Lake Golf Club Dining Room DINER/REGIONAL   This is one of the best bargains, and best kept secrets in town. It's right opposite the Oban Inn, perched along the river with wonderful views of the sailing boats and Fort Niagara. The patio is one of the most scenic places to dine. And while the food is not gourmet by any means, it is substantial, with comfort food favorites like braised lamb shanks, back ribs, and spaghetti with meatballs. Members of the public are welcome.

143 Front St., Niagara-on-the-Lake. ✆ **905/468-3424.** www.notlgolf.com. Main courses C$12–C$32. MC, V. Daily 7am–10pm.

Olde Angel Inn Pub and Restaurant PUB   One of the oldest operating inns—and one of the only places up past bedtime in the area—they serve traditional hearty pub grub and a good variety of microbrews from beyond and locally. More than 16 draft beers are available, including their own lager and red, Creemore Springs Lager, and Toronto's own Steam Whistle Pilsner. Imported beers include Guinness Stout, Kilkenny Cream, and Stella Artois. Every Friday and Saturday, tap your feet to local musicians. Choose from English menu staples such as shepherd's pie, fish and chips, and bangers and mash—this last offering is delicious rather than alarming. Bangers and mash is a dish featuring pork sausage and garlic mashed potatoes with Guinness gravy. The pub also has North American roadhouse munchies such as bruschetta and spring rolls. A great place to relax and unwind. Look out for a secret little joke in the women's washroom.

224 Regent St. (in the Market Sq.), Niagara-on-the-Lake. ✆ **905/468-3411.** www.angel-inn.com. Main courses C$14–C$25. AE, MC, V. Daily 11:30am–1am.

Old Winery Restaurant ★ 🍴 ITALIAN   Finally! Niagara-on-the-Lake has a restaurant with a sophisticated menu in a cool atmosphere that won't break the bank. Located in a restored brick warehouse, this place is the area's best bet for a refined meal on a budget. Reminiscent of an Italian trattoria, the atmosphere is lively, and the food is simple Italian with some North American favorites thrown in. There's pizza from the wood-burning oven, several homemade pasta dishes, and organic steaks. As a plus, the restaurant offers half-size entrees. Appetizers are simple but flavorful: Prosciutto and peaches come with a dab of olive oil, and spicy mayonnaise adds zip to potato crab cakes. The wine list is vast, covering all the major international wine hot spots as well as a vast number of local wineries. I also like that they carry many varieties by the glass—eight choices each for reds and whites.

2228 Niagara Stone Rd., Niagara-on-the-Lake. ✆ **905/468-8900.** www.theoldwineryrestaurant.com. Main courses C$11–C$27. AE, MC, V. Daily 11:30am–9pm.

Inexpensive

The Pie Plate ★ BISTRO/CAFE   The sign outside has the daily pie posted. That's because they only serve what's in season. At the best pie destination in the region, you can expect fresh strawberry, blueberry, cherry, and my personal favorite, peach, baked in a delicate, flaky crust that makes Grandma's seem store-bought. Light

cooking up A STORM IN NIAGARA

Would-be iron chefs and weekend kitchen wizards will be pleased to discover the culinary playgrounds of the Niagara region. Spurred by the growth of the wine industry, cooking classes for weekend kitchen warriors have sprung up across the area.

The Wine Country Cooking School (1339 Lakeshore Rd., Niagara-on-the-Lake; ✆ **905/468-8304**) is Canada's first winery cooking school. Based at Strewn Winery, the cooking school highlights the close relationship between food and wine in its teaching philosophy. Its bright, airy classroom, featuring an entire bank of windows along one wall, is a pleasure to work in. Cooking stations designed for pairs of cooks to work together are equipped with utensils and appliances that will make home cooks sigh with delight. A separate dining room is available for students to enjoy their creations, matched with wines from Strewn's cellars. Strewn's winemaker and guest speakers often attend the dinners. Packages are available that include dinner at Terroir la Cachette, Strewn's winery restaurant, and overnight accommodations in nearby Niagara-on-the-Lake.

The Good Earth Food and Wine Co. (4556 Lincoln Ave., Beamsville; ✆ **905/563-7856**) is run by Nicolette Novak, a walking encyclopedia of the land and its fruits. "When people come down the rickety lane through the orchards, I want them to forget their stress and tune out for 3 hours." And that's just what you'll do—no more than 12 guests sit around the kitchen island and watch local chefs demonstrate how to make easy-to-replicate dishes. Don't be intimidated—Nicolette is a jeans and T-shirt kind of lady, and her open-cupboard kitchen is a gateway to good food no matter what your experience level. But do book ahead: Spring classes are posted online in February, and often fill up within a month. In the summer, sit outside and enjoy the demonstration beside the stone hearth. The beautiful potager garden, with its raised beds, provides many of the fresh ingredients for the cooking classes. Classes also include hands-on courses, 2-day team-building events, and kitchen parties. The new vineyard is producing excellent wines, and there are some gourmet finds to buy in the little food store, like duck fat and homemade stocks.

Niagara Culinary Institute (Glendale Campus, 135 Taylor Rd., Niagara-on-the-Lake; ✆ **905/735-2211**) is part of the Hospitality and Tourism Division at Niagara College. They offer a variety of courses, ranging from half-day courses in desserts and other delights to full-day classes in soup-making and a three-session bread-making course. More extensive part-time classes leading to certification in various aspects of the hospitality and tourism industry are also available, including sommelier training.

L'Escoffier (17 Lloyd St., St. Catharines; ✆ **905/685-7881**) is a retail kitchenware destination with a teaching kitchen on the premises. Local chefs teach evening classes in food preparation, presentation, and how to pair food and wine.

lunches are also available, including thin-crust pizzas. The Guinness and sirloin beef potpie main dish is a nice precursor to a dessert pie, as is the turkey burger, thin-crust pizzas, or fish tacos: two homemade soft corn tortillas stuffed with tilapia, fresh salsa, and cabbage. There are also cinnamon buns and other baked goods. Located in an old Victorian home with creaky hardwood floors, it feels like going to Grandma's.

Dine in one of two small rooms with jellybean-colored chairs, if you want to take in the wafts of freshly baked pie emanating from the kitchen. Outside, wrought-iron chairs line the gabled patio.

1516 Niagara Stone Rd., Niagara-on-the-Lake. ℂ **905/468-9-PIE** (905/468-9743). www.thepieplate. com. Most courses under C$14. AE, MC, V. Tues–Sat 8am–9pm; Sun 10am–4pm.

Willow Cakes and Pastries BAKERY This is a delightful little place to duck in for a quick coffee and a homemade croissant or an elegant dessert, like the irresistible chocolate caramel cheesecake. Beware: The thick buttery filling from the butter tart will spill onto your fingers and your napkin—just make sure it ends up in your mouth. The pastries are light yet loaded with sinful calories. Quiche, *pain au chocolat,* banana bread, *petits fours,* and more are on display in the brightly lit glass-fronted cabinets. The array of artisanal breads is extensive. The shop has the feel of a chic French patisserie, but the distinctive charm of small-town Ontario shines through. A few small bistro tables are available, or you can arrange takeout to enjoy outdoors.

242 Mary St., Niagara-on-the-Lake. ℂ **905/468-2745.** www.willowcakes.ca. Most items under C$10. AE, MC, V. Summer daily 8am–7:30pm; winter daily 8am–6pm.

WINE COUNTRY

The renaissance of the Niagara region's wine industry in the late 1980s and early 1990s attracted considerable interest from a handful of talented chefs. These chefs, with their innovative approach to cuisine and intimate understanding of the connection between the land and the cooking pot, nurtured the fledgling wine-country restaurant industry. Today, there are an amazing range of good dining options from which to choose. The bar is constantly being raised by the restaurateurs themselves, whose enthusiasm for food and wine continues to drive the industry to new heights. Relax, savor, and enjoy.

Very Expensive

Hillebrand Vineyard Café ★★ REGIONAL A large chunk of the C$3-million winery renovation in 2007 went into overhauling the restaurant and the menu; what was good was made even better. The menu changes seasonally, and the accompaniments almost daily. "You'll never see a strawberry on our menu in January," the waiter informs me. I began with seven varieties of local hothouse heirloom tomatoes—purple, green, and red—wedged between slices of goat cheese, washed down with a crisp Sauvignon Blanc Artist Series limited edition. Entrees offered during my visit included homemade ravioli with asparagus and goat cheese and the St. Canut smoked and sugar-glazed pork. I highly recommend the Tour of Niagara, which allows you to sample three entrees. On less busy nights, guests are invited to sample bottles inside the climate-controlled wine room.

1249 Niagara Stone Rd., R.R. 2, Niagara-on-the-Lake. ℂ **905/468-7123.** www.hillebrand.com. Reservations recommended. Main courses C$40. AE, DC, MC, V. Summer daily 11:30am–3pm and 5–9pm; winter daily noon–2:30pm and 5:30–9pm.

The Kitchen House Restaurant ★★ FRENCH/REGIONAL Previously known as the Restaurant at Peninsula Ridge, the restaurant was recently redesigned and renamed. Ask for a table facing the lake, which, depending on the time of year, will allow you to watch the sun set as you dine. The restaurant also offers Sunday

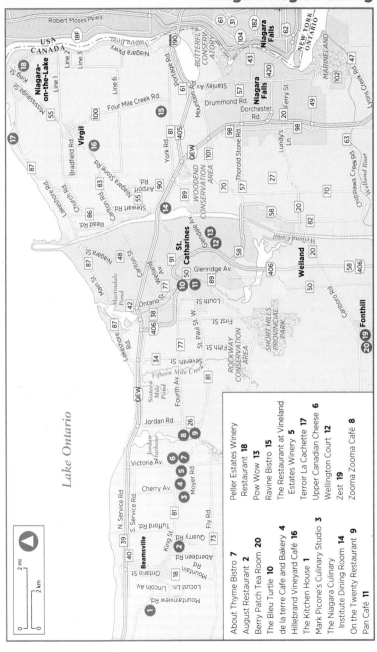

About Thyme Bistro **7**
August Restaurant **2**
Berry Patch Tea Room **20**
The Bleu Turtle **10**
de la terre Cafe and Bakery **4**
Hillebrand Vineyard Café **16**
The Kitchen House **1**
Mark Picone's Culinary Studio **3**
The Niagara Culinary
Institute Dining Room **14**
On the Twenty Restaurant **9**
Pan Café **11**

Peller Estates Winery
Restaurant **18**
Pow Wow **13**
Ravine Bistro **15**
The Restaurant at Vineland
Estates Winery **5**
Terroir La Cachette **17**
Upper Canadian Cheese **6**
Wellington Court **12**
Zest **19**
Zooma Zooma Café **8**

brunch that is leagues above your typical ham and eggs: Scrambled eggs with lobster and sautéed mushrooms are flavored with tarragon vermouth and truffle oil. Lunch on the patio is also exemplary.

5600 King St. W., Beamsville. © **905/563-0900.** www.peninsularidge.com. Main courses C$22–C$32. AE, DC, MC, V. Wed–Sun 11:30am–3pm and 5–9pm; Sun brunch 11am–3pm.

On the Twenty Restaurant ★★ REGIONAL   As the pioneer of Niagara's estate winery restaurants, On the Twenty has a lot to live up to, and it has achieved consistency in the quality of its food over the years. What sets this place apart is its romantic ambience. Situated in quaint Jordan Village, it's a relaxing retreat from the busy wineries; make it a weekend destination and stay at the Inn on the Twenty across the street. Guests of the Inn have breakfast here. The salads were some of the most imaginative I've had in the region, featuring several tastes and textures: Baby greens wrapped in prosciutto were surrounded by slices of Bartlett pear with blue cheese and drizzled with pomegranate vinaigrette; a Gewürztraminer was paired with blue cheese and buttermilk dressing. The wine list covers all the bases. The decor is very pleasing, with warm Tuscan colors, and a spectacular view over the Jordan Valley and Twenty Mile Creek. Service is professional and courteous.

3836 Main St., Jordan Village. © **905/562-7313.** www.innonthetwenty.com. Reservations recommended. Main courses C$24–C$38. MC, V. Daily 11:30am–3pm and 5–9pm.

Peller Estates Winery Restaurant ★★ FRENCH/REGIONAL   Diners looking for an adventurous meal should experience Peller's tasting menu in an unpretentious and inviting room. I think this is the prettiest dining room in wine country. The view of the vineyards from the patio is idyllic. An ever-changing menu, to keep up with the seasons, is fresh and creative. Standouts served during my visit included a puree of green pea soup; foie gras cheesecake topped with apple; a lobster truffle; and an audacious dish consisting of, from top to bottom, scallop, aged cheddar, braised beef short rib, zucchini confit, and toasted brioche, all sitting on a small bed of leeks braised in cabernet. The dessert continued the playful tone, with a new take on a camping favorite: Icewine cherry s'mores. Enjoy the cheese garden on warmer days between 1 and 6pm. Each server is trained in wine tasting, with mandatory continuing education.

290 John St. E., Niagara-on-the-Lake. © **888/673-5537.** www.peller.com. Reservations recommended. Main courses C$32–C$42. AE, MC, V. Summer daily noon–3pm and 5–9pm; winter daily noon–3pm and 5:30–8:30pm.

The Restaurant at Vineland Estates Winery ★★ CONTINENTAL   The bucolic surroundings—a vineyard amidst rolling hills set in an old Mennonite village—make a visit here an event. The menu, which changes seasonally and makes good use of local ingredients, is traditional fine-dining fare but it's accented with subtle changes and fresh additions. Chef Justin Downes concentrates on local fresh market ingredients and a varied menu. Vineland's version of a tasting menu is a five-course creative dinner, which costs C$75; add another C$35 if you opt for paired wines, C$45 for Reserve wine pairing, and C$75 for vintage wines. The wine selection is mainly comprised of Vineland Estates wines, nearby Tawse Winery and a few international selections.

3620 Moyer Rd., Vineland. © **888/846-3526.** www.vineland.com. Reservations required on summer weekends; recommended in winter. Main courses C$22–C$34. AE, DC, MC, V. Summer daily 11:30am–2:30pm and 5–8:30pm; winter Wed–Sun noon–2pm and 5:30–8:30pm.

Expensive

Ravine Vineyard Bistro ★★ BISTRO   This bistro has evolved from a small bites deli place into a definitely cool French-style bistro, fast becoming a favorite for its mussels and steak frites. The cuisine is local fresh market with a French twist, inspired by Niagara. The menu is the same for lunch and dinner, and the wine list is an excellent one, with not just Ravine Vineyard wines but also wines from their wine-maker friends, all VQA. You can still get fresh bread baked in the outdoor brick oven, delectable pastries, charcuterie, and artisanal cheeses for a picnic from the counter at the back of the tasting room. If you arrive late afternoon, order a glass of wine, a slice of still-warm bread, and a chunk of good cheese, and go sit out on the lawn to enjoy it. Lovely.

1366 York Rd., Box 340, St. Davids. © **905/262-VINE** (8463). www.ravinevineyard.com. Reservations recommended. Main courses C$11–C$28. AE, MC, V. Daily 11am–8:30pm.

Terroir La Cachette ★★ FRENCH/REGIONAL   For fresh Niagara produce given a French accent, Quebecois chef Alan Levesque creates superb dishes. Grilled Delft Blue Corner Farm veal T-bone with green peppercorns, shallots and roasted portabella mushrooms is just one memorable dish. The entrance to the restaurant is unimpressive, but the interiors and the patio are lovely. Large, panoramic picture windows overlook the Four Mile Creek. The restaurant is located inside Strewn Winery, and although the ownership is independent, there is a strong relationship between the restaurant and the winery; a great selection of Strewn wines is available. Other Niagara wines are on the list: Whites include Featherstone, Daniel Lenko, and Stoney Ridge, and reds are available from Creekside, Palatine Hills, and Malivoire.

1339 Lakeshore Rd. (inside Strewn Winery), Niagara-on-the-Lake. © **905/468-1222.** www.strewn winery.com. Reservations recommended. Main courses C$24–C$35. AE, DC, MC, V. Summer Mon–Fri 11:30am–3:30pm and 5–9pm, Sat 11:30am–10pm, Sun 11:30am–9pm; winter Wed–Sat 11:30am–3:30pm and 5–9pm, Sun 11:30am–3:30pm and 5–8pm.

Moderate

About Thyme Bistro BISTRO   You could easily miss this little boîte of a place. It looks quite unassuming from the outside. But inside you will find a professional French-style bistro that serves the best steak frites in the area, complete with house-made ketchup. Chef Ryan Shapiro's bistro charcuterie plate has his own smoked bacon and sausages, and on the menu you will find foie gras, duck confit, and a great wine list. A three-course fixed price dinner menu for C$30 includes duck confit, veal steaks, and fresh trout. Don't miss the bistro poutine with duck confit, old cheddar and foie gras sauce—it is a meal in itself. The restaurant embraces the province's "bring your own wine" policy, and customers are encouraged to buy local wines and bring these bottles to the restaurant. The patio has become the place where local winemakers come for lunch or dinner, bringing their wines with them. It's a place with real authenticity.

3457 King St., Vineland. © **905/562-3457.** www.aboutthymebistro.com. Fixed-price dinner C$30, mains C$30–C$39. AE, MC, V. Wed–Sun 11am–3pm and 5–9pm.

August Restaurant ★★ BISTRO   This is a bistro with heart and energy, a sassy but serious place that searches for the best local ingredients and celebrates what Niagara does best. Locals hang out here, and the tapas menu that runs on summer evenings is a big hit. Dishes are carefully plated, made with love and complexity without being overwhelming. Try the crispy duck rolls to start, and follow with the lobster mac & cheese.

5204 King St., Beamsville. 📞 **905/563-0200.** www.augustrestaurant.ca. Reservations recommended. Main courses C$16–C$26. AE, MC, V. Tues–Sat 11:30am–3pm and 5–9pm. Sun 9am–3pm.

Benchmark Restaurant, The Niagara Culinary Institute Dining Room ★ 🍴 REGIONAL   Meet the next Jamie Oliver at the dining room of the Glendale Campus of Niagara College. Students enrolled in the Hospitality and Tourism Division assist in menu design, work in the kitchen, and perform front-of-house duties as part of their course requirements. With dishes such as chilled cucumber and dill soup with crème fraîche and pâté de champagne with chardonnay jelly and toast, the restaurant aims high and meets expectations, but for a lot less money than you'd expect. Fresh herbs are supplied by the college's horticultural students, and the wine list features wines made by students at the Niagara College Teaching Winery, along with bottles from almost a dozen Niagara wineries. Most bottles are priced under the C$30 mark. The restaurant features panoramic windows and a casual atmosphere; student servers are charming and eager to please.

135 Taylor Rd., Niagara-on-the-Lake. 📞 **905/641-2252.** www.niagaracollege.ca. Reservations recommended. Main courses C$17–C$24. AE, MC, V. Lunch Tues–Sun 11:30am–2pm; dinner Wed–Fri 5–9pm, Sat 5–9:30pm.

Zooma Zooma Café ★ BISTRO/CAFE   This is a great place for a light, casual lunch or midafternoon pick-me-up if you are touring wine country or hitting Jordan for its boutique shops, galleries, and antiques retailers. Striking, acidic tones of chartreuse, orange, and fuchsia wake up your senses before the first sip of espresso or cappuccino passes your lips. Their grilled vegetable pizza—with sweet peppers, zucchini, and eggplant—is a highlight, as is the warm brie with apricot Riesling jelly on flatbread. A regular concert series of music on the patio makes for a great summer night.

3839 Main St., Jordan. 📞 **905/562-6280.** Main courses C$8–C$11. AE, MC, V. Sun–Thurs 10am–6pm; Fri 10am–10pm; Sat 10am–5pm. Winter daily 10am–5pm.

Inexpensive

de la terre Cafe and Bakery ★ BAKERY/CAFE   Chef Jan Campbell-Luxton hand-shapes his lovely organic multigrain loaves, and all the breads are artisanal and organic. This is more a bakery than a cafe, although they serve fair-trade coffee and tea, and use only biodegradable and recyclable take-out containers. This is the place to pick up great bread for a memorable picnic: fat round loaves of honey and walnut, olive bread, and multi-seed sourdough. Or pick up a dozen fresh cookies or butter tarts.

3451 King St., Vineland. 📞 **905/562-1513.** www.delaterre.ca. Tues–Sat 8am–6pm.

WELLAND CANAL CORRIDOR

The Welland Canal corridor takes in the communities of Old Port Dalhousie on the shores of Lake Ontario, the city of St. Catharines, and the town of Welland, among others. If you're exploring the area, or traversing it on the way to or from Niagara Falls, here are a few places you might like to stop for a bite to eat or a longer, more elaborate meal.

Expensive

Wellington Court ★★ INTERNATIONAL/REGIONAL   Local artists' paintings tastefully decorate the intimate rooms, and photographs line the hallway of this restaurant, located in an Edwardian town house where the chef's mother was raised. If you're a seasoned restaurant aficionado, you won't be bored here by the predictable. In this modest 40-seat restaurant, the menu has some original pairings that are pleasantly surprising. For instance, roasted chicken breast, truffled potato puree, and braised leeks are lapped with a sweet sherry and chicken stock reduction. For appetizers, they make their own pâté on dried cranberry crostini with pear compote. Menu items change with the seasons. Complement your dinner with a fine selection of regional wines. The waitstaff is subtle, floating in and out without interrupting a word of conversation.

11 Wellington St., St. Catharines. ✆ **905/682-5518.** www.wellington-court.com. Reservations recommended. Main courses C$24–C$32. AE, DC, MC, V. Tues–Sat 11:30am–2:30pm and 5–9:30pm.

Moderate

Pow Wow ★ 🏛ASIAN   When local chefs and winery employees want to exhale, they come here. The food isn't fine dining, but it's what chefs like: simple combinations that let the taste come through. The menu is extensive—a good mix of fish, meat, and pastas. The Komodo Dragon is a mix of Japanese udon noodles and sweet and spicy teriyaki sauce, loaded up with crunchy vegetables and tender beef tenderloin strips. The spicy Moroccan grouper is served on an herbed rice cake with passion fruit and pomegranate reduction. Starters include the popular firecracker shrimp, fried with sweet chiles, cashews, saffron, lemon, and lime. Tin painted ceilings, slanted hardwood floors, and partial brick walls make you think you're in a funky neighborhood in New York.

165 St. Paul St., St. Catharines. ✆ **905/688-3106.** www.powwowrestaurant.com. Main courses C$15–C$25. AE, MC, V. Mon 11:30am–2:30pm; Tues–Thurs 11:30am–9pm; Fri 11:30am–10pm; Sat 5–10pm. Closed Sun.

Inexpensive

The Bleu Turtle BISTRO   At the Bleu Turtle, the former chef from Peninsula Ridge Winery makes very special breakfasts, lunches, and take-away gourmet picnic dishes. Chef Robby bakes bread daily and prepares his own foods such as spreads, mayonnaise, ice cream, soups, pancake mix, and desserts. The meats and vegetables are roasted on-site. Try roasted pork belly or wild boar sausage with your eggs for a special breakfast, or the eggs Benedict with Alaskan king crab, potato, and hollandaise on brioche. For lunch or to take away, there are several sandwiches, like chicken flatbread with sundried tomato, asparagus, goat cheese, and caramelized onions—a bargain at C$12.

215 St. Paul St. W., St. Catharines. ✆ **905/688-0330.** www.bleuturtle.com. Main courses C$7–C$12. AE, MC, V. Wed–Sat 8am–2pm; Sun 8am–3pm. Closed Mon–Tues.

Pan Café CAFE   This cafe specializes in healthy breakfasts, lunches, and brunches. It has a fervent commitment to organic and local. The meat and dairy are grain-fed and drug and hormone free, eggs are free-range local, coffee is shade-grown and bird-friendly, and take-out containers are biodegradable. Everything in the kitchen is made from scratch, except the bread, which comes from de la terre Bakery in Vineland. Try the Cobb Salad with double smoked back bacon, Danish blue cheese, fresh avocado, tomato and a sunshine boiled egg on greens with a red wine vinaigrette. The place features friendly staff and a good atmosphere of exposed brick walls and lots of light. The mac & cheese is made with whole wheat.

120 St. Paul St., St. Catharines. ✆ **905/687-8704.** www.pancafe.ca. Main courses C$7–C$13. Tues–Sat 8am–3pm; Sun 10am–3pm.

FONTHILL

The village of Fonthill is home to a unique and unexpectedly superior restaurant whose reputation extends to the far reaches of the Niagara region.

Very Expensive

Zest ★ CANADIAN Many Torontonians make the 2-hour trek to this restaurant, and it has developed a cultlike following. I can see why. The interior is pretty and comfortable, and the central open kitchen provides the entertainment. It's a sophisticated restaurant full of ambience: distinctive teal blue walls, blonde wood floors, and leatherette-upholstered chairs. Using his Southeast Asian experiences, co-owner chef Michael Pasto prepares modern Canadian cuisine with an emphasis on local and seasonal ingredients. The fresh tomato soup is so simple, yet so full of flavor, with a soupcon of tarragon to add complexity. The calamari with spicy Thai dipping sauce is light and crunchy with a nice punch from the sauce. Mains include Cumbrae beef tenderloin with baco noir jus. Finish up with the house-made ice cream. The wine list is informative, with columns for the wine, vintage, origin, tasting notes, and price by the bottle and the glass.

1469 Pelham St., Fonthill. ✆ **905/892-6474.** www.zestfonthill.com. Reservations recommended. Main courses C$24–C$38. MC, V. Tues–Fri 11:30am–3pm and 5:30–9pm; Sat 5:30–9pm.

PRACTICAL INFORMATION
The Big Picture

The range of dining experiences in the Niagara region is wide. You can enjoy a leisurely lunch on a shady terrace with the lush vineyards spread out around you, dine by candlelight as you marvel at the rainbow colors of the illuminated Horseshoe and American Falls, or lounge around in a diner, eating pancakes and bacon washed down with a bottomless mug of coffee.

If you are enjoying the attractions at the Falls, the best bet for a quick lunch is along Clifton Hill and along Niagara Boulevard, where the fast-food outlets and small restaurants will get you fed and back out for the fun quickly.

Best bet for more casual dining in the area is to find an Italian restaurant. Due to the large local Italian population, Niagara Falls is famous for its Italian dishes.

If you are someone who really appreciates fine food and wine, Niagara-on-the-Lake and wine country is the place where you can indulge in some of the best cuisine in the country. Top chefs are turning the great local specialties into rave-review quality meals. Don't miss the opportunity to pair your food with one of the excellent local wines that may only be available at select restaurants or at the vineyard gate.

Pay attention to the wine prices in restaurants—they can be quite high, even for the local Niagara wines. Don't be surprised to find your favorite vintage at double the price you'd pay at the liquor store or sometimes even at the winery. Savvy diners can

WHERE TO STOCK UP FOR A picnic—AND WHERE TO ENJOY IT

With its lush green spaces, the Niagara region is ideal for a picnic. Here are a few places that will help you stock the perfect picnic hamper with delicious nosh.

The latest cheese store, the **Upper Canadian Cheese,** in Jordan (4159 Jordan Rd., Jordan Station; ✆ **905/562-9730**), offers two of its own cheeses—Comfort Cream is a semisoft rind cheese with an intense buttery taste, while the Niagara Gold has a washed rind with a mellower butter taste and nutty undertones. There's also fresh ricotta cheese and the newest product, Guernsey Girl, a delicious haloumi style cheese that grills beautifully. There's also a number of condiments such as cabernet jelly and gourmet crackers.

Ravine Vineyard Deli & Bakery in St. Davids (1366 York Rd.; ✆ **905/262-8463**) is the perfect stop to pick up goodies for a gourmet picnic. The selection of artisanal cheeses and cold meats is first class—just head to the back of the tasting room and you will find everything you need for an alfresco feast. There is also bread baked daily in the outdoor brick oven, as well as pizzas and delectable desserts.

Order a picnic from the **Shaw Festival Greenroom** chefs (Shaw Festival Box Office, 10 Queen's Parade, Niagara-on-the-Lake; ✆ **800/511-7429**). Book when you order your theater tickets or up to 24 hours in advance of pickup time. If you're in the vicinity of Port Dalhousie,

drop in to **Olson Foods and Bakery** (17 Lock St., Unit 112, Port Dalhousie; ✆ **905/938-8490**). This shop is now run by Anna's former staff who bought the store. It stocks a first-rate variety of European and Canadian cheeses. Gourmet pantry items and upscale kitchen gifts are also available.

Just a few minutes south of Niagara-on-the-Lake, on the Niagara Parkway, you'll find **Kurtz Orchards Gourmet Marketplace** (16006 Niagara Pkwy.; ✆ **905/466-2937**). This large food market and gourmet gift store has plenty of sampling stations, so you can try before you buy. The fresh pies, especially the peach, are fabulous, as are the jams and preserves.

As you drive along the Niagara region's rural roads, you will find many **roadside fruit stands** during the harvest season. Some are more substantial than others and stock additional food and beverage items.

If you are touring the wineries, keep your eyes open when you browse the **winery boutiques.** Many of them keep on hand a few loaves of local artisanal bread, packets of gourmet crackers, and a limited selection of cheeses for purchase.

As for where to enjoy your picnic—turn to "Parks & Gardens" or "Hiking & Biking" in chapter 6 and choose an idyllic swath of green on which to spread your picnic blanket, recline gracefully, and while the afternoon away.

take note of wine prices in the winery boutiques and compare them with those on the wine list in their chosen restaurant in order to better gauge how much markup has been applied.

If you find a bottle of wine from a winery that you want to bring to supper, some Ontario restaurants participate in the BYOB (bring your own bottle) program. At the time of publication, 15 Niagara region restaurants offer this service—for a complete list, visit **www.bringmywine.ca**. Diners can bring their bottle of wine, provided it's not offered on the restaurant's wine list. Diners pay a corkage fee—this pays for servers to open and serve your bottle; corkage fees range between C$12 and C$25, and during the winter season, some restaurants have no corkage fees—call ahead to find out. No partially consumed bottles are allowed. Visit the site for a full list of rules, which includes informing the restaurant you intend to bring your own bottle before you arrive.

Reservations

Reservations are recommended for dining, especially during high season. If you have a play to go to, tell the restaurant when you reserve and they will be sure that you are fed and have received your bill in time to make it to the performance.

Dining Hours

Generally speaking, most restaurants serve their most important meals in the evening, and it is not customary to dine late. Between seven and eight o'clock is an acceptable dining time for the evening meal, earlier if you have booked a visit to the theater.

Hours vary quite markedly between summer and winter. The "high season," when opening hours are long, runs approximately from May to October for restaurants. Some restaurants close 1 day or more during the week in the winter months. You should always call ahead if you have chosen a particular restaurant, in order to avoid disappointment.

Tipping & Taxes

Dining out in Niagara does not have to be an expensive venture, but be aware that taxes are high. Meals are subject to 8% provincial sales tax and 6% GST, so when you factor in an average tip, a whopping 27% is added to the bill. Tipping is usually left to the diner's discretion, although some establishments add 15% (the customary tip for good service) to the bill for parties of six or more. Note that a 10% liquor tax is added to alcoholic beverage purchases.

RESTAURANTS BY CUISINE

AMERICAN

Hard Rock Cafe (Niagara Falls, ON, $$, p. 75)

Rainforest Café (Niagara Falls, ON, $$, p. 76)

Red Coach Inn Restaurant ★ (Niagara Falls, NY, $$, p. 76)

Terrapin Grille ★ (Niagara Falls, ON, $$$$, p. 72)

ASIAN

Ginger Restaurant ★ (Niagara-on-the-Lake, $$, p. 83)

The Golden Lotus ★★ (Niagara Falls, ON, $$$, p. 75)

Pow Wow ★ (Welland Canal Corridor, $$, p. 91)

BAKERY

de la terre Cafe and Bakery ★ (Vineland, $, p. 90)

Willow Cakes and Pastries (Niagara-on-the-Lake, $, p. 86)

KEY TO ABBREVIATIONS:
$$$$** = Very Expensive **$$$** = Expensive **$$** = Moderate **$ = Inexpensive

BISTRO/CAFE

About Thyme Bistro (Vineland, $$, p. 89)

August Restaurant ★★ (Beamsville, $$, p. 89)

The Bleu Turtle (St. Catharines, $, p. 91)

de la terre Cafe and Bakery ★ (Vineland, $, p. 90)

De Luca's Wine Country Restaurant ★★★ (Niagara-on-the-Lake, $$$$, p. 78)

The Epicurean Restaurant ★ (Niagara-on-the-Lake, $$$, p. 82)

The Krieghoff Gallery-Café (Niagara Falls, ON, $$, p. 76)

Mide Bistro and Oxygen Bar (Niagara Falls, ON, $$$, p. 76)

Pan Café (St. Catharines, $, p. 91)

The Pie Plate ★ (Niagara-on-the-Lake, $, p. 84)

Ravine Vineyard Bistro ★★ (St. Davids, $$$, p. 89)

Zooma Zooma Café ★ (Wine Country, $$, p. 90)

CANADIAN

AG at the Sterling ★★★ (Niagara Falls, ON, $$$$, p. 73)

Elements on the Falls (Niagara Falls, ON, $$$$, p. 70)

Queenston Heights Restaurant ★ (Niagara Falls, ON, $$$$, p. 74)

The Rainbow Room by Massimo Capra ★ (Niagara Falls, ON, $$$$, p. 72)

Restaurant at the Oban Inn ★ (Niagara-on-the-Lake, $$$, p. 82)

Riverbend Inn & Vineyard ★★★ (Niagara-on-the-Lake, $$$$, p. 80)

The Shaw Café & Wine Bar (Niagara-on-the-Lake, $$$, p. 82)

Tiara Restaurant ★★ (Niagara-on-the-Lake, $$$$, p. 80)

Treadwell's Farm to Table Cuisine ★★ (Port Dalhousie, $$$$, p. 80)

Zest ★ (Fonthill, $$$$, p. 92)

CONTEMPORARY

Cannery Restaurant at the Pillar and Post (Niagara-on-the-Lake, $$$, p. 81)

Charles Inn Restaurant ★★★ (Niagara-on-the-Lake, $$$$, p. 78)

17 Noir ★★ (Niagara Falls, ON, $$$$, p. 72)

CONTINENTAL

The Restaurant at Vineland Estates Winery ★★ (Wine Country, $$$$, p. 88)

DINER

Betty's Restaurant (Niagara Falls, ON, $$, p. 74)

Bob Evans Farms Restaurant (Niagara Falls, NY, $$, p. 74)

Falls Manor Motel and Restaurant ★ (Niagara Falls, ON, $$, p. 75)

Little Red Rooster (Niagara-on-the-Lake, $$, p. 83)

Niagara-on-the-Lake Golf Club Dining Room (Niagara-on-the-Lake, $$, p. 84)

FRENCH

The Kitchen House Restaurant ★★ (Wine Country, $$$$, p. 86)

Peller Estates Winery Restaurant ★★ (Wine Country, $$$$, p. 88)

Terroir La Cachette ★★ (Wine Country, $$$, p. 89)

INTERNATIONAL

The Epicurean Restaurant ★ (Niagara-on-the-Lake, $$$, p. 82)

LIV Restaurant ★★ (Niagara-on-the-Lake, $$$$, p. 80)

Wellington Court ★★ (Welland Canal Corridor, $$$, p. 91)

ITALIAN

Antica Pizzeria ★ (Niagara Falls, ON, $$, p. 74)

Carpaccio Restaurant and Wine Bar ★ (Niagara Falls, ON, $$$, p. 73)

Casa D'Oro (Niagara Falls, ON, $$, p. 74)

Casa Mia (Niagara Falls, ON, $$, p. 75)

Old Winery Restaurant ★ (Niagara-on-the-Lake, $$, p. 84)

Ponte Vecchio ★★ (Niagara Falls, ON, $$$$, p. 72)

Romano's Macaroni Grill in the Hilton (Niagara Falls, ON, $$$, p. 77)

PIZZA

Zappi's (Niagara Falls, ON, $$, p. 78)

PUB

Coach & Horses Pub (Niagara-on-the-Lake, $$, p. 83)

Olde Angel Inn Pub and Restaurant (Niagara-on-the-Lake, $$, p. 84)

REGIONAL CUISINE

AG at the Sterling ★★★ (Niagara Falls, ON, $$$$, p. 73)

Benchmark Restaurant, Niagara Culinary Institute Dining Room ★ (Wine Country, $$, p. 90)

De Luca's Wine Country Restaurant ★★★ (Niagara-on-the-Lake, $$$$, p. 78)

Elements on the Falls (Niagara Falls, ON, $$$$, p. 70)

Hillebrand Vineyard Café ★★ (Wine Country, $$$$, p. 86)

The Kitchen House Restaurant ★★ (Wine Country, $$$$, p. 86)

Niagara-on-the-Lake Golf Club Restaurant (Niagara-on-the-Lake, $$, p. 84)

On the Twenty Restaurant ★★ (Wine Country, $$$$, p. 88)

Peller Estates Winery Restaurant ★★ (Wine Country, $$$$, p. 88)

Queenston Heights Restaurant ★ (Niagara Falls, ON, $$$$, p. 74)

The Rainbow Room by Massimo Capra ★ (Niagara Falls, ON, $$$$, p. 72)

Riverbend Inn & Vineyard ★★★ (Niagara-on-the-Lake, $$$$, p. 80)

Stone Road Grille ★★ (Niagara-on-the-Lake, $$$, p. 82)

Terroir La Cachette ★★ (Wine Country, $$$, p. 89)

Treadwell's Farm to Table Cuisine ★★ (Port Dalhousie, $$$$, p. 80)

Wellington Court ★★ (Welland Canal Corridor, $$$, p. 91)

Zee's Patio & Grill ★★ (Niagara-on-the-Lake, $$$, p. 83)

STEAKHOUSE

The Keg ★ (Niagara Falls, ON, $$$, p. 73)

WHAT TO SEE & DO IN THE NIAGARA REGION

The Niagara region has much to offer. The first stop for most visitors is its unique geographical formation, the mighty Niagara Falls, and all the attractions that have grown up around them. Beyond the Falls, the area is full of historical venues, child-friendly entertainment, lush parks, and some of Canada's best vineyards.

Many attractions are concentrated in the twin cities of Niagara Falls, Ontario, and Niagara Falls, New York, on either side of the border. The pretty town of Niagara-on-the-Lake, with its tree-lined streets and superbly restored and preserved historical homes, excellent live theater, and unique shopping, should be high on your list of priorities—it is one of my favorite places to visit in Canada. And no trip to Niagara is complete without a visit to the wine country to taste the award-winning VQA Ontario wines and sample the exceptional winery restaurant cuisine featuring local produce (an entire chapter is devoted to the wine region; see chapter 7, "The Wine-Country Experience").

As one of the most historic parts of Canada, the area is richly endowed with museums and historic homes. Of particular interest at the moment are the celebrations surrounding the anniversary of the War of 1812, which will include historic re-enactments, special exhibitions, and museum displays. To find out about specific historical events relating to the anniversary, visit the official website, www.Visit1812.com.

As you delve into this chapter, you will get a good grasp of the top attractions in Niagara—a mosaic of museums, historical landmarks, galleries in which to while away an hour or two, and a smattering of the light-hearted and entertaining. I've highlighted some activities that are ideal for families traveling with children. There are also many beautiful parks and gardens, which flourish in the unique microclimate of the Niagara Peninsula. Outdoor enthusiasts will find plenty of opportunities to enjoy hiking, cycling, and pastimes such as golf. Finally, I list some organized tours, and even provide a few self-guided ones.

Note that some advance planning may be required, since a few attractions eat up a fair bit of time, while others involve some driving. Call ahead to confirm admission hours, which are often seasonal and can change depending on the time of year.

THE TOP ATTRACTIONS

On the Canadian Side

HORSESHOE FALLS ★★★

Two key factors draw visitors in the millions to the Horseshoe Falls, or the Canadian Falls, as they are often called. One is the sheer magnitude of the volume of water that flows along the Upper Niagara River and cascades over the U-shaped rock shelf into the Niagara Gorge below; the other is the fact that you can get so thrillingly close to this remarkable natural display. There are numerous vantage points, each of which will give you a different experience, different emotions, and different souvenir snapshots to take home. To fully absorb the enormity of this natural wonder, take in as many of these as you can. Top it off with the spectacle of the illuminations, and a night of fireworks over the Falls. If you are only in the area for a day trip, don't go home until you've seen the Falls by night.

Maid of the Mist ★★★ ☺   A trip on the *Maid of the Mist* is a must for first-time visitors to the Falls. These small tour boats have been thrilling visitors to the Falls since 1846, when the first coal-fired steamboat equipped with two tall smoke stacks chugged daringly close to the thundering wall of water.

Before climbing aboard, you will be handed a large blue rain poncho (it's voluminous enough to cover even a backpack). You can drop the poncho into the recycling bin on the way out after your trip, but you might be better off keeping it as a souvenir. You might even want to keep it on, as a protector against the mist that often drifts (or blows!) in from the Horseshoe Falls at Table Rock House, a few hundred yards upstream from the *Maid of the Mist* boat launch. Another piece of advice: Resist the urge to bring out the electronics to record the event—you're better off with a waterproof disposable camera. Your camera may well get wet from the spray, but even worse, there is a large amount of lime in the water and the mist can leave a stubborn whitish coating on your lenses.

I must pass on a tip: Get a spot on the upper deck of the starboard side of the boat (landlubbers, that's the right-hand side). Most people crowd to the other side, eager to catch a close-up glimpse of the American Falls as soon as the boat leaves the dock. However, the Canadian *Maid* cautiously approaches the Horseshoe Falls with the starboard side closest to the waterfall, and then veers left to return to the dock,

---

    ### Catch the Rainbow

If you want to gaze upon the rainbow in the mist of the Horseshoe Falls, you need to view the Falls from the Canadian shore during the afternoon. Sunlight slants through the water droplets dancing in the air in mid- to late afternoon, depending on the time of year, creating the mystical band of color that is such a profound symbol of the wonder of nature.

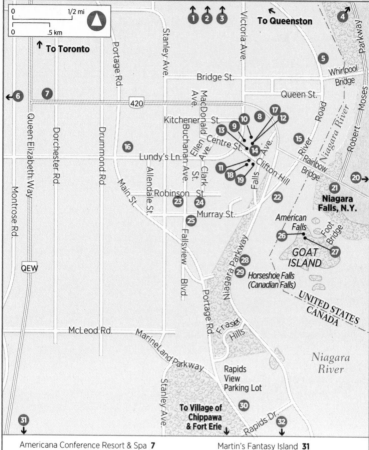

Americana Conference Resort & Spa 7
Aquarium of Niagara 20
Brick City 10
Butterfly Conservatory 1
Cave of the Winds 27
Chippawa Battlefield Park 32
Clifton Hill 9
Cosmic Coaster 12
Fallsview Casino 25
The Haunted House 14
House of Frankenstein 17
Journey Behind the Falls 28
Louis Tussaud's Waxworks 18
Maid of the Mist 22
Maid of the Mist (American Side) 26
Marineland 30

Martin's Fantasy Island 31
Niagara Airbus 6
Niagara Casino 8
Niagara Falls Aviary 15
Niagara Falls History Museum 16
Niagara Freefall Indoor Skydiving 23
Niagara's Fury 29
Niagara Helicopters 3
Niagara Skywheel 11
Ripley's Believe it or Not! Museum 19
Observation Tower 21
Old Fort Niagara 4
Skylon Tower 24
Strike Rock N' Bowl 13
Whirlpool Aero Car 2
White Water Walk 5

NIAGARA trivia—FACTS AND FIGURES

- The difference in elevation between Lake Erie and Lake Ontario is about 99m (325 ft.), with half of that difference occurring at the Falls themselves.
- The Niagara River, which connects Lake Erie and Lake Ontario, is about 58km (36 miles) long.
- At Grand Island, the Niagara River divides into two channels—the Chippawa (Canadian) channel on the west, which carries approximately 60% of the total river flow, and the Tonawanda (American) channel on the east.
- The deepest section of the Niagara River is immediately below the Falls. The depth of the river here is equal to the height of the Falls—52m (171 ft.).
- According to the U.S.G.S. (United States Geological Survey) of Niagara Falls, it appears that almost a third of the Canadian

- Falls lies within U.S. Territory.
- There are some 500 other waterfalls in the world that have a greater elevation than Niagara Falls. However, many of them have relatively little water flow. The grandeur of Niagara Falls is attributed to a combination of its height, water volume, and picturesque setting.
- The *Maid of the Mist* became famous for its role in the 1960 rescue of Roger Woodward, a 7-year-old boy who was the first person to survive a plunge over the Horseshoe Falls with only a life jacket. The boat that performed the rescue retired from service in 1983 and was relocated to the Amazon River to serve as a missionary ship.
- Niagara Falls is the largest producer of hydroelectric power in the world.

thereby rewarding starboard passengers with a close-up of the Horseshoe Falls, followed by a panoramic sweep past the American Falls as it returns to the dock. Stay below decks and you will miss the action. The trip is short, about half an hour, so get your cameras snapping right away. If you are visiting during July or August, schedule your boat ride for early- to midmorning (the first sailing is at 9am during peak season), before the lines begin to form.

5920 River Rd., Niagara Falls, ON (near the foot of Clifton Hill). © **905/358-0311.** www.maidofthemist. com. Admission C$17 adults, C$10 children 6–12, free for children 5 and under. Daily Apr to late Oct (opening date depends on ice conditions in the river). Sailing times vary by season: First trip of the day is at 9am in peak season, 9:45am in spring and fall; last boat sails btw. 4:45–7:45pm.

Journey Behind the Falls This self-guided tour takes you through tunnels bored into the rock behind the Canadian Falls, so if you suffer from claustrophobia, give this a miss—some people seem to find the idea of walking in a tunnel underneath the Falls quite unnerving. There are a couple of short offshoots from the main tunnel where you can peer through openings cut into the rock literally behind the Horseshoe Falls. There is not much to see except a wall of water, but it is nonetheless exhilarating to be on the "other side" of the mighty cascade.

The absolutely best part of the tour, though, is to venture outside onto the lower balcony at the northern edge of the base of the Falls. You will get wetter than wet (much more so than on the *Maid of the Mist*), but it is worth the inconvenience. Recyclable rain ponchos are provided (yellow, instead of the blue ones for the boat ride), but you're still likely to get drenched by spray or a rogue cascade of water, depending on the wind direction and strength. Of all the ways and means you can access the Horseshoe Falls, this is the place where you will feel the power of the Falls at its mightiest. The roar of the water is thrilling beyond compare.

The Journey Behind the Falls is one of the attractions included in the Adventure Pass. During peak season, the attraction operates on a timed entry system with a maximum number of visitors allowed through at any one time. You can visit the ticket booth early in the day and pre-book your entry time, saving you the inconvenience and frustration of standing in line.

6650 Niagara River Pkwy., Niagara Falls, ON (inside the Table Rock Complex). © **877/642-7275.** www. niagaraparks.com/nfgg/behindthefalls.php. Admission C$15 adults, C$8.95 children 6–12, free for children 5 and under. Sun–Fri 9am–7:30pm; Sat 9am–8:30pm. Last ticket sold 30 min. before closing.

Skylon Tower   One of the most distinctive structures on the skyline on the Canadian side of Niagara Falls is the 236m-high (774-ft.) Skylon Tower. Built in 1965, it dominated the landscape on the hill above the Falls for more than 30 years. In recent years, increasingly taller hotels have been sprouting up in the district, but the Skylon still attracts attention—it's almost a landmark. The brightly painted elevators that crawl up the outside of the tower are affectionately known as "yellow bugs." The view is panoramic, covering both the U.S. and the Canadian falls, but the journey to get there—stuffed in an elevator with tourists—isn't fun; you can get similar views from a restaurant nearby. In addition to the indoor viewing area, there is an outdoor deck

NIAGARA'S fury: THE CREATION OF THE FALLS

Niagara's Fury, the new installation at **Table Rock** (6450 Niagara Pkwy., Niagara Falls, ON; www.niagaraparks.com), is an experience that adds layers of significance to viewing the Falls.

The experience starts with an 8-minute animated pre-show, where woodland characters explain how the Ice Age formed Niagara Falls. Then, in a specially designed, 360-degree theater, the formation of the Falls is re-created in a 6-minute, multi-sensory show. The temperature drops 20 degrees, water bubbles, snow falls, and the floor tilts and trembles. Images produced with technology previously used only in satellites immerse the audience in a "4D" Universal Studios–style attraction. The seamless 360-degree screen is one of a kind, and a special nine-camera digital rig was developed specifically for this theater. A 360-degree rain curtain surrounds the audience, and water cannons and pool bubbles accent the 17m-wide (56-ft.) waterfall within the attraction.

Some scenes might be scary to those 7 years and under, so parental guidance is recommended. Persons with a history of heart disease or back/neck injuries are also advised to use caution.

Niagara's Fury is inside on the upper level at Table Rock, and is open year-round. The last ticket is sold a half-hour before closing time. Shows run every 20 minutes between 10:20am and 4:20pm daily. Paid parking is available across the street at Falls Parking Lot, or follow the signs to Rapidsview Parking Lot, just a few minutes' drive south of the Falls. Paid parking at this location includes a free shuttle ride back to the Falls at Table Rock.

Niagara's Fury is part of the Niagara Falls & Great Gorge Adventure Pass. Admission: Adults C$15; children 6–12 C$9.75; free for children 5 and under.

protected by a wire mesh screen. Be prepared for windy conditions outside, even if there is only a slight breeze at ground level. At the base of the tower, there is a maze of shops selling trinkets and a cavernous arcade zone, which can be overflowing with tourists. Ticket prices are rather high—if you are planning to ascend the tower, I recommend dropping into **Niagara Falls Tourism** (5515 Stanley Ave.; ℂ **905/356-5567**) to find out whether discount coupons are available (often there are booklets that have coupons for many of the attractions not included in the Great Gorge Adventure Pass), or ask at your hotel. Or purchase your tickets online, where the prices are almost one third lower.

5200 Robinson St., Niagara Falls, ON. ℂ **905/356-2651.** www.skylon.com. Admission C$14 adults, C$8.10 children 12 and under. Summer daily 8am–midnight; winter daily 11am–9pm.

BEYOND THE FALLS

Butterfly Conservatory A visit to the Butterfly Conservatory can be combined with a leisurely stroll around the Niagara Parks Botanical Gardens, as the building is located right on the grounds. The Conservatory is a bright and airy rainforest-like environment that is carefully climate-controlled. A multilevel pathway (stroller and wheelchair accessible) winds its way through the lush foliage. Two thousand tropical butterflies, representing 50 different species, live freely in the Conservatory.

This is an absolutely delightful place to spend an hour or so. The trick is to walk slowly and pause often, since the most rewarding discoveries are usually found through quiet observation. Often the butterflies will land on visitors, but it is important

---

 ## best-value CANADIAN NIAGARA FALLS EXPERIENCES

Take advantage of the special package put together by the Niagara Parks Commission, experience the top attractions, save a bundle, and avoid lines all at the same time. The **Niagara Falls Adventure Pass,** available between May and October, grants you entry to the *Maid of the Mist,* **Journey Behind the Falls, White Water Walk,** and the **Niagara Fury.** Or you can customize your pass by selecting the venues you want to see. Included with the pass is all-day transportation on the **People Mover** bus and **Incline Railway** that connect the Fallsview area on top of the hill with the complex in front of the Horseshoe Falls at the bottom. The price of just C$45 adults and C$33 children 6 to 12 (free for kids 5 and under) is a fantastic bargain. Buy this pass online at www.niagarafallsontario.com/adventurepass.html.

Between November and April, you can buy a **Winter Magic Pass,** which grants you entry to **Journey Behind the Falls, Niagara Parks Butterfly Conservatory, IMAX Theatre** *Legends and Daredevils* **movie,** and the **Bird Kingdom** at the Niagara Falls Aviary. Coupons are included with the Winter Magic Pass that give you discounts on admission to the Skylon Tower and Niagara Helicopter Tours rides.

You can book your ticket online from their website and print it, as well as, for a small fee or free with a purchased pass, download an MP3 audio tour. You can also arrange for an MP3 player already loaded with the audio tour for C$17. Another advantage is the ability to pre-book your entry time to the attractions at peak tourist periods. Rather than wasting time standing in line on busy days, use the People Mover to drop into the attractions and book your visit for later in the day.

Honeymoon Capital

Niagara Falls received its reputation as the "Honeymoon Capital of the World" when Aaron Burr's daughter, Theodosia, chose a Niagara Falls honeymoon in 1801. She was followed up by Jerome Bonaparte, Napoleon's brother, in 1804, and thus a tradition was born. John Lennon and Yoko Ono also spent their honeymoon here. Now more than 50,000 Niagara honeymoons are arranged each year.

not to touch them because they are extremely delicate and easily injured. It can be quite comical to see butterflies hitching a ride on the hat or shoulder of the person in front of you, who may be wandering around completely unaware of their natural adornment. There is a butterfly "nursery" with an observation window looking onto several stages of metamorphosis, and the window is opened several times daily to allow newly emerged butterflies to enter their new home in the Conservatory.

There is an abundance of natural light, and since the butterflies spend a considerable amount of time resting (you might almost believe they are posing for photos), it is a great place to bring your camera. The Conservatory doubles as the display greenhouse for the Niagara Parks Botanical Gardens. With more than 100 exotic plants in its tropical plant collection, the Conservatory also provides a rare opportunity to come into close contact with plants rarely seen in the Northern Hemisphere, and another reason for photographers to indulge in their passion.

The Conservatory is serviced by the People Mover bus and is one of the attractions included in the Adventure Pass. Due to space restrictions, the number of visitors allowed into the Conservatory at any one time is limited, and during peak season you may have to wait before entering.

2405 Niagara River Pkwy., Niagara Falls, ON. © **877/642-7275.** www.niagaraparks.com/nature/butterfly.php. Admission C$12 adults, C$7.95 children 6–12, free for children 5 and under. Daily 9am–5pm. Closed Dec. 25. Last ticket sold 30 min. before closing.

Whirlpool Aero Car Often called the Spanish Aero Car, because it was designed by Spanish engineer Leonardo Torres Quevedo and built in Bilboa, Spain, the Whirlpool Aero Car takes visitors on a hair-raising trip 75m (246 ft.) above the Niagara Gorge. Suspended between two points on the Canadian shore of the Niagara River, six sturdy cables support the uniquely crafted carriage, which holds 40 standing passengers. The car crawls along the cables on a 1km (⅔-mile) round-trip between Colt's Point and Thompson's Point, allowing tourists a bird's-eye view of the natural phenomenon of the Niagara Whirlpool. Although the car remains in its original form from when it began operating in 1916, the wheels, electric circuits, and track cable suspension system were modernized in the 1980s. The trip is only 10 minutes long, and you can see the whirlpool from the land, so if it's a busy day and the line is long, consider giving this attraction a miss. The winding stairwell that leads to the entrance to the aero car can be stifling on a hot day, despite the roof covering that gives some protection from the sun. And those who are afraid of heights should definitely stay on terra firma.

3850 Niagara River Pkwy., Niagara Falls, ON. © **877/642-7275.** www.niagaraparks.com/nfgg/aerocar.php. Admission C$12 adults, C$7.95 children 6–12, free for children 5 and under. Mon–Fri 9am–5pm; Sat–Sun 9am–6pm. Operation depends on wind and weather conditions. Last ticket sold 30 min. before closing.

💬 The Old Scow

If you look upriver from the Horseshoe Falls and scan the surface of the turbulent water, you will see an old scow that became stuck on the shoals way back in 1918. The scow, a flat-bottomed boat used for transporting cargo to and from ships, broke loose from its tugboat. Two men were stranded onboard as the scow made its way with increasing speed toward the Horseshoe Falls. In a desperate attempt to save themselves, the men opened the bottom doors of the scow and flooded it. Fortunately, the scow became wedged against a rocky ledge, but because of the complicated nature of the rescue operation it was 19 hours later when the men finally were brought on shore.

White Water Walk ★   As you make your way down the boardwalk at the base of the Niagara Gorge (an elevator takes you down to the river level), you can hear the thunder of water all around you. Stand next to the Class V and VI Niagara River rapids, one of the world's wildest stretches of white water. The ever changing display of waves, swell, foam, and spray is mesmerizing. Fidgety folks will do the walk amiably enough, but then ask what's next on the agenda. Others are drawn to the power of the water in motion and are quite content to stand and watch in fixed fascination, completely unaware of the passage of time.

Visit any time between April and November to see the rapids, but if you are in Niagara in the autumn, you absolutely must take this walk, as the wooden walkway is constructed under a canopy of deciduous trees. Warm autumn sunlight; orange, red, and gold leaves; the raging torrents of the rapids: It's a spectacular sight. And photographers take note—there are great nature shots here.

4330 Niagara Pkwy., Niagara Falls, ON. ℭ **877/642-7275.** www.niagaraparks.com/nfgg/whitewater. php. Admission C$9.50 adults, C$6.25 children 6–12, free for children 5 and under. Apr to late Nov Mon–Fri 9am–5pm, Sat–Sun 9am–6pm. Last ticket sold 30 min. before closing.

On the American Side

AMERICAN FALLS ★

The crest line of the American Falls, also sometimes referred to as the Rainbow Falls, is approximately 290m (951 ft.) wide; the depth of the water flowing over the crest line is only about half a meter (about 1⅔ ft.). Just south of the main waterfall, there is a smaller waterfall, which is a mere 17m (56 ft.) wide at the crest line. This pretty waterfall resembles a bride's veil, hence the name Bridal Veil Falls, although it is also known as Luna Falls and Iris Falls. Bridal Veil Falls is separated from the American Falls by a thin strip of land called Luna Island. A massive amount of broken rock covers the base of the American and Bridal Veil falls, contributing to their dramatic appearance. As the sun rises in the east, rainbows can often be seen as the light shines through the mist of the Falls. In order to feel the magnitude of the power of the churning water, you need to get up close and personal. Take the *Maid of the Mist* boat tour, which will take you past the American Falls and daringly close to the base of the Horseshoe Falls, walk along the pathway to the "Crow's Nest" at the base of the Observation Tower, or take the Cave of the Winds guided walking tour, which leads you along boardwalks down into the gorge—only 6m (20 ft.) away from the falling water at its closest point. Note, however, that the best views of the Falls are from the Canadian shore.

Cave of the Winds This well-established attraction features a guided tour along wooden walkways at the base of the Bridal Veil Falls, and has recently been updated. Accessed from Goat Island, an elevator takes you 53m (174 ft.) down into the Niagara Gorge. Sporting a yellow recyclable waterproof poncho and Velcro-closure souvenir nonslip sandals, follow your tour guide along the boardwalks to the "Hurricane Deck," where you stand just 6m (20 ft.) from the thundering waters of Bridal Veil Falls. You are likely to get doused with a generous spray of water, so consider yourself warned. A second deck has been constructed 45m (148 ft.) away from the base of the Falls, designed especially for physically challenged visitors and adults carrying small children. For a really wild experience, descend after nightfall to see the illuminations surrounded by multicolored cascading torrents of water.

Goat Island, Niagara Falls State Park, Niagara Falls, NY. ☎ **716/278-1730.** www.niagarafallsstatepark. com. Admission US$11 adults, US$8 children 6–12 (must be at least 1.1m/43 in. tall), free for children 5 and under; those under 1.1m/43 in. tall must be accompanied by an adult, and admission is restricted to certain areas of the walkway. Seasonal operation daily 9am–11pm.

 Famous Visitors

Marilyn Monroe visited the falls to film portions of the thriller *Niagara Falls,* released in 1953. Other notable visitors have included King George the V in 1939, Princess Diana with her sons in 1991, and Brad Pitt and his children in 2009.

Maid of the Mist ★★★ This is a must-do for visitors to the Falls—it might seem touristy, but it's well worth the trip. The *Maid of the Mist* operates on both sides of the Niagara Gorge, but each boat essentially provides the same experience, passing close to the base of the American Falls and into the horseshoe of the Canadian Falls. Boats on the American side dock at the base of the Observation Tower near Prospect Point in the Niagara Falls State Park. Recyclable blue rain ponchos are issued, which you can keep as a souvenir if you wish. Tickets include entry to the Observation Tower because access to the boat dock is via the tower elevators. Admission is included with the purchase of a Passport to the Falls. Tour lasts 30 minutes.

Inside Niagara Falls State Park, at the base of the Observation Tower, Niagara Falls, NY. ☎ **716/284-8897.** Admission US$14 adults, US$7.85 children 6–12, free for children 5 and under. Apr–Oct daily 10am–8pm (depending on weather conditions).

Observation Tower Included with the Niagara Falls State Park Passport to the Falls, this 85m-high (279-ft.) tower has an outside observation deck that extends past the Niagara Gorge cliff face to allow visitors a bird's-eye view of the American Falls. Take the elevator to the top for the best views. The elevator also descends to the base of the gorge to provide tourists with access to the *Maid of the Mist* boat ride. At the base of the observation tower are a groomed pathway and stairs leading to the "Crow's Nest," an observation deck close to the huge boulders at the base of the American Falls—a unique perspective that is worth the journey.

Inside Niagara Falls State Park, just north of the American Falls. ☎ **716/278-1762.** Admission US$1 adults and children 6 and over, free for children 5 and under. Late Mar–Dec daily 9am–8pm.

BEYOND THE FALLS

Aquarium of Niagara Experience marine life up close at the Aquarium of Niagara, just a short walk over the bridge from the Niagara Gorge Discovery Center, one of the stops on the Niagara Scenic Trolley route. Several times daily, you can

The Original Cave of the Winds

The original Cave of the Winds was a true cavern, located behind the Bridal Veil Falls. It measured approximately 40m (131 ft.) high, 30m (98 ft.) wide, and 9m (30 ft.) deep. Prior to the mid-1900s, tourists could enter the cave via a pathway. In 1954, a major rockfall occurred at Prospect Point, followed by several smaller rockfalls at Terrapin Point. Subsequently, an overhanging ledge of dolostone at the entrance to the cave was deemed to be in danger of collapse, and in 1955 the cave was demolished by a controlled dynamite blast.

watch the penguin feeding, sea lion shows, and harbor seal sessions. Tidal pool and shark feedings are available for observation on alternate days. Kids can buy a bucket of fish for US$5 and feed the seals. More than 40 exhibits contain a total of 1,500 aquatic animals from around the world. It's a great place to take the kids for a few hours. Not as extensive as Marineland, and there are no rides, but it's also less chaotic.

701 Whirlpool St., Niagara Falls, NY. ℂ **800/500-4609** or 716/285-3575. www.aquariumofniagara.org. Admission US$10 adults, US$8 seniors, US$6 children 4–12, free for children 3 and under. Late May to early Sept daily 9am–7pm; early Sept to late May daily 9am–5pm.

MUSEUMS & HISTORICAL LANDMARKS

From the War of 1812 to the American Revolution to the Underground Railroad for slaves, today's Niagara museums remain to tell the rich stories. With the anniversary of the War of 1812, local museums have been enlarged and improved, as a result of some serious government funds invested in heritage preservation. The area already boasted some of the best reconstructed forts and historical sites in North America, as well as walking tours throughout the sites. Old Fort Erie has been substantially upgraded and improved and is now an easier and more compelling showcase for period life and the 1812 War years. **Chippawa Battlefield Park** marks the site of the bloodiest and longest battle during the War of 1812; visitors can walk a path reading storyboards placed around a memorial cairn. Walkers can access the trail to **Fort Mississauga,** a post-1812 defense site made from postwar rubble, on the corner of Simcoe and Front streets. Spanning from Niagara-on-the-Lake across to the Welland Canal, where thousands of ships come through every year, Niagara's museums present a broad range of artifacts and history that come to life with educational interpreters and costumed guides at some of the larger venues.

As a special attraction for visitors during the War of 1812 celebrations, the Niagara Parks Commission is offering a **Niagara Heritage Trail Pass,** which will include admission to four heritage properties for C$18.12 (Laura Secord Homestead, MacFarland House, Mackenzie Printery, and Old Fort Erie). Included with the Pass are coupons for discounts at other attractions, such as the Niagara Parks Butterfly Conservatory and Sir Adam Beck Power Tours.

Niagara Falls, Ontario & New York

Niagara Falls History Museums   One benefit of the War of 1812 anniversary is the refurbishing of local historical properties. Lundy's Lane Historical Museum, closed until its official re-opening as the Niagara Falls History Museum on July 21, 2012, will display important War of 1812 artifacts in brand new galleries. Located on the very spot where the Battle of Lundy's Lane was fought, this museum mounts a proud show thoroughly explaining Niagara's heritage. The limestone building dating back to 1874 includes everything from historical prints of the Falls to War of 1812 artifacts, the uniforms of soldiers and firefighters, and costumed guides.

Outside the entrance, the Queen Victoria Memorial Fountain commemorates Victoria's reign of 64 years. Built in 1901 from 82 pieces of limestone, each stone represents a year of the queen's life. In addition to the History Museum, there is the Battleground Hotel Museum and the adjacent Willoughby Historical Museum.

5810 Ferry St., Niagara Falls, ON. © **905/358-5082.** Fax 905/358-0920. www.niagarafallsmuseum.ca. Admission C$3 adults, C$2.50 students and seniors, C$2 children 6-12, free for children 5 and under. Jan-May daily noon-4pm; May-Oct 31 daily 10am-5pm; Nov-Dec Tues-Sun noon-4pm.

Old Fort Niagara ★ ☺   Built as an outpost, it gradually became a fortress. Constructed in 1726 on the bluffs above Lake Ontario by the French, and strategically located at the mouth of the Niagara River, this fort held an important position that helped to shape Canada. The French maintained the first post here, but in 1759, during the French and Indian War, the British took over and retained control throughout the American Revolution. During the two world wars, Fort Niagara served as a barracks and training station. Restoration was completed in the mid-1930s.

Educational tours are available. Inside, costumed interpreters provide tours three to four times a day in the summer, which typically last an hour (tours are included in admission price). There are also fabulous fundraisers and events throughout the year; my favorite was the winter tour called Castle by Candlelight. It feels like you step back in time—bring your flashlight! Group tours are also available with advance

---

 Best Value Niagara Falls American Experience

Take advantage of the special package put together by the Niagara Falls State Park to experience the top attractions and save a bundle at the same time. The **Niagara Falls USA Discovery Pass** grants you entry to the *Maid of the Mist,* Observation Tower, Festival Theater, Aquarium of Niagara, and the **Niagara Gorge Discovery Center.** Included with the pass is all-day transportation on the **Niagara Scenic Trolley,** which takes you on a 4.8km (3-mile) guided tour of Niagara Falls State Park, with frequent stops to allow visitors to hop on and off at the major attractions and scenic vistas throughout the park. The price of just US$33 adults and US$26 children 6 to 12 (free for kids 5 and under) is a fantastic bargain. The Discovery Pass also includes discounted admission to Artpark, Old Fort Niagara, and the Historical Wax Museum. Discounts at snack centers and gift shops are also included. You can purchase the Passport at the Niagara Falls State Park Visitor Center, the Niagara Gorge Discovery Center, and at American Automobile Association (AAA) offices in Buffalo, Rochester, and Syracuse, New York.

notice only (1–2 hr.). In the summer, don't miss the musket-firing demonstration. The gift shop is a treasure-trove of interesting historical literature.

Fort Niagara Historic Site, Youngstown, NY. ✆ **716/745-7611.** www.oldfortniagara.org. Admission US$10 adults, US$6 children 6-12, free for children 5 and under. Daily from 9am year-round; closing hours vary with seasons.

Niagara-on-the-Lake & Queenston

For many history buffs, a collection of outdoor sites on well-groomed landscapes makes for great picnic spots. Originally a group of 19 buildings acting as the British Indian Department site, **Butler's Barracks** was named after Colonel John Butler, the deputy superintendent. A handful of buildings are left—the Korean War building, the gun shed, and the officers' quarters, to name a few. Take a tour through the outside area, guided by interpretive plaques. This is worth a visit to get a history lesson. Another historical attraction with interpretive plaques is **Fort Mississauga.** Built to help defend the British against subsequent attacks from the Americans after the War of 1812, the fort is now home to the Niagara-on-the-Lake Golf Club. **Navy Hall** (26 Queen St., Niagara-on-the-Lake; ✆ **905/468-4257**) isn't open to the public but is of historical interest and is in a scenic spot. Originally a group of barracks buildings built in 1765, today only one building remains.

One building that is open to the public and is worth a quick visit is **Niagara Apothecary** (5 Queen St., Niagara-on-the-Lake; ✆ **905/468-3845**). It's one of the oldest continually operating pharmacies in Canada, having dispensed medicines from 1820 to 1964. Many of the original containers, prescription books, and account books have been recovered and are on display. Stop in for a peek while shopping on Queen Street.

Fort George ★ ☺   If you have time for only one fort on your trip, this is the one to see. As a headquarters for the British army during the War of 1812, this fort played a pivotal role in keeping the Niagara region in Canadian hands. Built between 1796 and 1799, this fort was constructed to complement the existing Navy Hall buildings in safeguarding the region. Commander-in-Chief Major-General Sir Isaac Brock was killed by a sniper when the Americans invaded Queenston in 1813 and destroyed the fort. The British reclaimed the fort and garrisoned the area. Reconstructed in the 1930s, the fort became a military base for the new Dominion of Canada Army until 1965.

Today, visitors can step back in time and relive the days of the War of 1812. Enter through the enormous main gates made of heavy timber secured with iron spikes. Tour through the elegant officers' quarters, offices, and the artificers, where war tools and artillery were made and repaired. Walk outside alongside the cannons facing the American Fort Niagara and get a sense of how intense the fighting must have been 200 years ago. During the main season, there are regular reenactments staged throughout the day, narrated by knowledgeable and highly entertaining costumed interpreters. See the "soldiers" prepare and fire the noon-hour cannon. Watch a musket drill or enjoy the military band. Children will enjoy being "enlisted": Wee soldiers receive a fake musket and a shilling for their duty.

The Day the Falls Stopped

In 1848, Niagara Falls actually stopped flowing for 30 hours when ice fields from Lake Erie jammed at the source of the river.

Butler's Barracks **15**

Doug Forsythe Gallery **9**

Fort George **11**

Fort Mississauga **1**

The King Street/
Poulin Art Gallery **2**

Laura Secord Homestead **17**

MacKenzie Heritage Printery
and Newspaper Museum **18**

McFarland House **14**

Navy Hall **6**

Niagara Apothecary **12**

Niagara Historical Society
and Museum **13**

Niagara Pumphouse Visual
Arts Centre **5**

Niagara World Wine Tours **10**

Old Fort Niagara **4**

RiverBrink **16**

Simcoe Park **8**

Sir Adam Beck Generating
Station **19**

Whirlpool Jet Boat Tours **3**

Zoom Leisure **7**

26 Queen St., Niagara-on-the-Lake, ON. ✆ **905/468-4257.** www.pc.gc.ca. Admission C$12 adults, C$10 seniors, C$5.80 children 6–12, free for children 5 and under. May to end of Oct daily 10am–5pm; April and Nov weekends 10am–5pm.

Laura Secord Homestead The former home of Laura Secord—a Canadian heroine of the War of 1812—is only a 10-minute drive along the Niagara Parkway from Niagara Falls. A visit to the homestead will give you a good sense of Secord's heroic journey and the local history of the era. This museum has recently been enlarged and spiffed up: A new Visitors Centre, with gift shop and a small food bar, adds to the experience, and interactive displays help give an insight into the lives of particular women during the War of 1812. The home includes examples of Upper Canadian furniture from the era (1803–35) along with remnants of dishes and other artifacts. Costumed staff members add to the authenticity of the tours, which run every half-hour. There's also a lovely white chapel, once home to Canada's oldest congregation, on the property.

THE STORY OF laura secord: IT'S NOT JUST ABOUT CHOCOLATE

You may know the brand of chocolate, but its namesake is a lady with her own tale. Laura Ingersoll Secord, wife of British Loyalist James Secord, was born in Massachusetts but resided in Queenston, Upper Canada, during the War of 1812, as the Americans were fighting against the British (Canadians). In May 1813, three American soldiers invaded the Secord homestead in Queenston, demanding lodging and food. As Secord tended to her husband, who suffered injuries from the Battle of Queenston Heights, she overheard the officers speaking: American Colonel Boerstler was planning a surprise attack on British Lt. Fitzgibbon at Beaverdams. The fate of the Canadian Niagara Peninsula was at stake. She told the soldiers she was going to visit her brother so as not to arouse suspicion, and in the morning began the 32km (20-mile) trek to warn the British of the invasion.

After walking through enemy lines and climbing the treacherous Niagara Escarpment, she finally met up with Natives allied with the British. The Natives took Secord directly to Fitzgibbon. Thanks to Laura Secord, the American attack was thwarted, leaving the

Niagara Peninsula in Canadian hands. There are many renditions of the story—some say Secord walked barefoot along the way; others reported that she brought a cow with her as an excuse to leave home. What is for certain is that Canada as we know it wouldn't be the same without her courageous feat.

Years later, at the age of 85, Secord finally received recognition: The Prince of Wales heard of her heroic act and gave her £100. In 1913, the centennial anniversary of Secord's journey, a small Toronto-based chocolatier named Frank P. O'Connor chose the name Laura Secord for his single Yonge Street location. O'Connor wanted his company to represent the same wholesomeness, purity, domesticity, and cleanliness that Laura Secord espoused. Today, her silhouette still appears as the company logo. Visitors to the Niagara region can visit the old Secord homestead, complete with costumed tour guides and a monument dedicated to Laura Secord, located in the Queenston Heights Park (14184 Niagara Pkwy.). And while Canadians may view this intrepid lady as a heroine, Americans may not hold the same view.

29 Queenston St., Queenston. © **905/262-4851.** www.niagaraparks.com/heritage/laurasecord.php. Admission C$9.50 adults, C$6.25 children, free for children 5 and under. Mid-May to mid-Oct Wed–Sun 12–4pm.

McFarland House   Get a taste of living back—way back—in the 1800s in the old homestead of John McFarland. John and his sons constructed the house using bricks made in a kiln right on the property. The house later became a British military headquarters and then served as a makeshift hospital during the War of 1812 for both American and British soldiers. The home was badly damaged while McFarland was held prisoner during the war, and he was deeply saddened by its dilapidated state when he eventually returned from New York. Today the house, with re-created 19th-century herb garden, rooms, clothing displays, and teahouse, has been brought back to its glory days. Enjoy tea, home-baked goods, and light lunches while taking in the spectacle of flowers and greenery in a new glass conservatory. Costumed interpreters educate visitors about the history of tea and the tumultuous history of the house and its era.

15927 Niagara Pkwy., Niagara-on-the-Lake. © **905/468-3322.** Admission C$5 adults, C$3.75 children, free for children 5 and under. Mid-May to Labour Day 11am–5pm.

Mackenzie Heritage Printery and Newspaper Museum ★ ☺   See how far communication has come at Canada's largest working printing museum. Publisher William Lyon Mackenzie first printed *The Colonial Advocate* here on May 18, 1824. Mackenzie championed land rights, fair court practices, and improved schools and roads from these very presses. See the Linotype in action as 5,000 moving parts work in conjunction to bring the news. Equally impressive is the 1760 "Louis Roy Press," known to be the oldest press in Canada and one of a very few wooden presses remaining in the world. The entire collection is composed of 10 operating presses ranging from the mid-1800s to the 1900s. Visitors can arrange their own type and print out pages using a hot metal typecaster.

1 Queenston St., Queenston. © **905/262-5676.** www.mackenzieprintery.ca. Admission C$5 adults, C$3.75 children, free for children 5 and under. Mid-May to mid-Sept Wed–Sun 11am–5pm.

Niagara Historical Society & Museum   This museum serves as a repository for artifacts and treasures from Niagara-on-the-Lake's history. The Niagara Historical Society, formed in the mid-1890s by a local retired schoolteacher, began collecting local artifacts and documents at a time when most museums were focused upon acquisition and display of foreign objects of interest. The museum is a rich source of local knowledge, offering guided tours of the town, lectures, and special exhibitions. If you're a history fan, this place will take a good hour or two to visit. Prearranged tours are available. New to the museum is a War of 1812 walking tour. While the museum does not provide tours in multiple languages, handouts are available in French, German, Japanese, Chinese, and Korean.

43 Castlereagh St., Niagara-on-the-Lake. © **905/468-3912.** www.niagarahistoricalmuseum. Admission C$5 adults, C$3 seniors, C$2 students, C$1 children 5–12, free for children 4 and under. May–Oct daily 10am–5:30pm; Nov–Apr daily 1–5pm.

Sir Adam Beck Generating Station   The Niagara River is one of the world's most important sources of hydroelectric power, generating clean, low-cost, renewable, and reliable electricity. Sir Adam Beck Generating Station No. 2, one of Ontario's largest hydroelectric facilities, is built into the side of the Niagara Gorge, 10km (6¼ miles) downstream from Niagara Falls near Queenston. Water from the

THE welland canal CORRIDOR

The 44km-long (27-mile) **Welland Canal** connects **Lake Ontario** with **Lake Erie** via a series of eight locks and roughly divides the Niagara region in half. The present canal, which is used primarily by bulk carriers transporting commodities such as grain and iron ore, was built in 1932. It is the fourth in a series of canals, the first of which was constructed in 1829.

At the head of the Canal sits the port city of **St. Catharines**, where you will find the **Welland Canals Centre** and **Lock 3 viewing platform** (p. 113). The **St. Catharines Museum** is also located at this site. Moving south along the Canal, **Thorold**, with its **Lock 7 viewing area**, offers another great observation spot as well as a tourist information center with lots of information on the Canal and the ships that sail up and

down the waterway, a wooden outdoor deck for viewing, and a small snack bar (50 Chapel St. S.; ℂ **905/680-9477**). The world-famous Twinned Flight Locks are also located in Thorold, although there isn't a convenient place to stop and view them in operation. These locks raise and lower ships up and down the Niagara Escarpment (43m/141 ft.). This is the only place on the canal where there is two-way vessel traffic. Thorold also boasts an inn where you can stay and view the ships passing by your balcony. Farther south is the city of **Welland.** Finally, at the connection with Lake Erie lies the marine city of **Port Colborne.**

The Welland Canal is open between March and December. Call ahead for ship viewing times (ℂ **800/305-5134** or 905/984-8880).

Niagara River is delivered to the power plant through two 9km (5½-mile) tunnels built under the city of Niagara Falls. Take a comprehensive, fully guided public tour of the power station. Learn about the history of the station and how it was constructed and soak up plenty of statistics (the guides are engineers). The tour lasts approximately 40 minutes and includes a short film presentation. If you've never been to a generating station, this is a great overview of how one works. Note that all bags, including purses, must be secured in lockers during the tour. Good for all ages.

14000 Niagara Pkwy., Queenston. ℂ **877/642-7275.** www.opg.com. Admission C$9.50 adults, C$6.25 children 6–12, free for children 5 and under. Mid-Mar to early Dec daily 10am–4pm. June–Aug tours every 30 min., hourly remainder of the year.

St. Catharines

Morningstar Mill   This site is a unique example of early Ontario milling heritage, and the mill and miller's house have been designated as buildings of historical and architectural interest and value under the Ontario Heritage Act. The Morningstar Mill Park, Interpretive Centre, and Museum are operated by volunteers. A number of buildings are on the site—the gristmill, a turbine shed, the miller's house, an icehouse, a barn, and a sawmill. The sawmill is a recently completed reconstruction, since the original building was abandoned during the 1930s and eventually completely dismantled. The volunteers who work to restore and maintain the site have been working on adding a blacksmith shop and carpentry shop. Bags of flour, bran, and cornmeal that have been ground on-site are on sale at the mill. Admission is free, although donations from visitors are always appreciated.

2710 Decew Rd., St. Catharines. ℂ **905/688-6050.** www.morningstarmill.ca. Free admission. Mid-May to mid-Oct Tues and Thurs 9am–3pm, Sat–Sun noon–5pm; public holiday Mon noon–5pm. Since the Mill is run by volunteers, these hours are not guaranteed.

Welland Canals Centre at Lock 3 Here visitors can watch the ships pass by from a bird's-eye view atop a gigantic raised platform. Inside, watch the 15-minute film *Welland Canals Past and Present* to learn about the history of one of the tallest water staircases in the world—100m (328 ft.) high. This visit is worth at least a half-hour stop even if you're not a salty dog.

The **St. Catharines Museum,** housed in the same building, features an exhibit on the Underground Railroad as well as an impressive collection of maps, photographs, and more. Working models of the locks and bridges are on display. Don't leave without taking another half-hour to see this impressive museum.

1932 Welland Canals Pkwy., St. Catharines. ℂ **800/305-5134** or 905/984-8880. www.stcatharines lock3museum.ca. Admission C$4.25 adults, C$4 seniors, C$3.25 students (over 14), C$2.50 children 6–13, free for children 5 and under; family discount 15%. Mon–Fri 9am–5pm; Sat–Sun 11am–4pm.

Fort Erie & Port Colborne

Fort Erie Historical & Ridgeway Battlefield Site In June 1866, Irish-American veterans of the U.S. Civil War fought Canadian forces in hopes of gaining Ireland's independence from England. Today there is a commemorative cairn built on Hwy. 3, near Ridge Road, close to the old battlefield site; the site and cairn can be viewed at any time at the Ridgeway Battlefield Site. The Fort Erie Historical Museum tells a story dating back 10,000 years to the first aboriginal settlement—the outdated exhibits, viewed through glass cases, don't make it the most interesting visit but at least provide a thorough historical overview. The building, built in 1874, was once a jail turned town treasury, and still has the treasury vault. Ridgeway Battlefield Site is no longer a museum but instead an outside tour with interpretive plaques.

402 Ridge Rd., Ridgeway (within town of Fort Erie). ℂ **905/894-5322.** www.museum.forterie.ca. Admission C$1.50 adults, C50¢ children. Sept–May Sun–Fri 9am–5pm; June–Aug daily 9am–5pm. **Ridgeway Battlefield Site:** Hwy. 3 (Garrison Rd.), Ridgeway. Year-round.

Fort Erie Railroad ★ At one time, Fort Erie was the third-largest rail yard in Canada. The jet-black steam engine #6218 ran from its debut in 1948 into the early 1960s. Inside the museum, you'll find artifacts, such as tools and telegraphy equipment, and exhibits featuring photos and train-related paraphernalia. The original Grand Trunk Railway Station in Ridgeway and CN B-1 at one time monitored traffic movement over the International Railway Bridge. Today this relocated station, with wooden waiting chairs and stoves, re-creates the feel of a good old-fashioned train

The Hermit of Niagara

In 1829, a young man named Francis Abbott took up residence on Goat Island in an abandoned log cabin, despite not receiving permission to live there from the landowners. For the next 2 years, he was the sole inhabitant of the island and often entertained tourists with his antics, such as balancing on the wooden pier leading to Terrapin Tower. He died by drowning in June 1831, while bathing in the Niagara River.

station from back when steam billowed from the engines. Worth a visit even if you don't have a train collection at home.

400 Central Ave., Fort Erie. ℂ **905/871-1412.** June–Aug 9am–5pm.

Mildred Mahoney Dolls House Gallery ☺   This historical home has more than 140 dollhouses from around the world—England, Europe, Japan, the U.S., and Canada. Peek at rare miniature houses dating back to 1780. Inside each house, you'll find antique miniature furniture and crocheted pieces—some even made by Mrs. Mahoney herself. Mrs. Mahoney kept all the dollhouses (37 years' worth) in her home until 1983, at which point they were moved to Bertie Hall—a historical landmark. The doll collection is a unique, charming, and homey tribute to a woman's childhood dream come true. Bertie Hall also served as a stopping point for black slaves seeking freedom in Canada during the time of the Underground Railroad. Little girls will adore this place.

657 Niagara Blvd., Fort Erie. ℂ **905/871-5833.** Admission C$5 adults, C$4 seniors, C$3 students up to 16 years, free for children 5 and under. May 1–Dec 31 daily 10am–4pm, Jan 1–Apr 30 call for an appointment.

Old Fort Erie ☺   Built in 1764, this structure was the first British defense fort in the area. Only stone remnants of the original fort were used in the re-creation. The original building, built below the current structure, was a supply depot and port for ships along the Upper Great Lakes. Seeing battle during the American Revolution as a supply base for British troops, Loyalist Rangers, and Iroquois warriors, the tiny fort sustained much damage and another was built. During the War of 1812, the Americans occupied the fort, eventually destroying it when they vacated the premises. After the war, the fort continued to play an important role—most notably as a stop for American slaves seeking freedom in Canada during the mid-1800s. Today, visit impressively restored buildings such as the guardroom, soldiers' barracks, or the kitchen—where a fierce battle took place as the British tried to capture the fort from the Americans. The Curtain Wall that connected the two barracks together, with its 3m-thick (9¾-ft.) walls and wooden spikes, stands as an ominous reminder of a tumultuous era. Regular 1-hour tours are available with interpreters dressed in period costume. The fort has been extensively revamped for the War of 1812 celebrations, with a new Welcome and Visitors Centre and interactive activities.

350 Lakeshore Rd., Fort Erie. ℂ **877/NIA-PARK** (642-7275) or 905/371-0254. Admission C$12 adults, C$7.95 children 6–12, free for children 5 and under. May–mid Oct daily 10am–4pm.

Port Colborne Historical and Marine Museum ☺   Inside the museum is a re-creation of the history of Port Colborne. The Heritage Village is complete with a network of paths and buildings, including the log schoolhouse, the Sherk-Troup log home, the FW Woods Marine Blacksmith shop, the Graf Loom, and the Carriage House gift shop. Artifacts inside the museum include photos, textiles, glassware, marine artifacts, housewares, and community archives related to Port Colborne and the Welland Canal. You'll also find Canada's Century Car, the Neff Steam Buggy. Made in 1901, this car is one of the oldest automobiles in Ontario and was built in Port Colborne. More exhibits within the museum cater to the sea buff—check out the Wheelhouse from the *Yvon Dupre Jr.* tug boat, the anchor from the *Raleigh,* and a real lifeboat from the SS *Hochelaga.* The museum also hosts many events. In spring, enjoy the Pie Social, the History Fair, and the Antique Road Show; in summer,

NIAGARA freedom trail
(UNDERGROUND RAILROAD)

The Niagara Freedom Trail is a tribute to the estimated 40,000 black American slaves who came to Canada seeking freedom in the 19th century when Canada passed the Slavery Abolition Act, making their way through Fort Erie and Niagara Falls and into St. Catharines. The Freedom Trail, as it stands today, isn't so much a trail as it is a series of markers, historical sites, and plaques. The trail is marked with a running-man symbol.

Fort Erie has a significant plaque—**The Crossing**—which marks the spot where many slaves crossed over into Canada from Buffalo. Also in Fort Erie is **Bertie Hall**—today the Mildred Mahoney Dolls House Gallery (p. 114). This home was a site for refugees seeking shelter and has a secret tunnel entrance that led from the house to the riverbank. Fort Erie is also home to "Little Africa." In the late 1700s, the population grew from 80 to 200 black American slaves who made a living supplying lumber to the ferry and railway services. Here, Little Africa thrived—residents enjoyed working and farming walnut and hickory farms.

In Niagara Falls, the **Norval Johnson Heritage Library** houses more than 2,000 books by, about, and from black settlers on the subject of black heritage (5674 Peer St.; © **905/358-9957**).

Next-door is the **Nathaniel Dett Chapel,** built in 1836 and named after the church organist, a musician in his own right.

St. Catharines is home to the **Salem Chapel,** a British Methodist Episcopal church that served as a refugee safe haven (92 Geneva St.; © **905/682-0993**). Harriet Tubman, a former slave living in St. Catharines, helped an estimated 300 slaves to freedom and also attended the Salem Chapel. The **Anthony Burns Gravesite and Victorian Lawn Cemetery** honors Reverend Burns—the last man tried under the Fugitive Slave Act, which sent him back to slavery (Queenston St., west of Homer Bridge). He eventually moved to St. Catharines. The **Richard Pierpoint plaque** in Centennial Park commemorates an African-born slave who was brought to America and sold to a British officer. Pierpoint later joined the Colored Corps, an all-black military company, and was awarded land for his service.

If you can't tour the entire trail, the **St. Catharines Museum** at the Welland Canal Centre has a comprehensive gathering of facts and memorabilia, giving an impressive historical overview. The African Canadian Heritage Tour, the Central Ontario Network for Black History, and the Ontario Government have collaborated to produce a booklet outlining all 29 trail sites within the province.

participate in Canal Days; in December, savor the special Christmas pudding in Arabella's Tea Room—the original 1915 Edwardian-style homestead of Arabella Williams that serves steaming hot biscuits and homemade preserves. A great interactive village and educational museum to spend an hour or two with the kids. Tours are offered on request with knowledgeable locals.

The Museum, Heritage Village, and Gift Shop: 280 King St., Port Colborne. © **905/834-7604.** Free admission. May–Dec daily noon–5pm, including holidays. Arabella's Tea Room: June–Sept daily 2–4pm, including holidays.

GALLERIES

As you would expect in an area of such natural beauty, there is an active and accomplished artistic community in Niagara, along with a number of excellent galleries that feature the work of local artists and artisans, as well as works from artists throughout Canada.

Niagara-on-the-Lake

Doug Forsythe Gallery   Doug Forsythe is an established Canadian artist. Many of his collections feature landscapes—a golden field or a vineyard—seascapes that include vivid blues and blacks, marine themes, and figure studies. He works in computer graphics, watercolor, oil, and acrylics, and is skilled in etching, engraving, dry point, collagraphs, woodcuts, serigraphs, and woodcarving. Local scenes include Niagara-on-the-Lake, Niagara Falls, and Niagara vineyards. Forsythe also creates intricate guitars and fine scale-model ships. His photo-realist paintings artfully capture nature.

92 Picton St., Niagara-on-the-Lake. ✆ **905/468-3659.** www.dougforsythegallery.com. Free admission. Apr–June 10am–5:30pm; July–Sept 10am–6pm; Oct 10am–5:30pm; Nov–Dec 10am–5pm; Jan–Mar Fri–Sun 10am–5pm, Mon–Thurs by chance or call.

The King Street Gallery/Poulin Art Gallery   This gallery in a historical house in Niagara-on-the-Lake features works by Canadian artist Chantal Poulin. It's a small collection of about a dozen paintings and sculptures residing in a single room. Poulin's works range from portraits of children to landscapes of the Niagara vineyards, still life, and contemporary art. The gallery also displays other artists' work, including a number from Quebec.

153 King St., Niagara-on-the-Lake. ✆ **905/468-8923.** Free admission. Tues–Sun 10am–5pm.

Niagara Pumphouse Visual Arts Centre   The work of local artists—a mix of traditional still life and floral paintings to bold abstract shapes on canvas using mixed media—is displayed in the salon. Exhibitions range from raku ware and relief sculptures to etching, photography, and paintings. Lectures and programming for children and adults are offered throughout the year.

247 Ricardo St., Niagara-on-the-Lake. ✆ **905/468-5455.** www.niagarapumphouse.ca. Free admission. June–Aug daily 10am–4pm; Sept–May Sat–Sun 1–4pm.

RiverBrink ★   Home of the Samuel E. Weir Collection (1898–1981), this gallery features a fascinating collection of more than 1,000 pieces, consisting predominantly of Canadian works. Of particular interest are the works by Tom Thomson and

---

💬 **Hold the Foam**

The brown foam you can see floating on the water below the Falls is not caused by pollution. It is simply a suspension of clay particles and decayed vegetative matter, originating mostly from the shallow eastern basin of Lake Erie. The foam is a natural consequence of the tons of water that plummet over the crest line of the Falls.

the Group of Seven, who were the first artists to capture the power and spirit of Northern Canada. The jewel of the collection is a large painting done by an officer, James Dennis, who fought in the War of 1812, called *The Battle of Queenston Heights*. This important canvas was acquired by Mr. Weir in England in 1967 and brought "home" to Queenston. You'll also find many Quebec landscapes, Georgian portraiture, and War of 1812 pieces, plus a number of paintings of Niagara Falls, which give visitors a pristine view of the Falls and the surrounding area before mass development. The collection also includes many antiques and an impressive 4,000-volume reference library. I recommend calling ahead to book a guided tour—you'll get great insight into Canadian history and the story behind the paintings. Exhibits change annually.

116 Queenston St., Niagara-on-the-Lake. ℂ **905/262-4510.** www.riverbrink.org. Admission C$5 adults, C$4 seniors, free for children 11 and under when accompanied by parent. May–June Wed–Sun 10am–5pm; July to mid-Oct daily 10am–5pm. –mid-Oct. to Apr by appointment only.

St. Catharines

Rodman Hall Arts Centre   The house and surrounding gardens are more inter-esting than the majority of the art inside. The Walker Botanical Garden includes plants from all around the world, such as blue atlas cedar from North Africa; crypto-meria and magnolia from Japan; and dawn redwood, dogwood, and blue fir from China. However, there are a few gems in the gallery's collection, including a whale-inspired piece by Newfoundland artist David Blackwood and a landscape painting by British Columbia artist Emily Carr. International paintings include a small piece by French artist Marc Chagall. The gallery features a permanent display of more than 850 works. Established in 1960, Rodman Hall recently became part of Brock University's School of Fine and Performing Arts.

109 St. Paul Crescent, St. Catharines. ℂ **905/684-2925.** Free admission. Tues–Wed 11am–5pm; Thurs 11am–9pm; Fri–Sun 11am–5pm. Closed Mon.

Jordan Village

Jordan Art Gallery ★   Quaint and local, this gallery is owned by a group of local artists who also staff the store, so there is always a knowledgeable and enthusiastic steward on hand to chat about the art on display. In addition to the showcased work of the gallery owners, other selected artists' works are exhibited. The styles and media of these artists are quite remarkable. This gallery should be marked as a must-see if you are in the Twenty Valley area.

3845 Main St., Jordan Village. ℂ **905/562-6680.** Free admission. Summer Mon–Sun 10am–6pm; winter Wed–Sun 10am–5pm.

Grimsby

Grimsby Public Art Gallery   This gallery features local work and promising young artists. Monthly exhibitions, tours, and programs are featured. Recent exhibi-tions have included "Flights of Fancy: Niagara Realism & Other Imaginings" curated from the gallery's permanent collection.

18 Carnegie Lane, Grimsby. ℂ **905/945-3246.** Free admission. Mon and Fri 10am–5pm; Tues–Thurs 10am–8pm; Sat–Sun 1–5pm.

NIAGARA FALLS FOR THRILL SEEKERS

Amusements

CASINOS   It is difficult to ignore the casinos here. The Fallsview Casino is a soaring edifice that dominates the Niagara Falls skyline, and gambling brings in a large proportion of the visitors to the city. Even if you are not a gambler, there is a glamour and allure to the casinos that makes for an entertaining spectator sport.

The **Fallsview Casino** (6380 Fallsview Blvd., Niagara Falls, ON; ✆ **888/ FALLS-VU** [325-5788]; www.fallsviewcasinoresort.com) is for the high rollers and the gamblers who like a little sophistication and drama with their game. Try a "flutter" at a slot machine—there are machines that work on as little as a quarter—or roll the dice to raise your pulse. Even if you don't fancy a dance with Lady Luck, sit by the incredible metal fountain, the Hydra-Teslatron, in the lobby and watch the action. There are some good shops, pleasant restaurants, and great views of the Falls from the restaurants and bars here. Try a bowl of udon at the Noodle Bar, enjoy a martini in the stylish R5 bar, or take in a show at the Avalon Theatre. You don't have to deal a hand to appreciate the spectacle, enjoy the food, and sample the entertainment.

The original **Niagara Casino** (5705 Falls Ave., Niagara Falls, ON; ✆ **888/WIN-FALL** [946-3255]) is less flamboyant and more for the serious regular gambling crowd.

CLIFTON HILL   Clifton Hill is a compact entertainment district wedged between Victoria Avenue at the top of the hill and Falls Avenue at the bottom. The lights, noise, and nonstop mayhem spill over its edges and seep along the side streets, but the Hill is without a doubt the center of the maelstrom. The contrast between the party mood of the Clifton Hill district and the breathtaking natural beauty of the Falls could hardly be more extreme. The area is sensory overload both day and night. You'll either hate it or love it.

Just be sure to bring plenty of cash—admission prices for the novelty tourist attractions are steep. For example, **House of Frankenstein** (4967 Clifton Hill; ✆ **905/ 357-9660**) charges C$7.95 for adults and C$5.95 for children, and **Ripley's Believe It or Not! Museum** (4960 Clifton Hill; ✆ **905/356-2238**) will set you back C$14 for adults and C$7 for children. Often you'll find promotional brochures that contain discount coupons for some of the novelty attractions at hotels, some restaurants, and tourist information centers, so if you're planning to head to the Hill it's worth your while to hunt down one of these booklets before you step into the madness. If you plan to stay long enough to eat a meal or snack in the area, it also helps if you're a fast-food fanatic.

But beware: While some of the facades of these attractions may look enticing, new, and flashy, what's inside can be a huge disappointment. **The Louis Tussaud's Wax-works,** which feels like it hasn't changed inside since opening in 1949, does have well-constructed celebrity clones, if that's your style (5907 Victoria Ave.; ✆ **905/356-2238**). **Ripley's Believe It or Not!,** despite its showcase of freaky events, people, and animals (a buffalo with eight legs), isn't worth the trip.

On a scare scale from least to most, the **Haunted House** and its fake ghoul sounds is the least scary but best suited for kids; the **House of Frankenstein** hires real actors to make sounds; and **Nightmares,** on Victoria Avenue, may give little ones actual nightmares—I don't suggest sending kids through.

The best of the rides includes the **Cosmic Coaster,** where you strap onto a moving floor and watch a futuristic roller coaster set to Grateful Dead–like music. For the really small ones, **Brick City,** made from over one million LEGO blocks, is fun (they even have the Falls made of LEGOs). For the older set, the view from the Niagara **Skywheel** is cool. The giant Ferris wheel (C$10 adults, C$6 for children under 10) includes three turns, lasting 7 minutes, in an air-conditioned or heated gondola, and this gives you a great opportunity to get spectacular photos of the Falls. Beware: On a sunny day, no amount of air-conditioning will keep this box cool.

The Falls are Falling

Scientists speculate that at the present rate of erosion, the Falls will no longer exist in 50,000 years, although a river will still flow between Lake Erie and Lake Ontario.

If the day is overcast and the kids need diversion, **Strike Rock N' Bowl** (4946 Clifton Hill, Niagara Falls, ON; ✆ **905/358-4788**), a massive bowling and entertainment center located in the heart of the Clifton Hill tourist area, will keep them happy. There are 14 full-sized bowling lanes, multiple billiard tables, an amusement arcade, a dining area, and a sports bar. Up to six people can bowl on a single lane. There's also a full Boston Pizza food and bar menu available, plus a high-tech video arcade. It's open daily from 10am to 2am.

THEME PARKS Niagara Falls has many theme parks to keep the kids running around and the parents trying to catch up. The most popular is **Marineland,** where whales are the main attraction (7657 Portage Rd., Niagara Falls, ON; ✆ **905/356-9565;** www.marinelandcanada.com). Walkways allow visitors to view the marine mammals above and below water. Live performances featuring trained dolphins, walruses, and sea lions are scheduled several times daily. Fish, deer, black bears, and elk can also be seen. Marineland has an amusement park with a dozen or so rides, including roller coasters, a Ferris wheel, and a carousel. Day admission isn't cheap at C$42 adults and C$35 for children. A season pass is available for an additional C$5 when purchasing a regular-price day admission to the park. Younger kids can easily spend a full day here—but be sure to bring a lunch, as cafeteria prices are expensive and the food isn't especially healthy. However, older kids may find the rides tiresome, lacking the thrill factor in comparison to facilities that specialize in rides.

Martin's Fantasy Island (2400 Grand Island Blvd., Grand Island; ✆ **716/773-7591;** www.martinsfantasyisland.com) is a seasonal amusement park with wet and dry rides, water slides, a wave pool, carnival-type rides, and live shows. Many of the attractions, such as Kiddie Land and a petting zoo, are geared toward the younger kids. The Silver Comet roller coaster is tame in comparison to other parks. One admission price (adults, US$25, children under 48 in. US$20, seniors US$17; after 5pm, all ages US$13) covers all shows, rides, and attractions, including a petting zoo, canoes, and the water park. Parking is free.

Americana Conference Resort and Spa (8444 Lundy's Lane, Niagara Falls, ON; ✆ **800/263-3508;** www.americananiagara.com; Mon–Thurs C$20 per person, Fri and Sun C$25, Sat and holidays C$30, Niagara residents C$16) is a 2,325-sq.-m (25,026-sq.-ft.) indoor water park with beach-entry wave pool, tube slides, body slides, kiddy pool interactive play structure, and whirlpools. There's an arcade and lounge area, but this facility isn't as large or fun as the outdoor counterparts. Young kids will appreciate half a day to get wet without insanely scary rides.

THE BRAVE AND THE FOOLHARDY— NIAGARA'S daredevils

Barrel, tightrope, rubber tube, jet ski, kayak, or only the clothes on their backs—thrill-seekers worldwide have used every conceivable contraption to go over, under, or through the Niagara Falls. Some made it—some didn't.

In 1861, **Captain Joel Robinson** set out onboard the *Maid of the Mist II* to conquer the gorge rapids and whirlpool. During the ordeal, the smokestack snapped, but all crew and Robinson survived the journey in one piece. Their reward was a mere $500; Robinson retired soon after. **The Great Blondin,** aka Jean François Gravelot of France, balanced over the Falls on a precarious 335m-long (1,099-ft.) tightrope. On June 30, 1859, Blondin walked from Prospect Park in New York City to Oakes Garden in Niagara Falls, ON. Subsequent walks included carrying his manager on his back and pushing a wheelbarrow across. On one occasion, Blondin cooked omelets on a small stove and lowered them on a cord to passengers on the *Maid of the Mist.* On her 63rd birthday on October 24, 1901, New York native **Annie Taylor** was the first human to go over the Falls in a barrel, without any prior experience. The widow emerged from the barrel saying, "No one ought ever to do that again."

But many more daredevil stunts followed, including those by **William "Red" Hill, Sr.,** who rode through the Great Gorge rapids and whirlpool in a steel barrel contraption. The 290-kilogram (639-lb.) red barrel had to be rescued from the whirlpool vortex. But ever determined, Red continued on to Queenston. Wishing to carry on his father's legacy, **William "Red" Hill, Jr.,** went over the Falls in a tower of inner tubes tied together precariously with fish net and canvas. "The Thing," as it was called, sank down into the bubbling water. Moments later, detached inner tubes surfaced—but no Red in sight. His body was recovered the next day.

In the "not intending to seek fame" category, on July 9, 1960, **Roger Woodward,** a 7-year-old American boy, was boating on the Niagara River with his sister and a family friend when the engine of their boat cut out and the force of the rapids propelled the boat toward the Falls. The 40-year-old family friend didn't make it, but Woodward, in what is dubbed "the miracle of the Falls," survived a trip over the Horseshoe Falls wearing only a lifejacket and bathing suit. His sister was rescued by horrified bystanders only seconds before she would have been swept over the brink.

Please note: It is illegal to perform any kind of stunt pertaining to the Niagara Falls under the regulations of the *Niagara Parks Act.* In addition to legal prosecution, individuals performing stunts can be fined up to C$10,000.

Hours at the various parks vary, but all generally open late in the morning (11:30am) and close just before dark, while Marineland is open until 10pm.

Thrill Rides

Niagara Helicopters Limited   This is a pricey adventure, but it gives you a view of the Falls, and a perspective on their vastness that you couldn't get any other way. It is truly thrilling. Make sure, if you have the choice and are a good flyer, that you get the seat up front next to the pilot for the best and most exhilarating views. A 9-minute ride covers 27km (17 miles): over the hydroelectric waterways system and Niagara Parks Botanical Gardens, along the Niagara River and Gorge to the American and Horseshoe falls, past Queen Victoria Park, and returning to base. Complimentary headsets with commentary are provided on the flight. Photographs taken as you enter the helicopter cost C$25 and include pictures of the Falls from above. Founder Rudy Hafen recently saved two New York police officers from death when he plucked them from the brink of the Falls as their boat was swept toward the edge.

3731 Victoria Ave., Niagara Falls, ON. ⓒ 800/281-8034 or 905/357-5672. www.niagarahelicopters. com. C$132 adults, C$82 children 2–12, free for children 1 and under. Family and group rates, call first. Daily flights 9am–sunset, weather permitting.

Whirlpool Jet Boat Tours This tour entails getting a little, or a lot, of splash from the Niagara River, depending on which boat you ride. You have a choice of two boats—a "Wet Jet" boat, which is open to the elements (you're going to get soaked), or a "Jet Dome" boat, which is enclosed. Life jackets, splash suits, and wet boots are provided, but a complete change of clothing is recommended for riders of the Wet Jet. The trip, about 1 hour on the water if you climb aboard at Niagara-on-the-Lake and about 45 minutes if you board at Lewiston, takes you upriver through the Niagara Gorge, the white water of Devil's Hole, and the famous Whirlpool. A photography team takes digital photos of the jet boat (offered on the Wet Jet and the Jet Dome) that are electronically transferred back to the dock for passengers to view upon their return, with an option to purchase. The Jet Dome has undergone a redesign to allow easier and safer boarding and seating on the boat. The original dome glass has been replaced in order to improve visibility for passengers. Book online for either experience and you may get a discount of up to C$10 per person. Jet Dome departs from Niagara Glen in June, July, and August and from Niagara-on-the-Lake in April, May, September, and October. Wet Jet departs from Niagara Glen in June, July, and August and from Niagara-on-the-Lake from May through September.

61 Melville St., Niagara-on-the-Lake. ⓒ **888/438-4444** or 905/468-4800. www.whirlpooljet.com. Access also available on the U.S. side (the dock is at the end of Center St. in Lewiston, NY). Admission C$52 adults, C$42 children (6–13 years and minimum height of 1.1m/44 in. required for Wet Jet boat ride; children 4–13 years and minimum 1m/40 in. tall for Jet Dome ride). Passengers 15 and under must be accompanied by a parent or guardian. Children 5 and under are not permitted to ride on the Wet Jet boats and 3 and under are not permitted on the Jet Dome boats. Reservations recommended.

ESPECIALLY FOR KIDS

Here's a lineup of the best things for kids to see and do in the Niagara region. It's a good mix of entertainment that will have kids either squealing with joy careening down a water slide or oohing and ahh-ing walking through a historical fort. There is a plethora of places to go with kids—it seems Niagara Falls was built with them in mind. Here are my top picks that will make them want to return:

o **Maid of the Mist** (p. 98): You can't get much closer to the Falls than this. Kids will love the intense mist and thunderous sound of the Falls. They'll also appreciate the disposable poncho that matches the one you get.

o **Mackenzie Heritage Printery and Newspaper Museum** (p. 111): Kids can learn how to make a newspaper page the old-fashioned way. This museum is full of interactive and unique pieces that will have them busy for hours.

o **Marineland** (p. 119): Younger kids won't want to leave the rides and the magnificent animals here. It's one of the main draws for children in the area.

o **Fort George** (p. 108): Little soldiers will love the musket firing, cannons, and giant wooden wall fortifications, not to mention, they can enlist! Come on a July weekend, when kids can see reenactments of War of 1812 drills.

- **Brick City** (p. 119): Famous structures such as the Statue of Liberty and the Greek Acropolis are made of more than one million pieces of LEGO here. Kids can make their own creations.
- **White Meadows Farms** (p. 129): While in Rome, er, Canada, kids should experience the true Canadian experience of "sugaring off"—eating maple syrup poured on crisp white snow during February and March.
- **Puddicomb Farms** (p. 124): Kids of all ages will love a visit to this working farm/ vineyard. There's a train ride through the orchard, a playground, and lots of animals to visit, like goats, emu, peacocks, and bunnies. The country store on site sells homemade treats too.
- **African Lion Safari** (p. 213): Drive through this safari park to see elephants, lions, giraffes, and monkeys (who may hitch a ride on your windshield). There are lots of activities and a picnic area. Kids can get a close look at the animals they have only read about, and learn about their habits and habitats.

HorsePlay Niagara   Trail rides are available year-round. Take a 1- or 2-hour ride through the woods and past the ponds and abandoned quarries of adjacent Wainfleet Conservation Area. Themed activities include sunset rides and half-day adventures such as a cowboy cookout including wieners over an open fire. Children's play area includes a hay maze, playground, and petting zoo. Riders must be 6 years of age and up.

Hwy. 3, west of Port Colborne. ℰ **800/871-1141** or 905/834-2380. www.horseplayniagara.com. C$40 1 hr. Daily year-round 10am–5pm.

Looff Carousel   One of the largest and best-preserved examples of a Looff menagerie carousel, the carousel at Lakeside Park on Lake Ontario in Old Port Dalhousie is a fantastic sight. There are 69 carousel animals arranged in four rings. And the cost is only a nickel a ride! This beautifully preserved carousel celebrated its 100th birthday in 2005 and is one of only nine historic carousels in Canada. A recently constructed children's playground is situated between the carousel and the harbor walkway, in Lakeside Park.

Lakeside Park, accessed from Lakeport Rd., Old Port Dalhousie, St. Catharines. Admission C5¢. Mid-May to early Sept daily 10am–9pm.

Niagara Falls Aviary—Birds of the Lost Kingdom   This is a handy place to take the kids for some diversion, since it's within easy walking distance of the Falls as you travel upriver on River Road alongside the Niagara Gorge. Tropical plants, a waterfall, and moss-covered carvings combine to re-create a rainforest experience, complete with exotic species of birds from Australia, South America, and Africa.

 Keeping the Kids Entertained

When you're traveling with children, if you can put their needs first when planning your itinerary and include activities that all ages will enjoy, then everyone will have a more pleasant vacation. Be sure to schedule plenty of time for relaxation (and naps, if your children are very young). The best advice you can follow is not to over-schedule. Don't expect your kids to act like adults—young children have short attention spans. When they start to wiggle and fidget, let them have a half-hour to blow off steam in a playground, sit with them on a park bench and lick ice-cream cones, or take them to a movie.

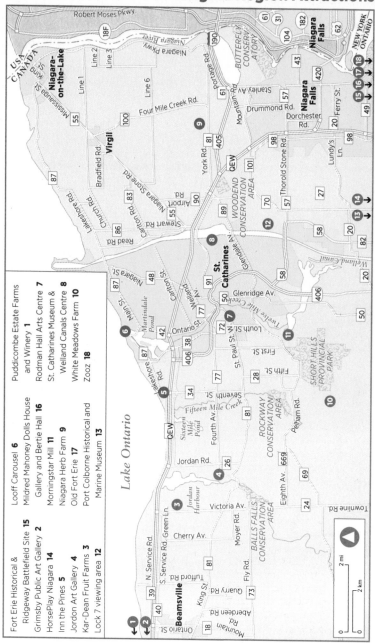

Fort Erie Historical &
Ridgeway Battlefield Site **15**

Grimsby Public Art Gallery **2**

HorsePlay Niagara **14**

Inn the Pines **5**

Jordon Art Gallery **4**

Kar-Dean Fruit Farms **3**

Lock 7 viewing area **12**

Looff Carousel **6**

Mildred Mahoney Dolls House
Gallery and Bertie Hall **16**

Morningstar Mill **11**

Niagara Herb Farm **9**

Old Fort Erie **17**

Port Colborne Historical and
Marine Museum **13**

Puddicombe Estate Farms
and Winery **1**

Rodman Hall Arts Centre **7**

St. Catharines Museum &
Welland Canals Centre **8**

White Meadows Farm **10**

Zooz **18**

THE MYSTERY OF THE whirlpool—SOLVED!

The Whirlpool is a natural phenomenon in the Niagara River, occurring at the point where the river makes a sharp right-angled turn. The Whirlpool is a huge basin 518m (1,699 ft.) long by 365m (1,198 ft.) wide and 38m (125 ft.) deep at its deepest point.

When the Niagara River is at full flow, the water travels along the 1.6km (1-mile) stretch known as the Whirlpool Rapids, at speeds up to 9m per second (30 ft./sec.). The water enters the basin, and then travels counterclockwise around the pool and past the natural outlet.

As the water tries to cut across itself to reach the outlet, pressure builds up and forces the water under the incoming stream. This creates the whirlpool effect. The water then continues on its way to Lake Ontario.

More than 300 tropical birds are housed in the aviary—some free flying and some contained in observational exhibits. Newly added, the interactive Reptile Encounter allows kids to feel pythons, turtles, and more. Check online for discounts on advance purchases.

5651 River Rd., Niagara Falls, ON. ℂ **888/994-0090** or 905/356-8888. www.niagarafallsaviary.com. Admission C$17 adults, C$12 children 5–12, free for children 4 and under. Purchase tickets online for a substantial savings. July–Aug 9:30am–7pm; Sept–June 10am–5pm. Last admission 1 hr. prior to closing.

Niagara Freefall Indoor Skydiving For something entirely different, consider flying without a plane. In this wind tunnel experience, you can experience free-fall, do tumbling tricks, and float on a current of air. The staff will train you and supply the helmets and equipment. A flight pass costs C$70 per person for 3 minutes in the tunnel. There's also Lazer Ball and a climbing wall.

6357 Stanley Ave., Niagara Falls, ON. ℂ **905/356-9764.** www.niagarafreefall.com. One ride C$70. Daily 9am–9pm.

Puddicombe Estate Farms and Winery The kids can have fun while the grown-ups try out the winery. A petting zoo, a pick-your-own-fruit, and a miniature train that tours the orchards will surely keep the kids entertained. There's also a general store, a bake shop, and a cafe.

468 Hwy. 8, Winona. ℂ **905/643-1015.** www.puddicombefarms.com. Free. Petting zoo and miniature train May to Oct 10am–4pm.

Simcoe Park This beautiful park has a gently rolling landscape, colorful flower beds, plenty of mature shade trees, and lush green lawns. There is a children's playground and a wading pool. Located in pretty Niagara-on-the-Lake.

Bordered by Picton St., King St., and Byron St. in Niagara-on-the-Lake.

Zooz Kids love animals, and Zooz features more than 400 of them, both exotic and domestic, and all housed in natural habitats. Lots to keep young ones busy for hours on end—a splash pad, Gator Express tram rides, catch-and-release fishing in a stocked pond, paddleboats, kite-flying, a petting area, and a children's play zone. Live interactive animal presentations and guided educational tours.

2821 Stevensville Rd., Stevensville. ℂ **866/367-9669** or 905/382-9669. www.zooz.ca. Admission C$19 adults, C$17 seniors, C$14 children 4–12, children 3 and under free. Seasonal operation: Hours may change, so call ahead. Daily May 12–31 9am–5pm; June–Sept 3 9am–6pm; Sept 4–Oct 8 10am–4pm.

PARKS & GARDENS
Niagara Parks Commission

While the area around the Falls and Clifton Hill is always busy and full of activity, Niagara Falls offers a number of quiet oases. In the heart of Niagara Falls is the **Queen Victoria Park,** which features half a million daffodils in the spring. **Oakes Garden Theatre** marks the entrance to Queen Victoria Park, which extends south along the Niagara Parkway to the Horseshoe Falls. Many open-air concerts are held here throughout the summer season. **The Niagara Parks Greenhouse** (7145 Niagara Pkwy., Niagara Falls, ON; www.infoniagara.com/attractions/green.html) is a 1,025-sq.-m (11,033-sq.-ft.) greenhouse and surrounding gardens, located just a short distance south of the Horseshoe Falls on the Niagara Parkway. Themed horticulture events occur throughout the summer.

Those who like to dine alfresco have a number of spots to choose from. Originally formed by a glacier drift, today a labyrinth of trails and several bridges make **Dufferin Islands** a great place to picnic and explore for the day (7400 Portage Rd., Niagara Parks Commission, Niagara Falls, ON; ✆ 877/642-7275). These eight islands, connected by bridges, take about 15 minutes to walk, or less to bike; it's a quiet area of about 16.2 hectares (28 acres), with 2km (1.2 miles) of walking trails. **Kings Bridge Park** (7870 Niagara River Pkwy.; ✆ 877/NIA-PARK [642-7275]), just south of the Falls near Chippawa, is another ideal picnic spot, with its picnic pavilion, picnic tables, restrooms, and playground and splash pad for children. On summer weekends and holidays, there is a parking fee of C$10.

Perhaps the quietest retreat in the area is **Navy Island** (✆ 905/356-1338; www.niagaraparks.com/nature/zh/navyisland.php), which is accessible only via boat. More than 10,000 years ago, natives used the island for fishing and canoe building. Today, you can find solace and wild raspberries, grapes, pawpaw, hickory, oak, and blue beech. Camping fees are C$8 adult, C$4 between 12 and 17 years old, and free for children 11 and under.

One not-so-quiet stop that is visited by tour bus after tour bus is the **Floral Clock** (14004 Niagara River Pkwy., Niagara Falls, ON). The design is changed twice a year, with violas providing color in spring, followed in late May by a labor-intensive operation to install 16,000 carpet bedding plants to form the 12m-diameter (40-ft.) clock face. Spring is the best time to see the clock, with the intense smell of more than 1,200 mature lilac trees representing 225 varieties. I've never seen the appeal of the Floral Clock myself, and I'm an avid gardener, but people seem to be perennially interested in visiting this fixture, which has been drawing visitors since 1950. There must be a million pictures of people from around the world standing in front of this floral display.

 Peek Inside the Clock

If you walk *behind* the Floral Clock (most people are much too occupied taking pictures of their family and friends standing in front of the clock to ever do this), you may be able to peek inside; the door is often open to allow visitors to see the drive mechanism of the clock. There is also a collection of photos of the clock in past years so you can compare the wildly different designs and colors as they change from year to year.

Please Don't Feed the Geese

A breed of nonmigratory Canada geese has made a comfortable year-round home throughout southern Ontario, thanks to the unwitting generosity of folks who feed them grain and bread. These geese have no natural predators, and their numbers are growing unchecked, causing city parks and walkways to be overrun with geese in some areas. Goose droppings, ripped-up sod, and damaged grass are just a few of the problems that have resulted. Park authorities are pleading with the public *not* to feed Canada geese, in order to encourage them to fly south in the winter and keep the population in check.

Niagara Parks Botanical Gardens   This is one of the most endearing places to me in the Niagara region, particularly in the spring when the bulbs are in full bloom. The beds and borders have provided much inspiration over the years for my own gardening projects. The formal herb garden, planted in a symmetrical design, has benches tucked into niches in the clipped hedges that surround the display. On a warm summer's day, you can sit in contented solitude for awhile, taking in the beauty of the plants or just dreaming about the future transformation of your own garden at home. There are numerous vegetable beds in an area adjacent to the herb garden and a rock garden. The plants in the perennial garden are handily labeled for reference, so bring a notebook and pen if you are a really keen green-thumber. The arboretum holds one of Canada's finest collections of ornamental trees and shrubs.

The Botanical Gardens were originally established in 1936 to provide a teaching facility for the School of Apprentice Gardeners. The site received its declaration as a botanical garden in 1990, as a result of the expansion of the variety and quality of the plant collections living in its extensive grounds. The Botanical Gardens continue to serve as a training ground for students of the School of Horticulture. The students gain practical experience through the maintenance and development of the gardens, although they also attend classroom lectures in horticultural theory.

The gardens are a short drive north of the Falls along the Niagara Parkway, about 9km (5½ miles) north of the Horseshoe Falls. The site is serviced by the People Mover bus.

2565 Niagara Pkwy., Niagara Falls, ON. ⓒ **877/NIA-PARK** (642-7275). www.niagaraparks.com/nature/botanical.php. Free admission. Daily dawn–dusk.

Queenston Heights Park   Only a few minutes' drive north of the Butterfly Conservatory and the Niagara Parks Botanical Gardens, this popular summertime destination is particularly good for families, history buffs, and those who enjoy hiking and cycling. Facilities at the park include two picnic pavilions, washrooms, and a band shell. During the summer, a small snack bar is in operation. On hot summer days, let your kids wade in the shallow water of the splash pad or burn off their energy in the children's playground. There are plenty of mature shade trees and open grassy areas for ballgames and family fun. For those who like to hike and bike, you'll be pleased to learn that Queenston Heights Park is the southern terminus of the Bruce Trail, Canada's oldest and longest continuous footpath. The trail runs along the Niagara Escarpment, spanning a distance of 850km (528 miles); the northern terminus is at Tobermory in southwestern Ontario. See "Hiking & Biking," in the section titled "Outdoor Pursuits," later in this chapter for more details.

A walking tour of the Battleground of the Battle of Queenston Heights is clearly marked throughout the park, and takes about 45 minutes to 1 hour to complete, if you're walking at a leisurely pace. Five plaques stationed along the way explain various stages of the battle and their consequences. See the section on tours later in this chapter for a more detailed description of the walking tour. **Queenston Heights Restaurant** provides an elegant setting with a spectacular view of the Niagara River, looking north toward Lake Ontario. The restaurant is perched on the edge of the Niagara Escarpment. For more detailed information on the restaurant, see the listing in chapter 5, "Where to Eat." To the right of the restaurant, you will find a monument dedicated to **Laura Ingersoll Secord,** who risked her life by taking a grueling 32km (20-mile) trek through trackless frontier forest to reach Lieutenant Fitzgibbon's headquarters and warn him of an impending attack on his forces by American soldiers. Free parking is available on the left as you enter the park.

14184 Niagara Pkwy., Queenston. ℂ **905/262-4274.** Free admission to park.

Niagara Falls, New York

The oldest state park in the United States, the **Niagara Falls State Park** (ℂ **716/ 278-1796**) is located on the eastern shore of Niagara River in downtown Niagara Falls, New York. It's a great spot to enjoy a snack or watch a short film on the history of the Falls (nominal admission fee charged to view the film). Attractions vary in their admission price; the best deal is to obtain a **Passport to the Falls** (see "Best Value Niagara Falls American Experience," earlier in this chapter). If you want to learn more about the natural and local history of Niagara Falls and the Niagara Gorge, the **Niagara Gorge Discovery Center** is located inside the Niagara Falls State Park. A multiscreen theater gives you a 180-degree perspective on how the Niagara Gorge was formed as the Niagara River eroded rock and soil over a time span of 12,000 years. The **Niagara Gorge Trailhead Building** is next to the **Discovery Center.** From this point, you can access hiking, walking, and cycling trails. Call ℂ **716/278- 1780** for more information. Also on the site is a 9m-high (30-ft.) outdoor climbing wall with three degrees of difficulty.

St. Catharines

The city of **St. Catharines** has earned the title of Ontario's Garden City. More than 1,000 acres of gardens, parks, and trails are within the city limits, all open for the public to enjoy. One of St. Catharines's jewels is **Burgoyne Woods,** accessed from Edgedale Road, off Glendale Avenue. Families will find this park particularly appealing, as there are swimming and wading pools, a playground, and plenty of picnic areas and nature trails. Paved trails are wheelchair accessible. **Ontario Jaycee Gardens** is one of Niagara's prettiest garden displays and St. Catharines's largest single planting of annual and perennial flowering plants. The northern perimeter of the park overlooks Old Port Dalhousie, including Martindale Pond and the Royal Canadian Henley Rowing Course. The land was originally part of the third Welland Canal. The Gardens are located on Ontario Street, north of the QEW and south of Lakeport Road. On the edge of the downtown core, **Montebello Park** is designated under the Ontario Heritage Act. Noteworthy features in the park include a magnificent rose garden with more than 1,300 rose bushes, and a band shell and pavilion dating from 1888. Mature shade trees cast their majestic branches over walking paths, picnic tables, and a children's playground. The park is located at the corner of Lake and Ontario streets in downtown St. Catharines. Avid gardeners will enjoy the **Stokes Seeds Flower Trial Gardens,**

farm living IS THE THING FOR ME

Experience the fruits of the earth up close—Niagara soil nurtures juicy fruit orchards, world-class vineyards, and expansive lush farms. As you drive around the Niagara region, stop by one of the many roadside stands for fresh produce, just hours from the vine or branch to the basket. Or spend a happy hour or two picking your own strawberries in June, sour cherries in mid-July, or pumpkins in October at farms such as **Kar-Dean Fruit Farms** (3320 First Ave., Vineland Station; C **905/562-4394**), **Sommers' Family Farm** (290 Main St. W., Grimsby; C **905/945-4448**), or **Mathias Farms** (1909 Effingham St., Fonthill; C **905/892-6166**).

If you're interested in touring a working farm, try one of the many agritourism farms, such as **Puddicombe Estate Farms & Winery** (1468 Hwy. 8, Winona; C **905/643-1015;** www.puddicombe farms.com). This 208-year-old family farm has lots to do. Learn about wine grapes on a wagon-ride tour, or taste estate wine while munching on some cheese and crackers on a wine tour on the farm, starting at C$10. Pick your own in-season fruits or buy already-picked cherries, pears, or apples. Enjoy a hearty lunch at the bakery cafe and bring home some goodies from the general store.

For specialty food items, visit the huge gourmet marketplace at **Kurtz Orchards,** located at 16006 Niagara Pkwy., Niagara-on-the-Lake (C **905/ 468-2937;** www.kurtzorchards.com). In the marketplace, sample homemade mustards, specialty teas, maple syrup, Ontario honey, oils and vinegars, and chunky cookies. Watch how they're made at demonstrations, or try a workshop—visit the website for event times. Tour the 40-hectare (100-acre) farm on a tractor-pulled tram led by Mr. Kurtz himself, starting at C$20, which includes a farm lunch.

one of the official sites of All-American Trial Gardens. July and August are the peak months for viewing the flowers, which are spread over several acres of farmland. It's located off Lakeshore Road, between Seventh and Fifth streets.

Happy Rolph Bird Sanctuary is a 6-hectare (15-acre) municipal park on the shores of Lake Ontario. The Sanctuary boasts one of Canada's most exotic collections of flowering rhododendrons. The petting farm, which operates from Victoria Day to Thanksgiving weekend, houses a variety of farm animals, including chickens, pigs, horses, rabbits, sheep, and goats. Hundreds of ducks, geese, and native birds live in the adjacent pond. The pond inlet, sheltered by evergreens and bordered by grassy banks and willow trees, provides food and shelter for the resident waterfowl and migratory birds.

Since the acquisition of this property in 1974, the city has extended pathways to the lake, added a parking lot and bird feeders, and renovated the barn and pond area. Picnic and playground facilities were expanded to include a pavilion and washrooms. The park offers a unique opportunity to experience nature firsthand. It is located on Read Road off Lakeshore Road.

Also here is the **9/11 Walkway,** a tribute to the 27 Canadians who died at the World Trade Center. The victims are memorialized by 27 varieties of deciduous trees. The wheelchair-accessible walkway has benches that enable those on the trail to enjoy the beautiful vistas on the shores of Lake Ontario.

Cheryl and Barney Barnes share the bounty of their market farm at a farm stand at **Inn the Pines** (1320 Seventh Louth St., St. Catharines; ✆ **905/353-5887;** www.innthepinesonline.com). They begin in spring with early spring onions, beets, peas, and lettuce (which is dug fresh for you while you wait), and follow with all that summer has to offer: 35 heirloom tomato varieties, sweet corn, zucchinis, peppers, beans, cucumbers, and so much more. Autumn brings the comfort foods: pumpkins, potatoes, and squash. In addition to produce, there are home-grown herbs, home-made preserves, farm-fresh eggs, or fresh-cut flowers, and, always, time for a friendly chat with Cheryl and Barney.

White Meadows Farms (2519 Effingham St., Pelham; ✆ **905/682-0642**) is a maple syrup farm where visitors can get their fill of all things maple. They also grow grapes and raise dairy cows. White Meadows offers a year-round

sweet shop, with maple sweets and syrup. Spring (Feb to mid-Apr) includes pancake weekends complete with preserves. When the sap starts to flow—February and March—join events revolving around "sugaring off," where visitors can make and taste fine Canadian maple syrup.

For something less sweet but also a good bet for the taste buds, visit the **Niagara Herb Farm** (1177 York Rd., Niagara-on-the-Lake; ✆ **905/262-5690**). Stroll through gardens with more than 350 varieties of culinary, medicinal, fragrant, and native herbs (book tours during summer months only). There is also a retail barn open March through December. Spend a summer Sunday afternoon at an herbal or craft workshop. Events include the Annual Open House, National Herb Week, and the Lavender Festival. Take home a satchel of lavender or jar of herbal jelly at the gift barn, open year-round.

OUTDOOR PURSUITS
Birding

The **Niagara River Corridor** has been designated as a "Globally Significant Important Bird Area" by major conservation groups in Canada and the United States. The river is a significant winter feeding zone for migrating birds, since the swiftly moving water keeps the river free of ice at a time of year when many other waterways are frozen over. Gulls, in particular, use the Niagara River as a major stopping-off point on their migratory flights. Almost half of the world's 43 species of gull have been identified by birders along the Niagara River. Species that have been noted include Bonaparte's gull; Franklin's and Sabine's gulls; and rarely seen species such as the California, Slaty-backed, and Ross's gulls. The best time of year to view gulls is from mid-November to mid-January.

The **Niagara Gorge** is a prime spot for birders, not only because small fish are abundant in the river, but also because large fish are sucked into the hydro turbines and chopped into pieces, which in turn attract gulls to the area. Overlooking the gorge at the site of the Sir Adam Beck power station, located on the Niagara Parkway north of the Butterfly Conservatory, many birds can be seen. The **Hydro Reservoir** is home to many gulls, ducks, geese, and herons. A footpath circles the reservoir and can be accessed from behind 2058 Stanley Ave. in north Niagara Falls, Ontario. Just upriver from the Horseshoe Falls on the Canadian side, opposite the Niagara Parks

Greenhouse, a variety of birds may be seen, including purple sandpiper, harlequin duck, and red-necked and red phalarope. Other spots include the Niagara Glen Nature Reserve, the Niagara Parks Botanical Gardens, and the Whirlpool Rapids Overlook (by the Whirlpool Aero Car). **The Beamer Memorial Conservation Area** (mentioned later in this chapter) is also a wonderful forest for exploring and watching wildlife—experience views of Forty-Mile Creek Valley, Lake Ontario's shoreline, and the Escarpment ridge.

Boating

Opportunities for boating are plentiful in the Niagara Region, including the major waterways of **Lake Ontario, Lake Erie,** the **Niagara River,** and the **Welland Canal.** Numerous smaller waterways are suitable for canoes and kayaks. Docking and boat-launching facilities are of good quality and are situated along the Niagara River, Lake Ontario, and Lake Erie shores. For detailed information and contact addresses on all aspects of recreational boating in Niagara, obtain a copy of the annual *Ontario Marina Directory* by contacting the **Ontario Marine Operators Association** (**OMOA;** Village Square Mall, 2 Poyntz St., Ste. 49, Penetanguishene, ON L9M 1M2; ✆ **888/547-6662;** omoa@omoa.com).

WELLAND CANAL If you wish to navigate a leisure craft through the Welland Canal between Lake Erie and Lake Ontario, contact the St. Lawrence Seaway Management Corporation at ✆ **905/641-**1932 for information, regulations, and fees involved in traveling via the canal.

ST. CATHARINES Canoeists, kayakers, and yachtsmen and -women are fond of the Lake Ontario shoreline and its connecting tributaries. Call ✆ **800/305-5134** for more information, or visit **www.stcatharines.ca.** In 1999, St. Catharines was host to the World Rowing Championships and, since 1903, has been a major rowing attraction.

PORT DALHOUSIE You'll find **Martindale Pond** located between the Henley Bridge on the QEW and Port Dalhousie harbor. The **Henley Rowing Course** is home of the annual **Royal Canadian Henley Regatta** (www.henleyregatta.ca).

NIAGARA RIVER If you are looking for a public marina on the river, the only one on the Canadian side is **Miller's Creek Marina** at 2400 Niagara Pkwy., Fort Erie (✆ **905/871-4428**), which allows Upper River access only. There are 135 seasonal docks, a boat launch ramp, a gas pump, showers, and washroom facilities.

PORT COLBORNE Port Colborne is a popular center for sailing and power boat enthusiasts; the town hosts a number of sailing regattas and dockside events during the summer months. Port Colborne has three marinas, the largest of which is **Sugarloaf Harbour Marina,** featuring 350 seasonal berths, 150 guest docks, showers, washrooms, a restaurant, a four-lane boat launch ramp, and more (3 Marina Rd.; ✆ **905/835-6644**).

Cross-Country Skiing

The Niagara region has a multitude of trails, which can be accessed in the winter for cross-country skiing. The most easily accessible for visitors is the **Niagara River Recreational Trail,** which runs alongside the Niagara River Parkway between Fort Erie in the south and Niagara-on-the-Lake in the north. The trail is ungroomed, but it is popular with skiers and you are likely to find tracks to follow. Just park your vehicle in any designated parking area along the east side of the Niagara Parkway, step into your skis, and off you go. Many of the conservation areas are also open to skiers, including **Short Hills Provincial Park** in St. Catharines, **Ball's Falls** in Vineland, and **Niagara State Park** on the U.S. side.

Fishing

Some of the best sportfishing in North America is found in Niagara, home to more freshwater species than anywhere on the continent. Game fish found in the waters of the Niagara region include coho salmon, rainbow trout, lake trout, walleye, yellow perch, smallmouth bass, northern pike, and muskellunge. Chinook salmon can be found in Lake Ontario between April and September; from September to November you can try your luck in the Niagara River. Some species have open and closed seasons; contact the Ontario Ministry of Natural Resources (see below) for more information. For information on dock fishing, boat launching, and annual fishing derbies, call the **Game & Fish Association** at ✆ **905/937-6335.**

To fish in Ontario, those aged 18 and over must obtain a valid fishing permit, as stipulated by the Ministry of Natural Resources. Ontario residents, other Canadian residents, and nonresidents all need different licenses. More information is available by calling ✆ **800/387-7011,** or visiting www.mnr.gov.on.ca/en/Business/LetsFish/index.html. Fishing is permitted on the Welland River, along the Niagara River, and on Lake Ontario and Lake Erie. Note that there is a catch-and-release program in the Dufferin Islands, located just a short way upriver from the Falls on the Canadian side.

Golf

The Niagara region is becoming a hot golf destination. Its varied topography and gentle climate are ideal attributes for hosting golf courses, and Niagara is teeming with them—more than 40 courses are contained within the Niagara Peninsula. The diverse landscape provides beginner and experienced golfers with a range of challenges on Niagara's well-designed and professionally maintained public and semiprivate golf courses.

The **golf season** in Niagara runs for 7 months, from April to October. Temperatures range from an average of 59°F (15°C) in April, to 82°F (28°C) in midsummer, and a comfortable 66°F (19°C) average monthly temperature in October. Greens fees vary widely, dependent upon the season, day of the week, time of day, whether it is an advance reservation or walk-in, and other factors. Expect to pay around C$100 and up for a round, including a cart.

Thundering Waters Golf Club (6000 Marineland Pkwy., Niagara Falls, ON; ✆ 877/833-DALY [833-3259] or 905/357-6000; www.thunderingwaters.com), located just south of the Falls, is near falls-view accommodations and the entertainment district in Niagara Falls, Ontario. Course designer John Daly attempted to hit a golf ball from Table Rock, next to the Horseshoe Falls in Canada, to Goat Island in the U.S., the island that lies between the Canadian and American falls. He failed, but the publicity was positive, and Daly proved to be a great ambassador for Niagara Falls and the new golf course. **Legends on the Niagara** (9561 Niagara Pkwy., Niagara Falls, ON; ✆ 866/GOLF-NIA ([465-3642]; www.niagaraparksgolf.com/legends), another relatively new course, with 45 holes along the Niagara River, has earned a distinguished Platinum rating (based upon KPMG's scoring criteria). The course at the **Grand Niagara Resort** (8547 Grassy Brook Rd., Niagara Falls, ON; ✆ **905/384-GOLF** [384-4653]; www.grandniagararesort.com) was designed by Rees Jones, one of the top golf-course architects in the world. Currently there's an 18-hole course with a lounge and restaurant, and plans to expand into a hotel and more. **Royal**

Niagara Golf Club (1 Niagara-on-the-Green Blvd., Niagara-on-the-Lake; ℂ 905/685-9501; www.royalniagara.com) is situated alongside the Niagara Escarpment and is one of Niagara's most scenic courses.

In a move that is sure to boost the profile of Niagara golf, our own Canadian golf star, Mike Weir, has plans to build a winery and a golf museum to be located on the Niagara Parks **Whirlpool Golf Course.** (3351 Niagara Pkwy., Niagara Falls, ON; ℂ 866/GOLF-NIA [466-3642]; www.niagaragolftrail.com). The plans are currently on hold until an organizational review of the Niagara Parks Commission has been conducted and the Commission has a clearer sense of its future plans. The course is one of Canada's most highly rated and renowned public golf courses. It is owned and operated by the Niagara Parks Commission and is located in a spectacular setting against the backdrop of the Niagara River whirlpool and gorge. The course was designed by the famous golf-course architect Stanley Thompson.

For more information on Niagara's golf courses, contact these online resources: the **Niagara Parks Commission** at **www.niagaraparks.com** and **www.niagaragolf trail.com**, the **Golf Association of Ontario** at **www.gao.ca**, or **Ontario's Online Golf Course Guide** at **www.ontgolf.ca**.

Hiking & Biking

No matter what your speed—whether you like to take a leisurely bike ride stopping at every historical site, or if you love mud flying in your face while whipping down a "bum over the saddle" hill, Niagara's varied topography caters to all. If you're a hiker, spend a day in one of the more than 35 conservation areas, which vary from wetlands to waterfalls to lush forests full of rare and exotic wildlife. Most parks and conservation areas touch into the **Niagara Escarpment** (www.escarpment.org) and can make for challenging climbs—on bike or on foot. The Niagara Escarpment is a UNESCO World Heritage Site, hits heights up to 510m (1,673 ft.), and is home to more than 300 bird species, 53 mammals, 36 reptiles and amphibians, and 90 fish and flora, including 37 types of wild orchids. The sedimentary rock here formed more than 450 million years ago. What remains today is an outdoors enthusiast's playground. The Escarpment rises near Rochester, New York, and runs west through the Niagara Peninsula, south of Lake Ontario, and then to Hamilton, where it takes a turn north and heads straight up to the end of the Bruce Peninsula. Bring maps, water, and a friend, if venturing out.

The Niagara community has also made huge strides in organizing well-maintained, paved, multiuse paths that pass by various historical sites and waterways of the region. And if you're so inclined, put a basket on the front of a rented bike, visit some wineries, and take home some goodies.

Go Transit has made biking Niagara even easier. Their award-winning *Bike Train* (www.biketrain.ca) helps visitors get active, travel local, and cycle Niagara in the summer. Originally developed by Toronto cyclist Justin Lafontaine and launched in partnership with VIA Rail between Toronto and Niagara in 2007, the Bike Train has proven to be a fun, economic, and environmentally friendly way to enjoy a cycling getaway. Getting to the destination is made easy as passengers travel in comfort while their bicycles are safely secured in a baggage car with bike racks. Knowledgeable Bike Train staff members are available onboard to provide cycling maps and useful information. Passengers join a community of travelers who are happy to share stories and anecdotes about their trips during the train journey.

Now called the **Toronto-Niagara Greenbelt Express,** this innovative train/bike transit provides service between Toronto's Union Station and Niagara Falls Station, with a number of stops in St. Catharines. Niagara Falls Station is ideally situated 1 block from the Niagara River Recreation Trail, a primarily off-road 56km (35-mile) paved path. Cycle north on a beautiful 20km (12-mile) ride to see the Niagara Gorge, abundant wineries, and historic Niagara-on-the-Lake. Cycle south on the path to see the magnificent Niagara Falls and beyond to Fort Erie. The St. Catharines station is located a short ride from the city's compact downtown. It is also a great starting point to explore Port Dalhousie, the historic Welland Canal, 20 Valley wine routes, and mountain biking trails around the Niagara Escarpment. There are a number of trails and routes to enjoy wherever you stop. The *Toronto-Niagara Greenbelt Express* runs eight weekends from June to October with stops in Toronto, Niagara Falls, and St. Catharines. The cost is C$20 adult (one-way) from Union Station in Toronto to Niagara Falls, C$9.60 for seniors and children.

BIKE RENTALS

If you want to pick a path and go it alone, rent a bike from **Steve's Place Bicycle & Repair** (181 Niagara Blvd., Fort Erie; © 888/649-BIKE [649-2453]). Steve rents hybrid bikes (cross btw. a road and a mountain bike) for C$25 a day or C$100 for a full week. Rentals include a lock, but you must provide your own helmet. The store is just off the Niagara River Trail—great location. Another spot to pick up a bike is **Zoom Leisure** (2017 Niagara Stone Rd. [Hwy. 55], Niagara-on-the-Lake; © 866/811-6993). Choose from Trek hybrid bikes, tandems, kids', or mountain bikes for off-road riding. Every bike comes with map, helmet, and bike lock. Prices are around C$12 per hour; C$20 half-day up to 3 hours; or C$30 for full day, until dark.

THE BRUCE TRAIL

The **Bruce Trail** is a meandering path that begins at Queenston Heights and ends almost 850km (528 miles) later in Tobermory, on the northern tip of the Bruce Peninsula. Hikers experience fantastic views overlooking waterfalls, opening up through lush fauna and flora and a kaleidoscope of colors (biking is not permitted on the trails). Opened in 1967, it is proudly the oldest and longest trail of its kind in Canada. For more information, including maps, visit the Bruce Trail Association website: **www.brucetrail.org**. Bring a map and follow the trail markings: Single white blazes (15×5cm/6×2-in. marking on tree, created by chipping off a piece of the bark) mean walk straight ahead, while a double blaze, with another slightly lower, indicates a turn ahead—look ahead for another single blaze to confirm the path's direction, or simply go in the direction of the upper blaze. Side trails are marked in blue.

The **Niagara Bruce Trail section** runs between **Beamsville** and **Queenston,** overlooks the Niagara River, and passes through countless orchards and wineries, yet feels secluded and wild. Within this area there are six recommended hiking routes. The first and most popular is the Brock's Monument to **Woodend Conservation Area.** An hour into the trek provides undulating terrain that requires proper hiking shoes. Stay on the single white–marked trail. The 18km (11-mile) hike, east to west, has parking on either side. You'll get a great workout here and perhaps a few blisters to boot! Starting at the east end of Queenston Heights Park from the cairn, you'll first come across the **Queenston Quarry** (Queenston Trails) 2km (1.25 miles) into the hike, which deviates onto its own set of trails that highlight more of the Niagara Escarpment. For mountain biking, the area's fat-tire mecca is **Short Hills Provincial Park** in Pelham—a multiuse trail system with more than 10km (6.25 miles) of single-track trails (call **Ontario Parks** at © 800/667-1940, or **Short Hills Provincial Park** directly at © 905/774-6642 in summer, or 905/827-6911 in winter). Visit **www.friendsofshorthillspark.ca** for a downloadable trail map. The expansive

735-hectare (1,816-acre) day-use park includes six trails and the Bruce Trail and has a distinctly different landscape from the rest of Niagara. Short Hills is a series of small but steep hills formed during the last ice age. The **Swayze Falls** (6.2km/3.9-mile) trail and **Black Walnut** (4.3km/2.7-mile) trail are open for mountain bikers, as well as hikers and horse riders—follow the yellow trail markers. The Black Walnut starts on a wide fire road with single-track trails that lead into the forest and loop back to the main fire road. With plenty of roots and steep climbs, these offshoots will please intermediate-level mountain bikers. Also note that the Scarlet Tanager, Hemlock Valley, Terrace Creek, and Paleozoic trails are for hikers only. The Terrace Creek is the best for hikers of intermediate ability (loads of hills). It takes about 2 hours to complete the trail and includes two waterfalls within the park. A great jumping-off point is the St. John's Education Centre.

A new mountain-bike trail, maintained by local riders, is the **12-Mile Creek** trail. It makes a 12-mile loop (obviously), which is about 20km of twisty single track. Starting at the foot of the Burgoyne Bridge, off Glendale Avenue in St. Catharines, the trail will provide hard-core riders a good fix. For a longer trail that follows the creek, park at Brock University and start riding behind the school to access the 12-Mile Creek trail.

In Lincoln County, just down the road from Rockway Glen, **Louth Conservation Area** has two magnificent waterfalls and a cornucopia of flowers. Intersecting with the Bruce Trail, there's also a 3km (1.75-mile) side trail with harder terrain. This place is quite secluded—don't be surprised if you don't see anyone. A far busier spot, and the touristiest, is **Ball's Falls Conservation Area,** which is just off the QEW. The trail is a flat, family-friendly jaunt that takes about 30 minutes to finish. The area is best known for its 19th-century hamlet—a barn, pavilion, church, and two waterfalls spread across 80 hectares (198 acres). The falls themselves are two-thirds the height of Niagara Falls, although the volume of water is considerably less.

OTHER TRAILS

Greater Niagara Circle Route   Closer to civilization is the Greater Niagara Circle Route (© **905/680-9477**), which is a 150km (93-mile), mostly paved path for cyclists, in-line skaters, and walkers—the 3m-wide (10-ft.) trail spans from Lake Erie to Lake Ontario. The trails are wheelchair accessible, save for a few railway crossings. The trail includes four sections:

o **The Friendship Trail,** part of the Trans-Canada Link Trail, extends from Port Colborne to Fort Erie along Lake Erie—about 14km (8⅔ miles). The route can be accessed in Fort Erie near the Ridgeway Battlefield site (1km/⅔ mile north on Ridge Rd.), and along Lake Erie on Windmill Point Road and Stone Mill Road. The trail follows the abandoned CN Rail line, passing through some quiet residential streets, and is great for a short ride or walking and jogging. Not the most picturesque ride.

o **The Niagara River Recreation Trail,** which spans all the way from Fort Erie to the tip of Niagara-on-the-Lake, is a great family ride, with plenty of grassy sections to stop and have a snack. Approximately 60km (37 miles), it is also part of the Trans-Canada Link Trail—access points include the north entrance from Fort George in Niagara-on-the-Lake. The trail is divided into four sections, each taking about an hour or two to complete on a bike: Niagara-on-the-Lake to Queenston is the busiest stretch and feels too congested on summer weekends; Queenston to the Whirlpool Aero Car; Chippawa to Black Creek; and Black Creek to Fort Erie (this is the least busy and frankly just as scenic). While strolling or riding, take in the hundred or so historical plaques that tell of soldiers defending the frontier and of significant Upper

Canadian historical sites such as Fort George, McFarland House, and early battle sites. Seasonal washrooms and free parking are available throughout.

o **The Waterfront Trail** picks up from the Recreation Trail going all the way to Brockville (outside of the Niagara Circle). But beware: During the majority of the Niagara-on-the-Lake section, there is neither waterfront nor a trail—riders are stuck on the side of the road and the lake is not even in view! Starting in St. Catharines, the trail signage to the gravel path is poor, but once you find your way, the trail finally follows the lake. The upside is that passing through more than 31 communities, including several farmlands and wineries, there's a chance to pick up wine and local fruit. In total, it spans 450km (280 miles). Access points include Lakeshore Road and another near Port Weller in Niagara-on-the-Lake, and Ansell Park in St. Catharines. For a detailed downloadable map, visit **www.waterfronttrail.org**.

o **The Welland Canal Recreation Trail** spans all the way from Lake Ontario to Lake Erie on a single paved path that hugs the canal waterway and passes through St. Catharines, Thorold, and Welland, finishing at Port Colborne. This is my favorite easy leisure ride. On hot days, a cool breeze comes off the water. Watching the ships in the canal is an added bonus. Access this section north of Lock 3 in St. Catharines or at the southern end of Seaway Park in Port Colborne. This trail is a bit busier, as it passes through towns and the sometimes-busy ports of the Welland Canal.

Niagara Conservation Areas ★   There are 36 separate conservation areas in the Niagara Region, operated by the **Niagara Peninsula Conservation Authority** (© **905/788-3135;** www.conservation-niagara.on.ca). Visit the website for a complete list; and remember that these trails are open for hiking only! A good majority of the trails are for beginners and offer great scenery and wildlife viewing, but if you're a hiker looking to cross streams and develop some well-earned blisters, I suggest the following.

The **Rockway Glen Conservation Area** is part of the Bruce Trail. The terrain features roller-coaster terrain crossing streams, rock faces, roots, and logs near a deep canyon; this is my idea of great hiking. Park your car at the Rockway Glen Community Centre (Pelham Rd., St. Catharines). Quite the opposite, in terms of terrain, but a spectacular place to view the Escarpment, is **Beamer Memorial Conservation Area,** Ridge Road, Grimsby. The trail itself is a flat path that makes a loop and takes about 40 minutes to walk. There are also four lookout points—a great vantage point for bird-watching. Take the Lookout Trail to see the 23m (75-ft.) falls. Three wheelchair platforms lead to observation areas. About halfway through the loop, there's a side trail that jumps onto the Bruce Trail; the steep stairs going up the escarpment lead to a path that goes all the way into Grimsby. If you're looking for a harder climb, do the path to Grimsby and back to Beamer, which will take a couple of hours. Moving down the QEW to the east in Beamsville, there's another unique hike. Feeling more like Middle-earth (from *Lord of the Rings*) with trees strewn across the forest floor and giant ferns, I spent most of the time looking at the path to secure my steps on top of the mossy rocks at **Mountainview Conservation Area** (Mountainview Rd., Beamsville). Occasionally there's a gap between the rocks leading to dark crevices—a golem is rumored to live here. And still in the same area, **Louth Conservation Area** (Staff Rd., Lincoln County) has undulating terrain, perhaps because a good chunk of it touches the Escarpment; the trails also access the Bruce Trail. Louth is also blessed with two waterfalls.

If you're in the Port Colborne area, I suggest the **Wainfleet Wetlands,** Quarry Road, Wainfleet. The area has informal trails, where hikers can see fossils—but please, don't take them home. **Wainfleet Bog,** Erie Peat Road, Wainfleet, near Port

Organized Tours

WHAT TO SEE & DO IN THE NIAGARA REGION | Organized Tours

On both sides of the border, you can take a leisurely drive alongside the Niagara River and Niagara Gorge. On the Canadian side (western shore), you can follow the Niagara Parkway all the way from Fort Erie at the southern end of the Niagara River to Niagara-on-the-Lake at the northern end, where it empties into Lake Ontario. On the U.S. side (eastern shore), start farther upriver, where the Robert Moses Parkway begins, first heading west at the junction with I-90 and following it as it turns north with the natural bend in the river. You will pass through Niagara Falls State Park (or head through downtown Niagara Falls, although it is a less picturesque route), then through several other state parks, including Whirlpool, Earl W. Brydges Artpark, and Joseph Davis, ending at the northern end of the Niagara River in Fort Niagara State Park.

Colborne, has more than 800 hectares (1,977 acres) of land—be sure to bring a compass. Trails are short, but the wetland scenery is worth the trek.

Niagara Glen Nature Reserve ★★ "The gorge" trail follows the river alongside rushing water. With side paths that take you onto flat rocks right at the water level, it's your best bet for an up-close view of the water at work—and it's free. It is located alongside the Niagara Gorge between the Whirlpool and the Niagara Parks Botanical Gardens, and you must descend the gorge to get to the trail, which is a steep, steep drop. There's a series of seven different pathways that link through this nature reserve ranging in length from .4km (.2 mile) to 3.3km (2 miles). Along the **Eddy Path,** you will see the Wilson Terrace Passages, which are narrow passageways between huge boulders that toppled from Wintergreen Cliff many thousands of years ago. Along the **River Path,** you will see Devil's Hole, which is the narrowest point of the Niagara River. Rock beds cover a good portion of both paths, so wear good shoes—I can't imagine running on these trails either. You'll know you have reached the end when you start to see painted blue symbols on trees. Then watch for a purple circle painted around the tree symbols. When you spot the one that says "Up," you'll start making your way up the side of the gorge to the top. Note that all the paths, or the access to them, are steep in places. (River Path is the flattest path, but you need to descend the cliff to reach it.)

The Niagara Parks Commission produces an excellent small field guide (C$10) in a miniature hard-backed binder with a history and description of the Glen and listings of the trees, vines, flowers, insects, and birds to be found in this unique habitat, complete with beautiful color photos to aid identification of species as you explore the Glen. The reserve has a parking lot, gift shop, small cafe, and washrooms located at the side of the Niagara Parkway on a table of land known as Wintergreen Flats (1km/⅔-mile north from Whirlpool Golf Course on Niagara Pkwy., Niagara Falls, ON; © **877/NIA-PARK** [642-7275]; www.niagaraparks.com/nature/rectrailarea.php).

ORGANIZED TOURS

By Bus

Grayline Niagara I wouldn't necessarily stop at all the spots offered on these tours on my own, but I did appreciate the guide's commentary on the gorge, the Falls, and the history of the area. I recommend the Illumination Tour (6–10pm), which includes the Journey Behind the Falls, Skylon Tower, Sir Harry Oaks Gardens, and a view of the Whirlpool. But if you're used to doing your own research before you visit a place, I don't recommend this tour; besides the Journey Behind the Falls, the rest of the attractions are free. The oldest and largest of the bus tour companies, Grayline is accessible from selected hotel lobby desks or by prearranged pickup. Tours are also available through Expedia, Travelocity, and other web-based travel companies. A full-day tour, lasting 7 to 8 hours, includes similar sights and more, with dinner and boxed luncheon. Advance reservations or same-day reservations are accepted, and there are discounts for groups of 10 or more.

3466 Niagara Falls Blvd. N., Tonawanda, NY. ✆ **800/695-1603.** www.grayline.com. Half-day from US$85 adults, US$50 children. Tours and times vary.

Niagara Airbus This company offers bus tours to wineries, sightseeing tours, and packages that include lunch. The Niagara Falls tour, for example, includes lunch and a ride on the *Maid of the Mist* (or a journey behind the Falls in winter). See the Floral Clock, Botanical Gardens, Queenston Heights, and Spanish Aero Car Observation Area, then stop in Niagara-on-the-Lake for free time to stroll the pretty streets and do some shopping. Buses will pick up guests at any hotel or bed-and-breakfast in the region.

8626 Lundy's Lane, Niagara Falls, ON. ✆ **905/374-8111.** www.niagaraairbus.com. Tours start from C$58. Book online and receive 10% discount.

By Bike

Niagara World Wine Tours This is your best bet for leisure rides. The guide takes you through less-traveled (meaning away from the tourists) paths in the forest and behind the vineyards. The guide stops occasionally to impart some history and juicy gossip (about historical figures, of course). Tours are geared toward adults. Two bike tours are run a day; the one that leaves at 11:30am includes a lunch under a canopy in the woods and stops at four wineries (including two tours—a good mix of large and small wineries), while the later tour includes three wineries. For hard-core riders, there are longer tours offered in nearby Beamsville and Jordan.

92 Picton St., Niagara-on-the-Lake. ✆ **800/680-7006.** www.niagaraworldwinetours.com. Tours C$65–C$120.

Zoom Leisure There's more *leisure* than zoom as you meander through the streets in between the vineyards on these tours—but that's just about the speed you need for tasting wines all afternoon. There are two tours a day, and guides are matched to the personality of the riders; you can opt for a harder ride (i.e., more hills and faster terrain). Providing more than 100 bikes to choose from, Zoom Leisure provides child-friendly bike accessories such as trailers and child seats that mount on the bike. Other amenities include handlebar bags, bells, water-bottle cages, and kickstands. One tour leaves at 11am and includes a packed lunch—riders cycle for about an hour before having a big-spread picnic, and then it's on to three or four wineries for wine tastings, which may include a tour. The shorter ride, leaving at 1pm, includes three winery stops. Each bike has an optional basket in the front to bring home goodies from your voyage. Reserve tours in advance (48–72 hr. ahead for most).

2017 Niagara Stone Rd., Niagara-on-the-Lake. ✆ **866/811-6993** or 905/468-2366. www.zoomleisure.com. Tours C$69–C$119.

CITY STROLLS

Niagara-on-the-Lake is a picturesque town, so I provide two tours, one for those equipped with a bike and the other for people wearing comfortable walking shoes, with plenty of chances to stop and shop. I also add a tour of St. Catharines, which is inland and has a different feel, for another tour of a historical area.

CYCLING TOUR: HISTORICAL NIAGARA-ON-THE-LAKE

START:	**Fort George parking lot, link onto Greater Niagara Circle.**
FINISH:	**Fort George.**
TIME:	**Plan to spend 1 to 2 hours, with time for stopping.**
BEST TIME:	**Take this tour in the morning as shops begin to open and the town is at its most peaceful.**

This tour will take cyclists through some of the most historical areas of the town and Lake Ontario views.

1 Indian Council House

Cross Queen's Parade to the Otter Trail recreational pathway. Near the small bridge stands the Indian Council House (ca. 1796), headquarters of the British Indian Department. During the War of 1812, British and Natives met here to discuss politics.

2 Butler's Barracks

The Barracks were constructed to replace Fort George after the War of 1812. It was here that soldiers trained to fight in the Boer War, World War I, World War II, and the Korean War. Turn right, crossing King Street, and continue on Mary Street.

3 Brockamour Manor

At the corner of King Street and Mary Street stands Brockamour Manor (433 King St.). Here it is said that Sophia Shaw became engaged to General Sir Isaac Brock. Brock never returned home, coming to an untimely death at the Battle of Queenston Heights. The ghost of Sophia is said to walk the halls sobbing. Follow Mary Street to Simcoe Street and turn right.

4 Green House

First occupied as a private home, and then becoming a residential school, Green House (20 Simcoe St.) has been substantially altered and changed during its existence. Continue straight on Simcoe Street.

5 Storrington House

One of the first homes built after the War of 1812, Storrington House (289 Simcoe St.) was residence to Adam Lockhart, the secretary for the Niagara Harbour and Dock Company. Servants' quarters were built for the hired help.

6 Keily House

Continue on Simcoe and cross Queen Street, passing by Keily House (ca. 1832). Built for lawyer Charles Richardson, this house is built on the soil of Fort

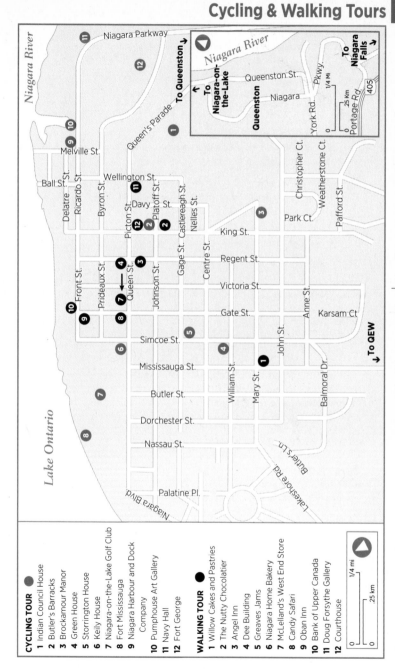

Niagara Parkway

Niagara River

To Queenston →

Niagara River

To Niagara Falls →

Queenston St.

Niagara

Queenston

To Niagara-on-the-Lake

York Rd.

Pkwy.

Portage Rd.

405

1/4 Mi

.25 km

Queen's Parade

Melville St.

Ball St.

Wellington St.

Delatre St.

Ricardo St.

Byron St.

Davy St.

Platoff St.

Picton St.

Castlereagh St.

Gage St.

Nelles St.

Park Ct.

Christopher Ct.

Weatherstone Ct.

Pafford St.

King St.

Centre St.

Regent St.

Front St.

Prideaux St.

Queen St.

Johnson St.

Victoria St.

Gate St.

Anne St.

Karsam Ct

John St.

Simcoe St.

Mississauga St.

William St.

Mary St.

Balmoral Dr.

→ To QEW

Butler St.

Dorchester St.

Nassau St.

Butler's Ln.

Lakeshore Rd.

Lake Ontario

Niagara Blvd.

Palatine Pl.

CYCLING TOUR
1 Indian Council House
2 Butler's Barracks
3 Brockamour Manor
4 Green House
5 Storrington House
6 Kelly House
7 Niagara-on-the-Lake Golf Club
8 Fort Mississauga
9 Niagara Harbour and Dock Company
10 Pumphouse Art Gallery
11 Navy Hall
12 Fort George

WALKING TOUR
1 Willow Cakes and Pastries
2 The Nutty Chocolatier
3 Angel Inn
4 Dee Building
5 Greaves Jams
6 Niagara Home Bakery
7 McLelland's West End Store
8 Candy Safari
9 Oban Inn
10 Bank of Upper Canada
11 Doug Forsythe Gallery
12 Courthouse

1/4 mi

.25 km

Mississauga. The sweeping veranda around the house was built in the late 19th century. In the cellar is a long vaulted chamber—a tunnel that connects to Fort Mississauga. The house is now operating as the Charles Inn.

7 Niagara-on-the-Lake Golf Club

Behind the Charles Inn is the oldest golf course in Canada. Back in the day, golfers started here for 9 holes, and then moved on to Fort George to finish the game. Behind the Niagara-on-the-Lake golf course sits Fort Mississauga.

8 Fort Mississauga

Built at the end of the War of 1812, this was built to replace Fort George. A few parts of the tower were built from limestone from Ontario's first lighthouse, which was burned here by enemy forces in 1813.

9 Niagara Harbour and Dock Company

Follow on to the end of Simcoe onto Front Street. Front Street is renamed Ricardo Street beyond King. To the left is the dock area used in the early 1780s. Many large steamboats were built in the yards of Niagara Harbour and Dock Company. Continue along until the end of the street.

10 Pumphouse Art Gallery

At one time, the engine that pumped water into the town was housed at what is now the Pumphouse Art Gallery. Go straight along the Niagara Parkway.

11 Navy Hall

Lieutenant-Governor John Graves Simcoe lived and worked for the Executive Council of Upper Canada on this site in 1792. American cannons destroyed the original buildings in 1813; they were rebuilt in 1815. To the right are ramparts of Fort George. At Navy Hall, Ricardo Street becomes the Niagara River Parkway, which leads all the way to Niagara Falls. Continue from here to Queen's Parade, and cross the street to link up with John Street, where the path continues. Continue along the path, and then take a right to link up with the Otter Trail once again.

12 Fort George

From 1796 until its capture by the American army in 1813, this fort was the British military headquarters. Unfortunately, the Americans destroyed the original fort, and after the war it was completely abandoned by the British. In 1930, it was reconstructed. Stop by for a tour, complete with costumed guides and a history lesson or two.

WALKING TOUR 1: # NIAGARA-ON-THE-LAKE SHOPPING DISTRICT

START:	**Willow Cakes and Pastries, corner of Mary and Mississauga streets.**
FINISH:	**The Courthouse.**
TIME:	**A slow 1-hour walk.**
BEST TIME:	**Midafternoon, when the lunch crowd has gone—stop for tea and browse the stores.**

Niagara-on-the-Lake offers some one-of-a-kind stores filled with unique gifts and tasty delights. Stroll and enjoy.

1 Willow Cakes and Pastries

Stop at 242 Mary St. for coffee and a croissant. You can read the local paper and fuel up for your walk to come.

2 Nutty Chocolatier

Just past Platoff Street, find the Nutty Chocolatier (233 King St.)—a great place to fill up on homemade fudge, truffles, and creamy Belgian chocolate. On Loonie Tuesday, stop in for a C$1 ice-cream cone.

3 Angel Inn

Proceed along Market Street and turn left onto Regent Street. Pass by the Angel Inn (224 Regent St.; ca. 1825)—a fine place for a pint of ale or glass of Niagara wine. But beware—they say this house is haunted by a solider from the War of 1812. Turn left onto Queen Street.

4 Dee Building

This two-story limestone building (54–58 Queen St.; ca. 1843) has housed everything from a clothing store to grocers. Take note of the original shop front facing Regent Street.

5 Greaves Jams

For a homemade souvenir, stop off at Greaves Jams (55 Queen St.; ca. 1845). Take note of the architectural features of this building—deep boxed cornices on the hip roof.

6 Niagara Home Bakery

And for something to put under the jam, pick up a bag of goodies at 66 Queen St. (ca. 1875). Enter the store through a double leafed door and enjoy the sunlight streaming in through the glassed transom over the doorway.

7 McLelland's West End Store

To accommodate the boom in population during the 1830s, locals could pick up groceries and their fix of wines and spirits at McLelland's West End Store (106 Queen St.; ca. 1835). The large T sign is a sign of a provisioner—the store that sold everything! The store expanded into 108 Queen St.

8 Candy Safari

This Gothic Revival house (135 Queen St.; ca. 1835) was originally built as a residence and shop for shoemaker and leatherworker John Burns. Today, it satisfies the sweet-tooth cravings of shoppers.

9 Oban Inn

Turn right onto Gate Street; on the corner of Front and Gate, take a peek at the Oban Inn. The original inn was built in 1822, and became a hotel in 1895. A fire destroyed the building in 1992. But, as with all good things, it came back and remains true to its original form.

10 The Bank of Upper Canada

Turn right onto Front Street and walk toward 10 Front St. With a stucco front and rough-cast side treatment, this old bank was rebuilt after the War of 1812. It still has the original steel vaults and is the location of a grand bed-and-breakfast now. Walk until Queen becomes Ricardo Street, then turn left onto Wellington Street and right onto Picton Street.

11 Doug Forsythe Gallery

Stop in to browse the fascinating Doug Forsythe Gallery (92 Picton St.). Find unique etchings and paintings using fascinating print-making techniques.

12 The Courthouse

Turn right on King Street, then right onto Queen Street to view the Courthouse (26 Queen St.; ca. 1847). This national historical site changed its function from a courthouse and jail cells to the town hall. The Shaw Theatre Festival was founded here and still performs in the Court House Theatre of the Shaw. From jail to theater—if only the walls could talk.

WALKING TOUR 2: **HISTORIC DOWNTOWN ST. CATHARINES**

START:	**Old Courthouse.**
FINISH:	**Same location.**
TIME:	**2 hours.**
BEST TIME:	**Take a midafternoon stroll through the area just after lunch.**

Known as the garden city, St. Catharines's city streets are busting with color against the backdrop of well-maintained historical homes.

1 Old Courthouse

Start at the Old Courthouse, constructed in 1849. Note the beautifully ornate stained-glass transom and curving balustrades. On the St. James side, notice the steer's head and wheat sheaf, recognizing the nearby market. The water fountain is a gift from Mayor Lucius Oille.

2 St. Catherine of Alexandria Cathedral

Northeast on Church Street, you will find this beautiful church built in 1845 for Irish Catholic immigrant workers—many of them working on the canal. The facade today is a wonderful example of English neo-Gothic.

3 134 Church St.

The lovely home at 134 Church St. was a wedding gift from farmer Stephen Parnell to his daughter and son-in-law, local merchant James Wood, who would later become a prosperous merchant.

4 173–175 King St.

Turn onto King Street and look for nos. 173–175. This stream of row houses is typical of its era in 1860. Notice the red brick, popular frieze, and brackets at the roofline. Now, follow Academy Street east.

5 224–226 St. Paul St.

Turn right onto St. Paul Street and note nos. 224–226. This Italianate facade, with bulging exterior, reveals window shapes and large openings for windows, which were unique by 19th-century standards. It also resembles a palace on the Grand Canal in Venice, Italy.

6 88 St. Paul St.

At this home, built in 1869, marvel at the ornate decoration of the windows and the roofline with cast-iron markers on the facade.

7 37 and 39 Ontario St.

Turn onto Ontario Street, where nos. 37 and 39 are the former Masonic temple buildings of 1873. Notice the cast-iron columns and window frames—a new material replacing brick and stone during its era.

8 Statue of William Hamilton Merritt

Returning back to St. Paul Street, overlooking Twelve-Mile Creek to the south is the statue of William Hamilton Merritt. Merritt was a prominent business-man of the 19th century. He also conceived of a water channel from Lake Erie to Lake Ontario, which became the Welland Canal. Cross to Yates Street and enter into the Yates Street heritage district.

9 24 Yates St.

This was the home of miller John Woodward and is representative of an elegant 19th-century style, in contrast to the Italian style mentioned above.

10 7 Norris Place

Turn right onto Norris Place. A carriage maker built the home at 7 Norris Place; its sidelights and transom above the doorway are typical of its day.

11 105 Ontario St.

Turn left off Norris; on a diagonal you will see 105 Ontario St., where there's another example of row houses from 1860 built for Josiah Holmes and his part-ner W. W. Greenwood.

12 83 Ontario St.

This is the former home of J. F. Mittleberger, another prosperous businessman of his day. Take a look at the unique faces on the door.

13 Welland Canal House Hotel

Across the street is this hotel, built in the 1850s. Today, it is a student residence. Walk 2 blocks farther to Queen Street and turn left.

14 64 Queen St.

This is the last house on the tour, former home of Chauncey Yale, an American manufacturer. Notice the familiar style of home and fence, which represents a traditional home (ca. 1851).

THE WINE-COUNTRY EXPERIENCE

7

Niagara has arrived as a winegrowing area, winning international awards and challenging the world. Its Icewine, Canada's liquid gold, has long been appreciated worldwide, but now its sophisticated and varied table wines are highlighting the unique and wonderful *terroir* of the Niagara peninsula.

It's the result of maturing vines, financial investment in state-of-the-art winemaking methods and equipment, and the increasing breadth of the education of its winemakers and growers.

INTRODUCING THE NIAGARA WINE REGION

History of the Niagara Wine Region

Niagara's vibrant wine industry had humble beginnings, with the first European settlers making use of the native *Vitis labrusca* grapes, which were ideal for juice, preserves, and desserts but unfortunately did not produce the light, dry, sophisticated style of table wines that dominates the world's markets today. During the mid-1900s, Niagara vintners achieved modest success with Canadian hybrids.

In the 1970s, a number of enterprising growers began planting *Vitis vinifera* vines, the so-called noble grape varietals that produce many of the world's finest wines, such as chardonnay, cabernet, gamay, and Riesling. Fertile, rich soils and a unique microclimate make Niagara a prime grape-growing region; and, contrary to the expectations of most, the *vinifera* vines thrived.

The biggest contributor to the transformation of Ontario's wine industry was the introduction of international trade agreements in 1988. The loss of tariff and retail price protection put the retail price of Ontario wines on par with imports from the world's most respected and well-established wine regions. The industry had to reinvent itself as a worthy contender. Growers, wineries, and the provincial government decided to revitalize the wine industry, and together they rose to the challenge.

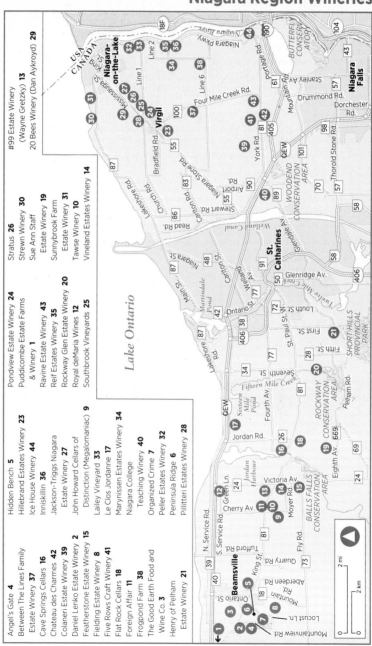

Angel's Gate **4**
Between The Lines Family Estate Winery **37**
Cave Springs Cellars **16**
Chateau des Charmes **42**
Colaneri Estate Winery **39**
Daniel Lenko Estate Winery **2**
Featherstone Estate Winery **15**
Fielding Estate Winery **8**
Five Rows Craft Winery **41**
Flat Rock Cellars **18**
Foreign Affair **11**
Frogpond Farm **38**
The Good Earth Food and Wine Co. **3**
Henry of Pelham Estate Winery **21**

Hidden Bench **5**
Hillebrand Estates Winery **23**
Ice House Winery **44**
Inniskillin **36**
Jackson-Triggs Niagara Estate Winery **27**
John Howard Cellars of Distinction (Megalomaniac) **9**
Lailey Vineyard **33**
Le Clos Jordanne **17**
Marynissen Estates Winery **34**
Niagara College Teaching Winery **40**
Organized Crime **7**
Peller Estates Winery **32**
Peninsula Ridge **6**
Pillitteri Estates Winery **28**

Pondview Estate Winery **24**
Puddicombe Estate Farms & Winery **1**
Ravine Estate Winery **43**
Reif Estates Winery **35**
Rockway Glen Estate Winery **20**
Royal deMaria Wines **12**
Southbrook Vineyards **25**

Stratus **26**
Strewn Winery **30**
Sue Ann Staff Estate Winery **19**
Sunnybrook Farm Estate Winery **31**
Tawse Winery **10**
Vineland Estates Winery **14**

#99 Estate Winery (Wayne Gretzky) **13**
20 Bees Winery (Dan Aykroyd) **29**

The mark of quality

When you purchase a Niagara wine in a restaurant, wine boutique, or retail store, check the label for the designation VQA (Vintners Quality Alliance). Wine-producing regions around the world establish governing bodies to dictate the conditions under which that region's wine is produced. The VQA in Ontario requires that wines with this designation have been made exclusively with grapes grown in one of the four recognized Ontario viticultural areas—Niagara Peninsula, Lake Erie North Shore, Pelee Island, and Prince Edward County. In addition, the wine must be made entirely in Ontario from officially approved grape varieties. These specifications ensure the consumer will receive a quality product and serve to protect the wine industry's reputation.

Between 1989 and 1991, growers removed almost half of Ontario's *labrusca* and hybrid vines and replaced them, over time, with traditional European varieties, as part of a government-initiated program to move toward increased production of higher-quality table wines. The focus was firmly and permanently shifted to *Vitis vinifera* production.

Today, Niagara has approximately 5,504 hectares (13,600 acres) under vine, in an area stretching from Niagara-on-the-Lake in the east to Grimsby in the west. It is the largest planted areas of all viticultural areas in Canada. Close to 80 wineries now make their home in Niagara, many with fine restaurants and boutiques on-site. A large number offer wine tasting and tours to the public. Niagara wines consistently bring home medals and awards from many of the world's most prestigious wine competitions.

World attention has turned to the Niagara wine industry, not least because of the superb quality of its Icewine, a dessert wine produced from grapes that have been left on the vine after the fall harvest to freeze naturally. The frozen grapes are handpicked and immediately pressed to capture the thick, yellow-gold liquid, high in natural sugars and acidity.

The Heart of a Wine Region's Success—Terroir

Winegrowing, or viticulture, is more or less restricted to two temperate bands around the world—where the summers are warm enough to consistently ripen the grapes and the winters are cold enough to allow the vines a period of dormancy.

Although the macroclimate of a district is the major factor determining whether grapes can be grown at all, it is the microclimate, soil, topography, and the effects that each of these characteristics has on the others, that influence the type of wine that can be produced in a particular area. The French have coined a term for this combination of climate, soil, and topography as it relates to the world of winemaking: ***terroir.***

The Niagara wine region is situated in one of the world's most northerly grape-growing regions. Despite Niagara's emergence onto the world wine stage over the last quarter-century, many people are still surprised to learn that the Niagara Peninsula is an ideal zone for the production of high-quality grapes. In fact, the growing season in Niagara enjoys a similar climate to that of Burgundy, France.

The area is designated a "cool-climate viticulture region." However, although many vine growers in cool climates have to contend with summers that are not warm enough to fully ripen the grapes, the unique climate of the Niagara Peninsula provides a more conducive environment. The moderating influence of Lake Ontario and Lake Erie protects the region from extreme temperature fluctuations. The presence of the Escarpment further moderates the climate.

Finally, the soil in the Niagara Peninsula is composed of deposits of clay, loam, sand, and gravel, which vary by district. The soil is also rich in essential minerals and trace elements originating from the variety of bedrock present in the region, providing important nutrients to the vines and contributing to the complexity of the wines produced.

ESSENTIALS
The Wine Region in Brief

The Niagara Peninsula appellation covers a large and diverse area. It is the largest planted viticulture area in Canada and is characterized by rich, fertile soil and unique microclimates, which provide ideal conditions for producing wine grapes with more complexity and intense flavor than those produced in many warmer climates. Lake Ontario, one of the deepest of the Great Lakes, moderates air temperatures year-round. Together with the Niagara Escarpment, this shapes the perfect climate to nurture grape vines. The classic cool-climate varieties such as Riesling, chardonnay, gamay noir, pinot noir, and cabernet franc flourish here, one of the reasons why the area is home to over 85% of Ontario's VQA wineries.

Because of the size and diversity of climate conditions—influenced by factors like lake effect, south-facing slopes, elevation, and soil—this large appellation can be more easily understood and accessed by looking at the 12 sub-appellations that neatly compartmentalize each unique area. There are three standalone sub-appellations and two regional appellations—Niagara Escarpment and Niagara-on-the-Lake—within which are three and four sub-appellations, respectively. It sounds confusing, but all it is, really, is a system for differentiating the small pockets of unique growing characteristics so wine neophytes and wine connoisseurs alike can appreciate, enjoy, and compare the subtle variations.

NIAGARA-ON-THE-LAKE

This regional appellation includes four sub-appellations: Niagara River, Niagara Lakeshore, Four Mile Creek, and St. David's Bench.

WHAT IS AN appellation?

An appellation is a named region in which grapes used for the production of wine are grown. Most of the major wine-producing nations have administrative bodies that oversee appellations and set rules for what standards a vineyard must follow to be considered a part of the appellation. In Canada, that body is the VQA (Vintners Quality Alliance).

Sub-appellations are smaller areas within an appellation that have been identified with unique geographical conditions. Sub-appellations in the Niagara Peninsula were identified after a lengthy technical study identifying common and unique traits related to geology, soils, topography, climate, and growing conditions.

NIAGARA RIVER The Niagara Parkway winds along this narrow band that borders the Niagara River. Vines dig deep into well-drained sandy soils, and air currents from the river moderate temperatures and help protect vineyards from damaging spring or fall frosts. The reddish-hued soils also tend to warm earlier in the spring. Tender grape varieties thrive here. **Wineries:** Peller Estates Winery, Lailey Vineyard, Reif Estate Winery, and Inniskillin Winery.

NIAGARA LAKESHORE From the Welland Canal toward the town of Niagara-on-the-Lake, lush vineyards border the shores of Lake Ontario. The land gently slopes, and vineyards and orchards receive abundant sunlight. Temperatures are moderated by lake breezes, and light sandy and silty soils provide good drainage. The area's grapes and fruit produce full-bodied, flavorful wines. **Wineries:** Stonechurch Winery, Palatine Hills, Konzelmann Estate Winery, Strewn Winery & Cooking School, and Sunnybrook Farm Estate Winery.

FOUR MILE CREEK This is the largest of the four sub-appellations in Niagara-on-the-Lake. It lies below the Escarpment, slightly inland, and stretches into an expansive flat, fertile plain. Red shale soils contain silt and clay, retaining water well. Days are warm, with lots of sunshine, and nights are cool. Conditions are optimal for growing many premium grape varieties. Wineries: Cattail Creek, Coyote's Run Estate Winery, Hillebrand Winery, Pillitteri Estates Winery, Joseph's Estate Wines, Jackson-Triggs, and Marynissen Estates.

ST. DAVID'S BENCH The topography is varied in this area, which was carved by glaciers to form a natural bench below the Escarpment. The region follows the Escarpment from the Niagara River to Beechwood Road, and vineyards are planted on gentle slopes to allow for good drainage in the silty clay soils. The Escarpment location helps vineyards warm early in the spring and provides frost protection. Throughout the growing season, vineyards located in the upper bench receive steady moisture from groundwater. Wineries: Maleta, Niagara College Teaching Winery, and Château des Charmes.

NIAGARA ESCARPMENT

This regional appellation includes three sub-appellations: Short Hills Bench, Twenty Mile Bench, and Beamsville Bench.

SHORT HILLS BENCH Short Hills Bench is the most easterly of the sub-appellations located within the Niagara Escarpment. It encompasses the land rising up from the plain of the Peninsula (south of Regional Rd. 81) to the Escarpment brow and situated between Twelve Mile Creek and Fifteen Mile Creek. The warm, sunny days and cool nights characteristic of this area are perfect for developing the intense grape flavors derived from its complex soils. **Wineries:** Henry of Pelham and Hernder Estates.

TWENTY MILE BENCH With its relatively high elevation and double bench formation, Twenty Mile Bench enjoys long periods of sun exposure during the summer and fall. Lake breezes pushing up against the Escarpment circulate the warm air and extend warm daytime temperatures into the evening, encouraging an even and continuous ripening process. **Wineries:** Flat Rock, Rockway Glenn, Featherstone, Vineland Estates, Ridgepoint, Kacaba, Lakeview Cellars, and John Howard Cellars of Distinction.

BEAMSVILLE BENCH The area is characterized by sloping benchlands and limestone- and mineral-enriched soils. The Beamsville Bench runs from west of

NIAGARA wineries IN THE U.S.

Nestled between the Escarpment and Lake Ontario, in an area northeast of Niagara Falls, New York, lie a handful of wineries. A brochure entitled *Niagara Wine Trail USA,* with descriptions of the wineries and a map showing their locations, can be obtained from tourist information centers in Niagara Falls, New York, and at tourist information centers inside Niagara Falls State Park; or you can visit **www.niagarawinetrail. org**. Opening hours vary quite markedly among vineyards; some are limited to weekends in the colder months, so call ahead to avoid disappointment.

Eveningside Vineyards (4794 Lower Mountain Rd., Cambria; ✆ **716/867-2415;** www.eveningside.com) is a family-owned and -operated boutique winery. Production of their European-style wines is limited. **Niagara Landing Wine Cellars** (4434 Van Dusen Rd., Lockport; ✆ **716/433-8405;** www.niagaralanding. com) has vineyards dating back to the 1800s. They produce wine from native *labrusca* grapes and European *viniferas*. **Vizcarra Vineyards at Becker Farms** (3760 Quaker Rd., Gasport; ✆ **716/772-7815;** www.beckerfarms.com) is a family destination, with pick-your-own produce; a playground; and a store filled with pies, jams, and other treats in addition to their winery. **Warm Lake Estate Vineyard and Winery** (3868 Lower Mountain Rd., Lockport; ✆ **716/731-5900;** www.warmlakeestate.com) is located on the south shore of Lake Ontario. The winery offers a picnic area, winery tours and tasting, and numerous summer events.

Cherry Avenue to Park Road west of Beamsville. Although a small appellation, the area provides a unique set of conditions that result in a natural complexity to the wines grown here. **Wineries:** Cave Springs, Hidden Bench, Organized Crime, Peninsula Ridge, Malivoire, EastDell, Fielding, Angel's Gate, Thirty Bench, Daniel Lenko, Mountain Road, and Crown Bench.

STANDALONE SUB-APPELLATIONS

CREEK SHORES   Characterized by gently sloping vineyards, Creek Shores is almost surrounded by waterways, with Lake Ontario to the north, Twelve Mile Creek to the east, and Twenty Mile Creek and Jordan Harbour to the west. The complex glacial soils of the Lake Iroquois Plains and lots of unobstructed sunlight define the *terroir* of Creek Shores and contribute to concentrated, full-bodied wines. **Wineries:** Creekside Estates, Harbour Estates, 13th Street, King's Court Estate, and Harvest Estate.

VINEMOUNT RIDGE   Vinemount Ridge lies just above and south of the brow of the Niagara Escarpment. The area is characterized by south- and east-facing slopes, early spring warming, and hot summers. Farther set back from Lake Ontario than other Niagara appellations, and with a slightly shorter growing season, the hot summers ensure that grapes are fully mature at harvest. **Wineries:** De Sousa and Calamus.

LINCOLN LAKESHORE   The Lincoln Lakeshore runs along the Lake Ontario shore from Winona Road to Jordan Harbour and Twenty Mile Creek, and is backed by the foot of the Escarpment bench on its south boundary. The area has an especially long and temperate growing season and a mild winter climate, owing to the full exposure to the moderating effect of Lake Ontario. Ideally suited to viticulture, even tender varieties, this area is also a major producer of tender fruit. **Wineries:** Stoney Ridge, Willow Heights, Thomas & Vaughn, Corner Stone, Magnotta, Legends, Birchwood, Puddicombe Estates, Foreign Affair, and Royal DeMaria.

Visitor Information

The **Wine Education and Visitors Centre** at Niagara College (135 Taylor Road, S.S. #4, Niagara-on-the-Lake; © **905/641-2252;** www.nctwinery.ca) is the best place to begin gathering information about the Niagara wine country. The center is designed for use by both the general public and by students in the teaching winery. Here you will find a wine-tasting room, maps, an information kiosk, an interactive computer kiosk for planning your visit, a wine store, interactive displays, and classes on wine tasting, wine storing, and wine education.

The **Wine Council of Ontario (WCO),** a nonprofit trade organization, produces an excellent map of Niagara's wine country with the official *Wine Route* clearly marked. As you drive along the highways and byways of the Niagara Peninsula, you will see these distinctive road signs, which feature the symbol of a bunch of white grapes against a deep blue background, often with names of vineyards, distances, and arrows added to aid your navigation. The map is available as a pocket fold-out and also appears as a pull-out centerfold in the annual *Official Guide to the Wineries of Ontario.* The guide and pocket map are widely available throughout the Niagara region—at tourism offices, wineries, and retail stores that carry wine. Visit their website at **http://winesofontario.org** for a wealth of information, including an events calendar, advice on pairing wine and food, trip-planning advice, maps, a list of winemaker members and their wineries, an explanation of the various grape varietals, and a history of Niagara's wine region—and much, much more.

Note: Not all wineries are members of the WCO. A number of establishments, either because they are smaller in size or brand new, are not listed in the guide, although you will see signposts directing you to their properties as you tour around. Many of them produce award-winning wines, and they all have their unique stories to tell. I urge you to venture into these wineries to enrich your experience of Niagara's wine country.

For year-round tourism information for the entire area, visit or call **Tourism Niagara at the Gateway Information Centre,** 424 South Service Rd. (exit 74 off the QEW), Grimsby (© **800/263-2988** or 905/945-5444; www.tourismniagara. com). Twenty Valley Tourism Association produces an excellent guidebook to the area called *Discover Twenty Valley,* which lists accommodations, dining, events, and more. Find out more at **www.20valley.ca**. The Welland Canals Centre at Lock 3 services the St. Catharines area (© **800/305-5134;** www.stcatharines.ca).

For information on wineries in Niagara-on-the-Lake (and loads of other tourist information on the immediate area), visit the **Niagara-on-the-Lake Visitor &**

Wine on the Radio or by Podcast

Check out the **Frugal Oenophile** at **www.frugal-wine.com** to listen to podcasts of interviews with wine producers and wine connoisseurs. Another great resource is wine expert Konrad Ejbich's 2-hour radio program, which is aired the last Friday of every month on **CBC** from noon to 2pm.

DINE AMONG THE vines

A number of wineries have restaurants or cafes on their premises. As you would expect in a wine region, the cuisine is exceptional. Opening days and times vary considerably depending on the property and the season, so call ahead. Reservations are recommended, although not required. For reviews and full descriptions of many of the following dining destinations, see chapter 5, "Where to Eat."

The region's longest established estate winery restaurant is **Inn on the Twenty Restaurant and Wine Bar,** located in the center of pretty Jordan Village, across the street from Cave Spring Cellars (3836 Main St., Jordan Village; ℭ **905/562-7313**). **The Kitchen House Restaurant** can be found in a historical Queen Anne–revival Victorian house on the grounds of Peninsula Ridge Estates Winery (5600 King St. W., Beamsville; ℭ **905/563-0900**). There are picnic and patio facilities at **Henry of Pelham Family Estate Winery** (1469 Pelham Rd., St. Catharines; ℭ **877/735-4267** or 905/684-8423); their **Coach House Café** offers casual light fare, cheese platters, and picnic baskets. **Hillebrand Winery Restaurant** is open for lunch and dinner (1249 Niagara Stone Rd., Niagara-on-the-Lake; ℭ **800/582-8412** or 905/468-7123). For great

value, sample the fare and service of the students of Niagara College at the **Niagara Culinary Institute Dining Room** (135 Taylor Rd., Niagara-on-the-Lake; ℭ **905/641-2252**, ext. 4619). Enjoy the creations of Marc Picone and his culinary team in a picturesque setting at **Vineland Estate Winery Restaurant** (3620 Moyer Rd., Vineland; ℭ **888/846-3526**, ext. 33, or 905/562-7088, ext. 33). At the western end of Niagara's wine region, along the Beamsville Bench on the Niagara Escarpment, lies EastDell Estates' **The View Restaurant,** named for its panoramic view of the surrounding vineyards and Lake Ontario (4041 Locust Lane, Beamsville; ℭ **905/563-9463**). Wine-country cuisine awaits at **Peller Estates Winery Restaurant** (290 John St. E., Niagara-on-the-Lake; ℭ **888/673-5537** or 905/468-4678). **Terroir La Cachette Restaurant & Wine Bar** features Provençal-style cuisine and is located within Strewn Winery (1339 Lakeshore Rd., Niagara-on-the-Lake; ℭ **905/468-1222**). **Angels Gate Winery** (4260 Mountainview Rd., Beamsville; ℭ **877/264-4283**), as well as Featherstone Estate Winery (which has a beautiful wraparound patio), has seasonal lunches that include cheese platters to have with your wine (3678 Victoria Ave., Vineland; ℭ **905/562-1949**).

Convention Bureau, 26 Queen St., Courthouse Building, Lower Level, Niagara-on-the-Lake (ℭ **905/468-1950;** www.niagaraonthelake.com).

This facility also operates an accommodations service, whereby you can give them your accommodations requirements and preferences and they will find a property for you (a small fee applies for this service).

Getting Around

Driving a car is probably the best way to see the wineries, as they are spread out over the entire Niagara region. Keep in mind that a tour of four to six wineries a day is more than enough. If you want to bike your way through your tour, choose a section and pick a couple of wineries. For example, the Greater Niagara Circle route (see

Buying Wines

When looking specifically for Canadian wines to buy, be aware that the label "Cellared in Canada" doesn't mean that the wine in the bottle is all Canadian. It is a misleading and confusing designation, and few consumers are aware that wines with this on the label can have as little as 1% Canadian wine in the blend.

The rest can come from foreign vineyards, and too often the quality of that imported wine is very poor. To be absolutely certain you are buying wine made from all Canadian-grown grapes, look for the VQA designation on the label.

chapter 6, "What to See & Do in the Niagara Region," for bike-path info) hits many wineries en route. Another great option is to cycle the quiet country roads—they're wide open and there are not many road hazards. If you opt for the bus, note that public transit does not visit individual wineries. Instead, check out the bus tour options below that cater to the wine-hopping crowd.

Wine-Tasting Tours

Crush on Niagara Not just a regurgitated tour, your guide reveals unique facts and tidbits about the wineries and the town that you won't find in a brochure. And because the owner is a sommelier, this is the best bet for in-depth wine tours. For a unique experience, visitors get to taste wine straight from the barrel and then compare it with the same wine in a bottle. Tours depart in the morning or afternoon, last for 4 hours, and take you through the Niagara Escarpment or the wineries of Niagara-on-the-Lake. Choose from a three-winery tour with lunch, the Sip and Savour, from C$99, or custom tours (with groups of six or more) for C$65; A Sense of the Bench Tour visits four wineries and includes a winery lunch (C$99). Call ahead to reserve a ticket; Saturdays fill up fast. Crush will pick up guests at their hotels (within the wine region) or select a meeting place. Tours run twice daily, 7 days a week.

4101 King St., Beamsville (administration office only). ℂ **866/408-WINE** (409-9463) or 905/562-3373. www.crushtours.com. Mon–Fri 9:30am–5pm; Sat 9:30am–2:30pm.

Niagara-on-the-Lake Trolley Wine Country Tours Sit back and relax onboard a vintage trolley, while your tour guide narrates the way through Niagara's wineries. Tours are approximately 2½ to 3 hours long, inclusive of pickup and drop-off and wine tastings at the wineries.

48 John St., Niagara-on-the-Lake. ℂ **888/669-5566** or 905/468-2195. Tours C$58. May–Oct daily. 2 tours each day.

Niagara World Wine Tours These guys are the kings of tours, offering bicycle, van, or coach excursions through the Niagara wine region. Choose from winery tours, dinner and wine, or a gourmet wine and culinary tour, which is my favorite as it takes visitors through the rolling vineyards near the Escarpment. The tour includes lunch at one of the wineries and stops at some of the smaller wineries, including Featherstone and Fielding. Areas covered include the Niagara Escarpment, the Niagara Peninsula, Jordan, and Beamsville. The cycling tour goes through Niagara-on-the-Lake, and be sure to ask about customized tours. If you prefer, tour the area in a luxury SUV, van, or minicoach, stopping at wineries, and then tasting fine cuisine at restaurants such as Terroir La Cachette. The ultimate package is the Niagara Rail and Lunch package, which includes a round-trip train ticket in Via Rail comfort class from Toronto to Niagara Falls, pickup in Niagara Falls by local guide/chauffeur, a three-course gourmet lunch at Terroir La Cachette, visits to four wineries (with a tour of one), and private wine tastings at each (C$165). Other packages are also available.

92 Picton St., Niagara-on-the-Lake. © **800/680-7006.** www.niagaraworldwinetours.com. Tours C$65–C$165.

Zoom Leisure With more than 100 bikes to choose from and a list of wine tours, this is a great place to start touring the region. Tour three wineries, sampling the wine as you go, or choose an extended package (with optional lunch), which includes four wineries. Each bike has an optional basket in the front to bring home goodies from your voyage. Group and custom tours—where you can choose different routes, different places to lunch, and different wineries to visit—are also available. Reserve tours in advance; call 48 to 72 hours ahead for most tours. If you want to purchase wine, the van will bring it back to the office for you.

2 Market St., Niagara-on-the-Lake. © **866/811-6993** or 905/468-2366. www.zoomleisure.com. Tours C$69–C$119.

Strategies for Touring Niagara's Wine Region

It would be impossible to visit Niagara's 80-plus wineries in one trip, unless you happen to have a couple of free weeks on hand and devote yourself to the task full-time. And touring the wine country is an activity that you must savor, not rush! My advice is to decide ahead of time which of the areas you would like to explore, keeping in mind that some of the appellations are quite far apart.

Have a good idea of which wineries you want to visit and be sure to look at the map. The routes to some of the wineries follow beautiful tree-lined roads, an enjoyable part of the experience, but they can also be confusing without a good map. If you have a GPS in your car, program in the addresses of the wineries you want to visit before you leave.

But don't be too rigid. Trust me when I say that you may very well discover a wine gem that you knew nothing about, by turning in to a humble and unpretentious small winery that just has a sign out on the road. You don't necessarily have to have your production facility designed by a famous architect to make good wine.

Tour smarter, not harder are the words of advice to keep close to your heart as you leaf through this chapter in the process of planning your Niagara wine-country

 Tasting a Flight

A *flight* is an array of wines, with each showing different characteristics ranging from the origin of the grapes used and production methods to the year the wine was produced and the producer her or himself. Tasting a flight allows you to get a sense of how influences such as age, production, origins, year of harvest, and winemaker styles can affect the bouquet and flavor. It's a great way to become more familiar with a particular **varietal.** You can also experience a **vertical tasting,** which includes several vintages of the same wine, or a **horizontal tasting,** which includes several producers' products from the same vintage.

trip. First decide whether you would like to tour in your own vehicle, travel by bicycle, or join an organized tour. Bicycle rental companies are listed in chapter 6, "What to See & Do in the Niagara Region," and there are a few tour options listed above.

If you are new to the world of wine, begin with a guided tour of one of the larger wineries to get a good grounding in how wine is made. Next, I recommend taking part in a **tutored tasting.** Even if you are a seasoned wine aficionado, a refresher may well rekindle your passion for the noble grape. **Hillebrand Winery** offers several educational seminars daily. I highly recommend the **Art of Wine Making,** an hour of instruction that follows the grape from vineyard to bottle. It's a unique experience to learn about winegrowing, fermentation, and barrel aging.

As you draw up your shortlist of the wineries you will call upon, **aim for a balance** among the larger, well established wineries and the smaller independents, the sophisticated estates and the modest tasting rooms.

I would tour a few wineries in each of St. David's Bench, Niagara River, and the Four Mile Creek appellations together and savor the differences in *terroir.* Short Hills Bench, Twenty Mile Bench, and Creek Shores make another geographically sensible grouping.

Also, plan to stop to **enjoy wine-country cuisine.** It's a given that wine begets great food, and Niagara has blossomed as a food destination in recent years. Many of the larger wineries have excellent restaurants—Peller Estates, for example, has one of the prettiest and best-rated dining rooms in the area. Other wineries, like Henry of Pelham with its very French patio cafe, have more modest bistrolike dining. Some, like Ravine Bistro, will sell you bread and cheese and whatever you may need to make your own picnic. (See chapter 5, "Where to Eat," for more suggestions on dining in wine country.)

Take it slowly—**aim to visit between three and six wineries** for a day's outing. You'll be able to really savor the wines and also learn the story behind each winery: its history, the types of wines it makes, where the grapes are grown, and the passionate people behind the scenes who make it all happen. Only by visiting the Niagara wine region will you gain a deep appreciation of the effort and experience that goes into every bottle produced. The winery staffs are quite approachable and knowledgeable;

 NEVER DRINK & drive

There are lots of options to explore to ensure everyone gets to enjoy their visit to the wine country.

o Designate a driver. If you are staying more than a day, rotate the responsibility.

o Contact a tour company and allow them to transport you. You'll have the added bonus of a knowledgeable guide.

o If you are touring wineries in the Niagara-on-the-Lake region, there is a step-on/step-off bus service. Several wineries in the area provide shuttle buses, too.

o Become adept at tasting like a professional. Discipline yourself to spit the wine you taste and discard the remaining wine. There are vessels for just this purpose at every tasting bar.

And don't think you're okay as long as you're wobbling along on a bicycle—if you are under the influence of alcohol, you are a potential danger to yourself and other road or trail users.

2007 Wines

The year 2007 was the vintage of the century, perhaps of all time, in Niagara. When you are tasting wines, ask to try one from 2007 and compare it with other years. If you like what you're tasting, pick up a bottle or two, before they disappear.

it's not unusual to have a long chat about the intricacies of a good bottle of pinot noir with a winemaker. You are likely to enjoy getting to know the winemakers just as much as the wines.

If you are looking for the undivided attention of the tasting-room staff, **tour in the morning.** Most wineries open at 10am. Later in the day, when the winery parking lots are filling up with vehicles, you'll be enjoying an after-lunch glass of wine.

Whether you are a seasoned oenophile or a wine novice, there are wineries in Niagara that will help you discover the delights of Niagara Peninsula *terroir*.

NIAGARA REGION'S WINERIES

In comparative terms, Niagara is a young wine producing region. But there is a history here already, and many of the industry's founding fathers are still at the helm. People like Karl Kaiser and Donald Ziraldo of Inniskillin, Andrew Peller of Peller Estates, Paul Bosc of Château des Charmes, Len Penachetti of Cave Springs, John Howard formerly of Vineland Estates and now the proud proprietor of John Howard Vineyards, and the Speck Brothers of Henry of Pelham—these are the names you will come across again and again as people discuss where Niagara has come from and where it is heading. In fact, you are likely to run into one of these winemakers when you visit their wineries. They are all still frequently hands-on owners, still involved, still innovating.

With close to 80 wineries in the Niagara region, choosing the ones you want to visit may be difficult. The following classifications, while unofficial, put many of the wineries into categories that may make it easier to design your visit. The categories are not based on the quality of the wine produced (each of the wineries on the list produces excellent, though different wines), but more on the character, the history, and the direction of the winery. It's not an exhaustive list—there isn't room here to cover all the wineries—and some of the wineries would fit just as well in one or more of the other categories, but this will give you a general overview of the personalities of some of our most intriguing winemakers and the wines they are producing.

Iconic Niagara Wineries: For First-Time Visitors

These are the largest wineries, generally the oldest, and the ones that have largely defined the winemaking business in the area. They were often the pioneers of new practices and directions, and they are frequently the flag-bearers for Niagara wines internationally. First-time visitors to Niagara wine country and novice wine aficionados should visit at least one of these legendary wineries.

Cave Spring Cellars ★   (Beamsville Bench) Cave Spring Cellars' tasting room, wine shop, and cellars are located in a historical building (1871) on the main street in the village of Jordan, which makes it a great destination winery. Cave Spring Cellars has been producing wine from *Vitis vinifera* grapes for 20 years, on land first scouted by plane and chosen for its hillside location, heavy clay soils, and proximity

NIAGARA'S JEWEL—icewine

Icewine is a truly sensational experience for the palate. Its key characteristic is a perfect balance of sweetness and refreshing acidity. Icewine delivers delicious aromas, ranging from lychee, apricot, pear, and vanilla in a vidal Icewine to strawberries and raspberries in a cabernet franc. Complex fruit flavors explode in the mouth with each and every sip. Officially classed as a dessert wine, Icewine also may be served as an aperitif with pâté or foie gras or on its own.

The grapes used to produce Icewine are left untouched on the vines and covered with a layer of protective netting once the fruit has reached full ripeness in October. Close attention is paid to the falling temperatures as winter envelops wine country. When the temperature drops below 18°F (-8°C; although most vintners prefer to operate at temperatures a few degrees colder) and the grapes are frozen solid, there is a sudden flurry of activity in the vineyards. Dozens of volunteers arrive, usually at midnight or later, when there is the least danger of the temperature rising.

The grapes are handpicked and quickly transported to the winery to be de-stemmed and crushed, then immediately pressed while still frozen. The water in the grape juice remains frozen, and a relatively minute amount of sweet juice is extracted, so concentrated that its consistency is like honey.

After the sediment has been cleared, the juice undergoes a slow fermentation process, which takes several months, and is then aged. Both fermentation and aging take place in stainless-steel

to the moderating influences of Lake Ontario. Tutored tastings are held on weekends at 3pm Friday through Sunday in the winter, and daily at 3pm in the summer; expect a fun, lighthearted approach to wine. The Cabernet/Merlot (Beamsville Bench) 1998 is bottled heaven. Ripe berry and chocolate tastes are prominent. On the white side, the Cave Spring Cellars 2007 Estate Riesling has notes of peach, apple, and lime. For tastings, expect to pay C75¢ per tasting and C$4 for Icewine. A late-harvest wine sample is C$2. Tasting fees are waived if a bottle is purchased. Packages are available in partnership with the adjacent Inn on the Twenty (see chapter 4, "Where to Stay," for listing information) and its prestigious fine-dining restaurant, which include overnight accommodations, a winemaker's dinner, and a private tutored tasting. Bottles of wine cost C$13 to C$30 for table wines and up to C$60 for Icewines.

3638 Main St., Jordan. © **905/562-3581.** www.cavespringcellars.com. June-Oct Mon-Thurs 10am-6pm, Fri-Sat 10am-7pm, Sun 11am-6pm; Nov-May Mon-Thurs 10am-5pm, Fri-Sat 10am-6pm, Sun 11am-5pm. Tours June-Sept daily noon and 3pm; Oct-May Fri-Sun 3pm.

Château des Charmes ★★ (St. David's Bench) The Bosc family's French roots permeate one of Niagara's original wineries. Paul Bosc, Sr., helped transform the Niagara wine landscape, planting the largest single *vinifera* in Ontario in 1978. Gone were the days of Baby Duck (an embarrassing but popular Canadian sparkling wine from days gone by), thanks in part to the vision of Paul, Sr. Today, the 113 hectares (279 acres) of vineyard, located on four different properties, emphasize single-vineyard bottles. The vineyard continues to break new ground, offering wines unique to the area, including the only *vinifera* clone in Canada, called the Gamay Noir Droit; the deviant gamay vine ripens later than gamay and is higher in sugar. Their pinot containers at cool temperatures in order to maximize fruit concentration.

Icewine was first discovered in Germany in the late 1700s by farmers trying to rescue their semifrozen grape crop after a sudden cold snap. However, German winters are not consistently cold enough to freeze the grapes—it happens only once or twice every 10 years or so. Moving forward to Niagara in the mid-1980s, insightful and enterprising winemakers realized that Ontario's cold winters would provide just the right conditions for producing an annual Icewine vintage.

Hillebrand Estates was the pioneer of Icewine production in Niagara, beginning in 1983. A year later, Inniskillin made its first vintage of Icewine. By the early 1990s, Niagara's Icewine entered the world stage when it began attracting favorable attention at international wine competitions, including the prestigious Vinexpo in Bordeaux, France.

Niagara Icewine is always produced as a varietal, with the majority being made from vidal and Riesling. Other varieties include Gewürztraminer, cabernet franc, merlot, pinot gris, chardonnay, muscat ottonel, and gamay. Winemakers vary slightly in their recommendations for serving. Chill the bottle for 1½ to 3 hours in the fridge, which will bring the serving temperature down to between 41° and 50°F (5°–10°C). Serve 1 to 2 ounces per person in a small tulip-shaped glass, which will encourage the wine to flow over the tip of the tongue (where most of the sweetness-detecting taste buds are concentrated) as you taste. A small white wineglass is an acceptable alternative.

noir, chardonnay, gamay, and aligote are notable. For a tasting treat, try the Equuleus, a bold blend of cabernet sauvignon, cab franc, and merlot. The Bosc family is often on the premises—sometimes Paul, Sr., rides his horses alongside the vineyard; the family has tried to preserve an old-world feel about the château—it feels very European and homey at the same time. Tours start with a hearty welcome from staff at the door and include a traditional tour of the winery and production facilities as well as a peek at the vines and a bit of history of the grapes. Daily tours start at 11am and 3pm; tours in several languages are available. Reservations are not required.

1025 York Rd., St. David's, Niagara-on-the-Lake. © **800/263-2541** or 905/262-4219. www.chateaudes charmes.com. Daily 10am–6pm.

Henry of Pelham Family Estate Winery ★★ (Short Hills Bench) Henry of Pelham was a founding member of the Vintners Quality Alliance (VQA). Started by their father and now run by the three brothers—Matthew, Daniel, and Paul—the winery has won numerous domestic and international awards, including those at VinItaly and the London Wine Trade Fair. Their first vintage was in 1988, and today their wines are served throughout the world. The winery is run with all the latest technology but also with a sincere concern for preserving the environment. Try their 2005 Reserve Baco Noir, a rich, jammy, and full-bodied wine that will age well. Their latest venture is the audacious Sibling Rivalry, red and white blended wines that are young and easy to drink, approachable but still good quality. My personal favorite is their Cuvee Catherine Rosé Brut, a delicious sparkling wine, pale peach in color, with a bright citrusy flavor—a perfect summer wine with a celebratory aura to it. Tours are offered daily for C$5 at 1:30pm from late May through October and by appointment

7

THE WINE-COUNTRY EXPERIENCE

Niagara Region's Wineries

in the winter. The 1-hour tour includes a detailed explanation of grape growing, wine-making, and wine appreciation. Also included is a visit to the naturally cooled barrel cellar, which is 6m (20 ft.) underground. A tasting of four table wines costs C$2. A limit of four 1-ounce samples per person applies. There is an additional charge for Icewine tastings.

1469 Pelham Rd., R.R. 1, St. Catharines. © **905/684-8423.** www.henryofpelham.com. Late May–Oct daily 10am–6pm; Nov–May daily 10am–5pm.

Hillebrand Estates Winery ★★ (Four Mile Creek) This winery is a great start-ing point for a tour of the wine country because of its extensive facilities, which just underwent a C$3-million renovation. With the addition of more outdoor tasting areas, including the Winemaker's Lookout—a two-story stone structure that over-looks the vineyard—the cobblestone village feels like it's growing. Established in 1979, Hillebrand is one of the original wineries in the area, and as such, has mastered the art of tours.

If you want to unveil the mysteries of how a wine interacts with your senses of sight, smell, and taste, then I recommend the Winery Experience Seminars (C$10 per person). The "Art of Winemaking" seminar is suitable for wine novices, but expe-rienced oenophiles may find this to be a welcome refresher course. Led by Hille-brand's knowledgeable and charismatic resident wine consultants, the seminar is a lesson on the inner workings of winemaking. Other seminars include specialized sparkling wine and Icewine sessions and an explanation of cellaring, with tips for identifying wines that will benefit from aging. My favorite seminar is "*Trius*—The Art of Red"—visitors can create their own red wine blend: Working in a team, you choose how much cabernet or merlot you want in your bottle as the winemaker takes you through the steps of creating a blended red wine. At the end, you can then create your own label, name it, and take it home.

The tasting bar offers a flight of three preselected wines for C$5 to C$10, or you can select your own wine to sample. Table wine prices run from C$10 to C$80. Hil-lebrand Estates Winery Restaurant is one of the top Niagara wine-country dining destinations, open for lunch and dinner. See the listing in chapter 5, "Where to Eat."

1249 Niagara Stone Rd., Niagara-on-the-Lake. © **800/582-8412** or 905/468-7123. www.hillebrand. com. Daily 10am–6pm; varies slightly by season.

Inniskillin ★ (Niagara River) Inniskillin is one of the largest Niagara wineries, producing about 150,000 cases a year, and with that size, it's a venue that has some-thing to offer a variety of tastes, from wine and food to architecture. The winery added a new tasting area in 2007; the Founders' Hall includes a demonstration kitchen where you can learn about wine and food pairings firsthand. The interior is rustic but sleek, with a glass facade, high beams, and a large open space with various tasting stations. Architecture buffs may appreciate the influences of Frank Lloyd Wright and J. D. Larkin in the winery's buildings. During the summer months, visi-tors can enjoy "small plate" dining, from dishes like fresh cauliflower soup with Niagara Gold cheese and cold-pressed canola oil drizzle for C$5, to a flatbread pizza with charcuterie, arugula, white truffle oil, and goat cheese for C$10. Or try a dessert, paired with a glass of Icewine. For tastings, samples are offered at C$1 for table wines—more for Icewines. Bottles range from C$12 and up. Guests are able to sample and go or linger and sit down for a formal flight tasting.

Guided tours are offered for C$9 daily between May and October until 4:30pm and until 2:30pm in the winter and include two tasting samples of table wines and

affordable ICEWINE?

There's no denying the fact that Icewine is expensive. In 2007, Royal DeMaria Wines sold a 2000 chardonnay for $30,000, making it the world's most expensive Icewine. But producers say the cost is justified by several hard facts. The grapes are at the mercy of nature in every vintage, and vintners cannot predict or control how much fruit will be left on the vines when the time for harvest eventually arrives, or what condition the grapes will be in. The process is labor-intensive, since the grapes are handpicked within a brief timeframe. Labor costs are high, since often trained workers (depending on the winery) must be enticed to go into the vineyards at short notice, in the middle of the night in extreme cold, to pick the frozen grapes. Yields are small—it takes 3 to 3.5kg (6⅔-7¾ lb.) of grapes to make one 375mL (13-oz.) bottle of Icewine. The same amount of grapes would make three 750mL (25-oz.) bottles of table wine.

Having said all of that, if your wallet will not stretch to Icewine's price tag, seek out one of the new, smaller 200mL (6¾-oz.) bottles. Watch out for sales of older vintage Icewines in the winery boutiques.

For exceptional value, try a select late-harvest dessert wine. This is made from the second pressing of the grapes, after they have thawed for several hours. The resulting wine retains much of Icewine's delectable aromas, but approximately one-third of the sugar content—and one-third of the price. Some people prefer its less sweet character at the end of a meal, and it is perfect when paired with good cheese and a ripe local pear.

one of Icewine. Other specialty tours include a Riedel Stemware seminar, an Inniskillin Classic Tour with Artisanal Cheeses, and an Icewine Experience, and range in price from C$10 to C$35 per person. If available, try their 2007 Pinot Grigio, which won double gold at the San Francisco International Wine Competition and has rich peach and melon notes. The winery has a well-stocked wine boutique housed in the barn, with gifts and accessories. Visit during the harvest (Sept–Oct) and you will be rewarded with the heady, blissful aroma of fresh juice as the grapes are gathered and processed right alongside the main visitor entrance.

S.R. 66, R.R. 1 Niagara Pkwy., Niagara-on-the-Lake. © **888/466-4754** or 905/468-2187. www.inniskillin. com. May–Oct daily 10am–6pm; Nov–Apr daily 10am–5pm.

Jackson-Triggs Niagara Estate Winery   (Four Mile Creek) If you have a keen interest in technology, you will be intrigued by the tour at Jackson-Triggs. Their state-of-the-art, gravity-flow-assisted production is one of the most technologically advanced in Canada. Hour-long tours are available for C$9 (refunded with purchase of wine) and include three tastings. Individual bottles of Jackson-Triggs wine range from C$9 and up for table wine and between C$45 and C$75 for Icewine. Although there isn't a full-scale restaurant on-site, small plates are available in the Tasting Gallery or outside on the Vineyard Patio during the summer months, and the winery holds special food and wine events throughout the year—including their popular "Savour the Sights," a unique dining experience with several courses, each served at different locations within the winery. Tucked away beyond the rear of the winery lies an open-air amphitheater, with rows of curved stone seating built into the grassy hillside. Seasonal entertainment is on offer between July and September—call ahead for details of who is performing and when. Past performers have included Chantal Kreviazuk, Hawksley Workman, Gord Downie, and the comedy troupe Women Fully Clothed. There are two tasting rooms—it's C$1 per sample at the tasting bar within the boutique, and at the premium tasting room with an outdoor terrace, each sample has a price tag of C$3 to C$4. Cheese platters can be purchased to accompany wines by the glass. Keep your eyes open for the half-dozen or so sample rows of different grape varietals growing in front of the winery. It's a great opportunity to see the vines and their fruit at close quarters.

2145 Niagara Stone Rd., Niagara-on-the-Lake. ℂ **905/468-4637,** ext. 3, concierge desk. www.jackson triggswinery.com. Summer daily 10:30am–6:30pm; winter daily 10:30am–5:30pm.

Marynissen Estates Winery (Four Mile Creek) Follow along the pretty Concession 1 side road and pull into the wood-clad tasting room and wine store. This small estate vineyard is family-owned and -run—you are likely to meet family members across the tasting bar counter. Some of the oldest vines in Canada thrive in the vineyards here. Founding winemaker John Marynissen was the first grower to successfully cultivate cabernet sauvignon grapes in Canada, at a time when the belief was firm that the Ontario climate was too harsh to support *vinifera* grapes. John's daughter Sandra is now the head winemaker and makes Sandra's Summer Blend, a nice, light summer white wine made from chardonnay, sauvignon blanc, and vidal. Because the winery is small, there are no formal tours available. From 10am to 5pm daily, come in for a taste for C50¢—no charge with purchase of wine. Varietals include sauvignon blanc, gamay, merlot, and their prestigious cabernet sauvignon. The Rolling Stones ordered several cases of Marynissen's wines when they were performing in Toronto.

R.R. 6, 1208 Concession 1, Niagara-on-the-Lake. ℂ **905/468-7270.** www.marynissen.com. May–Oct daily 10am–6pm; Nov–Apr daily 10am–5pm.

Peller Estates Winery ★★★ (Niagara River) One of Canada's largest producers of wine, Peller Estates is a grand property that echoes the distinguished château estates of the Old World. The interior of the main entrance immediately evokes a feeling of stepping into a splendid hotel lobby. Sweeping staircases, comfortable upholstered seating, a giant fireplace, wood paneling, warm caramel walls, and spacious public spaces all contribute to the luxurious setting. Excellent seminars are on offer, and they are carefully coordinated with nearby Hillebrand seminars so that they complement each other rather than repeat content between the two wineries. "The Art of Wine & Food" is an hour-long seminar that pairs three canapés with three

WINE COUNTRY touring PASS

One of the best ways to experience a range of wineries very affordably is with this pass. The Wine Country Touring Pass gives guests VIP access to Niagara's best wine experiences. Guests can spend a full day touring and tasting through Wine Country at four of the region's most unique wine destinations:

Peller Estates, Hillebrand Winery, Thirty Bench Wine Makers, and Wine Country Vintners. The Pass costs C$20 and can be booked online through the participating wineries. Bring your confirmation and pick your pass up at any of the four locations.

wines. In a formal boardroom, visitors are lead through a tasting and encouraged to give their opinions and to ask questions. Several types of winery tours are offered year-round starting at C$10. Tours start at 10:30am in the summer, running on the half-hour every hour, typically until 7:30pm. In the winter, tours start at 11:30am and run until 5:30pm. Individual samples range from C$1 to C$5 for Icewine selections. The reserve wines are reliably first-rate. If you are a sauvignon blanc devotee, make sure you taste one or more here. Wine prices start at C$10 and top at C$40 for table wine selections. Icewines can hit C$95. Peller Estates Winery Restaurant, led by chef Jason Parsons, is quite simply one of the best in Niagara's wine country. The chef also leads cooking and tasting demonstrations in the vineyards. See chapter 5, "Where to Eat," for more detailed information. A shuttle service is available between Niagara-on-the-Lake's old town district and the winery—call the winery for details. Packages that include lunch or dinner at the winery restaurant, tickets for the Shaw Theatre Festival, and overnight accommodations are available.

290 John St. E., Niagara-on-the-Lake. ℂ **905/468-4578** (winery) or 888/673-5537 for information on events in and around the vineyard. www.peller.com. Daily 10am–6pm; extended hours in summer.

Pillitteri Estates Winery (Four Mile Creek) This large family-run winery is t world's largest estate producer of Icewine. Free tours are offered at noon and 2 The tour includes a detailed walking tour of the facility, followed by a wine ta No reservations are required. Open to groups of 10 persons or fewer. Try th Shiraz Icewine, a ruby-colored wine with hints of candied cherry and an u note of spice, plus balanced acidity. It pairs perfectly with a dessert or che end of a fine meal. There's a good wine boutique, a small dining area, tables. It's a busy place and an interesting stop on the wine tour route.

1696 Niagara Stone Rd., Niagara-on-the-Lake. ℂ **905/468-3147.** www.pillitteri.com. Oct daily 10am–8pm; mid-Oct to mid-May daily 10am–6pm.

Vineland Estates Winery ★★★ (Twenty Mile Bench) Easily attractive wineries in the Peninsula, this winery is reached by dr lined country road. Set on a reconstructed 1845 Mennonite vi coach house and adjacent buildings nestle comfortably into the Estates is one of the largest wineries in Niagara, and is an ex the region. You will find Vineland wines in the U.S., U.K., countries around the world. In their stylish wine boutiqu accompaniments such as salsas and oils, as well as stemw the large tasting bar has a good selection of wines, and t to share their knowledge and personal points of view o for tasting. Summer lunch on the shaded terrace of the of the best locally sourced cuisine, will give visitors mate atmosphere that is Vineland's specialty. (See about the winery's restaurant.) Try their 2008 Ri medal at the American Wine Society Awards in 2 que, which was awarded silver at the Ontario V

Organized tours and tastings are available, yards, production area, and cellars to tour and and cheese, or specialized Icewine tours a twice daily between May and October, a in the fall and spring. Tours between Ja

THE WINE-COUNTRY EXPERIENCE

Lower-priced wines can be sampled free of charge; a nominal fee applies for premium wines. Bottles range from C$12 to around C$250.

3620 Moyer Rd., Vineland. (C) **888/846-3526** or 905/562-7088. www.vineland.com. May–Dec daily 10am–6pm; Jan–Apr daily 10am–5pm. Tours late May to Oct daily 11am and 3pm; Nov-Dec, Apr to mid-May Sat-Sun 3pm; Jan-Mar by appointment only.

The Iconoclasts: For the Connoisseur

These winemakers are fiercely independent, aggressively pushing the boundaries of winemaking convention, and often passionately striving for levels of quality that are only attainable in a small, personally run operation. These are the winemakers who are, or who will be, making headlines in the wine world. Oenophiles who want to explore the latest innovations and savor the character notes of handcrafted wines should visit these wineries.

Daniel Lenko Estate Winery ★★ (Beamsville Bench) Don't let the rustic shambles of the property fool you. Daniel Lenko is making some of the best chardonnay in Niagara. His tasting room is the farmhouse kitchen, his opinions are strong and strongly expressed, and his passion for winemaking is legendary. He is fiercely independent. The vineyards have the oldest chardonnay and merlot vines in Canada, producing fruit with intense and complex flavors. Due to small production, the wines are currently only available at the winery and some restaurants, and only occasionally at the LCBO (Liquor Control Board of Ontario). His 2007 Chardonnay is delicious, with orange blossom, apple, pineapple, and pear flavors, but he only sells it by the case. I particularly like his 2008 White Cabernet, a wonderful summer wine with elegant balance and raspberry and cassis notes. But it is only available by the case as well. If you aren't sure what you like, try the Taster Pack, a six-bottle cross-section of his wines for C$150. He also makes a viognier Icewine, totally unique to his winery, full of mango, melon, peach, apricot, and toffee flavors. He has also produced Charonnay, the first wine in celebration of Canada's diverse gay culture. For every bottle d, C$1 will be donated to AIDS research.

R.R. 81, Beamsville. (C) **905/563-7756.** www.daniellenko.com. Tastings Sat–Sun noon–5pm (call during the winter months).

ign Affair ★★★ (Lincoln Lakeshore) Len and Marisa Crispino fell in love he amarone style wines of Italy during a diplomatic posting in Milan. When turned to Canada, the love affair continued, and the couple opened a winery uld be devoted to developing Niagara wines produced using the appassimento It is the method of manually harvesting only perfect bunches of fruit, which n left on the vine longer than usual to concentrate sugars.

rvested grape bunches are laid out on straw or bamboo mats in controlled e rooms to allow air to freely flow around the grapes. The grapes are left to eral months, until they have lost from 35% to 40% of their weight, and have nigh concentrations of sugar and flavor. It is an expensive and labor inten-l of wine production, but the wines are considered to be some of the delicious, with rich raisin aromas, and powerful full-bodied flavors. hat used to be the Vineland Experimental Station, Foreign Affair has turning Niagara grapes into the Canadian interpretation of the Italian uction is limited and the prices range from C$28 to C$110, a reflec-, labor, and concentration of grapes required to produce the wines. A $110 Cabernet Franc 2007, with its hints of dried raisin, licorice, and a special and memorable treat.

Be Kind to Your Palate

If you're planning on visiting several wineries in a day, and therefore potentially tasting one or two dozen wines (law dictates that each winery may serve up to four 1-oz. samples of wine), try narrowing your tasting choices in order to make the most of your olfactory and taste experience. The simplest plan is to stick to red or white. Beyond that, you could choose a vintage known to be a particularly good year locally, or a single varietal, or only light or full-bodied wines. Have fun with it—taste whites in the morning and reds in the afternoon, or stick to Icewines and fruit wines. It's your choice!

4890 Victoria Ave. North, Vineland Station. ⓒ **905/562-9898** or 877/AMARON1 [262-7661]. www. foreignaffairwine.com. Thurs–Sun by appointment. The wines are available for purchase only at the winery or online, and are featured at selected area restaurants.

Hidden Bench ★★★ (Beamsville Bench) This artisanal winery is dedicated to producing ultra-premium wines solely from vineyards within the Beamsville Bench VQA sub-appellation. The winery sprang to national prominence with the award-winning Nuit Blanche, a white wine that combined sauvignon blanc and semillon. Their Terroir Series wines are produced in very limited quantities and represent the best premium wines that the Beamsville Bench can produce. Sometimes—because of stringent quality standards and small cuvee philosophy, coupled with old vine planting limitations—these wines will have a total production of only 100 to 250 cases annually and will only be produced when the vintage warrants. The Terroir wines frequently sell out quickly. Try their 2007 Locust Lane Riesling or the 2006 Terroir Cache. The meticulous care taken with every step of the winemaking process means that Hidden Bench wines are uncompromisingly evocative of the place where they are grown and are of very high quality. Winemaker Marlize Beyers brings a South African expertise to the wines, and Meg McGrath adds an Aussie accent to the retail store.

4152 Locust Lane, Beamsville. ⓒ **905/563-8700.** www.hiddenbench.com. Apr–Nov daily 10:30am–5:30pm; Dec–Mar Sat-Sun 10:30am–5:30pm.

John Howard Cellars of Distinction: Megalomaniac ★★★ (Twenty Mile Bench) Howard is one of the founders of Niagara wines, having created the blockbuster success of Vineland Estates. His retirement project, Megalomaniac Wines, is audacious and innovative. Housed in a winery that is mostly buried in the limestone of the Niagara Escarpment, the wines have achieved overnight success. And no wonder. The grapes for the Megalomaniac collection are harvested using European viticultural standards, from the 45 hectares (110 acres) of prime vineyards surrounding the Howard Estate. From the French vats to the French oak barrels, everything is the best. His winemaker, Sue-Ann Staff, comes from a long-established Niagara farming family. Howard produces affordable wines, most of which are under C$25, with such stylish labels and provocative names as Sonofabitch Pinot Noir, Narcissist Riesling, Big Mouth Merlot, and Cold Hearted Cabernet Franc Icewine. But the wines are winning prizes and praise. The Megalomaniac 2007 Narcissist Riesling is a perfect summer sipping wine, with aromas of clover, citrus, and peach. I recently did a barrel sampling of the 2007 reds (Howard barrels his wines for 22 months), and they were outstanding. The merlot was so full-bodied and fruity that it coated the glass like paint. His 2007 "Sous Terre" cab merlot Reserve won the Cuvee 2011 Gold award for best limited edition red wine, the equivalent in the Canadian wine world of winning Best Picture at the Academy Awards.

You can taste the wines at the winery on Cherry Avenue on weekends during the summer. There's a long oak bar set up right in the winery so visitors can watch the winemaking process while they sip. Megalomaniac wines can be purchased at the winery and are served in some select restaurants. Some are carried by the LCBO. The best way to buy the wines is to order them from the website.

3930 Cherry Ave., Vineland. ✆ **888/MEGALO-1** [634-2561] or 905/562-5155. www.megalomaniacwine. com. Tastings mid-May–Dec, daily 11am–5pm; Jan–mid-May by appointment.

Le Clos Jordanne ★★★ (Twenty Mile Bench) The winery is a partnership between the large Canadian firm, Vincor Canada, and the French house of **Boisset France,** a first for a Burgundy wine producer, and thus has attracted much attention. The winery employs the Burgundian traditions of mixing clones within planting blocks, spacing vines tightly, and using vertical shoot positioning to position the shoots toward the sun to ensure optimal photosynthesis, air circulation, and ripening. Only the best Burgundian clones were planted following organic/biodynamic farming methods. No synthetic fertilizers or pesticides are employed. The *terroir* is allowed to come through in the wines. Wild yeasts are used in their winemaking; the fermentation process is gentle and unhurried; and they minimize fining and filtration to preserve the flavor compounds. Le Clos is concentrating mainly on two types of grapes: pinot noir and chardonnay. Wisely, the winery engaged a good winemaker in Canadian-born Thomas Bachelder, who spent several years making wine in Burgundy. Le Clos Jordanne caught the attention of the wine community through a blind tasting held in Montreal for *Cellier* magazine. In the "Judgement of Montreal," 10 judges assessed 30 wines, primarily from France and California. Le Clos Jordanne's 2005 Claystone Terrace, a "pirate wine" in the tasting, rocked the wine world when it was chosen as the world's best chardonnay. This is a winery with big star power, producing superior wines. They are on the expensive side, ranging from C$35 to C$70, but represent some of the best wines from Niagara.

2540 South Service Rd., Jordan Station. ✆ **905/562-9404.** www.leclosjordanne.com. By appointment only.

Organized Crime (Beamsville Bench) Named after an incident involving a Mennonite church and a purloined pipe organ, this small winery makes limited production, handcrafted wines. Try their 2006 Pinot Noir with notes of dried cherry, silky and delicious.

4043 Mountainview Rd., Beamsville. ✆ **905/563-9802.** www.organizedcrimewine.com. May–Nov Wed–Mon 10am–6pm; Dec–Apr Fri–Sat 10am–6pm.

Sue-Ann Staff Estate Winery (Twenty Mile Bench) Sue-Ann is kind of the aristocracy of Niagara farming. Her family has been growing grapes and making wine in Niagara for five generations. She was named Winemaker of the Year in 2002 at the Ontario Wine Awards, and named one of the top four "Women in Wine" by the International Wine and Spirits Awards in London, England. She is the winemaster for John Howard Cellars of Distinction, and now she is the proprietor of her own winery and vineyard. There are plans to build a larger facility, but for now the tasting room will be in the farmhouse. If you are lucky, Brix the wonder dog, a lovely and friendly Bernese mountain dog (who loves to have his belly scratched), will be on duty. Sue-Ann's first vintage was bottled in July 2009. Keep an eye on her wines. She is one to watch.

3210 Staff Ave., St. Catharines. ✆ **905/562-1719.** www.staffwine.com. Sat–Sun, 11am–5pm.

SERVE YOUR WINE AT ITS IDEAL
temperature

You may not be aware, but as you wander in and out of tasting rooms and winery bars, the wine you taste will (hopefully) have been carefully stored and served at the optimum temperature for its particular characteristics.

Pay heed to the following practical advice, if for no other reason than that the wines you taste while touring and then lug home by the caseload will simply not taste the same at home unless you serve them at their intended temperature:

○ The cooler the wine, the less bouquet it will have, and conversely, the warmer the wine, the more bouquet will be detectable.

○ Acidity and tannins are accentuated at lower temperatures and diminished at higher temperatures.

Here are some simple guidelines for serving temperatures. Light, sweet white wines and sparkling wine may be refrigerated for 4 or more hours. Most other white wines and light reds may be chilled for 1½ to 2 hours in the fridge. Full, dry white wines may be served slightly warmer—1 hour in the fridge will do. Medium and full, rich red wines should be served slightly below room temperature, and certainly no more than 64°F (18°C). If you do not have a temperature-controlled wine fridge (and not many of us do), then you will have to get creative as to how you cool your red wines for serving. In the Rhône Valley in France, for instance, you will see bottles of wine sitting outside the door of many a home in the early evening. This is not an offering to St. Vincent, the patron saint of French *vignerons,* but a practical method of coaxing the wine to the correct serving temperature in time for the evening meal, which is served much later in the evening in France than in North America.

And finally, don't mistreat the wine you have just purchased by letting it cook in your car on a hot summer's day. Bring a cooler and a few ice packs with you to protect your wine from deteriorating due to exposure to high temperatures.

Sophisticated & Edgy

These are the wineries that are architecturally special, as well as lovely to look at while you taste their wines. Novices with an eye for style should check these out.

Peninsula Ridge Estates Winery ★★ (Beamsville Bench) An attractively restored and renovated Queen Anne–revival red-brick home at the end of the long, sweeping drive into the estate is the showpiece of this winery. The Kitchen House Restaurant, in the heritage building, is highly recommended for lunch or dinner (see chapter 5, "Where to Eat," for listing information). The Winery Retail Shop is located in a meticulously restored 1885 post-and-beam barn. The atmosphere manages to be sophisticated and casual at the same time, making the space an inviting one in which to linger. Allow the staff to guide you through a tasting of VQA wines. Tastings are C$2 for four samples, and C$2 for one sample of Icewine. No appointment for wine tours is necessary if you have fewer than 10 people in your party. Tours of the winery production facilities are informative for beginners. A daily wine tour (C$5) is conducted at 11am from June through August, otherwise by appointment. The traditional underground cellar tour is also available (C$10). Keep an eye out for their viognier—smooth, dry, and peachy. Icewine here is made with my number-one choice of grape for this delectable nectar—cab franc. The strawberry aroma and flavor is memorable. Wine prices vary between C$10 and C$55.

5600 King St., Beamsville. ☏ **905/563-0900.** www.peninsularidge.com. May–Oct daily 10am–6pm; Nov–Apr Mon–Fri 11am–5:30pm, Sat–Sun 10am–5:30pm. Tours daily at 11:30am and 3pm.

Southbrook Vineyards ★★ (Four Mile Creek) The first thing you notice is the 200m-long (656-ft.) lavender blue wall at the front of the Jack Diamond–designed pavilion. It is constructed to make the winery blend seamlessly with the land and the sky, making it an organic part of the landscape. The winery is certified LEED Gold, the second-highest rating available, and produces the first biodynamic wine in Canada, the 2008 Cabernet Rosé, a pretty and drinkable wine, released with perfect timing on Earth Day. The winery is both certified organic and has Demeter certification in biodynamics. That is about as green as a winery can get. Southbrook's limited edition wines are called Poetica—an artist series celebrating the words of Canadian poets. The winery has a lovely outdoor patio with a view of the vineyards in summer months and offers light lunches with wine.

581 Niagara Stone Rd., R.R. 4, Niagara-on-the-Lake. ☏ **888/581-1581** or 905/641-2548. www. southbrook.com. Mon–Sat 10am–5pm; Sun 11am–5pm. Patio: June–Sept daily 11:30am–4:30pm.

Stratus ★★ (Four Mile Creek) Stratus is urbane, high-end, and sleek. It's well worth a visit. With its futuristic steel facade, the winery became the first Leadership in Energy and Environmental Design (LEED) building in Canada, and the first LEED-certified winery in the world. In addition to such features as geothermal heating and cooling technology and a system for composting organic waste, the winery is four stories high to allow a gravity-feed production system to function, a necessity on the relatively flat landscape of the Niagara-on-the-Lake region. Premium prices have been set for the narrow range of wines on offer. The French-born winemaker has chosen to create two signature blends, Stratus White and Stratus Red, with a small number of single varietals including chardonnay and merlot. Wine critic Konrad Ejbich has only one complaint of Stratus's Riesling Icewine. Garnering a 99 out of 100, its only imperfection was bottle size: It wasn't large enough. Table wines typically run between C$30 and C$45. Tastings are offered from Wednesday to Sunday and no reservation is needed. Sample three wines for C$10. Tours are by appointment only and cost C$15 per person.

2059 Niagara Stone Rd., Niagara-on-the-Lake. ☏ **905/468-1806.** www.stratuswines.com. Daily 11am–5pm. Seminars held weekly; call for times and to reserve a space.

Tawse Winery ★ (Twenty Mile Bench) This very successful winery was named Winery of the Year in 2010 by *Wine Access* magazine and won a record five gold medals at the Canadian Wine Awards. The 2008 Robyn's Block Chardonnay won the White Wine of the Year with a score of 93 out of 100, the highest ever achieved by a table wine in this competition. The modern architecture of the Tawse winery building features clean, simple lines, making its presence in the landscape unobtrusive. A large pond is situated in front of the winery, providing the building with geothermal energy for heating and cooling. Due to its position on the bench, the winery is able to use the hillside terrain to its advantage, and uses a six-level gravity-feed system for its winemaking process. The winery plans to focus on traditional burgundy-style wines, and its chardonnays are certainly stirring the hearts of local wine critics. Small amounts of cabernet franc, pinot noir, and Riesling wines are also produced here. Many of the grapes used for Tawse wines are from old-growth, low-yield vines, which have a tendency to yield greater depth of character when vinified. Try the Tawse 2008 Quarry Road Chardonnay, an award-winning wine described by the winemaker as

celebrity WINERIES

Niagara has taken on a Hollywood glow as celebrities bring their reputations to the vineyards.

In June 2007, Diamond Estates Wines and Spirits Agency introduced the first two **Dan Aykroyd**-branded varietals that included the Dan Aykroyd Discovery Series Chardonnay and the Dan Aykroyd Discovery Series Cabernet Merlot. Since being launched, the wines have generated over C$1.5 million in net sales. Recently, two new Dan Aykroyd wines were launched into the Ontario market, a sauvignon blanc and a cabernet-shiraz, which won the "Best LCBO Red Wine" award at the 2009 Cuvee Wine Awards. There isn't really a Dan Aykroyd winery—he's a label. His wines are made at **20 Bees Winery** (1067 Niagara Stone Rd., Virgil; © 905/641-1042; www.20bees.com) and are available there as well as at the LCBO. But his notoriety has raised the profile of Niagara wines, and his well-marketed wines continue to win accolades.

There couldn't be a more perfect partnership than that between **Mike Weir,** Canada's most famous golfer, and Niagara, Canada's largest wine-producing area and home to some of the best golf courses in the country. His move has focused an international spotlight on both the golf and wine industries in Niagara. **Mike Weir Wines** (www.mike weirwine.com) was launched in April 2005, with 5,000 cases, and now sells more than 30,000 cases annually. His 2008 Riesling won Best White Wine of the Year, and a gold medal in 2011 at the Ontario Wine Awards. Net proceeds from the sales of Weir Wines support the Mike Weir Foundation, which assists the physical, emotional, and educational welfare of children in Canada. Weir has forged a new partnership with Château des Charmes to produce his wines, and has an exciting project to locate the home of Mike Weir Wines on a 6-hectare (15-acre) parcel of land adjacent to the Whirlpool Golf Course. The partnership with Niagara Parks has been delayed, mostly due to a major reorganization within the board of the Parks Commission, but the plans involve the construction of the Mike Weir Winery, a winery retail and hospitality center, its food and beverage components, and a Mike Weir gallery, as well as the planting of grapes and on-site processing. You've got to love this guy. When he hosted the Champions dinner at Augusta National Golf Club in 2004 following his Masters win, he insisted that all the wine be VQA wines from Niagara. And when his wines were served at the Toronto Film Festival, actor George Clooney declared Mike's chardonnay to be "outstanding."

Wayne Gretzky is a Canadian ice hockey icon, having made the top 10 list of the CBC's Greatest Canadians, so when he turned his interest to Niagara wine, much attendant publicity ensued. While he is participating from a distance—he still lives in Arizona—he has played a significant part in the development of the wines. No. 99 Estates Winery (3751 King St., Vineland; © 905/562-4945; www. gretzky.com) has a small, casual restaurant and welcomes visitors for tastings. While the chances of seeing the Great One on your visit are slim, his celebrity aura adds a shine to the wine. His wines are available online, at the winery, and at restaurants and the LCBO. The winery is open daily 10am to 6pm in summer, and daily 10am to 5pm in winter.

having "a rich palate of lemony citrus, crisp green apple, and a pleasant, pronounced minerality." Tours of the innovative production facilities, which include sampling in the winery store and in the barrel cellar, cost C$20 per person and must be booked in advance. In the tasting room, you can get two 2-ounce samples for C$5. Wines hover around the C$30 to C$40 mark.

3955 Cherry Ave., Vineland. ✆ **905/562-9500.** www.tawsewinery.ca. May–Oct 10am–6pm; Nov–Apr 10am–5pm. Call ahead to confirm opening hours.

Benchmark Wineries: Something New, Something Different, Something for Everyone

These wineries are proving to the world that Niagara is a viable, dependable, and exciting winegrowing area. They are also proving that there's young and innovative new blood moving into wine territory to push the boundaries and raise the bar. The variety in character and product is so large that whether you're a novice or a connoisseur, you are sure to find a wine and a winemaker to suit your taste. Try to visit three or four different ones.

Angel's Gate (Beamsville Bench) The name comes from the building's former life as a convent. As you walk up to the winery door, you pass by a tranquil garden. Wine production—from receiving to crushing and fermentation—is carried on underground, where temperatures are constant. A waterfall lends a peaceful element to the open-air garden room. Facing a fabulous view of Lake Ontario is a generous-sized terrace used for warm-weather dining until October. The Terrace lunch includes nibbles such as a tapas platter, a cheese and artisan bread platter, and an herbed mushroom and goat cheese dip. On the wine side, Angel's Gate is producing some good full-bodied wines, including their flagship wine, Angels III, a merlot-dominant Bordeaux mix of two cabernets and estate-grown merlot. The 2006 Merlot is big-hearted and smoky. Tours, by appointment and costing C$5, include a guided tour of the vineyards, cellar, and barrel rooms, followed by a tasting and cheese platter. Your fee is refunded if you purchase a bottle of wine. Sampling of four wines is free, and Icewine samples are C$2. Expect to pay between C$12 and C$40 for individual bottles of wine. Seminars are held on the how and why of decanting, how to build and stock a home wine cellar, and other wine-related topics.

4260 Mountainview Rd., Beamsville. ✆ **877/264-4283** or 905/563-3942. www.angelsgatewinery.com. June–Oct Mon–Sat 10am–5:30pm, Sun 11am–5:30pm; Nov–May Sun–Fri 11am–5pm, Sat 10am–5pm.

Between The Lines Family Estate Winery (Four Mile Creek) This new winery is run by two brothers in an old red barn between Lines Five and Six on the Four Mile Creek Road near Niagara-on-the-Lake. Greg and Yannick are two of the youngest winemakers in the area, but their passion for winemaking is as old as time. Yannick is the winemaker, and Greg looks after the vineyard. Their first vintage was produced in 2009, consisting of wines ranging from a fresh and fruity Riesling to a robust cabernet merlot with lots of dark berry flavors. They are open daily, but call ahead to make an appointment if you plan to come for a tasting.

991 Four Mile Creek Rd., Niagara-on-the-Lake. ✆ **905/262-0289.** www.betweenthelineswinery.com.

Colaneri Estate Winery (St. David's Bench) This is a new winery from a family that has grown grapes on this spot for years. The winery is an oddball place—it is a work in progress, about half completed when I visited, and the estimate of a completion date is vague. But visit this unique winery to see the work in progress. When done, it will be Niagara's largest winery at 31,000 square feet. It is impressive and ambitious, with four floors, including large spaces for big events and floor-to-ceiling windows that give lovely views of the vineyards. The tasting room is elegant, and the barrel cellar is state-of-the-art. The building is curved in a C shape (for Colaneri).

The wines are impressive too, done mostly in the appassimento style, big and aggressive, and generally high in alcohol.

348 Concession 6 Rd., Niagara-on-the-Lake. ✆ **905/682-2100.** www.colaneriwines.com. Daily 11am–5pm; 11am–6pm Sat-Sun May–Oct.

Featherstone Estate Winery (Twenty Mile Bench) The smallest full-time winery in Niagara, this laid-back family-run business is located in the owners' 1830s farmhouse. Featherstone is a small but earnest winery with high standards of land and crop management, resulting in wines of high quality, although limited quantity—3,500 cases (Jackson-Triggs produces 150,000!). The estate is a modest 9 hectares (22 acres), but its size makes it amenable to the personal care and attention lavished upon it. In their former life, the family owned a specialty-food store, and they contend their wines are best served with food. Not coincidentally, the patio serves a fantastic selection of platters, including antipasto, cheese, and charcuterie. Growing some of the oldest Riesling vines, their whites are excellent, while their 2011 Rose won double gold/Best of Category at the All Canadian Wine Championships. Visitors looking for unique wines not available elsewhere would appreciate a visit here; this winery also subscribes to a natural philosophy: Most recently a flock of New Zealand sheep have been enlisted to prune the lower vines—something unique to the region and fun to watch. The vineyard also employs a resident Harris Hawk to help control the pesky birds that damage the grapes. The owners also provide tours, lasting about 40 minutes, for groups of eight or more people by appointment only. The C$5 tour includes three samples. Three to four tasting samples, without the tour, are complimentary.

A surprisingly wide choice of wines is available, but some wines are limited in production to as few as 40 cases, so buy a case or two right there and then if there's a wine that really speaks to you. Individual bottles cost about C$12 to C$30. Food is served between 11am and 4pm Fridays to Mondays from late May to early September.

3678 Victoria Ave., Vineland. ✆ **905/562-1949.** www.featherstonewinery.ca. Apr–Dec Wed–Mon 10am–6pm; Jan–Mar by appointment or chance.

Fielding Estate Winery (Beamsville Bench) Located on the Beamsville Bench near the Niagara Escarpment on a secluded plot of land, a contemporary white cottage made of cedar, glass, and stone overlooks the vineyard and Lake Ontario in the background. "Better a drop of the extraordinary than an ocean of the ordinary" is the philosophy of this winery, which produces a maximum of 10,000 cases a year. Because of this limited production, Fielding wines are available only through the on-site wine and gift shop, online, and through select LCBO vintage sections. The winery focuses on traditional wines of 15 varietals priced between C$13 and C$36, including merlot, cabernet franc, pinot noir, and syrah. The selection of white wines includes chardonnay, Riesling, pinot gris, and Icewine. The C$5 tour (10:30am and 1:30 and 3:30pm) is informative but not overburdened with information—you're invited to ask questions. Tours include three tastings. Try the 2006 Viognier, with its notes of pear, spice, and florals. It won gold at the 2008 Ontario Wine Awards. Named the Ontario legislature's official winery for 2007, this winery is producing some fine wines. Winter tours by appointment only.

4020 Locust Lane, Beamsville. ✆ **905/563-0668.** www.fieldingwines.com. May–Oct 10:30am–6pm; Nov–Apr 10:30am–5:30pm.

Five Rows Craft Winery (St. David's Bench) While the winery is quite new, the Lowrey family has been growing grapes on this property for five generations. In 1984, Howard Lowery ripped out some of his tender fruit and juice grapes and planted five

THE INS & OUTS OF shipping WINE HOME

Many of the wines you will encounter in the Niagara wine region are available only at the winery. A number of the larger producers do sell some of their series in Ontario retail stores across the province, and a few export selected wines to the United States. For the most part, however, the best way to get your case (or cases!) home is to arrange for the winery to handle shipment. Each winery has its own policy for delivery of wine—many deliver only in Ontario, some deliver across Canada and to selected U.S. states, still others are willing to send product overseas, while a few sell their wines only on the premises.

If you are a resident of Ontario, you can order Niagara VQA wines online from Wine Country at Home, a wine club that is run jointly by Peller Estates and Hillebrand Winery. It offers members benefits that include wine education and tastings, monthly wine specials, and visiting privileges at the two wineries. You can find out more about the program by visiting either www.hillebrand.com or www.pellar.com. It was established in response to customer demand for wines that are not usually available for purchase at places other than the wineries themselves. It's also worth visiting the websites of individual wineries for information on ordering and shipping their wines.

rows of pinot noir, the gesture for which the winery is named. With only 14 hectares (35 acres) , of grapes, this is a winery that is dedicated to small production, hand-cared-for vineyards and little interference with nature. They grow six main varietals, mainly pinot noir, but also cabernet sauvignon, pinot gris, shiraz, Riesling, and sauvignon blanc. If you taste a wine you like here, snap it up quickly. The yields are small and will disappear fast.

361 Tanbark Rd., St. David's. © **905/262-5113.** www.fiverows.com. Tastings Sat-Sun 11am-5pm, May 1 to Dec 31, or during the week by appointment.

Flat Rock Cellars ★ (Twenty Mile Bench) This young winery, opened in spring 2005, has stunning architecture, surpassed only by the view from the generous floor-to-ceiling windows over the vineyards and across Lake Ontario. On a clear day, you can see the CN Tower in Toronto. Perched up high, you get the feeling you're in a bird's nest. From the tasting bar, a short walk across a bridge takes you to the production facility. Free tours are available by appointment only and are highly recommended, as the production area is tour-friendly, with a catwalk around the perimeter that allows you to clearly see the various stages of production from an elevated position. The grapes, which have been deliberately restricted to Riesling, chardonnay, pinot noir, and vidal, are handpicked entirely from Flat Rock's own vineyards. The entire process from vine to bottle is handled as gently as possible—the juice for red wines is hand-stirred while skins are in contact rather than using a mechanically operated stirring device. The vineyard won Best Red Wine of the Year at the 2011 Ontario Wine Awards for their 2007 Rogue Syrah. One of the coolest attractions of this winery is El Gastronomo Vagabundo, a gourmet snack truck that locates at the winery for the summer weekends, serving surprising and inventive dishes like five spice pork belly or Moroccan lamb tagine. To bring a bottle home, you'll pay between C$15 and C$30 for table wine and up to C$40 for Icewine.

2727 Seventh Ave., Jordan. © **905/562-8994.** www.flatrockcellars.com. May-Oct daily 10am-6pm; Nov-Apr Sat-Sun 10am-6pm or by appointment. Tours available upon request.

The Good Earth Food and Wine Co. (Lincoln Lakeshore) Nicolette Novak wasn't satisfied to just run one of the best cooking schools in the country here, so she decided to start a winery as well, and has done that in her usual exemplary fashion. The Good Earth produced its first vintage in 2010. Their chardonnay, Riesling, pinot noir, and cabernet franc are hand-pruned to produce low-yield, high-quality grapes from their 15-acre (6 hectares) vineyard. The on-site wine boutique is the only place where you can purchase the wines. The Good Earth also offers a bistro and seasonal patio, food and wine pairings, in-depth wine and culinary tours, and gourmet picnics to go.

4556 Lincoln Ave., Beamsville. ℂ **905/563-6333.** www.goodearthfoodandwine.com. Winery hours, Nov–May 10:30am–5pm daily; May 20–Oct 31 11am–5:30pm daily.

Lailey Vineyard (Niagara River) A simple wood building with a glass facade marks this unpretentious and unique spot. Stand at the spotlessly clean counter, learn a little about the wines on offer from the approachable, knowledgeable staff, and enjoy an interesting variety of wines. Samples may include unoaked chardonnay (with an extremely pleasant green-apple note), dry Riesling, cabernet/merlot blend, or their Icewine. Lailey Vineyard and its winemaker Derek Barnett were the first commercial vintners to release wines fermented in Canadian oak barrels—their 2001 chardonnay. Four additional varietals have now been added to the Canadian oak method. The family has been making their exclusively estate-grown *Vitis vinifera* wines for more than 35 years, but the tasting room is a relatively recent venture where most samples are free. Wines start at C$12 and reach C$45. Because the winery is small, tours are available by appointment only. You're in for a treat if the winemaker or one of the owners conducts the tours (call ahead to ensure they conduct the tour)—they speak with passion, which is something that is missing from the tours at the larger wineries. Basic tours cost C$5, which includes four samples; tours including a cheese platter, four samples, and two Icewines cost C$15.

15940 Niagara Pkwy., Niagara-on-the-Lake. ℂ **905/468-0503.** www.laileyvineyard.com. May–Oct daily 10am–6pm; Nov–Apr daily 10am–5pm.

Niagara College Teaching (NCT) Winery (St. David's Bench) Members of the public are welcome to visit the Glendale Campus of Niagara College and see the students in action at the Niagara College Teaching Winery. There is a vineyard and winery on the campus, where students practice what they learn in the classroom. Their award-winning VQA wines are available for purchase at the wine boutique located near the entrance to Niagara College's Culinary Institute Dining Room (see chapter 5, "Where to Eat," for more information on the restaurant) and also at the Wine Education Centre across the road. Expect to spend between C$12 and C$50 for a bottle and between C$1 and C$3 for samples. With Terence van Rooyen on board as the new winemaker (from Stonechurch Winery), the college is expecting exciting new wines. Try the 2007 Dean's List Pinot Noir, with its flavors of beetroot and raspberry. While at the college, enjoy the beautiful multilevel display gardens designed to mimic the Niagara Escarpment, which forms a backdrop to the college. The Bruce Trail can be accessed nearby, and there are walking and biking trails on campus. The campus greenhouse is open to the public as well. Locals flock here to buy a wide variety of plants for home and garden, particularly in the spring bedding-plant season and in the weeks leading up to Christmas, when the greenhouse is filled with brightly colored poinsettias. For groups of eight or more, book a tour—choose from a half-hour guided walk with three samples for C$4 or an hour-long educational tour for C$16 (minimum 15 people). The Wine Education and Visitors Centre here will help you learn anything you want to know about Niagara and its wines.

Niagara College, Glendale Campus, 135 Taylor Rd., Niagara-on-the-Lake. ℂ **905/641-2252.** www.nctwinery.ca. Winery and retail store Mon–Sat 10am–5pm; Sun 11am–5pm.

Pondview Estate Winery   (Four Mile Creek) The owner of Pondview, Lou Puglisi, was named 2008 Grape king, a Ministry of Agriculture award for having the finest vineyard in Ontario. The winery is a newcomer, although the family has been growing grapes here since 1974. Their debut has been a notable one, with their wines already winning awards. The tasting room is large and the atmosphere is welcoming. All the wines are made from the estate-grown grapes including Riesling, pinot grigio, cabernet and award-winning chardonnays. The 2009 Bella Terra Cab Franc is a fine red with hints of black cherry, tobacco, and vanilla.

925 Line 2, Niagara-on-the-Lake. ℂ **905/468-0777.** www.pondviewwinery.com. Daily 10am–6pm.

Puddicombe Estate Farms & Winery ☺   (Lincoln Lakeshore) This 120-hectare (297-acre) working farm was established more than 200 years ago by the Puddicombe family, who still own and operate the business today. Along with its family-based activities (including a petting zoo and agricultural train ride; see chapter 6, "What to See & Do in the Niagara Region," for more details), the Puddicombes offer a wine shop that's worth a visit. Prices range between C$9 and C$28. Award-winning wines are available to sample at the tasting bar at C$1 for four samples. Try the sauvignon blanc or raspberry fruit wine. Grapes grown in their vineyards include colombard, viognier, and muscats. Hikers take note—the farm property backs onto the Bruce Trail. Light fare is available in the licensed Harvest Café and Tea Room. Pick your own apples, cherries, and strawberries, or choose a basket of prepicked fruit in season. Tours for 10 or more are available by appointment only and differ from regular winery tours; tastings are C$4 per person, and C$15 will get you a wagon ride tour and more.

1468 Hwy. 48, Winona. ℂ **905/643-1015** or 905/643-6882. www.puddicombefarms.com. Jan–Apr Mon–Fri 9am–5pm, Sat–Sun 10am–4pm; May–Dec daily 9am–5pm. Tours June–Oct daily 11am and 1pm; Nov–May by appointment.

Ravine Estate Winery ★★   (St. David's Bench) This winery feels historic, even though it has only been open since spring 2009. The William Woodruff House, which serves as a tasting room and wine boutique, is very old, very beautiful—and has a great story that you will have to ask about when you visit. The winery is located on a 14-hectare (34-acre) plot that has been in owner Norma Jane Lowrey Harber's family since 1867. The desire to save the property from housing development was the initial impetus for the winery. Harber built the business with her husband, Blair, and their three sons. A rebuilt fruit-packing shed was converted to house the Ravine Bistro and a fine food shop with an outdoor wood-burning bread and pizza oven. The house itself has been lovingly re-created, but all the most modern winery equipment, as well as the working part of the restaurant, have been cleverly hidden in underground passages. The winery is one of the nicest places in the Peninsula to have a casual lunch and enjoy a glass of wine in relaxed surroundings. Try a glass of the 2007 Cabernet Franc Rosé. It is fresh and delicious, reminiscent of cranberries, strawberries, and spice.

1366 York Rd., St. Davids. ℂ **905/262-VINE** (262-8463). www.ravinevineyard.com. Daily 11am–6pm.

Reif Estates Winery   (Niagara River) With a new retail space, Reif finally has a venue befitting its wine. Enter the European country cottage through oversized oak doors, which lead to a large cherrywood tasting bar. Outside, not far from the water fountain, a wine sensory garden was created with help from local horticulture students: Four sections of flora and plants are meant to mimic the aromas and styles of each wine. A light-bodied white such as Riesling has pear smells, and a bold red has the smell of bell peppers. This attention to horticulture is natural to Reif Estates; their wines are produced using only grapes from their own vineyards. The first tasting sample is free, and it's C$1 for subsequent tastings. Icewine is C$4 per sample. Reif is well known for its Late Harvest Vidal, and its Riesling, vidal, and cabernet franc Icewines (high-end varieties cost C$55 per bottle). Wine prices vary between C$9 and C$50 (for premium first-growth reds).

The wine boutique has gifts as well as locally made jams, jellies, and fudge. There is a limited selection of Canadian cheese and crackers available for takeout if you decide on an impromptu picnic. Facing the car park are sample rows of the types of grapes grown at Reif, so you can get a close-up view of the vines and fruit. Winter tours are not available, but in summer two daily tours are on offer for C$5: at 11:30am and 1:30pm. The price includes three tastings, one of which is an Icewine. No appointment is required. Tours are generic, but the new venue is worth visiting.

15608 Niagara Pkwy., Niagara-on-the-Lake. (**C**) **905/468-7738.** www.reifwinery.com. Apr–Oct daily 10am–6pm; Nov–Mar daily 10am–5pm. Tours May–mid-Oct daily 11:30am and 1:30pm; mid-Oct–Apr by appointment only.

Rockway Glen Estate Winery (Twenty Mile Bench) This winery is somewhat unusual because it shares space with Rockway Glen Golf Course, an 18-hole championship course with full amenities, including a clubhouse restaurant (on the same premises as the tasting bar, wine boutique, and wine museum), driving range, and putting and chipping greens. The *musée du vin* is worth a visit, particularly if you opt for a guided rather than self-guided tour, since you will get a much more in-depth explanation of the artifacts on display and will have an opportunity to ask questions to further your knowledge of the history of the winemaking process. The museum's collection features a variety of antique implements and accoutrements from French vineyards, and depicts the journey of the noble grape from the vine to the bottle. The *musée du vin* is open 11am to 4pm daily. Guided tours must be pre-booked. Admission is C$5 per person, whether guided or self-guided. Three wine samples are complimentary.

Rockway Glen's Baco Noir (2005) is excellent and has the medals—such as the silver at the 2007 Ontario Wine Awards and bronze at the All Canadian Wine Championships—to back it up. Wine prices range between C$8 and C$20 for a special Reserve cab franc and C$40 for Icewines.

3290 Ninth St., St. Catharines. (**C**) **877/762-5929** or 905/641-1030. www.rockwayglen.com. Mon–Sat 11am–7pm; Sun 11am–5pm.

Strewn Winery ★ (Niagara Lakeshore) Your first impression as you pull into the parking lot at Strewn may leave you feeling a little puzzled; the industrial nature of the site is in stark contrast to many of the wineries in the district. You'd be right in thinking industrial, since the concrete-block winery buildings, in fact, are located in what was once an abandoned cannery. The exterior could use some sprucing up—cracked concrete and peeling paint give it an unkempt look from the outside. Step inside, however, and you will find a wood-clad wine boutique on your left, a state-of-the-art cooking school on your right, and to the rear of the building, a tasting bar and restaurant, serving Provençal-inspired cuisine and backing onto the picturesque woodland bordering Four Mile Creek. Public tours of the vineyard, barrel cellar, and production facilities are daily at 1pm for groups of 10 or more—call to make an appointment first. Tours are an informal walk through the property. No scripted lines here. Ask for owner Joe Will if he's around—he's a hoot.

MICROBREWERIES

If you'd rather gulp a frosty brew, don't weep in your empty pint glass. Here are three microbreweries amongst the grapes.

Visitors to Niagara-on-the-Lake can have a tasting and production tour of the production facilities at **TAPS** (10 Walker Rd., Virgil; ✆ **905/468-TAPS** [468-8277]; www.tapsbeer.ca). Choose from Red Cream Ale, a premium lager, or, for the true aficionado, a vanilla wheat beer offered seasonally. If you're around during September's Grape and Wine Festival, try TAPS's wine barrel lager, which is aged in stainless steel, then in red wine barrels. Tastings and tours are free. Call ahead to make sure they're not busy (summer Wed–Sat 11am–6pm, Sun 11am–5pm; winter Wed–Sat 11am–6pm).

The Niagara area is home to two other microbreweries. Syndicate Restaurant & Brewery, formerly **Niagara's Best Brewery,** has relocated to Niagara Falls. The brewery has become popular for their West Coast–inspired Blonde Premium Ale. Tasting rather hoppy with a full body, this beer is a favorite with the beer connoisseur. Their lager, which caters to the everyday beer drinker, is a light, refreshing drink. Tours of the production facility and samplings are free. The pub restaurant is a good bet for lunch and a cold one. (6863 Lundy's Lane, Niagara Falls ✆ **289/477-1022;** www.niagarasbestbeer.com). **The Merchant Ale House** is a pub that has hopped (forgive me) into the microbrewing business in the past few years. Sadly, their beer is only sold on the premises (98 St. Paul St., St. Catharines; ✆ **905/984-1060;** www.merchantale house.ca). Featuring between five and seven beers at any time, one staple is strawberry blonde fruit ale that tastes just like it sounds. The Drunken Monkey, which has prompted locals to bring in a slew of stuffed monkeys that sit above the bar, is a chewy-tasting dark oatmeal stout. The Old Time Hockey ale is an easy-drinking ale brewed with lager malts and English hops (chocolate was used to enhance its flavor). The Extra Special Bitter is dubbed the "King of English ales," and the Blonde Bombshell is a lager/malt that is combined with ale. The Merchant Ale House also offers seasonal beers such as their Halloween favorite, pumpkin beer.

Special events are held throughout the year; check the website for up-to-date information. Past events have included invitations to take part in pruning the vines in early spring; a fall participation event that includes grape picking, assisting with the grape crushing, and a sample of grape juice to take home; and an interactive seminar on identification of the characteristics of wines made from different grape varieties. *Terroir la Cachette* is Strewn's winery restaurant, featuring the French-Provençal cooking expertise of chef Alain Levesque, with an emphasis on local ingredients. The Wine Country Cooking School offers a variety of classes that feature food and wine. One-day classes, 2-day culinary weekends, and 5-day culinary vacations are available. (See chapter 5, "Where to Eat," for more detailed information on the restaurant and the cooking school.) To walk in and sample a wine, tastings range between C50¢ to C$2 for Icewine varieties. To take a wine home, expect to pay between C$11 and C$34 per bottle.

1339 Lakeshore Rd., Niagara-on-the-Lake. ✆ **905/468-1229** (winery), 905/468-1222 (restaurant), or 905/468-8304 (cooking school). www.strewnwinery.com or www.winecountrycooking.com. Daily 10am–6pm. Free tour daily 1pm.

Specialty Wineries

Frogpond Farm ★   This small country winery produces the only certified organic wine in Ontario. The proprietors are on-hand to enthusiastically discuss their organic farming methods and offer free tastings of their organic Riesling and cabernet merlot. The country screen door slams behind as you enter the small room with a thick wooden table set up for tastings. Try the oak-aged Riesling, which has been aged in huge 2,500-liter (660-gal.) oak casks, an unusual treatment for a Riesling (it is much more common to find oak-aged chardonnay). The barrels are old, so they allow air to reach the wine but do not impart the typical vanilla, toast, or caramel notes you would find from a young oak barrel. Rather, the flavor is richer and more complex than an unoaked Riesling. Prices are reasonable, ranging from C$12 to C$16.

If you are in a position to transport them home, when you drop in ask if there are any eggs for sale that day. (That's why I always travel with a cooler in the trunk!) You will even see the chickens they came from running around the farmyard. And when the peaches and cherries are ripe, they're free for the picking. The self-guided tour takes you around the property, past the frog pond (yes, there are frogs in the pond!) and vines. There are a few benches where you can sit and relax.

1385 Larkin Rd., Niagara-on-the-Lake. ℂ **905/468-1079.** www.frogpondfarm.ca. Tues–Sat 1–5pm. Free guided tours on Sat afternoons or by appointment.

The Ice House Winery   This winery specializes in producing Icewine. The Ice House Winery's 2005 Vidal Icewine, Northern Ice, was awarded the highest honor accorded wine—Grand Gold at the 2007 Monde Selection in Brussels. A visit here is a great chance to stock your cellar or pick up some Christmas gifts. Try one of the excellent Icewines as a pairing with a fruit dessert or a rich cheese, or, if you feel experimental, try a glass with seared foie gras.

14778 Niagara Pkwy., Niagara-on-the-Lake. ℂ **206/426-5381.** www.theicehouse.ca. Call to arrange a visit.

Sunnybrook Farm Estate Winery   (Niagara Lakeshore) Sunnybrook Farm, a short drive west of Niagara-on-the-Lake along the southern shore of Lake Ontario, is unique among the Niagara wineries because it exclusively produces fruit wines, many of which are made with fruit from their own orchards. This small family-owned and -operated fruit winery is proud of the many awards its wines have accumulated over the years. When you visit the cozy tasting room, you will see the bottles displayed on the shelves with their medals hanging around their necks. No formal tours are available, but staff members are ready to pour samples 7 days a week—it's C$2 for four tastings. Notable wines include black currant, spiced apple, and black raspberry. Peach, pear, and other fruit wines, many of them dry or off-dry, are a nice refreshing alternative to—or change from—grape wines. Their Ironwood Hard Cider has received critical praise. All of Sunnybrook's wines are Quality Certified (QC), which is the fruit wine equivalent of VQA for Ontario grape wines. Sunnybrook Farm currently produces about 3,500 cases of peach, pear, apple, plum, apricot, and berry wines, including distinctive iced fruit wines. The wines are light and balanced, naturally fermented, not fortified, and not grape-based. Get ready to be pleasantly surprised here. Sip on Iced Apple Dessert Wine and award-winning Ironwood Hard Cider—this is one of the best ciders you will ever taste. Prices to pick up a bottle range from C$15 to C$30.

1425 Lakeshore Rd., Niagara-on-the-Lake. ℂ **905/468-1122.** www.sunnybrookfarmwinery.com. May–Oct daily 10am–6pm; Nov–Dec daily 10am–5pm; Jan–Feb Thurs–Mon 10am–5pm; Mar–Apr daily 10am–5pm.

SHOPPING

E ven if shopping isn't your thing, somehow the urge to buy becomes irresistible when holidaying. Whether it is something that will remind you of the good times you had, or a memento for friends and family, or perhaps a reward for the lady who came in and fed the cat, there are few travelers who don't find an excuse to shop when on vacation.

You'll find the usual T-shirts, maple syrup, and stuffed moose on Clifton Hill, often made in China, but elsewhere in the Niagara region you will discover some truly exceptional shopping finds. My favorite souvenirs are consumable—food and wine specialties that convey the flavor of the region. There are few places quite as well equipped to offer gourmet and winery shopping as the Niagara region.

A one-of-a-kind piece of art, a remarkable chapeau, a Canadian Christmas tree ornament, or an antique bowl—you'll find them in the better stores in Niagara Falls, in Niagara-on-the-Lake, at the winery shops, and in the small villages throughout the winery district.

And don't overlook the outlets. Two large outlet malls, one near the Falls and one just over the border in New York State, are found here, and the bargains are worth the trip.

For specific shops and their specialties, check out the "Shopping A to Z" section later in this chapter.

THE SHOPPING SCENE

As you would expect in a high-volume tourist area like the Falls, souvenir shops and knickknack stands abound. But you'll also come across some shops that sell authentic and desirable made-in-Canada objects well worth investing in. On the American side of the Falls is one of the best outlet malls around, while farther afield, in Niagara-on-the-Lake and the wine country, there are numerous opportunities to pick up quality items in upscale shopping districts.

Since wine country is one of the big tourist draws, it's logical that a good bottle of wine would make an excellent gift. Several of the wineries sell wines that are only available at the cellar door and, in addition, sell wine-themed souvenirs, Icewine chocolates, cookbooks, flavored vinegars and oils, and specialty foods. Antiques lovers will find a large range of heritage furniture, silver, china, and collectibles, both Canadian and American, in the Twenty Valley district and in the vicinity of the town of Virgil, just south of Niagara-on-the-Lake.

Niagara Falls Shopping

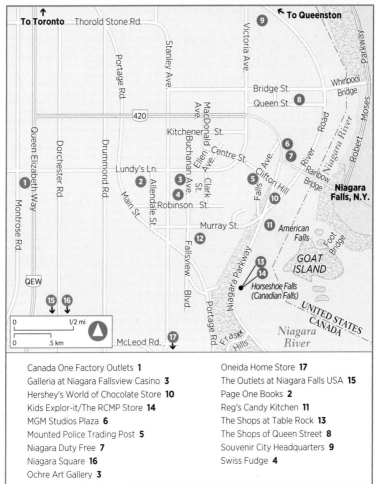

Canada One Factory Outlets **1**	Oneida Home Store **17**
Galleria at Niagara Fallsview Casino **3**	The Outlets at Niagara Falls USA **15**
Hershey's World of Chocolate Store **10**	Page One Books **2**
Kids Explor-it/The RCMP Store **14**	Reg's Candy Kitchen **11**
MGM Studios Plaza **6**	The Shops at Table Rock **13**
Mounted Police Trading Post **5**	The Shops of Queen Street **8**
Niagara Duty Free **7**	Souvenir City Headquarters **9**
Niagara Square **16**	Swiss Fudge **4**
Ochre Art Gallery **3**	

GREAT SHOPPING AREAS

Fonthill

Visit this pretty town for the scenic drive as well as some awesome shopping. The Niagara Gallery showcases the work of local artists and the Wildflower Market supplies organic vegetables and groceries as well as artisan crafts. Just outside of the town is an area well worth a morning's browse—the Shoppes of Ridgeville. Here you'll find gourmet delights and high-end kitchen supplies at the Whisk & Ladle, fresh baked goods at Nature's Corner, handmade chocolates at Sweet Thoughts, or home decor finds at In the Village. A little farther along, you'll find the Berry Patch Tea Room, with the opportunity to enjoy afternoon tea as well as buy loose tea and tea-making paraphernalia. A bit farther down the Canboro Road, you'll find Chez Fromage, the perfect place to pick up hard-to-get cheeses from Quebec to go with your artisanal bread.

Jordan Village

Jordan Village is compact enough to explore on foot. Two large, century-old warehouses have been converted into an eclectic assortment of retailers, punctuated by a luxurious inn, an award-winning fine-dining restaurant, and a well-established Niagara winery. In addition, numerous retailers are scattered along Main Street and Nineteenth Street, bounded on the south by Hwy. 81 (King St.) and on the north by Wismer Street. Shopping is higher-end in focus, with a mix of art galleries, designer fashions, giftware, antiques, home and garden accessories—and even a shop catering to dogs.

Niagara Falls

If you are a souvenir hound, you don't need a guidebook to give you suggestions for where to buy souvenirs. Head for Clifton Hill, and just follow the crowds. You will see trinkets at every turn. If you want upscale shops, visit the Galleria inside the Niagara Fallsview Casino Resort or the Canadian Treasures and other excellent shops at Table Rock. For duty-free shopping, see "Duty-Free Shopping" below.

Niagara-on-the-Lake

Niagara-on-the-Lake, dubbed "Canada's prettiest town," boasts great shopping along a stretch of road through the middle of town, spilling over onto a few of the cross streets. This area will appeal to the more conservative, affluent shopper. Clothes are top quality but tend to be more traditional than haute couture, with a preponderance of Tilley hats and Irish linen skirts. It's amusing to see the men sitting in the sun on park benches while their wives shop in the stores. You'll find indulgences such as homemade fudge, Brit imports, kitchen gadgets, wine, fine dog apparel, and scented soaps and bath oils. The town is full of flowers in summer and pretty as a Thomas Kinkade painting in the winter. There are many cafes for rest and refreshment in between purchases.

Port Colborne

When you've seen the Locks and the lakers, spend some time on historic West Street, which stretches along the Locks and has some very attractive shops and cafes. Find antiques at Treasures on West; lovely things for babies and for the home at Harmony on West; and clothing at Serendipities, Glam Girl, and Urbannity—there's a shop for every taste. Then stop for a cool drink and a sandwich at the Canalside Pub, where you can watch the ships pass through the Locks while you dine.

Port Dalhousie

This waterfront village, nestled on the south shore of Lake Ontario, has attracted some interesting boutiques and specialty stores. Its market is a mixture of stores and features a popular bakery. Port Dalhousie is small enough that you can park the car in one spot and walk around the village center. There are restaurants and bars in addition to gift stores, women's fashions, and a candy store.

Niagara-on-the-Lake Shopping

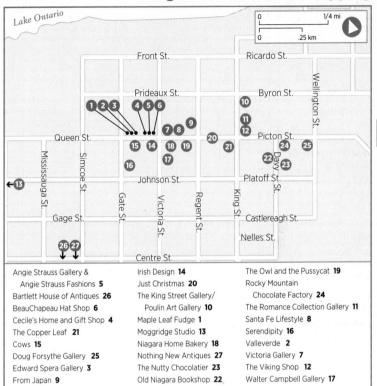

Angie Strauss Gallery &
  Angie Strauss Fashions **5**
Bartlett House of Antiques **26**
BeauChapeau Hat Shop **6**
Cecile's Home and Gift Shop **4**
The Copper Leaf **21**
Cows **15**
Doug Forsythe Gallery **25**
Edward Spera Gallery **3**
From Japan **9**

Irish Design **14**
Just Christmas **20**
The King Street Gallery/
  Poulin Art Gallery **10**
Maple Leaf Fudge **1**
Moggridge Studio **13**
Niagara Home Bakery **18**
Nothing New Antiques **27**
The Nutty Chocolatier **23**
Old Niagara Bookshop **22**

The Owl and the Pussycat **19**
Rocky Mountain
  Chocolate Factory **24**
The Romance Collection Gallery **11**
Santa Fe Lifestyle **8**
Serendipity **16**
Valleverde **2**
Victoria Gallery **7**
The Viking Shop **12**
Walter Campbell Gallery **17**

Wine Country

After you've tasted some wines at one of the wineries, nip in to the wine boutiques located in most of them to pick up a bottle of the wine that you just tasted and loved. Chances are you won't be able to buy it anywhere else, and chances are that the wine will be gone next time you visit. I really loved Château des Charmes Gamay Droit 2007, much better than the 2006, and bought two bottles, but I'm pretty sure that vintage will be sold out the next time I visit. Wineries like Peller Estates and Hillebrand sell more than wine—coasters, wine glasses, Icewine jellies, table linens, and many more food and wine products that make an excellent memento of your time in Niagara wine country.

MALLS & SHOPPING CENTERS
Niagara Falls, Ontario & New York

Canada One Factory Outlets True factory outlet deals can be found here; items are up to 75% off regular retail prices. Stores include Roots, Escada, Garage, the Body Shop Depot, Club Monaco Outlet Store, Samsonite Company Stores,

Ecco, Tootsies Factory Shoe Market, Esprit, and Mexx. The number of retailers here is only a fraction of those at the huge outlet mall in Niagara Falls, New York, but if you're looking for Canadian or European-based stores (for example, Roots, the Body Shop, Rocky Mountain Chocolate Factory, or Mexx), then Canada One will serve you better. Call ahead or visit the website before your trip for an up-to-date listing of retailers. The outlet is open 364 days of the year (closed Christmas Day), Monday to Saturday from 10am to 9pm (Jan–Apr the outlet closes at 6pm on Sat). On Sundays and holidays, the hours are 10am to 6pm. 7500 Lundy's Lane (at QEW), Niagara Falls, ON. © **866/284-5781** or 905/356-8989. www.canadaoneoutlets.com.

Galleria Fallsview Casino   The architecture, decor, and construction materials are all luxurious, in keeping with the upscale atmosphere of the casino—although some of the styles can be a bit garish. Whether you're a shopper, a gambler, or neither, it's worth a wander around the Galleria. Stroll up past the shooting fountains and waterfalls with their ever-changing multicolored lights and enter by the main doors. You'll come face to face with Hydro-Teslatron, a "living" sculpture. At regular intervals, H-T comes alive with a sound-and-light show, startling and fascinating bystanders. At the rear of the Galleria is a huge rotunda under a multistory glass-domed ceiling. There are some high-end retailers, including Swarovski Austrian crystal, Linea di Mano for elegant accessories, and Philippe Artois imported Italian menswear. For more affordable fashion, there's Cotton Ginny, La Vie en Rose, and Tabi. Enjoy treats from Swiss Fudge, or indulge in specialty teas from Teaopia. From Sunday to Thursday, the stores are open from 10am to 11pm; on Fridays and Saturdays, they close at midnight. 6380 Fallsview Blvd., Niagara Falls, ON. © **905/371-3268.** www.fallsviewcasinoresort.com.

Niagara Square   This regional shopping center is anchored by the Bay and Sport Chek. A separate Cineplex Odeon movie theater complex is on-site. A small food court serves shoppers. Several mall stalwarts cover the women's fashion scene, including Cotton Ginny, Suzy Shier, Tabi, La Senza, and Tan Jay, but men's and youth fashions are not as well represented. Bargain stores include Payless ShoeSource and Dollarama. The mall is open Monday to Friday from 10am to 9pm, Saturdays from 9:30am to 5:30pm, and Sundays from noon to 5pm. 7555 Montrose Rd. (corner of McLeod Rd. and the QEW), Niagara Falls, ON. © **905/357-1110.** www.niagarasquare.com.

The Outlets at Niagara Falls USA   This huge outlet mall is often very busy, and you may find yourself cruising the parking lot for awhile, especially on a weekend, to find a parking space. It's worth it, though. Many Canadians make the trek across the border to this clean and well-designed mall. The closest border crossing is the Rainbow Bridge, but you can zip down I-90 from Fort Erie or up from the Lewiston–Queenston Bridge. With the Canadian dollar so strong, however, shoppers are making the trip across the border in droves, so check to see that wait times at the border crossings are not too long (websites like www.borderlineups.com are helpful). Around 150 brand-name stores offer everyday discounts on their stock, as high as 60% or more off the regular retail prices. If it's famous, it's here. J. Crew, Banana Republic, Polo Ralph Lauren, Guess, Gap, Calvin Klein, Burberry, Liz Claiborne, Rockport, Cole Haan, Hugo Boss, Juicy Couture, kate spade, Michael Kors, Jones New York, and Saks Fifth Avenue Off 5th are just a handful of the fashion retailers. Housewares are available at Corningware Corelle Revere. Kid's clothing can be found at OshKosh B'Gosh, the Children's Place, Nautica, Carters Childrenswear, and more. Luggage, accessories, shoes, and menswear are well represented throughout. Specialty stores include a Fragrance Outlet, KB Toy Outlet, and Lindt Chocolate. You can browse the shops from 10am to 9pm Monday to Saturday, and 11am to 6pm on Sundays. 1900

duty-free SHOPPING

Check for the current duty-free allowances before making your purchases. Canadian residents, please note: If you are traveling to the U.S., you may purchase goods you wish to bring back to Canada at duty-free stores before leaving Canada. If you will be out of Canada for 48 hours or more, you may also purchase duty-free alcohol and tobacco. U.S. residents may purchase up to $200 of duty-free goods (excluding alcohol and tobacco) for trips across the border that are less than 48 hours. U.S. residents who stay in Canada for 48 hours or longer can bring back up to $800 worth of duty-free goods, which can include one liter of liquor and one carton of cigarettes. Please note that Customs rules and regulations are subject to change, and visitors to both sides of the border should check current rules and regulations before making out-of-country purchases they intend to bring home with them, whether those goods were purchased duty-free or not.

Niagara Duty Free   An array of duty-free goods is available, including perfume, cosmetics, jewelry, Swiss watches, china, crystal, chocolate, wine (including Niagara wines and Icewines), and liquor. There is a currency-exchange service. Save up to 50% on regular retail prices. Located beside the Rainbow Bridge on the Canadian side—the closest duty-free store to the Falls. The Rainbow Bridge is the shortest route to I-90 from Niagara Falls, Ontario, and is a truck-free route. 5726 Falls Ave. (beside the Rainbow Bridge), Niagara Falls, ON (✆ **905/374-3700;** www.niagaradutyfree.com).

Peace Bridge Duty Free   Billed as North America's largest duty-free shopping complex, the Peace Bridge Duty Free has a wide variety of items and is open 24 hours. In addition, there is a handy Travel Services Center, which offers currency exchange, customized maps, tourist information, and business services. Other amenities include a food court with branded fast-food outlets, restrooms, an ATM, and phones. Duty-free goods include Canadian souvenirs, leather goods, imported chocolate and gourmet foods, perfumes, china and crystal, wine, Icewine, beer, liquor, and tobacco. 1 Peace Bridge Plaza (beside the Peace Bridge), Fort Erie (✆ **800/361-1302;** www.dutyfree.ca).

Peninsula Duty Free   This duty-free shop is next to the Queenston–Lewiston Bridge, the most northerly of the three public border crossings in the Niagara region (the Whirlpool Bridge is reserved for Nexus subscribers). All of the usual duty-free items are available here, including souvenirs, perfumes, wine, beer, and liquor. Beside the Queenston–Lewiston Bridge, Queenston (✆ **905/262-5363**).

Military Rd., Niagara Falls, NY (take I-90 to exit 22 to Factory Outlet Blvd.). ✆ **800/414-0475** or 716/297-2022. www.fashionoutletsniagara.com.

The Shops of Queen Street   This historic part of downtown Niagara Falls is enjoying a rejuvenation. It is an area that now has a perceptible buzz, attracting shoppers, diners, and gallery-goers. Great little cafes, like Mide Bistro and Paris Crepes, perch next to galleries and antiques shops, with new ones opening almost daily. This is the place to shop for an art photograph or painting to take home as an enduring souvenir, or to just spend some time browsing the unique stores. You can find some amazing buys here. www.queenstreetniagarafalls.com.

The Shops at Table Rock   This new shopping area has the great advantage of being right beside the Falls, so it's easy to take a shopping detour while you are enjoying the sites. The shopping area is called Canadian Treasures and features one of

Canada's iconic shops, Roots (our Olympic athletes were outfitted in Roots fashions for years, as were the American athletes in 2002–06), which carries high-quality clothing, bags, shoes, and outdoor wear. There are also Traditions, which sells Canadian glassware and jewelry; Canadian Diamonds; First Nations Arts & Crafts; and the Royal Canadian Mounted Police Boutique. If you get hungry, there's Ah-So Sushi, which I highly recommend, and the new Niagara Pizza Company makes great homemade pizza. When you are done, the incline railway is just outside the door, to take you effortlessly up to your hotel. 6650 Niagara Pkwy., Niagara Falls, ON.

St. Catharines

Fairview Mall This mall serves local residents and features around 60 stores and services. Anchors are Zellers, Chapters, Mark's Work Wearhouse, Future Shop, and Zehrs. Winners clothing store and HomeSense home furnishings are new additions. Mall hours are Monday to Friday, 10am to 9pm, Saturday, 9:30am to 5:30pm, and Sunday, noon to 5pm. 285 Geneva St. (near the QEW—take the Lake St. exit), St. Catharines. © **905/646-3165.**

The Pen Centre This large indoor mall has approximately 180 stores and is the largest mall in the Niagara region. Anchor stores include the Bay, Gap, Pier 1, Sears, Zehrs, Zellers, HomeSense, Sport Chek, Winners, Old Navy, and my favorite spot for trendy and cheap clothes: H&M. There are a half-dozen full-service restaurants, a food court, and numerous snack retailers. If you want a break from shopping, there is a Famous Players Silver City on-site with eight movie theaters. There are dozens of women's and unisex fashion stores, although less in the way of children's and men's fashions, over more than 93,000 sq. m (1 million sq. ft.) of shopping. The mall is open Monday to Friday from 10am to 9pm, Saturday from 9am to 6pm, and Sunday from 11am to 6pm. Hwy. 406 and Glendale Ave., St. Catharines. © **800/582-8202** or 905/687-6622. www.thepencentre.com.

Welland

Seaway Mall Serving Welland and the surrounding district, Seaway Mall has a cinema complex and is anchored by Sears, Winners, and Zellers. A good selection of mall chain sportswear, shoes, unisex fashions, and women's fashion retailers can be found here. There are also banks, a post office, and a food court. Shopping hours are Monday to Friday 10am to 9pm, Saturday 9:30am to 5:30pm, and Sunday from noon to 5pm. 800 Niagara St., Welland. © **905/735-0697.** www.seawaymall.com.

SHOPPING A TO Z

Antiques & Collectibles

Bartlett House of Antiques This antiques store specializes in historical military paraphernalia, china, jewelry, and fine furniture, particularly oak, mahogany, and walnut pieces. 1490 Niagara Stone Rd., Niagara-on-the-Lake. © **905/468-1880.**

Blue Barn Antiques & Collectibles Located in an old barn in the Twenty Valley antiques district, this store offers two floors of antiques and collectible treasures. 4107 Cherry Ave., Vineland. © **905/562-4606.** www.bluebarnantiques.ca.

Europa Antiques Located in an old red-brick church, this is a charming store, with stained glass, furniture, and decorative items. It is an easy stop on the way to the theater or when touring wine country. 1523 Niagara Stone Rd. (Hwy. 55), Virgil. © **905/468-3130.** www.europa-antiques.com.

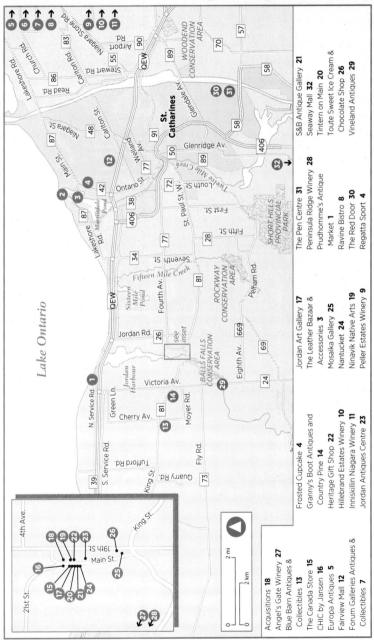

Lake Ontario

St. Catharines

WOODEND CONSERVATION AREA

SHORT HILLS PROVINCIAL PARK

ROCKWAY CONSERVATION AREA

BALLS FALLS CONSERVATION AREA

Jordan Harbour

Fifteen Mile Creek

Twelve Mile Creek

Sixteen Mile Pond

Martindale Pond

Glenridge Av.

Ontario St.

Fourth Av.

Fifth Av.

Seventh St.

First St.

St. Paul St.

Fourth St.

Victoria Av.

Cherry Av.

Green Ln.

Moyer Rd.

Pelham Rd.

Eighth Av.

Jordan Rd.

Main St.

Niagara St.

Welland Av.

Carlton St.

Stewart Rd.

Airport Rd.

Glendale Av.

Read Rd.

Lakeshore Rd.

Church Rd.

Carlton Rd.

Niagara Stone Rd.

Lakeshore Rd.

N Service Rd.

S Service Rd.

Tufford Rd.

King St.

Quarry Rd.

Fly Rd.

19th St.

4th Ave.

21st St.

see inset

QEW

406

0   2 km
0   2 mi

Acquisitions **18**
Angel's Gate Winery **27**
Blue Barn Antiques & Collectibles **13**
The Canada Store **15**
CHIC by Jansen **16**
Europa Antiques **5**
Fairview Mall **12**
Forum Galleries Antiques & Collectibles **7**

Frosted Cupcake **4**
Granny's Boot Antiques and Country Pine **14**
Heritage Gift Shop **22**
Hillebrand Estates Winery **10**
Inniskillin Niagara Winery **11**
Jordan Antiques Centre **23**

Jordan Art Gallery **17**
The Leather Bazaar & Accessories **3**
Mosaika Gallery **25**
Nantucket **24**
Ninavik Native Arts **19**
Peller Estates Winery **9**

The Pen Centre **31**
Peninsula Ridge Winery **28**
Prudhomme's Antique Market **1**
Ravine Bistro **8**
The Red Door **30**
Regatta Sport **4**

S&B Antique Gallery **21**
Seaway Mall **32**
Tintern on Main **20**
Toute Sweet Ice Cream & Chocolate Shop **26**
Vineland Antiques **29**

8

SHOPPING | Shopping A to Z

183

antiquing IN THE NIAGARA REGION

There are many fine antiques dealers in the Niagara region—although many have retired in the last few years—but if you want to hit a few places in a single neighborhood, then head for Virgil, a village just a few kilometers south of Niagara-on-the-Lake on Niagara Stone Road. Another good hunting ground is the Twenty Valley—its antiques retailers are located mainly around Jordan and Vineland. If you're a country-drive kind of person who likes to pull over now and then when an antiques market catches your eye, cruise along Victoria Avenue between the QEW and Fly Road (if you turn onto the North Service Rd. first, you can catch Prudhomme's 25-vendor market before heading south on Victoria toward Vineland), or Niagara Stone Road (Hwy. 55) between the QEW and Niagara-on-the-Lake.

Take note that opening hours for antiques retailers differ from typical shopping hours. Many are closed on Mondays (except holiday Mon) and some also close Tuesday and Wednesday, although most are open 7 days a week in July and August. As always, if there is a particular vendor you wish to visit, call ahead to avoid disappointment.

Forum Galleries Antiques & Collectibles　A variety of dealers showcase their wares at this large 745-sq.-m (8,0-sq.-ft.) antiques market. There are good-quality antiques at excellent prices. Consider a carved 1930s Art Deco sideboard, a steal at C$1,300; a pink and grey marble Art Deco clock for C$200; or an English walnut secretary from 1780 for C$3,500. The proprietors can arrange for delivery. There's also a large range of jewelry, glass, books, lamps, art, silver, china, toys, fine antiques, Canadiana . . . lose yourself for an hour or so as you wander the aisles. The Forum holds regular auctions, and now has an online bidding system. 2017 Niagara Stone Rd. (Hwy. 55), Niagara-on-the-Lake. ℂ **905/468-2777.** www.forumgalleries.com.

Granny's Boot Antiques and Country Pine　Handcrafted country pine pieces are a specialty at Granny's Boot. You'll also find a great selection of folk art, unique antiques, rustic furniture, and primitives. 3389 King St., Vineland. ℂ **877/211-0735** or 905/562-7055. www.grannysbootantiques.com.

Jordan Antiques Centre　This village marketplace carries inventory from 25 antiques dealers and features a permanent show year-round. Specialized items include antique toys, Christmas decorations, jewelry, and silver. The Centre has a sound local reputation as a gift resource and showcase for large pieces of antique furniture. 3836 Main St., Jordan Village. ℂ **905/562-7723.** www.jordanantiques.com.

Nothing New Antiques　This is the place for Canadiana, country furniture, and accessories. 1823 Niagara Stone Rd., Niagara-on-the-Lake. ℂ **905/468-7016.**

Prudhomme's Antique Market　Housed in a turn-of-the-20th-century farmhouse full of tiny rooms and hallways, this market has four floors of collectibles, with dealers' "cabins" outside. Most of what you will find here is Victorian or more recent, but the place is stuffed full. Every corner has something interesting, from vintage linens and hats to old books. I bought a copy of the first volume of Noel Coward's autobiography, *Present Indicative,* for C$2. Open year-round Thursday through Sunday from 10am to 5pm. 3319 North Service Rd., Vineland. ℂ **905/562-5187.**

S&B Antique Gallery　This store specializes in European, particularly French, items, including fine furniture, decorative arts, and collectibles. On display you will find dining-room suites, bedroom suites, occasional furniture, china and glass, estate jewelry, prints, paintings, and lighting. 3836 Main St., Jordan Village. ☎ **877/337-4577** or 905/562-5415. www.sbantiquegallery.com.

Vineland Antiques   Housed in the original general store in the village of Vineland, this antiques market is a multidealer enterprise. 4227 Victoria Ave., Vineland. ☎ **905/562-9145.** www.vinelandantiques.ca.

MORE ANTIQUES STORES

There are more antiques and collectibles destinations to check out, including **Lakeshore Antiques & Treasures,** 855 Lakeshore Rd., Niagara-on-the-Lake (☎ 905/646-1965), and **Antiques of Niagara-on-the-Lake,** 1561 Niagara Stone Rd., Niagara-on-the-Lake (☎ 905/468-8527). These destinations offer multiple dealers in a marketplace setting.

Art Galleries

8

Angie Strauss Gallery   Local artist Angie Strauss creates oil and watercolor paintings in the impressionist style and has a line of women's fashions (see below). In the recently expanded gallery, one of the largest private galleries in the Niagara region, you will find limited editions, prints, and originals. Strauss paints popular local scenes and landmarks, florals, landscapes, and country collages. 129 Queen St., Niagara-on-the-Lake. ☎ **888/510-0939** or 905/468-2255. www.angiestrauss.com.

Doug Forsythe Gallery   Doug Forsythe is an established Canadian artist. Many of his collections feature landscapes, seascapes, marine themes, and figure studies. He works in computer graphics, watercolor, oil, and acrylics, and is skilled in etching, engraving, dry point, collagraphs, woodcuts, serigraphs, and woodcarving. Local scenes include Niagara-on-the-Lake, Niagara Falls, and Niagara vineyards. Forsythe also creates intricate guitars and fine scale-model ships. 92 Picton St., Niagara-on-the-Lake. ☎ **905/468-3659.** www.dougforsythegallery.com.

Edward Spera Gallery   Spera paints predominantly wildlife, in carefully realistic detail. His original acrylics as well as prints are for sale in this attractive gallery. All reproductions have been personally signed, titled, and numbered by the artist and are printed on 100% acid-free paper. 135 Queen St., Niagara-on-the-Lake. ☎ **905/468-7447.** www.speraart.ca.

Jordan Art Gallery ★   This gallery is owned by a group of local contemporary artists who also staff the store, so there is always a knowledgeable and enthusiastic person on hand to chat about the art. In addition to showcasing the work of the gallery owners, other selected artists' works are exhibited. Joyce Honsberger creates large whimsical fiber and metal sculptures, while Mori MacRae's paintings are playful takes on portraits—think funky Mona Lisa. There's jewelry, wearable art, paintings, dishes, sculptures, and more—what a place! 3845 Main St., Jordan Village. ☎ **905/562-6680.** www.jordanartgallery.com.

The King Street Gallery/Poulin Art Gallery   This gallery in a historic home in Niagara-on-the-Lake features works by Canadian artist Chantal Poulin, whose works range from portraits of children to landscapes, still life, and contemporary art. A number of vineyard landscapes are available as well. The gallery also displays other artists' work, including sculptures from Quebecois collaborative artists Yann Normand and Nancy Ferland, and Olivier Henley. 153 King St., Niagara-on-the-Lake. ☎ **905/468-8923.**

Moggridge Studio   In a quiet residential area with a view of Lake Ontario, this gallery and framing studio handles a huge variety of categories. In addition, the work of Canadian wildlife artist Robert Bateman is available here. Other Canadian artists whose work you'll find here include Bev Doolittle and Trisha Romance. 285 Niagara Blvd., Niagara-on-the-Lake. © **800/265-4889** or 905/468-2009. www.artline.vaxxine.com/studio/aboutstudio.htm.

Mosaika Gallery   This small gallery specializes in handmade Canadian jewelry, one-of-a-kind pieces that are easy to pack and make a perfect gift. 3769 Main St., Jordan. © **905/562-1136.** www.mosaikagallery.com.

Ninavik Native Arts ★   This beautiful store features an impressive collection of Native art and sculpture. Initially the focus was purely on Inuit works, but the owners have expanded their product line to include Iroquois artists. Stunning pieces by established Native sculptors run as high as five figures. Works from younger, up-and-coming indigenous artists are also featured. Soapstone, ivory, bone, and antler are used to create the works of art. Fabrics, prints, pottery, paintings, and masks are also on display. Pieces may be purchased in person or online. 3845 Main St., Jordan. © **800/646-2848** or 905/562-8888. www.ninavik.com.

Ochre Art Gallery   Original paintings by Canadian artists are available for sale in this gallery within the Doubletree Resort in Niagara Falls. Paintings have been selected to reflect the beauty of nature and the great Canadian outdoors. 6039 Fallsview Blvd. (inside the Doubletree Resort Spa Fallsview), Niagara Falls, ON. © **800/730-8609** or 905/354-4132.

Victoria Gallery   Situated at the back of a tea emporium, this is a surprisingly elegant shop specializing in estate and antique jewelry, with some good china tea sets and plates. 108 Queen St., Niagara-on-the-Lake. © **905/468-5707.** www.victoriateas.com.

Walter Campbell Gallery   Campbell specializes in charming scenes of Niagara-on-the-Lake and other typical Canadian scenes, ideal for a souvenir. The store showcases his limited-edition prints in different sizes, framed or unframed. 108 Queen St., Niagara-on-the-Lake. © **905/468-4466.** www.artofwaltercampbell.com.

Books

Chapters   Chapters has become a familiar name and favored destination for Canadian book lovers. They sell an extensive selection of books and magazines; larger stores carry CDs and a growing selection of giftware. Fairview Mall, 285 Geneva St., St. Catharines. © **905/934-3494.**

Coles   Under the umbrella of Chapters Indigo, Coles is a mainstream general bookseller that favors mall locations. The store stocks a wide selection of new and established titles and authors, book-related accessories, and gifts. Niagara Square Shopping Centre: 7555 Montrose Rd., Niagara Falls, ON; © **905/357-1422.** The Pen Centre: Hwy. 406 and Glendale Ave., St. Catharines; © 905/685-4961. Seaway Mall: 800 Niagara St. N., Welland; © 905/735-6146.

Old Niagara Bookshop   This independent bookstore carries literary works, specializing in Canadiana and children's books. Most titles are new. They carry some out-of-print and collectors' items, but not secondhand books. 233 King St., Niagara-on-the-Lake. © **905/468-2602.**

Page One Books   Most of the books in stock here are used rather than new. Since they serve a relatively small community, the subject areas are wide-ranging—they try to carry a little bit of everything. Fun for a browse. 5984 Main St., Niagara Falls, ON. © **905/354-9761.**

CDs, Movies & Music

Larger shopping malls have at least one store specializing in CDs and DVDs, although they tend to limit their selection to mainstream bestsellers and charge full price. Three of the most popular chain stores in the Niagara region are **HMV Canada, Music World,** and **Sunrise Records.**

MGM Studios Plaza   If you're a film buff, you will enjoy the MGM store. Besides a wide selection of DVDs and CDs, there is a range of interesting movie memorabilia and licensed movie-themed gifts and clothing. Great collection of James Bond, Pink Panther, and Rocky stuff. 4915 Clifton Hill, Niagara Falls, ON. ℂ **905/374-2663.**

Chocolates & Sweets

Cows   They advertise that they make the best ice cream in the world. I'm no connoisseur, but it's pretty good, made with high butterfat content and the best of ingredients. Try a scoop of the Gooey Mooie or the Turtle Cow. The shop also carries clothing, cups, toys, and souvenirs, all with cows on them. 44 Queen St., Niagara-on-the-Lake. ℂ **905/468-2100.** www.cows.ca.

Foods at Ravine   The Bistro at Ravine is a wonderful place for lunch, but the deli is the place to stock up on delicious items for a picnic, like charcuterie and homemade bread, as well as artisan cheeses and decadent desserts. 1366 York Rd., St. Davids. ℂ **905/262-8463.** www.annaolson.ca.

The Frosted Cupcake   This nut-free shop produces darling cupcakes in every flavor and color you can imagine, and the ladies here even bake gluten-free and vegan versions. Every day there are at least six flavors to choose from, like Cocoa Chanel, Lu Lu Lemon, or Salted Caramel. 524 Lake St., St. Catharines. ℂ **905/934-0003.** www.thefrosted cupcake.ca.

Hershey's World of Chocolate Store ☺   As you stroll along Falls Avenue at the foot of Clifton Hill, keep your eyes open for the gigantic silver-colored Hershey's Kiss that marks the location of this sweet treat emporium. If you have a sweet tooth, you'll be delighted with the free samples of Hershey products—milkshakes, fudge, truffles, Kisses, and more. The 650-sq.-m (6,996-sq.-ft.) store's shelves are loaded with calories. Fudge-making demonstrations happen on-site. Parking is available in a garage immediately adjacent to the store. 5701 Falls Ave., Niagara Falls, ON. ℂ **905/374-4444.**

Laura Secord   Named after a local heroine of the War of 1812, Laura Secord is Canada's largest and best-known chocolatier. If you are looking for chocolate-themed gifts, Laura Secord is a winner. Every major holiday in the calendar has a theme at Laura Secord. They stock gift-wrapped boxes of chocolates and gift baskets. Niagara Square: 7555 Montrose Rd. (corner of McLeod Rd. and the QEW), Niagara Falls, ON; ℂ **905/357-1110;** www.niagarasquare.com. The Pen Centre: Hwy. 406 and Glendale Ave., St. Catharines; ℂ 800/582-8202 or 905/684-1227; www.thepencentre.com.

Maple Leaf Fudge   The aromas of chocolate, vanilla, and sugar hit you as soon as you open the door. This homemade fudge in several flavors is a ritual purchase for many visitors to Niagara-on-the-Lake. The fudge is cooked in copper kettles, creamed on solid marble slabs, and each slice is hand cut. Try the double chocolate with nuts or the Irish cream. 114 Queen St., Niagara-on-the-Lake. ℂ **905/468-2211.** www.mapleleaffudge.com.

Niagara Home Bakery   It's almost impossible to walk past the window of this little bakery. Fresh pies, cookies, butter tarts, and biscuits seem to be calling your name. 66 Queen St., Niagara-on-the-Lake. ℂ **905/468-3431.**

Reg's Candy Kitchen Reg Wall has been making fudge at this location for more than 36 years. You can watch him at work in his candy kitchen. Delicious flavors include chocolate mint, butterscotch, maple walnut, and vanilla. The shop is just one block from the *Maid of the Mist,* along River Road, right under the Rainbow Bridge. Rainbow Bridge Plaza, Niagara Falls, ON. ✆ **905/356-4229.**

Rocky Mountain Chocolate Factory Truffles, handmade chocolates, and fudge are available, but the real attraction is the caramel apples, dipped in everything from Reese's Pieces to miniature marshmallows. 70 Queen St., Niagara-on-the-Lake. ✆ **905/468-0800.**

Swiss Fudge High-quality chocolate and candy from around the world are featured in this scrumptious shop in the Galleria shopping complex inside Niagara Fallsview Casino Resort. Swiss Fudge has been making fudge in Niagara Falls since 1966. Whether your sweet tooth craves English, American, Italian, Canadian, or French candies, it will be satisfied here. Plenty of prettily packaged sweet gifts are on display. 6380 Fallsview Blvd., Niagara Falls, ON. ✆ **905/356-5691.**

Toute Sweet Ice Cream & Chocolate I always say you can never have too much ice cream, and if you are touring around the Twenty Valley, this little ice-cream parlor (with an outdoor patio for summer pleasure) in Jordan Village is just what you need. You can customize your ice cream by choosing fresh fruit, brownies, cookies, chocolate, or nuts, and they will blend it with their premium ice cream on a frozen granite stone while you wait. Chocoholics should stop by, too, for hand-molded Belgian chocolates. Icewine truffles are also available on the premises. Yum. 3771 Nineteenth St., Jordan. ✆ **905/562-9666.**

Christmas Stores

Just Christmas ★ You might think a store that sells only Christmas decorations wouldn't do much trade outside of the Christmas season, but you'd be wrong. People don't just browse out of season here, they buy. It's the perfect store for those who plan ahead. And the store is like Doctor Who's Tardis (deceptively small outside, very large inside). Every Christmas decorating theme you could imagine is here for you to discover as you make your way from room to room, following the crowds of shoppers. 34 Queen St., Niagara-on-the-Lake. ✆ **905/468-4500.**

Department Stores

The Bay Established in the Canadian North more than 300 years ago as a fur-trading post known as the Hudson's Bay Company, the Bay carries standard department-store collections of fashions and housewares. Sales and promotions are frequent, and merchandise is good quality. The Bay occupies an anchor spot at two Niagara-region malls—the Pen Centre in St. Catharines and Niagara Square in Niagara Falls, Ontario. The Pen Centre: 221 Glendale Ave., St. Catharines; ✆ **905/688-4441.** Niagara Square Mall: 7555 Montrose Rd., Niagara Falls, ON; ✆ 905/668-4441.

Sears Offering a comprehensive range of consumer goods, Sears anchors the Pen Centre in St. Catharines and Seaway Mall in Welland. Like at the Bay, sales and promotions are offered on an ongoing basis. The Pen Centre: 221 Glendale Ave., St. Catharines; ✆ **905/682-6481.** Seaway Mall: 800 Niagara St., Welland; ✆ 905/732-6100.

Fashion, Men's

Phillip Artois Exclusively Italian-made, high-end menswear, Phillip Artois specializes in smart casual clothing, including shirts, slacks, sportswear, and sweaters.

Leather shoes, accessories, better suits, dress shirts, and sports jackets round out the selection. Galleria, Niagara Fallsview Casino Resort, 6380 Fallsview Blvd., Niagara Falls, ON. © **905/356-7400.**

Fashion, Men's & Women's

Irish Design Find Irish books and music, Shetland wool sweaters, and Celtic jewelry at this shop. Irish descendants will appreciate exports such as Taytobrand chips, Inis Energy of the Sea lotions and perfumes, and Claddagh heart rings. The Irish tearoom in the back has Irish favorites such as Barry's imported teas, homemade scones, salmon dill fish cakes, and Bushmill's Irish coffee with a cinnamon shamrock served in your foam. There's also a quiet little patio, removed from the crowds out on the street. 75 Queen St., Niagara-on-the-Lake. © **905/468-7233.**

Roots Although Roots has been a well-known Canadian label for many years, their sponsorship of the Nagano Winter Olympic Games several years ago catapulted their coats, sweaters, and caps into the world spotlight. Demand has grown for their clothing line since that time, particularly in the United States. This casual clothing, in infant to adult sizes, washes and wears well. Only selected stores carry kids' merchandise. Roots has expanded their product line to include fragrances, jewelry, leather goods, and shoes. Table Rock Complex: Queen Victoria Park, Niagara Falls, ON; © **877/642-7275.** Canada One Outlet Mall: 7500 Lundy's Lane, Niagara Falls, ON; © 905/371-2322.

Fashion, Women's

Angie Strauss Fashions Featuring the creations of fashion designer and local artist Angie Strauss, this boutique stocks clothing, hats, jewelry, and accessories. Styles are aimed at more mature women; plus sizes are available. Mix and match separates. Some items feature Strauss's watercolor paintings. Accessories and gifts include gift cards, desk clocks, tote bags, silk scarves, aprons, and paper tole kits. 129 Queen St., Niagara-on-the-Lake. © **888/510-0939** or 905/468-2255. www.angiestrauss.com.

Nantucket Casual and high-fashion clothing and home and garden accessories. Fashion advisor Jennifer Thrasher fills the store with imports from Europe and handcrafted items from the South to create an eclectic assortment of merchandise. 3836 Main St., Jordan. © **905/562-9281.**

The Red Door This tiny white-and-red painted store features a mix of funky, yet conventional women's clothes—women in their 30s or 50s can shop here for clothes, but there's also costume jewelry, frames, dishes, cute and brightly colored bath mats, and a wall of bath soaps and Fruit Frappe lotions. On the trendier side, the purses are fun and well priced. 45 Front St. S., Thorold. © **905/680-2045.**

Tintern on Main Designer and boutique owner Jacqueline Del Col, under the label of Tintern Road, is a gracious host. Del Col's work utilizes higher-end fabrics and fine detailing, yet strives to combine style with practicality. A number of other fine designer labels, selected by Del Col, are also available and include Franco Mirabelli, Michael Kors, and Virani. Find some funky dresses and classy business-casual wear that is a trendier option than clothes available at the majority of the stores in the area. 3836 Main St., Jordan Village. © **905/562-5547.**

Valleverde Nothing form-fitting here; instead it's flowing, airy dresses and other women's clothing. Fine linens and flax organic materials make some naturally beautiful pieces of clothing. 55 Queen St., Niagara-on-the-Lake. © **905/468-3698.**

8

SHOPPING

Shopping A to Z

Gardening

The Copper Leaf   Gardeners will happily browse here for ages, wandering among the statuary, garden tools, furniture, garden decor items, and a small selection of live plants. 3845 Main St., Jordan. ✆ **905/562-0244.** www.thecopperleaf.com. Another location at 10 Queen St., Niagara-on-the-Lake. ✆ 905/468-5323.

Gift & Souvenir Shops

The Canada Store   One of Jordan's most recent Main Street retailers, the Canada Store has plenty of souvenirs and Canadian-made crafts. 3636 Main St., Jordan. ✆ 905/562-9714.

Cecile's Home and Gift Shop   A small shop full of attractive things for the home, china, linens, paper napkins, and soaps. 113 Queen St., Niagara-on-the-Lake. ✆ **905/468-0066.**

From Japan   This may be my favorite shop, even if I just hang out there for awhile. Compared to the noise and bustle of Niagara-on-the-Lake, this is an oasis of calm. The shop specializes in fine Japanese handicrafts. It's a spare and well-designed space, with lovely bowls, plates, kimonos, wood block prints, furniture, papers, incense, and even a stone fountain. 187 Victoria St., Niagara-on-the-Lake. ✆ **905/468-3151.** www.fromjapaninc.com.

Heritage Gift Shop   Proceeds from sales at this shop support the Jordan Historical Museum of the Twenty, which is just 2 minutes down the road on the valley side of Main Street. The museum has several old restored buildings and artifacts, a cemetery where a number of pioneers are buried, and access to the Twenty Valley hiking trails. In the shop, which is fully staffed by volunteers, you will find an assortment of gift items and pieces for the home, many of them with a Victorian flavor. Choose from china, pottery, glassware, candles, linens, and decorative seasonal florals. At the back of the store there is a fudge counter with slices of freshly made sweet, creamy fudge. 3836 Main St., Jordan. ✆ **905/562-4849.**

Mounted Police Trading Post   Royal Canadian Mounted Police collectibles and souvenirs abound in this small shop along with bears, figurines, hats, shirts, and a plethora of tacky souvenirs. 5685 Falls Ave., Niagara Falls, ON. ✆ **800/372-0472.** www.mounted policetradepost.com.

The RCMP Store   This is one of four specialty boutiques within the Table Rock Complex located on the Niagara Parkway, near the lip of the Horseshoe Falls. Merchandise is themed around the Royal Canadian Mounted Police. Shops of Table Rock, Queen Victoria Park, Niagara Falls, ON. ✆ **877/642-7275.**

Serendipity   A joy of a store especially for someone who loves to cook. There are dishes and cookware by Emile Henri, kitchen utensils, one-of-a-kind serving plates, tea towels, and tableware. The store also carries cards and gifts for babies. 44 Queen St., Niagara-on-the-Lake. ✆ **905/468-8881.**

Souvenir City Headquarters   This is a high-volume tourist souvenir stop packed to the rafters with trinkets such as tacky mass-produced beads and totem poles, valor eagle paintings, and personalized Niagara Falls coffee mugs. Groups and buses travel here in droves. The Chocolate Factory serves up fast food. The chocolate fudge is actually worth buying, and some of the maple syrup products (cookies) are also quite good. 4199 River Rd., Niagara Falls, ON. ✆ **905/357-1133.**

Swarovski   This store's world-famous fine Austrian lead crystal figurines can be dust collectors, but the crystal jewelry is quite fashionable, modern, and stylish. The prices, for the quality of necklaces and earrings, are also quite reasonable. Galleria, Niagara Fallsview Casino Resort, Niagara Falls, ON. ✆ **905/354-0118.** www.swarovski.com.

The Viking Shop   If you're an avid collector of ornaments, head here. The Viking Shop carries Hümmel, Royal Doulton, Precious Moments, Lilliput Lane, Peter Rabbit, Willow Tree Angels, Wedgwood, Waterford Crystal, Boyd's Bear, Cherished Teddies—the list goes on. Garden deck chimes and knickknacks abound. 42 Queen St., Niagara-on-the-Lake. © **905/468-2264.**

Hats

BeauChapeau Hat Shop ★   They declare that there is no such thing as a bad hair day, just a good hat day. There are literally thousands of hats in the store. Say fedora, homburg, bowler, or safari—they're all here. And that sexy number Harrison Ford sports in those Indiana Jones movies—yep, officially licensed Indiana Jones wool felt and genuine fur hats are available. Women's hats range from inexpensive knitted beanies to handmade cloches, with berets, upturns, buckets, and wide brims filling out the selection. The shop often supplies the male actors with their hats for productions at the Shaw Theatre Festival. 126 Queen St., Niagara-on-the-Lake. © **905/468-8011.** www.beauchapeau.com.

Home Decor

Acquisitions   For those who love to decorate their homes, room by room, with dedication to detail, look no further than Acquisitions, a retail store that also offers a professional interior design service. Fabrics, wall-coverings, decorative accents, custom furnishings, lighting, mirrors, and artwork can all be found here. 3836 Main St., Jordan. © **905/562-1220.**

CHIC by Jansen   Marrying traditional craftsmanship with modern technology, CHIC by Jansen offers an exclusive selection of hand-carved reproduction furniture. Here you can find original paintings, tiffanies, porcelains, unique bronzes, and elegant lighting to complete your home decor. 3836 Main St., Jordan Village. © **905/562-0083.** www.chicbyjansen.com.

Santa Fe Lifestyle   Home decor items and furniture abound here, but you will also find casual clothing, hand-blown glass, and jewelry. The theme is American Southwest, and there is a mix of authentic and reproduction pieces. K. John Mason, a third-generation blacksmith and sculptor (whose ironworks studio is close by and may be toured by appointment) exhibits his work here. Custom ironwork is available, as is pottery from parts of the southwestern states. 3836 Main St., Jordan. © **905/562-3078.**

Kitchenware

Oneida Home Store   This outlet store features Oneida-brand hollowware, stainless-steel flatware, and silver-plate flatware. Savings can be substantial, but some merchandise is imperfect and some patterns are ones that have been discontinued. 8699 Stanley Ave. S., Niagara Falls, ON. © **905/356-9691.** www.oneida.com.

Leather

The Leather Bazaar & Accessories   Leather goods of all kinds, from belts, pouches, and gloves to handbags, shoes, and clothing, are on offer. 50 Lakeport Rd., Port Dalhousie, St. Catharines. © **905/938-5016.**

Sports Equipment & Clothing

Regatta Sport   Whether you're a recreational athlete or national champion, you will find this specialist clothing and equipment store quite fascinating. This is the place for training and racing gear for rowers, dragon-boaters, cyclists, runners, and other types of athletes. The company was proud to make rowing sweaters for Prince William and his new bride Kate when they visited Canada in the summer of 2011. 50 Lakeport Rd., Port Dalhousie, St. Catharines. ✆ **905/937-7858.** www.regattasport.com.

Toys

Kids Explor-it ☺ Inside the Table Rock Complex located on the Niagara Parkway, near the lip of the Horseshoe Falls, is this shop just for children, designed to be an interactive store and play center. Shops at Table Rock, Queen Victoria Park, Niagara Falls, ON. ✆ **877/642-7275.**

The Owl and the Pussycat The Owl is chock-full of dresses for little girls and pajamas and blue jeans for little boys, as well as toys, teddy bears, and baby-sized sunglasses. 16 Queen St., Niagara-on-the-Lake. ✆ **905/468-3081.**

Turtle Pond Toys ☺ Play areas are set up around the store to encourage kids to try out the merchandise. Higher-quality toys, games, and puzzles for children of all ages. Galleria at Niagara Fallsview Casino Resort, 6380 Fallsview Blvd., Niagara Falls, ON. ✆ **905/357-7710.**

Wine & Spirits

Most of Ontario's wine, some beer, and all spirits are purchased through the provincial government-owned **Liquor Control Board of Ontario (LCBO)** retail stores. There are locations throughout the Niagara region. Look for the vintages section for the best selection of wines from around the world. Individual winery boutiques are also licensed to sell wine, but you can't buy alcoholic beverages in a grocery or convenience store in Ontario. Beer is also available at the Beer Store, a provincially owned and operated business with plenty of locations in the region.

Wine Boutiques

While all of the wineries sell wine at the cellar door, some of them have gone further and extended their offering to almost anything you can think of that has to do with wine and good food. There are many desirable objects that would make an excellent memento of a day in wine country.

All of the following wine boutiques have a range of wines and Icewines, food items, and wine-related gifts, including wine glasses, limited-edition prints, unique bottle openers and bottle stoppers, aprons, cookbooks, sauces, flavored oils and vinegars, and much more:

○ **Angel's Gate Winery,** 4260 Mountainview Rd., Beamsville. ✆ **905/563-3942.** www.angelsgatewinery.com.

○ **Hillebrand Estates Winery,** 1249 Niagara Stone Rd., Niagara-on-the-Lake. ✆ **800/582-8412.**

○ **Inniskillin Niagara Winery,** 1499 Line #3 at the Niagara Pkwy., Niagara-on-the-Lake. ✆ **905/468-3554.** www.inniskillin.com.

○ **Peller Estates Winery,** 290 John St. E., Niagara-on-the-Lake. ✆ **905/468-4678.** www.peller.com.

○ **Peninsula Ridge Estates Winery,** 5600 King St., Beamsville. ✆ **905/563-0900.** www.peninsularidge.com.

○ **Pillitteri Estates Winery,** 1696 Niagara Stone Rd., Niagara-on-the-Lake, ✆ **905/468-3147.** www.pillitteri.com.

NIAGARA REGION AFTER DARK

Nightlife in Niagara Falls has a special quality. This is a popular vacation town, and during high season, once the sun goes down, a party mood takes over and makes the city a pretty glamorous place to be. Where else would you have illuminations and fireworks to rival the Fourth of July every weekend of the summer? At night, both the American and Horseshoe falls are bathed in a spectacular rainbow of colors. Add to that the sizzle of a grand fireworks display on Friday and Sunday evenings during tourist season, and you have a floorshow that grabs everyone's attention.

In the casinos, the action heats up, the bars are busy, and several locations offer good live entertainment. A revitalized Queen Street offers live jazz and intimate cafes, and the crowds on Clifton Hill get very cheerful.

Farther afield, in Niagara-on-the-Lake, a number of pubs and wine bars start buzzing after the theater. While a performance at the Shaw Theatre Festival will take up most of the early evening, there's still time to enjoy a late glass of wine and maybe discover that the person on the barstool next to you is one of the actors you saw performing that evening.

If you're looking for live music or somewhere to dance the night away, St. Catharines has some unique places for the 30-something crowd, while some of the smaller winery towns, like Jordan, have pubs and taverns that showcase local musical talent. Jackson-Triggs Winery runs a series of concerts during the summer, and Henry of Pelham has a series of Shakespearean plays that are performed on an outdoor stage. From live entertainment to dance clubs, there's something to enjoy for pretty well any style of nightlife you are looking for.

Tip: For current shows and performers, look for **Niagara Hot Spots,** the free entertainment guide to what's happening around Niagara, or visit **www.niagaranights.com**.

THE PERFORMING ARTS

From May to October, Niagara's performing arts scene is in high gear. The best-known theatrical draw is the Shaw Theatre Festival, the only festival in the world that is devoted to the life and works of George Bernard Shaw (1856–1950) and his contemporaries, but the presence of this prestigious theater company has inspired several other theatrical and musical endeavors. Throughout the year, concerts, plays, and dance recitals are held in the **Centre for the Arts** at Brock University (500 Glenridge Ave., St. Catharines; ℂ **905/688-5550**). Several small theater companies perform regularly, and dinner theater is a popular draw. Other events in the performing arts arena take place as part of various festivals held in Niagara's many towns and villages (see "Niagara Region Calendar of Events," in chapter 2).

Theater

Gypsy Theatre at the Seneca Queen   This newly renovated theater in the upwardly mobile Queen Street area stages productions like *Cats, The Musical of Musicals,* and *The Chronicles of Narnia.* Performances are staged by the same troupe that operates Gypsy Theatre. Tickets vary for different events, but are generally C$30 per person for groups of eight or more, C$35 for seniors and students, and C$40 for adults. 4630 Queen St., Niagara Falls, ON. ℂ **905/871-4407.**

Shaw Theatre Festival ★★★   Shaw's long life provides the festival with a nearly bottomless source of material to present each year, and their eclectic offerings range from intimate dramas to social satire to entertaining musicals. The Shaw Theatre Festival is a nonprofit charitable organization as opposed to a commercial theater, which allows for a degree of freedom in the choice of productions. In 2011, for example, the theater performed Tennessee Williams's *Cat on a Hot Tin Roof* as well as Shaw's *My Fair Lady.*

The company's main season runs from April to the end of October, and has 1,700 theater seats in four theaters. The largest is the **Festival Theatre,** which at 856 seats is still intimate by most standards. This is where the grand season opening takes place each May and where the main large productions occur, and it also includes a cafe and outdoor patio as well as a theater shop. **The Court House Theatre,** located where the Shaw Theatre Festival began in 1962, has 327 seats in a "thrust" configuration. It is an intimate place to watch a performance, and the audience is provocatively close to the action. This building, interestingly, was also the site of Upper Canada's first parliament.

The Royal George Theatre, which seats 328, was built in 1915 as a vaudeville house for the purpose of entertaining troops stationed on the Commons in the town during World War I and acquired by the Shaw Theatre Festival in 1980. Through the generosity of philanthropist Walter Carsen, it was completely renovated and is now an attractive "opera house"–style theater. **The Studio Theatre,** which doubles as a rehearsal hall, is located in the newly constructed Donald and Elaine Triggs Production Centre attached to the Festival Theatre. The seating arrangement is flexible, depending on the needs of the particular show appearing in that space, with a maximum capacity of 175 seats.

To enrich your Shaw experience, plan to attend one of the many theatrical events that take place throughout the season. **Backstage tours** are held Saturday mornings from June to October. Between May and August, informal **preshow chats** give an introduction to the evening's play prior to most performances. On most Tuesday evenings, post-performance, the audience is invited to remain in the theater for an **informal Q&A session.** The public can **engage in discussions with members of the theater company** on selected Saturdays during July and August prior to the matinee performance. **Free concerts** are held on selected Sundays throughout the season in the lobby of the Festival Theatre at 11am. The festival also offers staged readings and workshops throughout the season; check their website for more information.

Ticket Bargains

There are several ways to get a discount on your Shaw tickets. One of the best promotions that the company offers, and a great way to encourage young people to attend performances, is the **under 30** promotion where those between 19 and 29 years can enjoy regularly priced and Preview performances at all theaters for just C$30. Proof of age required. Students can book C$30 seats in the Festival Theatre balcony for regularly priced performances. Valid student ID is required. **Super Sunday** tickets are discounted 25% to 50% for Sunday evening performances. There is an early-booking bonus of between 10% and 15%. See www.shawfest.com for details for the current season.

The Shaw announces its festival program in September. Tickets are difficult to obtain on short notice, so book in advance.

Contact the box office at the Festival Theatre for tickets for all four venues. 10 Queen's Parade, P.O. Box 774, Niagara-on-the-Lake, ON, L0S 1J0. © **800/511-SHAW** (511-7429) or 905/468-2172. www.shawfest.com.

Shakespeare in the Vineyard For two 3-day runs on adjacent weekends in July, one of Shakespeare's plays is performed in a temporary outdoor theater, under much the same circumstances as the plays were originally performed in Elizabethan London (except there are chairs to sit on, the female parts are played by females, and the person next to you will likely have brushed his teeth). The performances are staged adjacent to the Henry of Pelham Winery, and the wine bar is open from 6 to 7pm. The performance starts at 7pm. The acting may be a bit unpolished, and if it rains there are no refunds, only a ticket for another performance. But it is good fun, especially if you are a fan of the bard. Tickets are C$25. All proceeds go to the Niagara Peninsula Children's Centre. For reservations, call the Brock University Centre for the Arts at © **905/688-5550,** ext. 3257, or order tickets online at www.arts.brocku. ca. Henry of Pelham Winery, 469 Pelham Rd., R.R. 1, St. Catharines.

Repertory & Dinner Theater

Firehall Theatre The Niagara Falls Music Theatre Society is a community theater group, performing a selection of musicals, drama, and comedies, such as Neil Simon's *The Odd Couple.* They stage a three-play season through the fall and winter months. Tickets are C$15 for adults, C$14 for students and seniors. 4990 Walnut St., Niagara Falls, ON. © **905/356-4953.** www.firehalltheatre.net.

Garrison Little Theatre This is Fort Erie's live theater company, which has been performing since 1986. They perform matinees and dinner theater with three different productions running in November, February, and April. Italo-Canadian Club, 1101 DiPietro St., Fort Erie. © **905/871-3520.**

Greg Frewin Theatre This 700-seat dinner theater presents a Las Vegas–style magic show, complete with large cats, showgirls, and astounding illusions by Greg Frewin, the award-winning International Grand Champion of Magic. Matinees start at 3pm, and the evening show starts at 8pm all year; an optional preshow dinner is served at 6:30pm. After the show, you can get your picture taken with a tiger. Suitable for the entire family. 5781 Ellen Ave., Niagara Falls, ON. © **866/779-8778** or 905/356-0777. www. gregfrewintheatre.com.

Gypsy Theatre, Fort Erie Primarily a summer theater company, the Gypsy Theatre has a permanent professional acting company that performs an eclectic range of shows. Past performances include vivacious *Cats, Nunsense,* and *Shirley Valentine.* 465 Central Ave., Fort Erie. ℂ **877/990-7529** or 905/871-4407. www.gypsytheatre.com.

Niagara Falls Grand Dinner Theatre The Niagara Grand offers lunch and dinner shows. Plays are selected for their suitability for all ages; recent shows included the comedy *Greetings* by Tom Dudzick, and *Drinking Alone* by Norm Foster. The season runs from March to December. Queen Victoria Place, 6345 Niagara Pkwy., Niagara Falls, ON. ℂ **866/845-SHOW** (845-7469).

Oh Canada Eh! Dinner Show An evening of Canadian comfort food and squeaky-clean musical entertainment awaits. During the main tourist season, the "Oh Canada Eh!" show plays daily. Starting at 6:30pm (ending at 9pm), guests pass around four courses (just like home) during the performance, while actors double up as servers to clear the table. Matinees are scheduled on some days beginning at 3pm. You'll hear Newfie jokes and a host of Canadian songs made popular by such artists as Shania Twain and Anne Murray. Canadian audiences might appreciate—or cringe—from the Mounties, hockey players, lumberjacks, and even *Anne of Green Gables* references, but American visitors can appreciate a bit of border humor, too. For the most part, the jokes are quite corny and the constant clapping and screaming out "EH!" may not be for everyone. 8585 Lundy's Lane, Niagara Falls, ON. ℂ **800/467-2071** or 905/374-1995.

Port Mansion Dinner Theatre ★ I belly-laughed and was on the verge of tears watching the shows here—the theater is engaging and heartfelt. You can watch the play with a glass of wine at your table in the balcony-style seating—very cozy. The dinner beforehand is standard fare (steak, pasta, salmon) and might be worth skipping. The adjacent 88-seat cabaret-style Theatre in Port provides an intimate theater experience all year, performing musicals, comedies, and dramas, like *Breaking and Entering.* Lively nightlife hops nonstop at the PM nightclub. In the summer, PM stages theme nights, including Friday Miami Nights and Band Night Thursdays; and DJs from local radio stations spin tunes on Wednesdays and Saturdays. 12 Lakeport Rd., Port Dalhousie. ℂ **866/452-7678** or 905/934-0575. www.portmansion.com.

Showboat Festival Theatre A variety of comedy, drama, mystery, and musical performances is produced from mid-June to the end of August by the Showboat Festival Theatre. Professional shows include *Mending Fences, I'll Be Back before Midnight,* and *2 Across.* The intimate 220-seat theater-in-the-round is located in the historical setting of the Roselawn Centre for the Living Arts, a facility that incorporates Roselawn, a stone-and-brick 1860 Victorian building. 296 Fielden Ave., Port Colborne. ℂ **888/870-8181** or 905/834-0833. www.showboattheatre.ca.

Music

Although the Niagara region offers great live theater, its options for a night of music are a little more limited. **Pop performers** with a decidedly mainstream bent often perform at the Avalon Ballroom in the **Niagara Fallsview Casino Resort** (6380 Fallsview Blvd., Niagara Falls, ON; ℂ **888/836-8118**). More diverse fare, from folk to rock to classical, can be found during July and August at the 500-seat open-air amphitheater at Jackson-Triggs Winery (2145 Niagara Stone Rd., Niagara-on-the-Lake; ℂ **866/589-4637**).

Those who prefer classical or choral music will appreciate the professional offerings of **Chorus Niagara** and the **Niagara Symphony,** both of which perform at the

Centre for the Arts, Brock University (500 Glenridge Ave., St. Catharines; ✆ **905/ 688-5550**). Chorus Niagara's repertoire includes a diverse range of choral programs, from full orchestra accompaniment to a cappella, and from ancient music to premiere performances. The Niagara Symphony Orchestra plays both classical and pop concerts.

THE CLUB, LIVE MUSIC & BAR SCENE

Downtown Niagara Falls, Ontario, buzzes with noise and crowds, particularly along Falls Avenue and Clifton Hill. Niagara-on-the-Lake is much quieter, offering cozy and elegant hotel bars and a pub or two. St. Catharines caters to the student crowd. In the smaller towns, there are some neighborhood pubs and small entertainment venues that will give you a taste of the local talent.

Dance clubs, bars, and live entertainment venues, by nature, are constantly evolving, as they try to keep up with or keep ahead of their patrons' latest passions in terms of music and drinks. By the time you visit some of the venues listed here, they may have changed the type of music they offer, the decor, the beer, or even their name. The best thing to do is to head out and look for the action. You will definitely find lots of choices.

Comedy Clubs

House of Comedy   Stand-up comedians entertain in the House of Comedy's new venue, which is a larger and brighter space than the previous basement location. Those with tender ears should be warned that comedians can be quite raw in their subject matter—cursing is rampant. Entertainers like David Coulier from *Full House* and Sailish the Hypnotist perform, and a dinner-and-show package is available. Shows are Friday and Saturday nights. Doors open at 8pm; shows begin at 9pm. 4189 Stanley Ave., Niagara Falls, ON. ✆ **905/357-SHOW** (357-7469). www.thehouseofcomedy.com.

Dance Clubs & Lounges

Club Rialto   One of the few places catering to the over-30 crowd, with music that's a little less hip-hop and a little more Billy Joel. DJs and karaoke rule. You'll find it tucked away at the back of the Casa d'Oro Restaurant. 5875 Victoria Ave., in Casa d'Oro Restaurant, Niagara Falls, ON. ✆ **905/356-5646.**

CopaCabana's Brazilian Steak House   Imagine sipping a minty mojito on a hot summer night to a live Brazilian band and the Rio Samba Divas dancing. Every weekend, there's live Brazilian music with tasty—but expensive—Caribbean drinks. For eats, there's a Brazilian Churrascaria—a South American style of dining featuring a "full rodizo"; waiters come around with giant skewers of slow-cooked meat (12 kinds of Angus-grade beef) carved tableside onto your plate. A glass facade opens up to one of the largest patios in the city with an outdoor grill in the summer. 6671 Fallsview Blvd., Niagara Falls, ON. ✆ **905/354-8775.** www.copacabana.ca.

Dragonfly   Long red velvet curtains and exceedingly tall dark metal doors give this Asian-inspired nightclub an ominous and sensual feel. Over 930 sq. m (10,010 sq. ft.), this is Niagara's place to be for young sophisticates (20s and up). Open Tuesday, Wednesday, Friday, and Saturday. Orchid Fridays (C$10 cover) is ladies' night, featuring a DJ spinning R&B, house, party mix, and rock; Saturdays (C$15 cover) offer rock, club anthems, and R&B. Doors open at 10pm; call ahead to reserve a spot to

The Club, Live Music & Bar Scene

avoid the notorious line. The place gets hopping around 11pm. 6380 Fallsview Blvd., Concourse Level, Unit 109, Niagara Falls, ON. ☏ **905/356-4691.** www.dragonflynightclub.com.

Hard Rock Club   Can't decide what you want to do tonight? The Hard Rock Club has a dance floor with doors that open to the street, so you can see the Falls while you boogie. Not in the mood for dancing? Relax in the retro lounge, accented with red plush velvet, or check out the martini bar. The outdoor patio is popular in the summer. Local trendy 20- and 30-somethings like to hang here. 5701 Falls Ave., Niagara Falls, ON. ☏ **905/356-7625.**

Rumours Night Club   If you've got the energy to dance, dance, dance, then head to Rumours, smack in the middle of the carnival atmosphere of the "Street of Fun" at the top of Clifton Hill. This perennially popular club regularly sees lines out the door. Huge video screens, blasting sound, and a laser show are on tap here. Music ranges from retro '80s and '90s to Top-40 tunes, with an all-request mix on Sunday nights. Dress to impress. 4960 Clifton Hill, Niagara Falls, ON. ☏ **905/358-6152.** Cover $5 (Canadian and U.S. currency).

Eclectic

After Hours   This restaurant and lounge is frequented by an easygoing 30-plus crowd, dropping in for appetizers, dinner, or Niagara wines, and willing to take in whatever music is on offer. Entertainers include vocalists, quartets, and bands, singing and playing everything from Celtic tunes, acoustic guitar, and rock to jazz and blues. 5470 Victoria Ave., Niagara Falls, ON. ☏ **905/357-2503.**

The Moose & Goose   This student hangout has hosted some great live rock bands, including Billy Talent, Finger 11, Kim Mitchell, The Tea Party, and The Trews. 54 Front St., Thorold. ☏ **905/227-6969.**

365 Club   Located just steps away from the action on the vast gaming floor of the Niagara Fallsview Casino Resort, this intimate lounge and bar has no cover charge.

 DESIGNED FOR romance

If you're thinking quiet romance and conversation, one of the sexiest places to be in the evening is **R5** (6380 Fallsview Blvd., Niagara Falls, ON; ☏ **888/325-5788;** www.fallsviewcasinoresort.com), a hard-to-find little bar in the Fallsview Casino. Tucked away just above the Golden Lotus, and accessible by elevator, this is the essence of sophistication. The decor is sharp contemporary, with a "fire and ice" theme. Grey leather sofas are placed so you can look out full-length windows at one of the best views of the Falls, or stand out on the balcony—a spectacular place to view the evening fireworks. The bar serves standard drinks like mojitos and martinis and also stocks a 6,000-bottle wine collection including a 1942 Chateau Petrus for that night you really want to celebrate. There are also special drinks, like the Black Pearl, a C$1,200 shot of Louis XIII Remy Martin cognac. They also can arrange to serve a diamond ring or a tennis bracelet in a lovely cocktail, as a creative way to propose or just to give a little token of your love.

There are fireplaces in several locations of the multi-floored space, and you can order plates of tapas and sushi. R5 is open Monday to Thursday 4pm to 1am, Friday 4pm to 2am, Saturday 2pm to 2am, and Sunday 2pm to 1am. A live pianist plays Thursday, Friday, and Saturday from 8pm to 1am.

The Club, Live Music & Bar Scene

NIAGARA REGION AFTER DARK

Niagara Falls After Dark

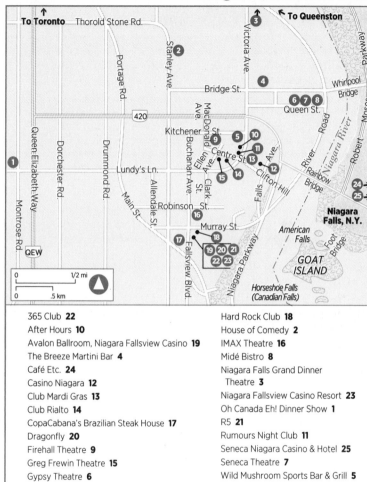

365 Club **22**
After Hours **10**
Avalon Ballroom, Niagara Fallsview Casino **19**
The Breeze Martini Bar **4**
Café Etc. **24**
Casino Niagara **12**
Club Mardi Gras **13**
Club Rialto **14**
CopaCabana's Brazilian Steak House **17**
Dragonfly **20**
Firehall Theatre **9**
Greg Frewin Theatre **15**
Gypsy Theatre **6**

Hard Rock Club **18**
House of Comedy **2**
IMAX Theatre **16**
Midé Bistro **8**
Niagara Falls Grand Dinner
  Theatre **3**
Niagara Fallsview Casino Resort **23**
Oh Canada Eh! Dinner Show **1**
R5 **21**
Rumours Night Club **11**
Seneca Niagara Casino & Hotel **25**
Seneca Theatre **7**
Wild Mushroom Sports Bar & Grill **5**

The 365 Breeze martini is a great fruity cocktail to sip (amongst other cocktails) while being entertained by a variety of cabarets, lounge singers, and other live stage acts. From Thursday to Sunday, a local band plays '60s and '70s tunes for an older crowd, from 8:30 until 10:30pm. Another band plays Top-10 radio picks until 2am. Inside the Niagara Fallsview Casino Resort, 6380 Fallsview Blvd., Niagara Falls, ON. © **888/FALLS-VU** (325-5788). www.fallsviewcasinoresort.com.

Wild Mushroom Sports Bar & Grill   This is one of those bars where everybody knows your name after just a few minutes. It's a bit on the rough-and-tumble side, but it's an authentic local bar, and you are bound to encounter some real characters. 5633 Victoria Ave., Niagara Falls, ON. © **905/357-2788.**

Jazz & Blues

Café Etc.   This cafe-cum-jazz-bar swings with live music on Friday and Saturday nights. 462 Third St., Niagara Falls, NY. ℂ **716/285-0801.**

Club Mardi Gras   Open 7 nights a week, 9pm to 2am, this is the place for those who like their evening fun to be a bit on the edge. There's some real partying "New Orleans Style," complete with the beads, the masks, the music, and a patio overlooking Clifton Hill. When you know that the club was the site for the Girls Gone Wild Canadian Tour 2005, you get an idea of the kind of dancing and partying that occurs. 4967 Clifton Hill, Niagara Falls, ON (entrance and parking off Oneida Lane). ℂ **905/356-9165.** www.clubmardigrasniagara.com.

Jordan Tavern   There has been a roadhouse on this site since 1844, and it has hosted everything from church services to vigilante meetings in its history. Today this spot, although freshly renovated, has retained the comfortable roadhouse style. There's live entertainment here every Friday and Saturday night, starting at 9pm. It's a very casual and local-style place, featuring acts like Mr. Rick and the Biscuits, the Bill Culp Duo, and Trigger Finger. 3751 Main St., Jordan. ℂ **905/562-9591.** www.jordanhouse.ca.

Midé Bistro   This interesting little bistro, which also has an oxygen bar, features live jazz every second Friday evening, from 7 to 10pm. There is a C$12 cover, and food and drink are available. They also do a Sunday jazz brunch. Call for current information. 4337 Queen St., Niagara Falls, ON. ℂ **289/296-5632.** www.midebistro.com.

Stella's   Imagine an industrial open-spaced apartment: brick walls, exposed wooden ceilings, and an expansive hardwood floor for dancing to DJ-spun Top-40 tunes on the weekend. There's a VIP area in the back and high-backed booths on either side for the 25-plus crowd to take a break. Nightly specials include half-priced drinks from 11am until 8pm on Friday, and half-priced martinis on Thursdays. An extensive menu includes Italian fare. 45 James St., St. Catharines. ℂ **905/685-3000.** www.stellasdowntown.ca.

Gay & Lesbian Clubs

In December 2007, the U.S.-based Travel Industry Association named Niagara Falls 6th in the top 10 "gay-friendly" destinations in Canada.

The Breeze Martini Bar   This is a small and cozy "leather" bar with Leather Night on Thursday, Martini Night on Friday, Party-Pick Up Night on Saturday, and Tea Dances on Sunday. 4776 Bridge St., Niagara Falls, ON. ℂ **905/348-6297.**

Club Rendezvous   Niagara's longest gay-owned and -operated business, this club features cabaret events, dinner buffets, movie nights, free pool nights, and karaoke. 151 Queenston St., St. Catharines. ℂ **905/684-0451.**

FILM

IMAX

IMAX Theatre   IMAX technology is a Canadian invention. The screen is more than six stories high, which is almost overwhelming in terms of visual stimulation. Add 12,000 watts of digital surround sound, and you've got the whole picture. The film *Niagara: Miracles, Myths, and Magic* has been the star of the theater for many, many years and has become a little dated, but it nevertheless gives tourists who

Niagara Region After Dark

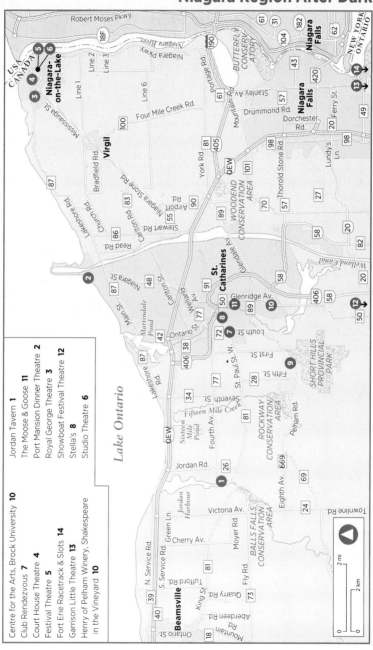

Robert Moses Pkwy.

Niagara River

Niagara Pkwy.

USA
CANADA

Niagara-
on-the-Lake

Virgil

Line 1
Line 2
Line 3
Line 6

Four Mile Creek Rd.

Bradfield Rd.
Church Rd.
Lakeshore Rd.
Read Rd.
Carlton Rd.
Niagara Stone Rd.
Stewart Rd.
Airport Rd.

Portage Rd.

Stanley Av.
Mountain Rd.

BUTTERFLY CONSERVATORY

Niagara Falls

New York Ontario

Niagara Falls

Drummond Rd.
Dorchester Rd.
Ferry St.
Lundy's Ln.

Welland Canal

St. Catharines

Glendale Av.
Glenridge Av.
Louth St.
St. Paul St. W.
First St.
Fifth St.
Seventh St.
Fourth Av.
Pelham Rd.

WOODEND CONSERVATION AREA

SHORT HILLS PROVINCIAL PARK

ROCKWAY CONSERVATION AREA

Martindale Pond
Fifteen Mile Creek
Sixteen Mile Pond

Main St.
Welland Av.
Carlton St.
Niagara St.
Ontario St.
Lakeshore Rd.

Lake Ontario

Jordan Rd.
Jordan Harbour

Victoria Av.
Cherry Av.
Green Ln.
Moyer Rd.
Eighth Av.
Quarry Rd.
Fly Rd.
Aberdeen Rd.
Mountain Rd.
Tufford Rd.
King St.
N. Service Rd.
S. Service Rd.
Townline Rd.

BALLS FALLS CONSERVATION AREA

Beamsville
Ontario St.

Centre for the Arts, Brock University **10**
Club Rendezvous **7**
Court House Theatre **4**
Festival Theatre **5**
Fort Erie Racetrack & Slots **14**
Garrison Little Theatre **13**
Henry of Pelham Winery, Shakespeare in the Vineyard **10**

Jordan Tavern **1**
The Moose & Goose **11**
Port Mansion Dinner Theatre **2**
Royal George Theatre **3**
Showboat Festival Theatre **12**
Stella's **8**
Studio Theatre **6**

SAVE ON imax TICKETS

Discounts on IMAX tickets are plentiful—if you know where to look. Most hotels offer discounted tickets—just ask at the reception desk. You can also purchase tickets online at a lower price than at the box office. Another way to save (if you are planning a trip up the nearby Skylon Tower) is to buy a SkyMax combo ticket.

are unfamiliar with the Falls and all its history a broad appreciation of the seventh, forgotten wonder of the natural world. The re-creation of such spectacles as the Great Blondin's tightrope antics over the gorge, Annie Taylor's foolhardy yet brave plunge over the Falls in a barrel, and the daring folks who have shot the rapids makes for interesting viewing.

There is an impressive collection of original daredevil barrels and other historical artifacts in the **Niagara Falls Daredevil Gallery,** which is free whether you have movie tickets or not. The containers are open for viewing and visitors are invited to touch, unlike in most museums. Also on-site is a **National Geographic** gift shop. 6170 Fallsview Blvd., Niagara Falls, ON. ℂ **905/374-IMAX** (374-4629).

Repertory Cinema

If you're a fan of independent, foreign, and second-run films, check out events at **Brock University,** 500 Glenridge Ave., St. Catharines (ℂ **905/688-5550**). The Brock University Film Society screens films on Sunday evenings in the David S. Howes Theatre on campus. Visit www.arts.brocku.ca/boxoffice.php for schedules, pricing, and parking details.

The **Niagara Indie Filmfest** is held annually in June at various downtown St. Catharines locations. The festival showcases Canadian short film and video works. For more details, visit **www.niagaraindiefilmfest.org**, or call the **Festival Hotline** (ℂ **905/685-8336**).

GAMING

Casino Niagara Niagara's original casino, this casino features more than 2,400 slot and video poker machines on two gaming levels. With its fake palm trees, joker face masks, and less contemporary carpets, the setting is reminiscent of old-style Las Vegas. The dress here is quite casual—jeans and sneakers. And even though the casino went nonsmoking, the smell still lingers in the carpets. Table games include blackjack, roulette, craps, Sic-Bo, Pai-Gow, baccarat, mini-baccarat, three-card poker, and Let it Ride. Lower-limit tables and an exclusive high-limit gaming area are offered on-site. Beginners can play the slots with ease; there are plenty of machines to go around, even on a busy night. You have a choice of valet parking or Park'n'Ride shuttle service from a nearby parking lot. Dining choices include Perks Café, the Market Buffet, and the Quench Bar. Lucky's Steakhouse offers a dark and romantic hideaway for some quiet time. The casino is open 24 hours a day, every day of the year. 5705 Falls Ave., Niagara Falls, ON. ℂ **888/WIN-FALL** (946-3255).

Fort Erie Racetrack & Slots   The Fort Erie Racetrack, more than 100 years old, features live thoroughbred racing in a season that stretches from late April to early November; the outdoor track runs around a beautiful garden and pond. The racetrack hosts one of the Canadian horse racing season's most prestigious events, the Prince of Wales Crown, which is the second leg of Canada's Triple Crown. Simulcast racing is also available. Inside, the venue isn't as pretty, to say the least, but it is popular with an older crowd. Those who like to gamble on the slots will find 1,200 slot machines to keep them occupied. Dining ranges from all-you-can-eat buffets to roadhouse-style menus. Bertie St., Fort Erie. 🕐 **800/295-3770.** www.forterieracing.com.

Niagara Fallsview Casino Resort   Romanesque in style—gold trim on the ceilings and crown molding, grand light fixtures and marble floors—this upscale casino is full of people who dress up and want to be seen. It features an 18,580-sq.-m (199,993-sq.-ft.) casino that operates 24 hours a day, every day of the year. There are 150 gaming tables and more than 3,000 slot machines in the vast gaming area; high rollers can enter the private salon (most tables start at C$100) with a members' lounge. For the novice gambler, there are slot machines that take bets as low as a quarter. If you want to take a break from the gambling, catch icons such as Diana Ross and Wayne Newton at the Avalon Ballroom or watch some live local entertainment while having a drink at the 365 Club. There is a 368-room hotel, a full-service hotel spa, and a luxury shopping galleria. A unique hydroelectric water sculpture dominates the main entrance to the resort. In front of the complex, a series of waterfalls provides an ever-changing display, complete with colored lighting after dark. Ten dining options—including some of the area's best sushi and Italian—ensure every pocketbook and palate is represented. 6380 Fallsview Blvd., Niagara Falls, ON. 🕐 **888/FALLS-VU** (325-5788). www.fallsviewcasinoresort.com.

Seneca Niagara Casino & Hotel   This American casino feels a bit raw: Waitresses, dressed in short hockey jerseys, serve free alcohol amidst thick cigarette smoke. There are 3,200 reel-spinning and video slot machines and almost 100 gaming tables on the large floor that once was a convention center, including blackjack, craps, roulette, and more. A separate poker room is available for play. Above the bar, in the center of the room, a band plays most nights; the music is geared toward an older crowd. Parking is free, as are all beverages. Patrons must be 21 years of age or over and must have photo ID available. Hungry gamblers can choose steak, buffet, or sports pub–style food. 310 Fourth St., Niagara Falls, NY. 🕐 **877/873-6322** or 716/299-1100. www.senecaniagaracasino.com.

Gambling Should Be Fun, Not Obsessive

Many people enjoy playing games of chance for entertainment. But for a minority of people, gambling becomes a real problem, and they find themselves unable to control the amount of money they spend. Information on dealing with a gambling problem can be obtained by calling the **Ontario Problem Gambling Helpline** at 🕐 **888/230-3505.**

SIDE TRIPS FROM NIAGARA

N iagara Falls dominates the region, and most visitors who stay for awhile will schedule their visit to the Falls on the first day. A stay for a few more days will take in excursions to the wine country and to Niagara-on-the-Lake to absorb both wine and history.

But if you have time and truly want to acquaint yourself with this area, several day trips will take you to some of the most historically rich and culinarily gifted towns in the region.

A drive to Port Colborne, on the shores of Lake Erie, takes you past historic Welland Canal and the Locks, as well as allowing you to enjoy an afternoon at some of the province's best white-sand beaches.

On a visit to Hamilton, you'll be rewarded with castles, historic homes, a world-class art gallery, and Canada's most famous gardens, the Royal Botanical Gardens.

For art lovers, an artists' studio trail introduces you to some of the best artists in Niagara, who take great delight in showing you around their studios.

Food lovers can enjoy tours of the abundant producers who grow and make such gourmet delicacies as artisanal breads and cheeses, organic lamb, herbs, honey, vinegars—a long list of delicious items to consume or to take home. It is also a trek that can supply the makings of a memorable picnic.

And with the celebrations for the 200th anniversary of the War of 1812, and the 200 years of peace that have followed, all of these day-trip destinations have festivals and events planned that will appeal to any history-loving traveler.

PORT COLBORNE & THE WELLAND CANAL

Port Colborne

The city of Port Colborne, a 42km (26-mile) or 30-minute drive from Niagara, has had close ties to the shipping industry from its inception. The original settlement was known as Gravelly Bay and dates from 1832. It was renamed after Sir John Colborne, a British war hero and the Lieutenant Governor of Upper Canada at the time of the opening of the southern terminus of the first Welland Canal in 1833.

Port Colborne & the Welland Canal

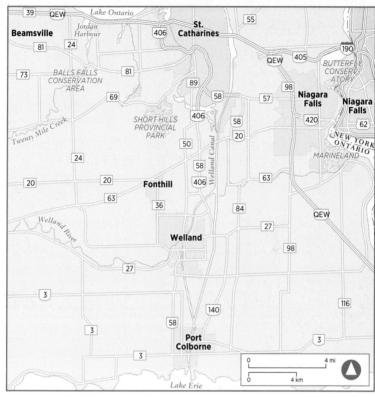

By the 1880s, Port Colborne had become an important summer tourist resort, as paddle-wheeled steamers and steam trains brought hundreds of tourists on a daily basis to lakeside resorts such as Lake View Grove and the exclusive Humberstone Club.

The city's position at the gateway of the southern entrance to the Welland Canal has played a pivotal role in its development. To celebrate that connection, the city hosts Canal Days Marine Heritage Festival in August, which highlights Lock 8, which at 420m (1,378 ft.) is one of the world's longest canal locks. Port Colborne was recently awarded the designation as a Fair Trade City, the first one to be awarded this designation in Ontario. Port Colborne is only the fourth community in Canada to earn the achievement.

The town today is an interesting blend of the old and the new, with a well-preserved historic center, a busy harbor, a varied and sophisticated shopping district along the canal side, and scenic sandy beaches. It is a town that really comes to life in the summer months. The historic shopping district on West Street by Bridge 21 provides visitors with plenty of shops and park benches to relax. It is not uncommon to see wooden tall ships quietly moored here along the canal wall as they wait for clearance to transit the canal.

A curiosity in town is the incredible shrinking mill, which is an optical illusion produced when viewing the federal grain elevator. When traveling east on Lakeshore Road, the mill appears to move farther away as one drives closer.

ESSENTIALS

GETTING THERE   The drive to Port Colborne is an easy and enjoyable one, taking you alongside the Welland Canal and the Locks, passing by some of the smaller towns like Thorold and Welland, and winding through farm country.

If you're traveling by **car** from Toronto, take the QEW Niagara to Regional Road 24 at Vineland. Take Hwy. 24 south to Hwy. 3. Follow Hwy. 3 to Port Colborne. From St. Catharines, take Hwy. 406 south to Hwy. 140. Take Hwy. 140 south to Hwy. 3. Turn right on Hwy. 3 to Port Colborne.

For a more active way to get to Port Colborne, you can **bike** from St. Catharines along the Welland Canals Parkway. To access the trail, turn north off the QEW onto Ontario Street. Follow Ontario Street, which turns into Lakeshore Road, until you reach the Welland Canal. There's a park on the west side where you can leave your car, and the trail begins here. This 45km (28-mile) paved trail follows the canal along its west bank from St. Catharines through Thorold, Welland, and Port Colborne. It is an easy route, with the exception of one short section where the trail climbs the Escarpment at Thorold. There is, however, a rest spot at the top, and a convenience store across the road. In Thorold, the path crosses onto the Thorold Island, between the old Third Canal and the current Fourth Canal. In Welland, it follows the old Fourth Canal through the city. The trail zigzags across the canal in Port Colborne until it meets the Friendship Trail at Seaway Park.

VISITOR INFORMATION   For visitor information about the Port Colborne area from mid-May to mid-October, visit the **Humberstone Hall Visitor Information Center,** 76 Main St. W., at Mellanby Ave. (✆ **800/PORT-FUN** [767-8386] or 905/834-1668; www.portcolborne.ca). From mid-October to mid-May, visitor information can be found at City Hall, 66 Charlotte St.

The Heritage Port Colborne Committee publishes a self-guided walking tour of 33 heritage homes, sites, and properties in the community. The tour follows two different routes: one 1.5km (1 mile) and another 3.8km (2⅓ miles) in length. Hard copies of the tour guide and map are available at Humberstone Hall Visitor Information Center, as well as City Hall, the library, and *The Leader* newspaper office. You can also download a map at www.portcolborne.ca.

   How Does a Lock Work?

The locks were a brilliant solution to the problem of getting ships and their cargo from Lake Erie to Lake Ontario. But in reality, it was gravity that provided the answer. Water flows downhill from the higher elevation of Lake Erie to Lake Ontario. A ship sailing from Lake Ontario to Lake Erie has to be raised through each lock to a higher water level. First the ship enters the lock and is secured with ropes or cables. Next, the gates are closed and large valves are opened to allow water from the canal above the lock to flow through large pipes. The ship begins to rise. When the water level has risen to the height of that in the canal above the lock, the gates are opened and the ship sails out. The process is repeated until the last lock raises the ship to the level of the lake.

The pride of the Port Colborne Historical Museum is the Neff Steam Buggy, the oldest Ontario-made car, and the second oldest car in Canada. Built by Benton Neff in his Port Colborne foundry in 1901, the car has had quite a career, traveling around North America to different car shows after it was rescued from the wreckers and restored by antique car aficionado Loren Holmwood. Holmwood donated the car to the museum so it could return to its birthplace. An operating replica is available so visitors can take a ride in a copy of what has been called "the finest antique automobile in North America."

WHAT TO SEE & DO

Ship-watching and the **Welland Canal,** at Main Street, draw tourists with a desire to watch "saltie" or "laker" ships, as they slip through the canal. One of the best ship-watching locations in Port Colborne is at Lock 8 Park.

Overlooking the Welland Canal and one of the world's longest locks, **Lock 8 Gateway Park** opened in November 5, 1979, to mark the 150th anniversary of the opening of the first Welland Canal. As a regulating, or guard gate, Lock 8 raises or lowers ships .3 to 1.2m (1–4 ft.), depending on Lake Erie water levels. The "Jack-knife" bridges at either end are raised and lowered as ships pass in or out of the lock. The park has an elevated viewing platform, flower gardens, fountains, a picnic pavilion, and washrooms. Information on the canal and on ship schedules and destinations is available at the Visitor Information Centre, located across Mellanby Avenue from the park.

At the **Port Colborne Historical and Marine Museum,** 280 King St. (© 905/834-7604), interpretive exhibits showcase the history of Port Colborne and the Welland Canal. Marine artifacts include the wheelhouse from the *Yvon Dupre Jr.,* the anchor from the *Raleigh,* and a lifeboat from the SS *Hochelaga.* Part of the museum is a heritage village, which includes the original 1869 Georgian revival–style carriage house of Arabella Williams, Humberstone's first log schoolhouse, the 1850 log home of John and Sally Sherk, the 1880 F. W. Woods and Sons Marine Blacksmith Shop, and a 1915 Edwardian cottage. The museum also houses Canada's Century Car, the 1901 Neff Steam Buggy. The museum is free, and it's open from May to December, daily from noon to 5pm. There's also a gift shop and Arabella's Tea Room, which is open daily from June to September from 2 to 4pm daily. Tours are offered on request.

The **Sugarloaf Marina,** on Elm Street at Sugarloaf Harbour, is a busy place in summertime, with 500 boat slips, a restaurant with a lively patio, shopping, fishing, scuba diving, and sailing. There is live entertainment on several weekends during the summer, and the marina also runs fishing derbies.

Located on Welland Street, fronting Lake Erie, **Nickel Beach** is perfect for nature lovers, who can explore the white-sand dunes. The public beach has shady picnic areas, washrooms, and unsupervised swimming. Keep an eye out for the homely but very rare Fowler toad, a protected species that makes its home there.

For history lovers, there are several themed walk/drive trips that can be taken, following the paths of the individuals and armies fighting the War of 1812. Visit www.discover1812.com for trip ideas, itineraries, and events around this important time in Niagara history.

10

SIDE TRIPS FROM NIAGARA

Port Colborne & the Welland Canal

OUTDOOR ACTIVITIES

Horseplay Niagara, Hwy. 3 (𝄞 **905/834-2380;** www.horseplayniagara.com) runs **horseback rides** along the beach and dune buggy rides over a dirt track. There are 1- and 2-hour horseback rides, sunset trail rides, cookouts, and romance packages. The routes travel along the Trans-Canada Trail, on secluded pathways, and along scenic lakes or beaches.

Because of its location on the north shore of Lake Erie, Port Colborne offers good opportunities for **bird-watching** during spring and fall migration periods. Local wetlands are nesting areas for waterfowl and stopping points for whistling swans. Significant numbers of gulls, terns, and cormorants nest on the shoreline near Nickel Beach. The nearby eastern breakwall has been designated as an Important Bird Area (IBA) because of its colonies of common terns, ring-billed gulls, greater black-backed gulls, herring gulls, double-crested cormorants, and black-crowned night herons. Local stands of Carolinian forest are popular with songbirds.

Situated on the pristine shores of Lake Erie, **Sherkston Shores** (www.sherkston. com) is set in 223 hectares (551 acres) of beautifully landscaped grounds, scattered with hidden **nature trails** amongst century-old forests in an area steeped in history.

Like many communities surrounding Lake Erie, Port Colborne is an excellent home port for **scuba diving** activities. Warm water and great visibility combine with 19th-century marine treasures to create a memorable diving experience. Twenty shipwrecks—lake schooners, barquentines, and tugs from the 19th century—can be found resting on the bottom of the lake. In 1917, a quarry near Sherkston Beach ceased operations and began to fill with water. Today it forms a large spring-fed lake that provides exciting diving. A 10m (33-ft.) dive below the lake's surface reveals train tracks, mining equipment, and even a locomotive, submerged when the quarry flooded.

Hard to imagine, but there actually is some pretty good **surfing** on the Great Lakes. Crescent beaches, relatively shallow waters, and lakeshore breezes create a perfect place to shred. Nickel Beach and Holloway Bay to the east, and Long Beach to the west have developed an international reputation as hot spots for wind and board surfing.

Special Events in Port Colborne

Other events may be scheduled in addition to the ones listed below, and dates may change from year to year. For more information, contact the Port Colborne visitor information center (𝄞 **905/835-2900**).

JUNE

Arabella's Pie Social, History Fair, and Antique Road Show. A pie-cooking contest, costumed interpreters from Old Fort Erie, historic displays, a plant sale, an antiques road show, and much more highlight this festival at 280 King St. For more info, call 𝄞 **905/834-7604.** First Weekend in June.

JULY

Flavors of Niagara International Food, Wine and Jazz Festival. Restaurants from around the region and Niagara VQA wineries offer their fare in a casual, outdoor environment with live musicians entertaining in the band shell. Held at H. H. Knoll Lakeview Park. For more information, call 𝄞 **905/834-1668.** First weekend in July.

Niagara Antique Power's Annual Display. Antique trucks and cars, vintage motorcycles, tractors, and a lawn garden display are the draws here. There's also a tractor pull and entertainment. For more information, call 𝄞 **905/892-8357** or visit www.niagara antiquepower.org. Early July

Canal Days Marine Heritage Festival. Celebrate the height of summer at the Annual Canal Days Marine Heritage Festival, held at H. H. Knoll Lakeview Park. The waterfront celebration includes historic tall ships, vendors, festival food, and entertainment including a fireworks display over the Welland Canal. More events are held at other venues throughout the city. For more information, call ℂ **905/834-1668.** First weekend in August.

Welland

Welland was first settled in 1788 by United Empire Loyalists. In 1814, Canadian forces led by George Hay met American invaders near the present-day town during the Battle of Cook's Mill. After 2 days of combat, the Americans retreated to Buffalo, New York, ending the second to last battle of the War of 1812 on Canadian soil. First called Cooks Mills, then Aqueduct after an old, wooden aqueduct on the Welland Canal, then later Merritsville, Welland gained its present name when it was incorporated in 1858. It became a city in 1917.

The Welland Museum, 140 King St. (ℂ **905/732-2215;** www.wellandmuseum. ca), in the Carnegie Building, opened in spring 2006. The original building was built in 1923, one of the last Carnegie libraries to be built in Canada. The museum holds area artifacts and hosts many revolving exhibits. There's also a resident ghost. Admission is C$3 for adults, C$2 for seniors and students ages 13 to 17; children 12 and under are free but must be accompanied by an adult, C$10 for a family.

IlluminAqua (ℂ **905/735-1700;** www.illuminaqua.com) is held throughout the summer. The event sees the canal illuminated by pods of fire, and local music and entertainment performed on stages floating in the canal and at the Merritt Park Amphitheatre. Food, drinks, and activities for everyone abound. IlluminAqua runs every second Friday evening from June through Labour Day weekend.

At the **Niagara Food Festival,** City Hall, 60 E. Main St. (ℂ **905/735-1700**), visitors can taste a large selection of food and wine from an assortment of vendors. There is a local food market, live music and entertainment, fun activities for the kids, contests, and exhibits. You can also learn exciting new cooking techniques from celebrity chefs at a new state-of-the-art mobile culinary theater.

Thorold

Thorold's slogan is "Where Ships Climb a Mountain." Water combined with gravity lifts and lowers ships and pleasure crafts in a watertight lock, which is the highest one in the Welland Canal system. More than 3,000 lake and ocean vessels carry an astonishing 40 million metric tons (89.6 billion lbs.!) of cargo through eight locks every year.

Thorold is rich in heritage homes, including the **DeCou House,** the destination of Laura Secord's quest to inform the British Army of the impending American invasion. It's also home to the largest murals in Canada, an incredible endeavor that covers 1,858 sq. m (20,000 sq. ft.), and recounts the history of Thorold. They are located along the Welland Canals Parkside Trail, between Lock 6 and 7.

Thorold is located 5 minutes from St. Catharines and 10 minutes from Niagara Falls. If you are driving from Toronto on the QEW, take Hwy. 406 south to Hwy. 58 east and exit at Pine Street; turn left to reach the downtown area. When coming on the QEW from Niagara Falls or Fort Erie, exit at Thorold Stone Road West. Pass through the Thorold Tunnel under the Welland Canal, and exit on Pine Street, turning right. If you follow the scenic route from Hwy. 20, take Hwy. 406 N., exit on Beaver-dams Road, and turn left on Pine Street.

The **Thorold Tourism Office** (✆ **905/680-9477**) is located at the Lock 7 Viewing Complex, 50 Chapel St. S.

Pelham, Ridgeville & Fonthill

These small communities are home to several interesting shops. The main street of Ridgeville is lined with boutique shops, from eco-friendly specialty products and organic baked goods at Nature's Corner to home decor pieces at In the Village, to unique kitchen tools or culinary gifts at the Whisk and Ladle. After shopping, head to Sweet Thoughts for a handmade chocolate treat or special gift. If you've brought along a cooler, stop in at Chez Fromage in Pelham to buy some hard-to-get Quebec cheeses to have with your bread from Nature's Corner.

Where to Eat

Berry Patch Tea Room CAFE   Stop in this busy tearoom for lunch or afternoon tea. Order from the selection of sandwiches, salads, wraps, quiches, quality loose teas, and generous helpings of homemade pie and ice cream, scones, and berry crumbles.

398 Canboro Rd., Ridgeville. ✆ **905/892-4209.** Full afternoon tea, C$18; sandwiches, $6.75–$8.50. MC, V. June–Sept daily 11:30am–4pm.

The Keefer Mansion Inn ★ REGIONAL   This heritage property has a fine dining room and an outdoor patio with views of the canal. The cuisine concentrates on local and fresh ingredients with a French twist. The inn also serves afternoon tea on Saturdays and Sundays from 2 to 4pm.

14 St. Davids Rd., Thorold. ✆ **905/680-9581.** www.keefermansion.com. Four-course tasting menu, C$48, with wine pairings C$68. AE, MC, V. Daily 11:30am–2pm and 5–9pm.

West Harbour Restaurant Bar & Grill CONTEMPORARY   Located on the second floor of the marina, this restaurant serves fare like burgers, quesadillas, wraps, pasta, and fish and chips. The patio overlooks the boats in the marina and the nearby park.

3 Marina Rd., Sugarloaf Marina, Port Colborne. ✆ **905/835-1895.** Main courses C$10–C$24. MC, V. Daily 11am–10pm.

Zest ★★ REGIONAL   Zest, one of the best dining rooms in the area, is located in the tiny village of Fonthill. Fresh and local dishes are served with finesse, great for a leisurely dinner at the end of a busy day of touring.

1469 Pelham St., Fonthill. ✆ **905/892-6474.** www.zestfonthill.com. Main courses C$24–C$38. MC, V. Tues–Thurs 11:30am–2:30pm and 5–8pm; Fri 11:30am–2:30pm and 5–9pm; Sat 5–9pm; closed Sun–Mon.

HAMILTON

Hamilton is a city that continues to transform itself. Located in southern Ontario on the western end of the Niagara Peninsula, the city wraps around the western part of Lake Ontario. It is the geographic center of the "Golden Horseshoe," at roughly the midway point between Toronto and Niagara Falls. Hamilton Harbour marks the northern limit of the city, and the Niagara Escarpment runs through its middle, bisecting the city into upper and lower parts. Once known for its steel mills and foundries, the city has become in recent years a center for higher education, medical services, and Internet technology. Through all the changes, its historic heart has remained unchanged.

Ancaster Mill **16**
Art Gallery of Hamilton **13**
Battlefield House Museum and Park **9**
Café Limoncello **8**
Canadian Warplane Heritage Museum **18**
Dundurn Castle **2**
The Earth to Table Bread Bar **10**
Griffin House **17**
HMS Haida **4**
James Street North Art Crawl **5**
Locke Street Shopping and Dining Area **11**
Museum of Steam and Technology **6**
Ottawa Street Shopping District **7**
Quatrefoile Restaurant **15**
Royal Botanical Gardens **1**
Westfield Heritage Village **14**
Whitehern **12**
Williams Coffee Pub **3**

History may well be the hallmark of Hamilton, and the range and number of the museums in the city are a testament to that fact. The jewel in the crown is Dundurn Castle, but there is also the historic estate of Whitehern, right next to city hall. A half-hour away is Westfield Heritage Village.

The Museum of Steam and Technology preserves the technology that powered the city 140 years ago, while the Canadian Warplane Heritage Museum has restored and displays aircraft from World War II, including the only operational Lancaster in North America. In nearby Ancaster, Griffin House preserves the story of Enerals Griffin, a Virginian slave who escaped to freedom and lived in this simple clapboard house, which is now a museum and an important cultural landmark of the Black Heritage Network.

HISTORIC & romantic beginnings

Robert Land, a United Empire Loyalist, was the first white settler in the Hamilton area, having fled from persecution in Pennsylvania, narrowly escaping execution. He settled at the head of the lake, believing his wife and children to be dead. His wife, Phebe, had managed to escape with her children to Nova Scotia, believing her husband was dead. When she journeyed to Niagara to claim farmland that was given to the loyalists, she heard rumors of a man called Land living in what would become Hamilton. She hired a boat, traveled to satisfy her curiosity, and discovered her long-lost husband.

The reunion, according to legend, was a joyous one, and the couple and their family, having been granted 405 hectares (1,000 acres) in the center of the future city of Hamilton, helped to build the community that would be home to generations of their descendants. Robert and Phebe are buried in the Hamilton Cemetery, alongside such characters as William Cook, a Canadian soldier who was killed with General Custer at the Battle of Little Big Horn, and Isabella Whyte, the secret half-sister of Queen Victoria. Tours of this Gothic cemetery are conducted regularly and offer a running commentary on the city's colorful past.

Hamilton boasts two stunning waterfronts, each with its own stretch of new trails. The Beach Strip Trail is a 10km (6 miles) paved pathway along Lake Ontario that leads to the popular water park, Wild Waterworks. The west-end Hamilton Harbour Waterfront Trail, is another 10km (6.2 miles) magnet for walkers, joggers, and in-line skaters. Also here are Hamilton's popular Bayfront Park and Pier 4, home to boaters, dragon-boat races, family picnics, and summer festivals. Attractions here include the Hamilton Waterfront Trolley, cruises on the *Harbour Queen*, the new Pier 8 skate rink, and a William's Coffee Pub.

Events, exhibits, and programs commemorating and celebrating the Bicentennial of the War of 1812 will take place in 2012, 2013, and 2014, in the Hamilton area. Expect a peak in activities during 2013 to mark significant events like the 200th anniversary of the Battle of Stoney Creek, the sinking of warships the *Hamilton* and the *Scourge,* the encampment at Burlington Heights, and the Burlington Races.

It has been said that, for a city to be truly civilized, it must nurture its talent and create a home for that talent to blossom. Hamilton has excelled at both of these. The city is the hometown for comedians Red Green (aka Steve Smith), Martin Short, and Eugene Levy; singer Stan Rogers; architect Bruce Kuwabara; ballerina Karen Kain; and 2007 Canadian Idol winner Brian Melo.

Essentials

GETTING THERE By **car,** Hamilton is just a short detour from the QEW. Travelers from Buffalo, Fort Erie, and St. Catharines can take the QEW over the Skyway Bridge to Hwy. 403, which takes you to the center of the city. Those coming from Toronto will exit at Hwy. 403 in Burlington, before the Skyway Bridge. **Bus** lines offer regular service to Hamilton from many different locations. Via Rail brings **train** travelers from across Canada to the station in Aldershot, a short distance outside the city in neighboring Burlington. **By air,** you can get to Hamilton via John C. Munro Hamilton International Airport (it's both accessible and less stress-inducing than flying into Toronto's Pearson International Airport), which serves Southern Ontario well with direct WestJet service to cities like Calgary, Halifax, and Edmonton.

VISITOR INFORMATION Hamilton's Tourist Information Centre (𝄞 **800/263-8590** or 905/546-2666; www.tourismhamilton.com) is downtown at Jackson Square (2 King St. W.). The center is open Monday through Friday from 8:30am to 4:30pm. The Tourist Board also operates a staffed information center at Hamilton International Airport throughout the summer (May–Oct).

What to See & Do

African Lion Safari African Lion Safari is a popular local attraction where 1,000 animals roam free in this expansive drive-through reserve, while visitors remain "caged" in their cars. The family-owned business boasts successful breeding programs for many endangered and threatened species. Family-friendly activities include live animal shows, the popular "elephant swim," the "African Queen" boat cruise, "Nature Boy" scenic railway, and Misumu Bay Wet Play.

1386 Cooper Rd., R.R. 1, Cambridge, ON. 𝄞 **800/461-WILD** (9453) or 519/623-2620. www.lionsafari. com. Admission C$30 adults; C$28 senior; C$25 children 3-12; children 2 and under free. Summer hours June 25–Sept 5 daily 9am–5:30pm; Sept 6–Oct 10 daily 9am–4pm.

Art Gallery of Hamilton ★★★ For the art lover, Hamilton is home to Ontario's third largest art gallery, the Art Gallery of Hamilton. After an C$18-million renovation and expansion designed by Hamilton-born architect Bruce Kuwabara, the AGH is now a beautiful exhibition space, and home to the Joey and Toby Tanenbaum collection of 19th-century European art. One of the best bargains in town is the "First Fridays" initiative, where visitors have free entrance to the gallery from 5 to 9pm on every first Friday of the month. Combine a tour of the gallery with a light meal in the gallery cafe and you've got a great evening on a shoestring. Special exhibitions occur regularly. And don't miss the work-in-progress, Bruegel-Bosch Bus by Kim Adams.

123 King St. W., Hamilton, ON. 𝄞 **905/527-6610.** www.artgalleryofhamilton.com. Admission C$10 adults, C$8 seniors and students, C$4 children 6-17, children 5 and under free. Tues–Wed noon–7pm; Thurs–Fri noon–9pm; Sat–Sun noon–5pm.

Battlefield House Museum and Park Like Dundurn and Whitehern, Battlefield is a National Historic Site. It is home to the annual re-enactment of the Battle of Stoney Creek, a pivotal battle in the War of 1812. In addition to the weekend-long event held every June, Battlefield House is a "living history" museum offering visitors year-round tours by period-costumed guides.

77 King St. W., Stoney Creek, ON. 𝄞 **905/662-8458.** www.battlefieldhouse.ca. Admission adults C$6.50, seniors C$5.50, students 13-17 C$5.50, children 6-12 C$4.50, children 5 and under free, families C$17. July to early Sept Tues–Sun 11am–4pm; Early Sept–June Tues–Sun 1–4pm.

Canadian Warplane Heritage Museum ★ ☺ The Canadian Warplane Heritage Museum showcases the aircraft used by Canadians or Canada's military from the beginning of World War II up to the present. The collection includes aircraft that really fly and several that remain on static display. Visitors can climb into the cockpit of a real World War II trainer or a real jet fighter. There are interactive flight combat simulators, interactive video displays, movies, photographs, and memorabilia from Canadian history. Its prized possession is probably the most famous Allied bomber of World War II, the Avro Lancaster, the only operational one in North America and one of only two air-worthy Lancasters in the world. It is also the only one you can buy a

10

SIDE TRIPS FROM NIAGARA

Hamilton

flight on for special occasions, although the cost is very steep (starting at C$2,500 for 1 hr.). The Hamilton International Air Show returned in 2011 and has been a great success. See http://airshow.warplane.com/hamilton-airshow-2011.aspx for details.

9280 Airport Rd., Mount Hope. ℂ **905/679-4183.** www.warplane.com. Admission C$10 adults, C$9 seniors and students 13-17, C$6 children 6-12, children 5 and under free. Daily 9am-5pm.

Dundurn Castle★★ Dundurn is a classic mid-19th-century Regency-style villa. Costumed guides give visitors a glimpse into the life of a prominent 1850s Victorian family and their servants. The gardens have been extensively restored, notably the kitchen garden. The plantings are all heritage varieties that would have been harvested here in the 1850s. The gift shop features Canadian handmade crafts, souvenirs, and special gifts. You can also visit the Hamilton Military Museum, all inside Dundurn Park.

610 York Blvd., Hamilton. ℂ **905/546-2872.** www.dundurncastle.com. Admission C$11 adults, C$9 seniors and students 13-17, C$5.50 children 6-12, children 5 and under free. July 1 to Labour Day daily 10am-4pm; Labour Day to June 30 Tues-Sun noon-4pm.

Griffin House Griffin House is a reminder of the bravery and determination of black men and women who journeyed to freedom in southern Ontario via the Underground Railroad. Griffin House offers tours and black history–related programs as part of the Black Heritage Network. The site is located on top of a hill overlooking the Dundas Valley and is managed as a joint project.

733 Mineral Springs Rd., Ancaster. ℂ **905/546-2424.** griffinhouse@hamilton.ca. Admission C$2, children 5 and under free. Open on public holidays from Victoria Day to Thanksgiving 1-4pm.

James Street North Art Crawl Part of Hamilton's emerging arts scene, the historic downtown street is becoming an arts hub with artists and young professionals moving into the area's affordable historic homes and downtown lofts and studios. The *National Post* newspaper called the area the "New Brooklyn," referring to artists and young people flocking to the area after being priced out of Toronto. The art crawl happens every second Friday of the month. Stores, restaurants, and galleries extend their hours and open their doors to the street, transforming the strip into a wonderful, art-loving street party, welcoming to young and old alike.

James St. North Art District, from King William St. to Strachan St. www.jamesstreetnorth.ca. Every 2nd Fri year-round 6pm-midnight.

The Harbourfront and HMS Haida Families will enjoy a visit to HMCS *Haida*, where you can walk the decks of Canada's most famous warship. The *Haida* saw service in World War II and the Korean War and is the last Tribal Class destroyer in the world.

Pier 9, 658 Catharine St., Hamilton. ℂ **905/526-0911.** Admission C$3.90 adults, C$3.60 seniors, C$1.90 children 17 and under. May-Sept daily 10am-5pm.

The Museum of Steam and Technology This example of 19th-century public works architecture preserves two 14m-high (45-ft.), 64-metric-ton (70-ton) steam engines, which pumped the first clean water to the city over 140 years ago. One engine operates as a demonstration every day. The only surviving facility of its time in North America, the museum is a National Historic Site and a Civil and Power Engineering Landmark. The museum offers various permanent and changing exhibits, as well as a wide range of special family-oriented events.

900 Woodward Ave., Hamilton. ℂ **905/546-4797.** steammuseum@hamilton.ca. Admission C$6.50 adults, C$5 seniors and students 13-17, C$4.50 children 6-12, children 5 and under free. July 1 to Labour Day daily 11am-4pm; Labour Day to June 30 Tues-Sun noon-4pm.

Royal Botanical Gardens ★★   The RBG is Canada's most famous gardens, with the largest lilac collection in the world. An exhilarating trip, the RBG takes you through five gardens, a 30km (19-mile) trail system, and four nature sanctuaries. A cafe and two teahouses are on the grounds.

680 Plains Rd., Burlington. ✆ **905/527-1158.** www.rbg.ca. Adult C$13; senior (65+) C$10; student/youth C$10; children 5-12 C$7.50, children 4 and under free; family (2 adults, 2 children 17 and under) C$34. Daily 10am-dusk.

Westfield Heritage Village ★   A restored 19th-century village, with over 30 buildings, including a schoolhouse and a blacksmith shop, this village brings history to life. It's quite common to see artists painting the old houses and shops. The buildings are all carefully restored and staffed with costumed interpreters, re-creating the spirit of early Canadian culture. Much of the village is handicapped accessible.

1049 Regional Rd. 552 (Kirkwall Rd.), Rockton. ✆ **800/883-0104** or 519/621-8851. www.westfield heritage.ca. Admission C$8.50 adults, C$6.50 seniors and students 13-17, C$5.50 children 6-12, children 5 and under free. Apr-Oct daily 12:30-4pm.

Whitehern ★★   Almost hidden gardens surround this home, which is part Georgian, part Edwardian, and part Victorian. The McQuesten family lived here from 1852 to 1968, and were instrumental in establishing the Royal Botanical Gardens McMaster University, and the Queen Elizabeth Way. In the 1930s, Misses Hilda and Mary McQuesten would hold a June tea for the Woman's Missionary Society. Whitehern has revived the affair with its own version, featuring music, lemonade, tea, and homemade ice cream, as part of its warm-weather program, "Picnic in the Park," which runs throughout the summer. Even without the tea, this is an inviting garden to visit. Lovingly restored to the design created in the early 1930s by landscape architect and founder of Sheridan Nurseries, Howard Dunnington-Grub, it is a green surprise in the center of the city. Costumed guides conduct tours.

41 Jackson St. W., Hamilton. ✆ **905/546-2018.** www.whitehern.ca. Admission C$6.50 adults, C$5.50 seniors and students 13-17, C$4.50 children 6-12, children 5 and under free. July 1 to Labour Day daily 11am-4pm; Labour Day to June 30 Tues-Sun noon-4pm.

Shopping

One of the little-known pleasures of Hamilton is the shopping, from the great bargains of Ottawa Street to the art finds of James North. It's one of the enduring charms of the city, where each neighborhood has a distinctly different character, and each offers the intrepid shopper an exceptional experience. Even if you don't buy, the walk through these small, distinct neighborhoods will be worth it.

There is no place in the country like Hamilton's **Ottawa Street.** It is the textile bargain capital of Canada. The street is lined with stores that specialize in everything you need to sew clothing or make draperies or upholster furniture. There are stores that specialize in buttons and trims, and those that provide curtain rods and rings. You can find authentic Chanel wool gabardine by the yard and Versace silk for a fraction of their value. Restaurants like Café Limoncello and Logans echo the relaxed European flavors of the neighborhood and are a great place to recuperate from shopping with a cappuccino or a plate of pierogi. And now, with rents in other parts of the city inching ever upward, galleries and artists' studios are appearing. This is now the place to browse for antiques and art. Add to that an excellent and authentic Farmers' Market on Saturday mornings, and it's clear that Ottawa Street is a very cool place.

In the little shops on **Locke Street,** you can discover great bargains on antiques and collectibles, designer clothes, and specialty items for the kitchen. Everything from a carved Victorian settee to vintage clothing can be found here, at incredible prices. A transit gallery displays work from contemporary artists from the area and from across the country. The Beach Road Butcher Shop, also on Locke Street, is famous for its lean spicy kielbasa, and Christina, the proprietor's daughter, makes a thousand delicious cabbage rolls a week. The Earth to Table Bread Bar is the perfect stop for coffee and freshly baked bread.

The James Street North neighborhood bubbles with an artsy avant garde style. Here you can discover the works of tomorrow's noteworthy artists while they are still affordable. Galleries, art supply stores, and a history museum, as well as artists' studios and little cafes, make this a great place to spend an afternoon shopping.

Where to Eat

Ancaster Mill ★★★ REGIONAL   If you have drifted up to Ancaster to visit the Griffin House, be sure to stop at the Old Mill. It has one of the prettiest settings of any restaurant in town, and serves excellent fresh and local cuisine along with a view of the waterfall. The Sunday brunch here is famous and Chef Jeff Crump ensures that ingredients are fresh, local, and top quality.

548 Old Dundas Rd., Ancaster. © **905/648-1827.** www.ancasteroldmill.com. Main courses C$22–C$40. Sun brunch, C$41 adults, C$20 children. AE, MC, V. Tues–Sat 11:30am–10pm; Sun 9:30am–2:30pm, and 5–9pm.

Café Limoncello ITALIAN   At this busy casual Italian restaurant, good solid Italian dishes are served. Bruschetta, pasta, veal parmigiana, and calamari are customer favorites.

226 Ottawa St., Hamilton. © **905/549-3556.** www.cafelimoncello.com. Main courses C$14–$C20. AE, MC, V. Sun–Wed 9am–9pm, Thurs–Sat 9am–11pm.

The Earth to Table Bread Bar BAKERY/CAFE   An artisanal bread bar by day and a superb pizzeria by night, this comfortable cafe is an inviting place any time of day. Bettina Schormann, the wizard of bread and pastry, turns out magical loaves and irresistible sweets. The cafe serves wine and beer as well as fair-trade coffee. One of my favorite places in the city.

258 Locke St. S., Hamilton. © **905/522-2999.** www.breadbar.ca. Pizzas C$11–C$14. AE, MC, V. Daily 8am–11:30pm.

Il Fiasco Café and Wine Bar ITALIAN   Picture this: In front of you is a chilled glass of sauvignon blanc and a plate of fresh crab cakes. Around you are blue walls with a lighthearted hand-painted mural. Just outside the large window, people are browsing through antiques shops, buying fresh bread in the little bakery, and sipping espresso in outdoor cafes. This could be a small Parisian street scene, or perhaps a street in a trendy Toronto neighborhood. But no. The restaurant is a tiny Italian-style gem, and is fast becoming the vibrant heart of bohemian cafe culture. It's a great place for lunch or dinner.

182 Locke St. S., Hamilton. © **905/522-8549.** www.ilfiasco.ca. Main courses C$11–C$25. AE, MC, V. Tues–Wed 11:30am–3pm and 5–9pm; Thurs–Fri 11:30am–3pm and 5–10pm; Sat 11:30am–10pm; closed Sun–Mon.

Quatrefoile Restaurant REGIONAL/INTERNATIONAL   This restaurant is as beautiful to look at as it is delicious to dine in, with white leather chairs, silver accents, and fresh flowers. It was chosen as one of the 10 best restaurants in Canada by *EnRoute* magazine. Chef Fraser Macfarlane produces French classics with a modern and local accent, and the service is gently attentive without being intrusive. Definitely worth the drive to Dundas.

16 Sydenham St., Dundas, ON. ℰ **905/628-7800.** www.quatrefoilrestaurant.com. Main courses C$32– C$44. AE, MC, V. Tues–Sat 12–3pm and 5pm–closing.

Williams Coffee Pub CAFE   This attractive coffee shop has a large patio with views of the harbor, good casual food, coffee, tea, and soft drinks, as well as free wireless Internet.

47 Discovery Dr., at the foot of James St. N., Hamilton. ℰ **905/522-5886.** Paninis and wraps C$6–C$7. AE, MC, V. Daily 8am–10pm.

THE ARTISTS' TRAIL

For those who love to discover a region through its visual arts, Niagara is rich in artists who interpret the local landscape and express the local spirit in paintings, sculpture, and glasswork. A day spent visiting the studios of these artists can lead to engaging encounters with local craftsmen and artists, as well as present an opportunity to purchase a great piece of art.

All of the following are the private studios of established artists. Since many of them are located in private homes, and since the artists may have changing hours, it is necessary to call ahead and make an appointment to visit each studio.

The studios are found from Niagara Falls right through to Stoney Creek, and all are within an easy drive of Niagara Falls. Check out the artists' work on their website galleries and choose a few whose works appeal. Any work you buy will be an investment as well as a memory.

Beverly Sneath   Sneath's work in watercolor is based on the beauty of nature, including florals, landscapes, local scenes, portraits, and figures. A secondary theme is humanity in both real and fictional settings. Her watercolor paintings capture valued moments from children playing with animals to a subtle breeze on a fall field to a nymph watching the full moon rising in the night sky. In bronze and clay sculpture, her focus changes to express her versatile creativity in three-dimensional forms. Sneath teaches watercolor classes for adults as well as art classes for children in schools, libraries, galleries, and summer art camps. She is co-owner of the Rainbow Artists company, which provides visual art, dance, music, and drama workshops.

1341 Effingam St., Ridgeville. ℰ **905/892-5868.** www.beverlysneath.com.

Bruno Capolongo   Bruno Capolongo is an internationally recognized artist with works in public and private collections the world over. While known mainly as a painter of contemporary oil, encaustic, and mixed media works, he is also known for his published work in the fine art reproduction world, books, and magazines. Capolongo is the winner of numerous art awards, including the international Elizabeth Greenshields award, of which he is a rare triple recipient. His exquisite encaustic paintings have earned him the reputation as a master of the medium. His studio is within the west Niagara wine region, between Kittling Ridge Estate and Puddicombe Estates Wineries.

10 Craig Blvd., Grimsby. ℰ **905/643-0590.** www.brunocapolongo.com.

Carolyn Dover   Carolyn Dover is a Hamilton-born professional artist who has lived and worked in Grimsby for the past 23 years. She studied at both McMaster University in Hamilton and Mount Alison University in New Brunswick, where she completed her bachelor of fine arts degree with distinction in 1985. Her paintings are part of private collections across Canada as well as the U.S., United Arab Emirates, and Hungary. Dover has exhibited extensively throughout southern Ontario. She continues to explore her interest in the local vineyards while teaching classes in oil painting and drawing at the Dundas Valley School of Art. Her studio is in Grimsby.

℗ **905/309-4166.** www.earlscourtgallery.ca. Call ahead to make an appointment.

David T. Wright David studied painting in England, receiving an MFA in painting in 1972. Since then he has maintained painting studios in Ontario and in central Mexico. He now lives and paints in the Niagara wine region, where his studio is right beside picturesque Ball's Falls. David's oil paintings are devoted to an interpretation of his environment, painting subjects to which he feels a personal attachment—interiors of his home, still lifes, cityscapes, and landscapes familiar to him. He has exhibited extensively in galleries in Canada, the U.S., and Mexico. His work is represented internationally in more than 100 corporate and public collections, and in many private homes.

3249 Sixth Ave., Jordan. ℗ **905/562 3727.** www.davidtwright.com.

Doug Mays Located near the western end of Niagara wine country, Arrows in the Quiver Studio/Gallery exhibits the exclusive watercolor and acrylic paintings of local artist Doug Mays. Known for his loose, impressionistic painting style, Doug's paintings maximize spontaneity and "expressive freedom." This award-winning artist is an elected member of the Canadian Society of Painters in Water Colour (CSPWC) and past president of the Central Ontario Art Association (COAA).

3 Macdui Dr., Stoney Creek. ℗ **905/643-4541.** www.arrowsinthequiver.com.

Jan Yates Painting primarily in "plein air," Yates explores the vineyards and changing seasons of Niagara, mostly in oil on canvas. While her works represent actual scenes from the Escarpment, many of them are also partly abstract. Her colors are strong, and she is interested in interpreting the sky and its changing moods. She studied fine art in Southern California for 10 years and then moved to the Niagara Peninsula in 1995.

℗ **905/309-0541.** www.janyates.com. Call ahead to make an appointment.

Lynette Fast Dr. Lynette Fast is a practicing water-media artist, a former teacher, and a retired associate professor of visual arts education. Lynette's glass-framed paintings are influenced by the natural environment, and in particular the Niagara Escarpment where she has lived and worked in her Vineland studio/gallery since 1983. Her intent is to capture nature's energy and rhythms and to encourage the viewer to participate in these impressions with heart and mind. Most works combine glazing, stenciling, and extensive layering of shape, texture, and tone from multiple perspectives.

3208 King St., Vineland. ℗ **905/562-7056.**

Michelle Teitsma This Niagara artist, who studied classical animation at Sheridan College, has been painting in the area for the past 9 years. She left animation behind to pursue air brush works and oil on canvas representations of people, landscapes, and still life. Her works are often suggestive of a whole story behind the painted form. She also creates murals.

www.michelleteitsma.com. Visit the website to make an appointment.

Susan Wilde   Susan Wilde is a classically trained contemporary oil painter excelling in the meticulous, highly realistic treatment of fruit in glass or silver vessels. Her compositions are simple studies applying the old advertising maxim, "less is more," with stunning effect. Studying the Renaissance period left her fascinated with the use of chiaroscuro (strong light against deep shadow), which is evident in her work today.
Fruitland Rd. off the QEW, on the lake in Stoney Creek. ✆ **905/564-1213.** www.susanwilde.com.

NIAGARA'S CULINARY TRAIL

There are few experiences more enjoyable than exploring backcountry roads and discovering the charms of small villages and artisanal shops. One of the best ways to experience the bounty of Niagara is on a foraging trip—visiting beekeepers, cheesemongers, bread bakers, growers of heritage tomatoes, and producers of artisanal vinegars.

The Niagara Culinary Trail works to link agriculture, tourism, and the food community to promote sustainable cuisine by celebrating the joys of local, seasonal, and artisanal cooking. These activities support a healthy Greenbelt and encourage support for healthy food and healthy growing practices. They also give locals and visitors a useful guide to some of the otherwise hard-to-find specialty shops, each with its own unique character and products.

It would be easy to miss **de la terre Café and Bakery** (3451 King St., Vineland, Ontario; ✆ **905/562-1513;** www.delaterre.ca) in Vineland, for example, and that would be a shame. Almost any time you drop in here, chef Jan will be hand-shaping his loaves of bread. Chat him up—he's friendly and a very knowledgeable source of information about local places worth a visit. He also serves fair-trade coffees and teas and the best bread and pastries around. In Fonthill is **Bow Ridge Herbs** (2 Orchard Hill Rd., Fonthill; ✆ **905/892-2045**), where Roxanna Bowman's retail shop sells over 300 varieties of herbs, specializing in rosemary.

A bit farther down a tree-lined country road, in the tiny community of Ridgeville, you'll come to the **Whisk & Ladle** (306 Canboro Rd., Ridgeville; ✆ **905/892-926;** www.thewhiskandladle.ca), where Stratford Chef School graduate Ruth Nixon offers top-of-the-line kitchen supplies, as well as prepared dishes like wild mushroom lasagna and strawberry rhubarb crumble.

Continue onto Fenwick for a stop at **Chez Fromage** (784 Canboro Rd., Fenwick; ✆ **905/892-7922;** www.chezfromageetc.ca) for a slice of Quebec Benedictine Bleu and a cheese discussion with owner Nathalie Kita.

Aceto Niagara Inc (Niagara-on-the-Lake; ✆ **905/468-4373;** www.acetoniagara.com) stocks a line of gourmet vinegars made from genuine Icewine and the best of Niagara's tender fruit. The company produces a variety of vinegars and aperitifs, including Icewine aceto aperitif; Icewine vinegar; tomato vinegar; peach vinegar; cherry vinegar; and an attractive cherry, peach, and tomato trio.

Inn the Pines (1320 Seventh St. S., St. Catharines; ✆ **905/353-5887**) sells fruits, vegetables, herbs, and organic eggs. Children will be thrilled to have a look at the chickens and bunnies. **Olson Foods at Ravine** (1366 York Rd., St. Davids; ✆ **905/262-8463;** www.ravinevineyard.com) sells homemade baked goods and wood-oven artisanal breads; there is also a cafe serving regional fare. At **Tree and Twig** (84039 Regional Rd. 45, Wellandport; ✆ **905/386-7388;** www.treeandtwig.ca), you'll find more than 1,000 varieties of organic and heirloom vegetables, with several rare varieties of heirloom tomatoes.

Essentials

VISITOR INFORMATION **Niagara Culinary Trail,** Queenston (© **905/262-4941;** www.niagaraculinarytrail.com), produces a map, available at the tourism information booths and at several merchants and wineries, as well as from their website. You can design your own trip, or join a guided bus tour to experience the best of Niagara's regional cuisine, or just wander until you find a place of interest.

Another great map is from the **Niagara AgriTourism Circuit** (www.agrotourisme niagara.com), which allows visitors to plan a self-guided tour of the local producers. The map is available at the tourist information centers, at many retail outlets, and from its website.

The **Niagara Culinary Trail Tours,** Port Robinson (© **905/384-1986;** www. winecountrytours.ca), offers three different bus tours of the culinary trail, each developed to give visitors a full range of food and wine experiences for groups of 20 or more. Participants will discover how to buy directly from the producer during the entire harvest season. Tours include visits to food producers when their produce is ripe and in season, a visit to an award-winning winery, a catered lunch, local cheese, and seasonal fruit on the bus. For those who like to take home a more permanent memory, pick up a copy of Niagara food writer Lynn Ogryzlo's recipe books: *Niagara Cooks, Niagara Cooks by Season,* and *The Ontario Table*.

PLANNING YOUR TRIP TO NIAGARA

Planning a trip to Niagara is easy—this is, after all, one of the oldest tourist areas in Canada, and the infrastructure is well established. There are excellent tourism information centers throughout the region, informative websites, and well-trained staff who are happy to help or answer questions, as well as downloadable iPhone apps that will guide you around the region. This chapter provides a variety of planning tools, including information on how to get there, tips on accommodations, and quick on-the-ground resources.

GETTING THERE
By Plane

When visiting the Niagara region, you have a choice of arriving in Canada or the United States. The majority of the attractions are on the Canadian side, but the Buffalo Airport is closer to the Falls than either Pearson (Toronto) or Hamilton.

Most flights arrive at **Pearson International Airport (YYZ)** in northwest Toronto, approximately a 2-hour drive from Niagara Falls. The trip usually takes 30-plus minutes longer during the weekday peak commuter times: 7 to 10am and 3:30 to 6:30pm. If you can, fly into **Hamilton (YHM)**—it's less busy.

Note that the term "direct flight" may include an en route stop but not an aircraft change.

FROM THE U.S. Canada's only national airline, **Air Canada** (✆ 888/247-2262; www.aircanada.ca) operates direct flights to Toronto (Pearson Airport) from most major American cities and many smaller ones. It also flies from major cities around the world and operates connecting flights from other U.S. cities.

A major discount Canadian carrier servicing select routes is **WestJet** (✆ 888/WEST-JET [937-8538]; www.westjet.com), with service between Toronto and San Francisco, Los Angeles, Phoenix, Palm Springs, Las Vegas, Hawaii, several Florida locations, and the Bahamas.

Porter Air (✆ 888/619-8622; www.flyporter.com) is an excellent choice for visitors, especially those who plan to take the train to Niagara. Porter flies in to the Toronto City Centre Airport (YTC) and runs a complimentary shuttle service every 15 minutes from the airport to the nearby Fairmont Royal York Hotel, across the street from Union Station, where trains depart to Niagara. The airline currently serves Toronto, Ottawa, Montreal, Quebec City, Halifax, Mont Tremblant, St. John's, Thunder Bay, Windsor, Moncton, Sault Ste. Marie, Sudbury, New York (Newark), Boston (Logan International Airport), Myrtle Beach (Myrtle Beach International Airport), and Chicago (Midway).

Among U.S. airlines, **American** (*©* 800/433-7300; www.aa.com) has daily direct flights from Chicago, Dallas, Miami, and New York. **United** (*©* 800/241-6522; www.united.com) has direct flights from Vancouver, Chicago, San Francisco, and Washington (Dulles); it's a code-share partner with Air Canada. **US Airways** (*©* 800/428-4322; www.usairways.com) operates directly into Toronto from a number of U.S. cities, notably Baltimore, Indianapolis, Philadelphia, and Pittsburgh. **Northwest** (*©* 800/225-2525; www.nwa.com) flies direct from Detroit and Minneapolis. **Delta** (*©* 800/221-1212; www.delta.com) flies direct from Atlanta, Detroit, Minneapolis, and Cincinnati.

The Hamilton International Airport is smaller, which also means less busy, and it is closer to the Niagara region—it takes about 45 minutes to drive from the airport to Niagara Falls. WestJet flies into Hamilton from Orlando, and from Canadian cities Halifax, Winnipeg, Calgary, and Edmonton.

WITHIN THE U.S. Niagara Falls International Airport is for charter and cargo planes only, so plan to fly into **Buffalo Niagara International Airport** (4200 Genesee St., Cheektowaga, NY; *©* 716/630-6000; www.nfta.com/airport), 25 miles (41 kilometers) from the Rainbow Bridge (a 35-min. drive). The airport is served by a number of airlines, including **JetBlue** (*©* 800/538-2583; www.jetblue.com), which has lots of cheap one-way flights from other parts of New York; **AirTran Airways** (*©* 800/247-8726; www.airtran.com); **American** (*©* 800/433-7300; www.aa.com); **Continental** (*©* 800/525-0280; www.continental.com); **Comair/ Delta Connection** (*©* 800/221-1212; www.comair.com); **Northwest** (*©* 800/ 225-2525; www.nwa.com); **Southwest** (*©* 800/435-9792; www.southwest.com); **United** (*©* 800/241-6522); www.ual.com); and **US Airways** (*©* 800/428-4322; www.usairways.com).

FROM CANADA Travelers whose departure city is within Canada are advised to fly to Toronto or Hamilton rather than Buffalo.

FROM ABROAD A number of major U.S. airlines fly into Buffalo Niagara International Airport (see "Within the U.S.," above). Visitors arriving from abroad can make connections to Buffalo from several major U.S. cities, including Atlanta, Boston, Chicago, Detroit, and New York.

ARRIVING AT THE AIRPORT

Arriving at Pearson International Airport in Toronto, every passenger on an international flight must pass through Customs. Please see the Customs section (p. 229) for more information. The lines may be longer for larger flights, but the Customs process generally takes about 10 minutes. If you possess a NEXUS card (a pre-approved Customs card), you can bypass lines but may still be subject to random searches. The NEXUS card is only available for U.S. and Canadian citizens. To apply, visit **www.cbsa-asfc.gc.ca**. In terms of airport services, porters in red coats will assist inbound travelers with transportation (bus, limo, or taxis). Should you be approached in the terminal, do not accept transportation from individuals; these are unlicensed drivers who will charge a higher fee for taxi service. Inside the airport, information kiosks will assist with hotel, car rental, or currency needs. Most recently, travelers can order takeout at any restaurant participating in the "Made to Fly" program. Visit the website **www.gtaa.com/en/home** for details and a complete listing of services.

GETTING TO NIAGARA FROM THE AIRPORT

If you land at **Pearson International Airport** in Toronto, renting a car may be your best bet. However, there is an **airport express bus service** that will take you to the bus station and train station in downtown Toronto, where you can get transportation to the Niagara region. The fare is C$16 per adult one-way to downtown Toronto. A one-way fare to Toronto Union Station from Pearson Airport is C$20, while a return trip is C$33. Car-rental companies with desks inside the terminals include **Avis, Budget, Dollar, Thrifty, Hertz, National,** and **Alamo.**

Car-rental companies at **Hamilton International Airport** include Avis, Hertz, and National.

Niagara Airbus (© **800/268-8111** in Canada, 716/835-8111 in Buffalo, or 716/625-6222 in Niagara Falls, New York; www.niagaraairbus.com) offers a flexible shuttle and taxi service from **Toronto (Pearson)** and **Buffalo Niagara International Airport** to any destination in the Niagara region in Canada and the Niagara Falls/Buffalo area in New York State. The one-way fare from Toronto Pearson Airport to Niagara Falls, Ontario, is C$69. The company also serves **Hamilton airport** with individual taxicabs rather than a shuttle service.

If you arrive at **Buffalo Niagara International Airport,** the closest airport to the Falls, the **ITA Shuttle** (© **800/551-9369;** www.buffaloairporttaxi.com) can take you from the airport to the American side of the Falls for $45 per person each way or to the Canadian side for $55 per person each way. Children under 6 years old ride free. Reservations must be made at least 12 hours in advance and can be made online or by phone. If you prefer to rent a car, Avis, Budget, Hertz, and Enterprise all have rental counters at the airport.

To find out which airlines travel to Niagara, please see "Airline Websites," p. 240.

By Bus

Greyhound Canada (© **800/661-8747**) provides coast-to-coast service with connections to Niagara Falls. The local bus station is Niagara Transportation, 4555 Erie Ave., Niagara Falls, Ontario (© **905/357-2133**). Book online or obtain schedule and fare information at www.greyhound.ca. **Greyhound Lines, Inc.** (© **800/231-2222;** www.greyhound.com), provides bus service between the U.S. and Canada. The local bus station on the U.S. side is at Niagara Discount Souvenir, 303 Rainbow Blvd., Niagara Falls, NY (© **716/282-1765**).

Traveling by bus may be faster and cheaper than the train, and if you want to stop to visit towns along the way, bus routes may offer more flexibility. But there's also less space to stretch out, toilet facilities are meager, and meals are taken at roadside rest stops, so consider carefully, particularly if you're planning to bring children with you.

Investigate offers such as unlimited-travel passes and discount fares. It's tough to quote typical fares because bus companies, like airlines, are adopting yield-management strategies, resulting in frequent price changes depending on demand.

International visitors can obtain information about the **Greyhound North American Discovery Pass.** The pass, which offers unlimited travel and stopovers in the U.S. and Canada, can be obtained outside the United States from travel agents or through www.discoverypass.com.

By Car

When driving from the I-90 in **New York State,** take Route 290 to Route 190 to the Robert Moses Parkway. This will put you in downtown Niagara Falls, New York, and you'll see signs for the Rainbow Bridge to Canada. Other crossing points to Canada from the U.S. are between Lewiston, New York, and Queenston, Ontario, and between Buffalo, New York, and Fort Erie, Ontario.

Driving distances from major U.S. cities to Niagara Falls include Boston (774km/481 miles), Chicago (861km/535 miles), Detroit (384km/239 miles), New York (677km/421 miles), and Washington, D.C. (768km/477 miles).

From **Toronto,** take the Queen Elizabeth Way (signs read **QEW**) to Niagara via Hamilton and St. Catharines. Driving time is approximately 1½ to 2 hours, depending on traffic. Note that rush hour snarl-ups can considerably lengthen your trip when traveling from Toronto. If possible, avoid driving on major highways in the Toronto and Hamilton area between 7 and 10am and between 3:30 and 6:30pm.

From **Windsor** and **Detroit,** take Hwy. 401 E. to Hwy. 403, then join the QEW to Niagara. Driving time from Windsor to Niagara Falls is approximately 4 to 4½ hours.

Exit from the QEW at Hwy. 55 if your destination is Niagara-on-the-Lake or if you would like to take the scenic route to Niagara Falls, which will lead you along the Niagara Parkway on the west side of the Niagara River. If you want to go straight to the Falls, continue on the QEW to Hwy. 420 and follow the signs. A third option is to continue on the QEW to Fort Erie, at the southern end of the Niagara River. You can visit the attractions in Fort Erie, and then make your way along the southern portion of the Niagara Parkway to the Falls, which is also a pretty drive.

Be sure to check for the wait times at the border. It can sometimes take an hour or longer to get through Customs during busy times. The **Canada Border Services Agency** (www.cbsa-asfc.gc.ca/general/times) lists the wait times for all U.S. and Canadian border crossings, and the site is updated hourly.

Be sure to carry your driver's license and car registration and insurance documents if you plan to drive your own vehicle. If you are a member of the American Automobile Association (AAA) or the Canadian Automobile Association (CAA), you can get assistance by calling (✆ **905/984-8585;** www.caa.niagara.net).

Many car rental agencies have non-negotiable age requirements, minimum and maximum. Check with individual agencies to see what their specific policies are.

See "Getting Around by Car," below, for special driving customs and technicalities.

For more information on car rentals and gasoline (petrol) in Niagara, see "Getting Around by Car," below.

By Train

Amtrak (✆ **800/USA-RAIL** [872-7245]; www.amtrak.com) and **VIA Rail Canada** (✆ **888/VIA-RAIL** [842-7245] or 416/366-8411; www.viarail.ca) operate trains between **Toronto** and **New York,** stopping in **Niagara Falls** and **St. Catharines** but not Niagara-on-the-Lake. Amtrak comes right into the Niagara Falls station in New York State at 27th Street and Lockport Road.

International visitors can buy a **USA Rail Pass,** good for 15, 30, or 45 days of unlimited travel on **Amtrak** (✆ **800/USA-RAIL** in the U.S. or Canada; ✆ 001/215-856-7953 outside the U.S.; www.amtrak.com). The pass is available online or through many overseas travel agents. See Amtrak's website for the cost of travel within the western, eastern, or northwestern United States. Reservations are generally required and should be made as early as possible. Regional rail passes are also available.

GETTING AROUND

By Car

The best and most efficient way to tour the Niagara region is by car.

While driving on the Niagara Parkway beside the Canadian Falls can be intimidating in high season, the traffic is much better since the many tour buses now stop at a nearby central bus stop to unload their passengers. Be prepared to drive slowly and be wary of sightseers crossing the streets. They don't always use the crosswalks.

You will be able to tour the wine region easily by car, as well as enjoy the drive along the Niagara River to Niagara-on-the-Lake. The Queen Elizabeth Way (QEW) is a multi-lane expressway that will take you quickly through the center of the region. For a more leisurely drive, and certainly a more historic one, leave the QEW past St. Catharines at exit 55 and head south to Regional Road 81. It is the oldest highway in the province and will lead you through the small towns, fruit farms, vineyards, and wineries. The road is tree-lined and hugs the lower edge of the Niagara Escarpment for the majority of its routing west of St. Catharines. Many small shops and flea markets line the highway, and numerous parks and conservation areas are marked along the route.

A car is necessary if you wish to tour the entire region during your visit, but you do not need a car to get around in Niagara Falls. Public transit is not available between Niagara Falls and Niagara-on-the-Lake, but a shuttle bus runs between the bus terminal and certain hotels in Niagara Falls to Fort George in Niagara-on-the-Lake (© 800/667-0256 or 905/358-3232). The bus leaves in the morning and returns in the late afternoon. Niagara-on-the-Lake is small enough that you don't need a car. Wine-country tours can be arranged through tour companies. See chapter 7 for details.

DRIVING RULES In Ontario, a right turn on a red light is permitted after coming to a complete stop, unless posted otherwise, provided you yield to oncoming traffic and pedestrians. Wearing your seat belt is compulsory. Fines for riding without a seat belt are substantial. Headlights must be on from dusk until dawn. While it is not mandatory to have lights on in daytime, all cars manufactured after 1989 have daytime running lights that go on automatically. Speed limits are posted and must be obeyed at all times. Always stop when pedestrians are using the crosswalks, and watch for pedestrians crossing against the lights. Radar detectors are illegal. American drivers should note the difference in speed limits—Canadian signs are calculated in kilometers per hour, while U.S. signs are in miles per hour. Use the kilometer display on your speedometer or, if your car doesn't have one, divide the kilometers by 1.6 to obtain the mileage.

In the winter, some of the roads in the Niagara region can be subject to bad weather, and are occasionally closed due to weather conditions. Always travel with caution in winter and plan ahead. For road closures and weather information, there are several sources that you can consult. **The Traveller's Road Information Portal (TRIP)** is a website that gives you easy 24/7/365 access to Ministry of Transportation (MTO) road information on provincially maintained highways: www.mto.gov.on.ca/english/traveller/trip/index.shtml.

Alternatively, for really instant information, check the MTO's Twitter feed: @_mto. You can also check www.highwayconditions.com/on.htm or call for road conditions at © **800/268-4686** or 416/235-4686. It's a good idea to carry water, blankets, and food when traveling in Ontario in the winter. A cellphone is always handy—charge it up before you leave.

Speed limits and distances are in kilometers (1km equals .62 mile). Unless otherwise posted, the speed limit in urban and residential areas is 50km per hour (31 mph); on the highway it's 80km per hour (50 mph). Driving under the influence of alcohol is against the law and carries stiff penalties.

PARKING Parking lots fill up quickly, especially those along the Niagara Parkway. I've found that the best choice is to park in a lot a few blocks away and walk to the Falls.

Note: Your best bet is to come early for the best parking spot at a good rate. The lot in front of Niagara Tourism on Robinson Street, just a short walk from the Falls, charges C$5 for the day, but like other lots here, the price doubles later if the lot starts to fill up. That's still about half the cost of parking right beside the Falls.

Parking meters generally accept quarters, loonies, and toonies. Always read the signs posted near parking meters to find out if there are any parking restrictions. If you must leave your vehicle on a city street overnight, ask hotel staff or your B&B host whether there are parking restrictions. Parking meters are available in the city of Niagara Falls, New York, but I recommend that you park your vehicle in the Niagara Falls State Park. Meters are plentiful on both the U.S. and Canadian sides. Meter payment is required 7 days a week.

For parking at the Falls, you can leave your vehicle at the **Rapids View Parking Lot** for C$10 for the day (south of the Horseshoe Falls on the Niagara Pkwy.). The price includes a free shuttle to and from the Falls. Other options include purchasing a **People Mover Pass** at the parking lot (C$7.50 adults, C$4.50 children 6–12; see below), which allows you unlimited on/off privileges on the People Mover transit system that runs between Table Rock, at the Horseshoe Falls, and the Floral Clock, north of the Niagara Gorge along the Niagara Parkway. The People Mover stops at most of the major tourist attractions along the route, including the *Maid of the Mist,* American Falls, Whitewater Walk, Whirlpool Aero Car, Botanical Gardens and Butterfly Conservatory, and the Floral Clock.

You can also elect to purchase a **Niagara Falls and Great Gorge Adventure Pass** at the parking lot (C$45 adults, C$33 children 6–12). This pass includes entry to major attractions and access to the People Mover for a single, discounted price. You can also custom design your adventure pass by adding or changing the attractions. Additional parking is available opposite the Horseshoe Falls (all day for a single fee ranging btw. C$12–C$18), and at the Niagara Parks Floral Showhouse, south of the Horseshoe Falls (Apr–Nov C$3 per hour to a maximum of C$12; free in the winter).

You will find a number of all-day parking lots with the reasonable fee of around C$5 in the Fallsview district at the top of the Escarpment. From here, you can take footpaths down to the Falls (ask your parking attendant for directions, since these paths are not well signposted), or travel on the Incline Railway (see below for details).

By Public Transportation

BUS Niagara Transit operates throughout the city of Niagara Falls and surrounding communities, including service to Brock University and Niagara College. The bus station is located at 4320 Bridge St., Niagara Falls, ON (© **905/356-1179**; www. niagaratransit.com). The buses operate on an exact-fare basis: C$2.50 adults, C$2.25 students and seniors, and C$1.25 children; ages 5 and under ride free. Buses run regularly until midnight. Welland Transit has regular routes, and the last run is 10:30pm (160 E. Main St.; © **905/732-6844**, ext. 6; www.welland.ca/transit/index. asp). The City of St. Catharines Transit Commission has regular bus routes and also services Thorold, with limited services in Niagara-on-the-Lake (© **905/687-5555**; www.yourbus.com). The last St. Catharines bus leaves at 11:45pm. Niagara Falls, New York, runs buses via the Niagara Frontier Transportation Authority (© **716/855-7300**; www.nfta.com). Rates depend on zones crossed, starting at US$1.75 within one zone to a maximum of US$2.65 for four zones.

Greyhound Canada (© **800/661-8747**) provides coast-to-coast service with connections to Niagara Falls. The local bus station is Niagara Transportation, 4555 Erie Ave., Niagara Falls, ON (© **905/357-2133**). Book online or obtain schedule and fare information at www.greyhound.ca. **Greyhound Lines, Inc.** (© **800/231-2222**; www.greyhound.com), provides bus service between the U.S. and Canada. The local bus station on the U.S. side is at Niagara Discount Souvenir, 303 Rainbow Blvd., Niagara Falls, NY (© **716/282-1765**).

THE FALLS SHUTTLE Owned and operated by the Niagara Transit Commission, the Falls Shuttle passes by tourist accommodations properties in the Lundy's Lane and River Road districts. The **Red Line** serves Lundy's Lane, the Via Rail Station, the Bus Terminal, the Falls, and points of interest along the Niagara Gorge. The **Blue Line** serves the Fallsview area, including the Konica Minolta Tower, Skylon Tower, and Clifton Hill, traveling as far as Marineland. When the fireworks display over the Falls is in operation, every Friday and Sunday (10pm) and holidays from May 24 until September, a special **fireworks shuttle** takes tourists to the brink of the Falls. The fare is C$6 per adult, and tickets are available from shuttle-bus drivers, the Niagara Bus Terminal, and most lodgings.

PEOPLE MOVER The Niagara Parks Commission runs the People Mover, a bus service that covers the 30km (19-mile) loop from Table Rock along the Niagara Parkway to the Floral Clock, stopping at all the Niagara Parks attractions. A full-day pass allows you to hop on and off all day.

This public transportation system is highly recommended for visitors to Niagara Falls. The spotless and air-conditioned buses shuttle from the main terminal beside Table Rock Plaza to the Horseshoe Falls and Queenston Heights Park along the Niagara River. Buses operate daily between April and October, although first and last trip times vary by season. For more information, call © **905/357-9340.** The People Mover departs every 20 minutes and costs C$10 adults, C$6.05 children 6 to 12, and children 5 and under are free. A pass includes unlimited rides on the Incline Railway. Strollers are permitted.

INCLINE RAILWAY This open-air car transports pedestrians up and down the cliff between the Fallsview tourist area and the Horseshoe Falls. The cost is C$2 per trip, or unlimited access with the purchase of a People Mover Day Pass.

By Bike

The Niagara region is very bike-friendly, and while the whole area is too large to cover completely by bike, the Niagara Parkway and much of the wine country around Niagara-on-the-Lake can be seen at its best from the seat of a bike. Trails along the river are paved and well marked, and active visitors can wheel it down the 31km (19-mile) parkway, passing parks, gardens, wineries, and historic sites, ending in the pretty town of Niagara-on-the-Lake. VIA Rail makes it easy with their Bike Train, which allows you to bring your bike with you to either St. Catharines or Niagara Falls. Several companies offer organized bike tours of the area (p. 137 has details).

By Taxi

You can hail a taxi on the street, but you'll also readily find one at taxi stands in front of major hotels. You can also summon a taxi by phone: ✆ **905/357-4000** for **Niagara Falls Taxi,** or ✆ **905/685-5463** for **5-0 Transportation.** Other cab companies are listed in the Yellow Pages. On the American side, call **LaSalle Cab Dispatch Service** (✆ **716/284-8833**).

5-0 SHUTTLE   For service between Niagara Falls and Niagara-on-the-Lake, you can use the 5-0 Transportation shuttle bus. Pickup is at major hotels in Niagara Falls and the Niagara Falls Bus Terminal. One-way fare is C$10 adult and C$5 child. For more information, call ✆ **800/667-0256** or 905/358-3232 (www.5-0taxi.com).

On Foot

If Niagara Falls is your main interest, you can easily get around on foot, especially if you book a hotel near the Falls. Many of the hotels are just a few blocks from Table Rock, the main viewing area. You can tour the Falls and the attractions, then walk through the colorful shops and activities of Clifton Hill.

TIPS ON ACCOMMODATIONS

Niagara has almost every kind of accommodation a traveler could want, with lots of choice, ranging from simple B&Bs to luxury boutique hotels. Prices range as well, from affordable to luxe. In high season, from about early June to late September, demand is high and you would be wise to book a room well in advance of your visit for optimum selection. You'll find the best prices for rooms are available by online bookings through hotel websites, and winter and shoulder season rates are much lower than high season. Hotels in Niagara Falls tend to be a bit more glitzy and entertainment-oriented, while the hotels you will find in Niagara-on-the-Lake or in the countryside will be a restored Georgian home or a vineyard château perhaps, with a quieter and often more sedate character. Several major hotel chains are present in Niagara Falls, including the Sheraton, the Hilton, and Embassy Suites.

[FastFACTS] NIAGARA

Area Codes   The telephone area code for the Niagara region is 905. The area code in Niagara Falls, New York, is 716.

Business Hours   Most **stores** are open Monday to Saturday from 9:30 or 10am to 6pm, and many have extended hours one or more evenings. Sunday opening hours are generally from noon to 5pm, although some stores open at 11am and others are closed all day. **Banks** generally open weekdays at 10am and close by 4pm, with extended hours one or more evenings; some are open Saturdays. **Restaurants** generally open at 11 or 11:30am for lunch and around 5pm for dinner, although many stay open all day. Hours for **attractions and museums** vary considerably depending on the season; refer to chapter 6,

"What to See & Do in the Niagara Region," for individual opening hours. **U.S. banking** hours are generally 9am to 5pm Monday through Thursday, 9am to 6pm Friday, and Saturday 9am to 1pm.

Car Rental   See "Getting There by Car," earlier in this chapter.

Cellphones   See "Mobile Phones," later in this section.

Customs   You'll pass through **Canadian Customs** (✆ **800/461-9999** in Canada, or 204/983-3500) upon arrival, and **U.S. Customs** (✆ **360/332-5771**), if you are traveling through the U.S., on your departure.

What You Can Bring into Canada   Your personal baggage can include the following: boats, motors, snowmobiles, camping and sports equipment, appliances, TV sets, musical instruments, personal computers, cameras, and other items of a personal or household nature. If you are bringing excess luggage, be sure to carry a detailed inventory list that includes the acquisition date, serial number, and cost or replacement value of each item. It sounds tedious, but it can speed things up at the border. Customs will help you fill out the forms that allow you to temporarily bring in your effects. This list will also be used by U.S. Customs to check off what you bring out. You will be charged Customs duties for anything left in Canada.

A few other things to keep in mind:

- If you're over 18, you're allowed to bring in 1.5 liters (53 oz.) of wine; or a total of 1.14 liters (40 oz.) of alcoholic beverages; or up to 8.5 liters of beer or ale; 40 ounces of liquor and wine or 24 12-ounce cans or bottles of beer and ale; and 50 cigars, 400 cigarettes, or 14 ounces of manufactured tobacco per person. Any excess is subject to duty.

- Gifts not exceeding C$60 and not containing tobacco products, alcoholic beverages, or advertising material can be brought in duty-free. Meats, plants, and vegetables are subject to inspection on entry. There are restrictions, so contact the Canadian Consulate for more details if you want to bring produce into the country, or check the Canada Border Services Agency website, www.cbsa-asfc.gc.ca.

- If you plan to bring your dog or cat, you must provide proof of rabies inoculation during the preceding 36-month period. Other types of animals need special clearance and health certification. (Many birds, for instance, require 8 weeks in quarantine.)

If you need more information concerning items you wish to bring in and out of the country, contact **Canada Border Services** (✆ **800/461-9999** in Canada, or 204/983-3500; **www.cbsa-asfc.gc.ca**).

What You Can Take Home from Canada   For information on what you're allowed to bring home, contact one of the following agencies:

U.S. Citizens: U.S. Customs & Border Protection (CBP), 1300 Pennsylvania Ave. NW, Washington, DC 20229 (✆ **877/287-8667; www.cbp.gov**).

Canadian Citizens: Canada Border Services Agency (✆ **800/461-9999** in Canada, or 204/983-3500; **www.cbsa-asfc.gc.ca**).

U.K. Citizens: Call **HM Customs & Excise** at ✆ **0845/010-9000** (from outside the U.K., 020/8929-0152), or consult their website at **www.hmce.gov.uk**.

Australian Citizens: Call the **Australian Customs Service** at ✆ **1300/363-263,** or log on to **www.customs.gov.au**.

New Zealand Citizens: New Zealand Customs, The Customhouse, 17–21 Whitmore St., Box 2218, Wellington (✆ **04/473-6099** or 0800/428-786; **www.customs.govt.nz**).

It is advised to always have at least one or two consecutive blank pages in your passport to allow space for visas and stamps that need to appear together. It is also important to note when your passport expires. Your passport must be valid for at least one day beyond your stay in Canada. Visitors to Canada may stay up to six months. Many countries require your passport to have at least 6 months left before its expiration in order to allow you into the destination.

Disabled Travelers   Generally speaking, Ontario is well equipped to help people with disabilities get around. A clearinghouse of official Canadian federal government information on disability issues, including those related to travel and transportation, is available from Persons with Disabilities Online at www.pwd-online.ca. Another website that has comprehensive information on services offered for those with disabilities is www.abilities.ca. Check websites of restaurants and hotels that you plan to visit, or call ahead, to be sure that the venue is accessible. Most disabilities shouldn't stop anyone from traveling. There are more options and resources out there than ever before.

To find out which attractions, accommodations, and restaurants in the Niagara region are accessible to people with disabilities, refer to *Accessible Niagara,* an annual guide available from local Visitor Information Centres, or visit their website at www.accessible niagara.com. The guide covers accommodations, tourist attractions, parks, religious facilities, restaurants, shopping malls, retail stores, wineries, and transportation. On the U.S. side, find www.cqc.state.ny.us, the New York State Commission on Quality of Care and Advocacy for Persons with Disabilities. There is designated parking for persons with disabilities right across from the Falls. Alert the parking attendant that you have a disability, and you will be led to the special areas for vans and vehicles with ramps. There is a ramp that leads from the parking lot down to the road. You can cross at the lights and arrive right in front of the Falls. There is also limited wheelchair parking upstream a little in front of the horseshoe-shaped driveway leading to the Niagara Parks Police building.

If you are seated on a scooter or in a wheelchair, you may have a problem seeing through the wrought-iron barrier around the gorge. The best place for seated visitors is on top of the Maid of the Mist center, not far from the Falls, or on the second-floor balcony of Table Rock House. You can take pictures and see the entire area from your vantage point at both of these places.

Blind and visually impaired travelers can obtain information on how to make the most of their trip to Niagara by calling the Canadian National Institute for the Blind (CNIB) Information Centre (✆ **905/688-0022;** www.cnib.ca) or the American Foundation for the Blind (✆ **800/232-5463;** www.afb.org).

Organizations that offer a vast range of resources and assistance to travelers with disabilities include MossRehab (✆ **800/CALL-MOSS** [2255-6677]; www.mossresourcenet.org), the American Foundation for the Blind (AFB; ✆ **800/232-5463;** www.afb.org), and SATH (Society for Accessible Travel & Hospitality; ✆ **212/447-7284;** www.sath.org). AirAmbulanceCard.com is now partnered with SATH and allows you to preselect top-notch hospitals in case of an emergency.

For more information specifically targeted to travelers with disabilities, the community website www.accesstotravel.gc.ca has destination guides and several regular columns on accessible travel. Also check out the quarterly magazine *Emerging Horizons* (www.emerginghorizons.com) and *Open World* magazine, published by SATH (see above).

Drinking Laws   You must be **19 years of age or older** to consume or purchase alcohol in Ontario. Bars and retail stores are strict about enforcing the law and will ask for proof of age, at their discretion. The **Liquor Control Board of Ontario (LCBO)** sells wine, spirits, and beer. Beer is also available through the Beer Store, with numerous locations in the Niagara region. Niagara wines may also be purchased at individual wineries by the bottle or case. You must be **21 years of age or older** to consume or purchase alcohol in the

United States. Beer, and sometimes wine, can be purchased at local convenience stores. Liquor is sold through private proprietors.

Do not carry open containers of alcohol in your car or any public area that isn't zoned for alcohol consumption. The police can fine you on the spot. Don't even think about driving while intoxicated.

Driving Rules   See "Getting Around: By Car" on p. 225.

Electricity   Like the United States, Canada uses 110 to 120 volts AC (60 cycles), compared to 220 to 240 volts AC (50 cycles) in most of Europe, Australia, and New Zealand. Downward converters that change 220–240 volts to 110–120 volts are difficult to find in North America, so bring one with you.

Embassies & Consulates   All embassies in Canada (more than 100 in total) are located in Ottawa; consulates are primarily located in Toronto, Montreal, and Vancouver. Embassies include the **Australian High Commission,** 50 O'Connor St., Ste. 710, Ottawa, ON K1P 6L2 (☏ **613/236-0841**); the **British High Commission,** 80 Elgin St., Ottawa, ON K1P 5K7 (☏ **613/237-1530**); the **Embassy of Ireland,** 130 Albert St., Ottawa, ON K1P 5G4 (☏ **613/233-6281**); the **New Zealand High Commission,** 727–99 Bank St., Ottawa, ON K1P 6G3 (☏ **613/238-5991**); the **South African High Commission,** 15 Sussex Dr., Ottawa, ON K1M 1M8 (☏ **613/744-0330**); and the **Embassy of the United States of America,** 490 Sussex Dr., Ottawa, ON K1N 1G8 (☏ **613/238-5335;** http://ottawa.usembassy.gov for general inquiries).

Emergencies   Call ☏ **911** emergency services for fire, police, or ambulance. For the **Ontario Regional Poison Information Centre,** call ☏ **800/268-9017.** For the **Western New York Regional Poison Control Center,** call ☏ **800/222-1222.** When in Ontario, call **Telehealth Ontario** ☏ **866/797-0000** to speak with a registered nurse and have health questions answered, including whether your health situation should be deemed an emergency, urgent care, or regular consultation.

Family Travel   Niagara Falls is one of the most family friendly destinations you can imagine. Many restaurants cater especially to a younger crowd, and places like Clifton Hill are completely designed for family fun. Most of the attractions around the Falls are perfect for a family outing. (See chapter 1, Best Activities for Families, p. 6) Luckily for visitors with kids in tow, the Niagara region has a good selection of hotels with suite accommodations, which are equipped with kitchenettes or full kitchens and one or two bedrooms; some have two bathrooms. You get the advantage of food-preparation facilities and accommodations for the entire family in one unit, which are important considerations when you have young children with you. When booking your accommodations, always ask if family packages are available.

When you're deciding which time of year to visit, try to schedule your trip during school vacation periods, which in Ontario run for 2 weeks during Christmas/New Year, 1 week in mid-March, and the months of July and August. Special events and festivals particularly aimed at families are held at various museums and other locations during school holidays.

Recommended family-travel Internet sites include Family Travel Forum (www.family travelforum.com), a comprehensive site that offers customized trip planning; Family Travel Network (www.familytravelnetwork.com), an award-winning site that offers travel features, deals, and tips; Traveling Internationally with Your Kids (www.travelwithyourkids.com), a comprehensive site offering sound advice for long-distance and international travel with children; and Family Travel Files (www.thefamilytravelfiles.com), which offers an online magazine and a directory of off-the-beaten-path tours and tour operators for families.

To locate accommodations, restaurants, and attractions that are particularly kid-friendly, refer to the "Kids" icon throughout this guide.

Gasoline (Petrol)   Taxes are already included in the printed price. One U.S. gallon equals 3.8 liters or .85 imperial gallons. The average price for regular gasoline, which most rental cars will take, is around C$1.30 cents a liter. But be aware that prices often increase during the busy summer months. New York State gas prices are about US$3.85 per gallon.

Holidays   Ontario celebrates the following holidays: New Year's Day (Jan 1), Good Friday and Easter Monday (Mar or Apr), Victoria Day (Mon following the third weekend in May), Canada Day (July 1), Simcoe Day (first Mon in Aug), Labour Day (first Mon in Sept), Thanksgiving (second Mon in Oct), Remembrance Day (Nov 11), Christmas Day (Dec 25), and Boxing Day (Dec 26).

For more information on holidays, see "Niagara Region Calendar of Events," in chapter 2.

Health   There are no specific health concerns to be aware of when traveling to Ontario. There is an excellent medical system, no disease threats, and little chance of encountering dangerous insects or disease-carrying bugs.

If you are not a Canadian resident and become ill while traveling in the country, you may have to pay all medical costs upfront and be reimbursed later. For U.S. travelers, Medicare and Medicaid do not provide coverage for medical costs outside the U.S. Before leaving home, find out what medical services your health insurance covers. To protect yourself, consider buying medical travel insurance.

If you suffer from a chronic illness, consult your doctor before your departure. Pack prescription medications in your carry-on luggage, and carry them in their original containers, with pharmacy labels—otherwise they won't make it through airport security. Carry the generic name of prescription medicines, in case a local Canadian pharmacist is unfamiliar with the brand name.

For conditions like epilepsy, diabetes, or heart problems, wear a MedicAlert Identification Tag (© **800/825-3785;** www.medicalert.org), which will immediately alert doctors to your condition and give them access to your records through MedicAlert's 24-hour hotline.

Health care is excellent in Canada and the chances of you contracting a serious illness are low. To be safe, carry your regular brand of anti-diarrheal and pain relief medication, although those medications, including generic equivalents, are easily available in Canadian drugstores.

Hospitals   Emergency services are available at Greater Niagara General Hospital, 5546 Portage Rd., Niagara Falls, ON (© **905/358-0171**), and St. Catharines General Hospital, 142 Queenston St., St. Catharines (© **905/684-7271**). Ontario hospital emergency rooms are extremely busy and wait times for nonurgent cases are typically several hours. If at all possible, use a walk-in clinic. Visit www.acurehealth.com/tools/walk-in-clinics/ontario/niagara_falls.htm for a list of urgent care clinics and their contact information. The Morrison St. Walk-In Clinic, 6453 Morrison St., in Niagara Falls, Ontario (© 905/374-3344), is the most central clinic to the downtown area.

On the U.S. side, Niagara Falls Memorial Medical Center offers emergency services (621 10th St., Niagara Falls, NY; © **716/278-4000,** or 716/278-4394 emergency room).

All doctors in Ontario hospitals speak English. If you become ill and require immediate assistance, dial 911. You will be required to pay for medical treatment as a walk-in at an Ontario hospital.

Insurance   Even though Canada is just a short drive or flight away for many Americans, U.S. health plans (including Medicare and Medicaid) do not provide coverage here, and the ones that do often require you to pay for services up front and reimburse you only after you return home. As a safety net, you may want to buy travel medical insurance. Travelers from the U.K. should carry their European Health Insurance Card (EHIC), which replaced the E111 form as proof of entitlement to free/reduced cost medical treatment abroad (© **0845/606-2030;** www.ehic.org.uk). Note, however, that the EHIC covers only "necessary medical treatment," and for repatriation costs, lost money, baggage, or cancellation, travel insurance from a reputable company should always be sought (www.travelinsuranceweb.com).

For information on traveler's insurance, trip cancellation insurance, and medical insurance while traveling, please visit **www.frommers.com/planning**.

Internet Access & Wi-Fi Almost all hotels will offer Internet service, usually wireless. There is often a daily charge for usage, but look carefully and you can find some hotels that have free Internet service. Often Wi-Fi is free in the lobbies. New wireless hotspots are popping up all over the place, so if you're equipped with the technology, you should find it fairly easy to go online. Otherwise, try the public library. The Victoria Avenue Branch, at 4848 Victoria Ave., is convenient to downtown. **UPS Stores** offering paid Internet access include locations in St. Catharines at the Pendale Plaza, 210 Glendale Ave. (© **905/682-5310**); in Niagara Falls, Ontario, at the Doubletree Resort Lodge & Spa (p. 49), and at 4025 Dorchester Rd. (© **905/357-4348**); in Fort Erie, 1243 Garrison Rd. (© 905/994-8339); and at the **Welland Plaza,** 200 Fitch St. (© **905/788-9993**).

Legal Aid If you are "pulled over" for a minor infraction (such as speeding), never attempt to pay the fine directly to a police officer; this could be construed as attempted bribery, a much more serious crime. Pay fines by mail, or directly into the hands of the clerk of the court. If accused of a more serious offense, say and do nothing before consulting a lawyer. Here the burden is on the state to prove a person's guilt beyond a reasonable doubt, and everyone has the right to remain silent, whether he or she is suspected of a crime or actually arrested. Once arrested, a person can make one telephone call to a party of his or her choice. International visitors should call their embassy or consulate.

Legal Aid Ontario (LAO) is an agency that provides legal assistance to financially disadvantaged persons in the province of Ontario. Legal aid is provided primarily for criminal, family, immigration, and refugee matters, for a few specific other types of proceedings, and for duty counsel support. Its mandate includes financial support for 80 independent community legal clinics in Ontario that provide "poverty law" services, including social assistance and disability, landlord and tenant disputes, and some specialized services. Contact **Niagara North Legal Aid Office,** 55 King St., Ste. 200, St. Catharines, ON L2R 3H5 (© **905/685-1012** TTY).

LGBT Travelers Ontario is a gay- and lesbian-friendly destination. Nearby Toronto, for example, hosts the largest gay pride parade in the world every July. The **International Gay and Lesbian Travel Association** (IGLTA; © **800/448-8550** or 954/776-2626; www.iglta.org) is the trade association for the gay and lesbian travel industry, and offers an online directory of gay- and lesbian-friendly travel businesses and tour operators.

For gay-friendly accommodations, bars, and restaurants and gay wedding arrangements in the Niagara area, visit www.gaycanada.com or www.gayniagara.com. Details of the region's annual Pride Weekend, held in St. Catharines in June, are posted on the Gay Niagara website. The Canadian website GayTraveler (http://gaytraveler.ca) offers ideas and advice for gay travel all over the world. On the U.S. side, see www.gayjourney.com/hotels/us_ny.htm.

Mail Mailing letters and postcards within Canada costs C59¢. Postage for letters and postcards sent from Canada to the United States costs C$1.03, and overseas C$1.75.

At press time, U.S. postage rates were 29¢ for a postcard and 44¢ for a letter. For international mail, a first-class letter of up to 1 ounce costs 98¢ (80¢ to Canada or Mexico); a first-class postcard costs the same as a letter. For more information, go to www.usps.com.

If you aren't sure what your address will be in the United States, mail can be sent to you, in your name, c/o General Delivery at the main post office of the city or region where you expect to be. (Call ✆ **800/275-8777** for information on the nearest post office.) The addressee must pick up mail in person and must produce proof of identity (driver's license, passport, etc.). Most post offices will hold your mail for up to 1 month, and are open Monday to Friday from 8am to 6pm, and Saturday from 9am to 3pm. In Canada, General Delivery (Poste Restante in French Canada) is also available to the travelling public for a period of up to four months. Contact Customer Service by email at: service@canadapost.ca or at ✆ 800/267-1177 to arrange for this service.

Always include zip codes when mailing items in the U.S. If you don't know your zip code, visit www.usps.com/zip4.

Mobile Phones   Most U.S. cellphone carriers have roaming agreements with Canadian cellphone carriers. Before leaving home, check with your carrier for rates and availability.

Money & Costs   Frommer's lists exact prices in the local currency. The currency conversions quoted below were correct at press time. However, rates fluctuate, so before departing consult a currency exchange website such as www.oanda.com/convert/classic to check up-to-the-minute rates.

THE VALUE OF THE CANADIAN DOLLAR VS. OTHER POPULAR CURRENCIES.

Can$	US$	UK (£)	Euro (€)	Aus$	NZ$
C$1	$1.04	62p	€.72	A$.96	NZ$1.24

Compared to many international destinations, the Niagara region is moderately priced. As in every tourist spot, prices for hotel rooms and some meals are higher during peak season, but remain affordable by world standards.

It's always advisable to bring money in a variety of forms on a vacation: a mix of cash and credit cards is best. You should also exchange enough petty cash to cover airport incidentals, tipping, and transportation to your hotel before you leave home, or withdraw money upon arrival at an airport ATM.

The currency of Canada is the Canadian dollar, made up of 100¢. Paper currency comes in C$5, C$10, C$20, C$50, and C$100 denominations. Coins come in 1¢, 5¢, 10¢, and 25¢ (penny, nickel, dime, and quarter) and C$1 (loonies) and C$2 (toonies) denominations.

The Canadian dollar is growing in strength; U.S. visitors will find that the heady days of highly favorable exchange rates have passed. At press time, the Canadian dollar was hovering around $1.04 in U.S. money, give or take a couple of points' variation. What this means is that your American money gets you about 5% less the moment you exchange it for local currency. By the time you read this book, however, the exchange rate may have changed. The British pound has been sitting at around C$1.40. (You might want to visit a website such as www.xe.com/ucc for up-to-the-minute exchange-rate information.)

Sales taxes are high in Ontario. You'll pay 13% tax on most retail items—a 5% federal goods and service tax (GST) and an 8% provincial sales tax (PST). Taxes for restaurant meals are even higher.

Traveler's checks in Canadian funds are universally accepted by banks (which charge a fee to cash them), larger stores, and hotels. If your traveler's checks are in a non-Canadian currency, you can exchange them for Canadian currency at any major bank.

U.S. denominated travelers checks are easily accepted at major Canadian banks. The easiest and best way to get cash in the Niagara region is from an ATM. The **Cirrus** (✆ **800/424-7787;** www.mastercard.com) and **PLUS** (✆ **800/843-7587;** www.visa.com)

WHAT THINGS COST IN NIAGARA

	C$
Double room, moderate	110
Double room, inexpensive	70
Three-course dinner for one without wine, moderate	15.00–25.00
Bottle of domestic Imperial beer	3.50
Cup of coffee	1.35–2.00
1 liter of regular gas	1.28
Admission to most museums	4.50–8.50
Admission to most national parks	10.00

networks span the globe; look at the back of your bank card to see which network you're on, and then call or check online for ATM locations at your destination. Be sure you know your personal identification number (PIN) before you leave home, and be sure to find out your daily withdrawal limit before you depart. Many banks impose a fee every time a card is used at a different bank's ATM, and that fee can be higher for international transactions than for domestic ones. On top of this, the bank from which you withdraw cash may charge its own fee. The 24-hour PLUS and Cirrus ATM systems are widely available throughout Ontario. The systems convert Canadian withdrawals to your account's currency within 24 hours. Cirrus network cards and the Visa Plus cards work at ATMs at **BMO Bank of Montreal** (© 800/555-3000), **CIBC** (© 800/465-2422), **HSBC** (© 888/310-4722), **RBC Royal Bank** (© 800/769-2511), **TD Canada Trust** (© 866/567-8888), and at all other ATMs that display the Cirrus or Visa logo.

Major U.S. credit cards are widely accepted in Ontario, especially American Express, MasterCard, and Visa. Diners Club, Carte Blanche, Discover, JCB, and EnRoute are taken by some establishments, but not as many. The amount spent in Canadian dollars will automatically be converted by your issuing company to your currency when you're billed—generally at rates that are better than you'd receive for cash at a currency exchange. However, the bank will probably add a 3% "adjustment fee" to the converted purchase price. You can also obtain a PIN on your credit card and use it in some ATMs. You usually pay interest from the date of withdrawal and often pay a higher service fee than when using a regular ATM card.

Beware of hidden credit card fees while traveling. Check with your credit or debit card issuer to see what fees, if any, will be charged for overseas transactions. Recent reform legislation in the U.S., for example, has curbed some exploitative lending practices. But many banks have responded by increasing fees in other areas, including fees for customers who use credit and debit cards while out of the country—even if those charges were made in U.S. dollars. Fees can amount to 3% or more of the purchase price. Check with your bank before departing to avoid any surprise charges on your statement.

Multicultural Travelers While Canada is officially a bilingual country, French and English, most people you will encounter in the Niagara region will speak English. Many of the main attractions offer commentary in other languages, however. Niagara Helicopters, for example, offers audio tours in several languages, and Casino Niagara has a language-pin program in effect. Employees who speak languages other than English wear a pin telling you what language they speak. Anyone unable to speak English may converse through them. The Niagara Parks Adventure Pass comes with an audio tour that is available in six different languages.

Newspapers & Magazines   The daily newspapers are the *Niagara Falls Review, St. Catharines Standard, Fort Erie Times, Port Colborne Tribune,* and the *Welland Tribune.* Several smaller communities publish weekly newspapers. For entertainment listings in the St. Catharines area, pick up a copy of *The Downtowner* or *Pulse St. Catharines. The Brock Press* is Brock University's student newspaper. *Niagara Life* is a glossy magazine featuring the personalities of the region.

There are two local dailies in Niagara Falls, New York: the *Niagara Gazette* and the *Tonawanda News. The Current* is a free weekly. Several smaller communities publish weekly newspapers. *Niagara This Week* is a free local paper that carries local news and a listing of community events in its "It's Happening" section. Also published is the smaller *Free Daily Press.* Both are available at tourist information centers. For information more closely tied to specific areas and towns, visit the websites of the tourist information centers listed in "Visitor Information," below.

Packing   Visitors to Niagara are often caught unaware by the heavy spray from the Falls. It's a good idea to bring along a raincoat and umbrella if you plan to walk by the Falls, even on a sunny day. Be prepared for some very hot days if you visit in the summer; bring sunscreen. Temperatures can exceed 95°F (35°C). That's when the cooling spray is really appreciated. In winter, you will need to wear something warm as well as rain gear. Ice on your eyelashes is a common occurrence in winter months.

Passports   See www.frommers.com/planning for information on how to obtain a passport. See "Embassies & Consulates," above, for whom to contact if you lose yours while traveling in the U.S. and Canada. For other information, please contact the following agencies:

Entry Documents for U.S. Citizens   It is no longer possible to enter Canada and return to the U.S. simply by showing a government-issued photo ID (such as a driver's license) and proof of U.S. citizenship (such as a birth or naturalization certificate). The **Western Hemisphere Travel Initiative (WHTI),** which took full effect in 2009, requires all U.S. citizens returning to the U.S. from Canada to have either a U.S. passport (this includes children under age 18), a Trusted Traveler Card (NEXUS, SENTRI, or FAST), a state-issued enhanced driver's license, or a new passport card (see box below) in order to get back into the U.S.

You'll find current entry information on the website of the U.S. State Department at **www.travel.state.gov** and on the **Canada Border Services Agency** website, **www. cbsa-asfc.gc.ca**.

Permanent U.S. residents who are not U.S. citizens should carry their passport and Resident Alien Card (U.S. form I-151 or I-551). Foreign students and other noncitizen U.S. residents should carry their passport, a Temporary Resident Card (form 1688) or Employment Authorization Card (1688A or 1688B), a visitor's visa, an I-94 arrival-departure record, a current I-20 copy of IAP-66 indicating student status, proof of sufficient funds for a temporary stay, and evidence of return transportation.

Entry Documents for Commonwealth Citizens   Citizens of Great Britain, Australia, and New Zealand don't need visas to enter Canada, but they do need to show **proof of Commonwealth citizenship** (such as a **passport**), as well as evidence of funds sufficient for a temporary stay (credit cards work well here). Naturalized citizens should carry their naturalization certificates. Permanent residents of Commonwealth nations should carry their passports and resident status cards.

Foreign students and other residents should carry their passport, a Temporary Resident Card or Employment Authorization Card, a visitor's visa, an arrival-departure record, a current copy of student status, proof of sufficient funds for a temporary stay, and evidence of return transportation. ***Note:*** With changing security regulations, it is advisable for all travelers to check with the Canadian consulate before departure to find out the latest in travel-document requirements. You will also find current information on the **Canada Border Services Agency** website, **www.cbsa-asfc.gc.ca**; follow the links under "FAQ."

For Residents of Australia You can pick up a passport application from your local post office or any branch of Passports Australia, but you must schedule an interview at the passport office to present your application materials. Call the **Australian Passport Information Service** at (C) **131-232,** or visit the government website at **www.passports.gov.au**.

For Residents of Ireland You can apply for a 10-year passport at the **Passport Office,** Setanta Centre, Molesworth Street, Dublin 2 ((C) **353/1671-1633** or 890/426-888; www.irlgov.ie/iveagh). Those under age 18 and over 65 must apply for a 3-year passport. You can also apply at 1A South Mall, Cork ((C) **353/21494-4700** or 890/426-900) or at most main post offices.

For Residents of New Zealand You can pick up a passport application at any New Zealand Passports Office or download it from their website. Contact the **Passports Office** at (C) **0800/225-050** in New Zealand, or 04/474-8100, or log on to **www.passports.govt.nz**.

For Residents of the United Kingdom To pick up an application for a standard 10-year passport (5-year passport for children under 16), visit your nearest passport office, major post office, or travel agency, or contact the **United Kingdom Passport Service** at (C) **0870/521-0410** or search its website at **www.ukpa.gov.uk**.

Police In a life-threatening emergency or to report a crime in progress or a traffic accident that involves injuries or a vehicle that cannot be driven, call (C) **911.** Non-emergency inquiries should be directed to (C) **905/688-4111.** The **Niagara Falls Police Department** in New York can be reached at (C) **716/286-4711** for non-emergency inquiries.

Senior Travel Some attractions and accommodations offer special rates or discounts for seniors, so always mention that fact when you make your travel arrangements. Carry a form of photo ID that includes your birth date. Becoming a member of a senior's organization may earn you a discount on travel arrangements. Consider joining the **Canadian Association of Retired Persons (CARP),** 27 Queen St. E., Ste. 1304, Toronto, ON M5C 2M6 ((C) **800/363-9736;** www.carp.ca). The website has a comprehensive travel section for members, which features hotels, packages, transportation, and travel insurance. The U.S. equivalent is **AARP** (formerly known as the American Association of Retired Persons), 601 E. St. NW, Washington, DC 20049 ((C) **888/687-2277;** www.aarp.org). Members get discounts on hotels, airfares, and car rentals. AARP offers members a wide range of benefits, including *AARP The Magazine* and a monthly newsletter. Anyone 50 or older can join.

Recommended publications offering travel resources and discounts for seniors include the quarterly magazine *Travel 50 & Beyond* (www.travel50andbeyond.com) and the best-selling paperback *Unbelievably Good Deals and Great Adventures that You Absolutely Can't Get Unless You're Over 50* (McGraw-Hill), by Joann Rattner Heilman.

Single Travelers While the area around the Falls can be crowded at peak times, this is a single-friendly destination. Restaurants are usually very welcoming to single customers, and the area is very safe, as long as you practice common sense.

For more information on traveling single, go to www.frommers.com/planning.

Smoking Smoking is not permitted in any indoor public places in Ontario. The smoking regulations for New York State are similar.

Student Travel The **International Student Travel Confederation** (ISTC; www.istc.org) was formed in 1949 to make travel around the world more affordable for students. Check out its website for comprehensive travel services information and details on how to get an **International Student Identity Card (ISIC),** which qualifies students for substantial savings on rail passes, plane tickets, entrance fees, and more. It also provides students with basic health and life insurance and a 24-hour helpline. The card is valid for a maximum of 18 months. You can apply for the card online or in person at **STA Travel**

(📞 **800/781-4040** in North America; www.statravel.com), the biggest student travel agency in the world; check out the website to locate STA Travel offices worldwide. If you're no longer a student but are still under age 26, you can get an **International Youth Travel Card (IYTC)** from the same people, which entitles you to some discounts. **Travel CUTS** (📞 **800/592-2887**; www.travelcuts.com) offers similar services for both Canadians and U.S. residents. Irish students may prefer to turn to **USIT** (📞 **01/602-1904**; www.usit. ie), an Ireland-based specialist in student, youth, and independent travel.

Students who would like to attend lectures, seminars, concerts, and other events can contact **Brock University**, 500 Glenridge Ave., St. Catharines (📞 **905/688-5550**; www. brocku.ca) or **Niagara College** (📞 **905/641-2252**; www.niagarac.on.ca) for information on all campuses (Welland, St. Catharines, Niagara Falls, and Grimsby).

Taxes   As of July 1, 2010, the Ontario government implemented a "harmonized" tax system, with a 13% sales tax on virtually everything for sale. (Previously, the federal GST was 5% and the Ontario sales tax was 8%, but the Ontario sales tax was not applied to purchases such as fast-food meals.) Taxes are added when you purchase an item, rather than being included in the original price, as is common in much of Europe. The Canadian government suspended the GST Visitors' Rebate Program in 2007. The accommodations tax is 5%.

In Niagara Falls, New York, sales tax is 8% on all goods and accommodations. There are no duty-free stores in the U.S. Visitors can receive tax-free purchases only if they ship their purchases home at the time of purchase. For more information, visit **www.tax.state. ny.us**, or call 📞 **800/972-1233.**

Telephones   Many convenience stores and packaging services sell **prepaid calling cards** in denominations up to C$50; for international visitors, these can be the least expensive way to call home. It's hard to find public pay phones; those at airports now accept American Express, MasterCard, and Visa credit cards. **Local calls** made from pay phones in most locales cost C50¢ (no pennies). Most long-distance and international calls can be dialed directly from any phone. **For calls within Canada and to the United States,** dial 1 followed by the area code and the seven-digit number. **For other international calls,** dial 011 followed by the country code, city code, and the number you are calling.

Calls to area codes **800, 888, 877,** and **866** are toll-free. However, calls to area codes **700** and **900** (chat lines, bulletin boards, "dating" services, and so on) can be very expensive—usually a charge of C95¢ to C$3 or more per minute, and they sometimes have minimum charges that can run as high as C$15 or more.

For **reversed-charge or collect calls,** and for person-to-person calls, dial the number 0 then the area code and number; an operator will come on the line, and you should specify whether you are calling collect, person-to-person, or both. If your operator-assisted call is international, ask for the overseas operator.

For **local directory assistance** ("information"), dial 📞 **411;** for long-distance information, dial 1, then the appropriate area code, and 555-1212.

Time   Niagara is on **Eastern Standard Time. Daylight saving time** is in effect from the second Sunday in March (clocks are moved ahead 1 hr.) to the first Sunday in November (clocks are moved back 1 hr.).

The continental United States is divided into **four time zones:** Eastern Standard Time (EST), Central Standard Time (CST), Mountain Standard Time (MST), and Pacific Standard Time (PST). Alaska, Hawaii, and Newfoundland have their own zones. For example, when it's 9am in Los Angeles (PST), it's 7am in Honolulu (HST), 10am in Denver (MST), 11am in Chicago (CST), noon in New York City (EST), 5pm in London (GMT), and 2am the next day in Sydney.

Tipping   The same rules apply in Niagara as in major North American cities.

In hotels, tip **bellhops** at least C$1 per bag (C$2–C$3 if you have a lot of luggage) and tip the **chamber staff** C$1 to C$2 per day (more if you've left a disaster area for him or her to clean up). Tip the **doorman** or **concierge** only if he or she has provided you with some specific service (for example, calling a cab for you or obtaining difficult-to-get theater tickets). Tip the **valet-parking attendant** C$1 each time you get your car.

In restaurants, bars, and nightclubs, tip **service staff** and **bartenders** 15% to 20% of the check, tip **checkroom attendants** C$1 per garment, and tip **valet-parking attendants** C$1 per vehicle.

As for other service personnel, tip **cab drivers** 15% of the fare; tip **skycaps** at airports at least C$1 per bag (C$2–C$3 if you have a lot of luggage); and tip **hairdressers** and **barbers** 15% to 20%.

Toilets You won't find public toilets or "restrooms" on the streets in most Canadian and U.S. cities, but they can be found in hotel lobbies, bars, restaurants, museums, department stores, railway and bus stations, and service stations. Large hotels and fast-food restaurants are often the best bet for clean facilities. Restaurants and bars in resorts or heavily visited areas may reserve their restrooms for patrons.

Visas While the citizens of most Western countries (including the United States, Australia, New Zealand, Ireland, and the United Kingdom) do not require a visa to visit Canada, there are several countries that must have a visa for a Canadian visitor's entry. Check **www.cic.gc.ca** for a current list of those countries requiring a visa. See "Passports," above, for further information on documents needed to enter Canada.

Visitor Information In the city of Niagara Falls, Ontario, visit **Niagara Falls Tourism** at 5515 Stanley Ave. (© **800/563-2557;** www.niagarafallstourism.com). Other major tourism offices include **Niagara-on-the-Lake Visitor and Convention Bureau,** 26 Queen St., Courthouse Building, Lower Level, Niagara-on-the-Lake (© **905/468-1950;** www.niagaraonthelake.com); **St. Catharines Tourism Services,** 1932 Welland Canals Pkwy., St. Catharines (© **800/305-5134;** www.stcatharineslock3museum.ca); and **Thorold Lock 7 Information & Viewing Centre,** 50 Chapel St. S., Thorold (© **905/680-9477;** www.thorold.com).

If you are traveling by car, drop in to one of the **Ontario Travel Centres: in Niagara Falls** at 5355 Stanley Ave. (west on Hwy. 420 from the Rainbow Bridge; © **905/358-3221**); in **Fort Erie** at 350 Bertie St., just off the QEW (© **905/871-3505**); or in **St. Catharines** at 251 York Rd., R.R. 4 (westbound QEW at east end of Garden City Skyway; © **905/684-6354**). If you are arriving in the Niagara region along the Queen Elizabeth Way, you can also visit **Gateway Niagara Information Centre** at 424 S. Service Rd., QEW, at Casablanca Blvd., at the Grimsby exit (© **905/945-5444**).

On the American side, the **Niagara Tourism and Convention Corporation** is at 345 Third St., Ste. 605, Niagara Falls, NY (© **800/338-7890** or 716/282-8992; www.niagara-usa.com). Office hours are Monday to Friday from 8:30am to 5pm.

Water Water quality is excellent throughout Ontario and New York State. You can drink the tap water without concern. There has been a move toward getting rid of plastic water bottles because of their impact on the environment, so, although water in bottles is easily available, consider bringing along a refillable metal water bottle.

Wi-Fi See "Internet Access & Wi-Fi," earlier in this section.

Women Travelers Check out the award-winning website **Journeywoman** (www.journeywoman.com), a "real life" women's travel-information network where you can sign up for a free e-mail newsletter and get advice on everything from etiquette and dress to safety.

For general travel resources for women, go to www.frommers.com/planning.

AIRLINE WEBSITES

Air Canada
www.aircanada.com

Air France
www.airfrance.com

Air India
www.airindia.com

Air Jamaica
www.airjamaica.com

Air New Zealand
www.airnewzealand.com

Air Tran
www.airtran.com

Air Wisconsin
www.airwis.com

Alaska Airlines/Horizon Air
www.alaskaair.com

Alitalia
www.alitalia.com

American Airlines
www.aa.com

Atlantic Southeast
www.flyasa.com

British Airways
www.british-airways.com

CanJet Airlines
www.canjet.com

Caribbean Airlines (formerly BWIA)
www.caribbean-airlines.com

Cathay Pacific
www.cathaypacific.com

Continental Airlines
www.continental.com

Cubana
www.cubana.cu

Delta Air Lines
www.delta.com

Directair
www.visitdirectair.com

Emirates Airlines
www.emirates.com

Iberia Airlines
www.iberia.com

Icelandair
www.icelandair.com

Japan Airlines
www.jal.co.jp

Jet Airways
www.jetairways.com

JetBlue Airways
www.jetblue.com

KLM
www.klm.com

Korean Air
www.koreanair.com

Lan Airlines
www.lanchile.com

Lufthansa
www.lufthansa.com

Olympic Airlines
www.olympicairlines.com

Porter Air
www.porter.com

Quantas Airways
www.quantas.com

SAS Scandinavian Airlines
www.flysas.com

Singapore Airlines
www.singaporeair.com

Southwest Airlines
www.southwest.com

Spirit Airlines
www.spiritair.com

Sunwing Airlines
www.flysunwing.com

United Airlines
www.united.com

US Airways
www.usairways.com

WestJet
www.westjet.com

Index

See also Accommodations and Restaurant indexes, below.

General Index

A

Abbott, Francis, 113
Academic trips, 31
Accommodations, 45–68, 228. *See also* Accommodations Index
  accommodations, 67
  best, 3–4, 45–46
  family-friendly, 54
  Niagara Falls, 46–54
  Niagara-on-the-Lake, 54–62
  practical information, 66–68
  prices, 48, 67–68
  reservation services, 68
  Welland Canal Corridor, 65–66
  wine country, 62–65
Aceto Niagara Inc, 219
Acquisitions, 191
Adventure Pass, Niagara Falls, 102
African Lion Safari, 122, 213
After Hours, 198
Air Canada, 221
AirTran Airways, 222
Air travel, 221–223
Americana Conference Resort and Spa, 119
American Airlines, 222
American Falls, 104–105
American Revolution, 13
Amtrak, 224
Amusements, 118–120
Angel Inn, 141
Angel's Gate, 168
Angel's Gate Winery, 192
Angie Strauss Fashions, 189
Angie Strauss Gallery, 185
Anthony Burns Gravesite and Victorian Lawn Cemetery, 115
Antiques and collectibles, 182, 184–185
Antiques of Niagara-on-the-Lake, 185
Aquarium of Niagara, 105–106
Arabella's Pie Social, History Fair, and Antique Road Show, 208
Area codes, 228
Art galleries, 116–117, 185–186
  Hamilton, 213, 214
Art Gallery of Hamilton, 213
Artists' studios, 217–219
Aykroyd, Dan, 167

B

Ball's Falls, 131
Ball's Falls Conservation Area, 134

Bank of Upper Canada, 142
Bartlett House of Antiques, 182
Battlefield House Museum and Park, 213
The Bay, 188
Beamer Memorial Conservation Area, 135
The Beamer Memorial Conservation Area, 130
Beamsville Bench wineries, 148–149, 155–156, 162–165, 168, 169
Beamsville Strawberry Festival, 26
BeauChapeau Hat Shop, 191
Bertie Hall, 115
Between The Lines Family Estate Winery, 168
Bike Train, 132
Biking, 31, 132–136, 227–228
  to Port Colborne from St. Catharines, 206
  rentals, 133
  tours, 137–140
Bird-watching, 28, 129–130, 208
Black Walnut, 134
Blue Barn Antiques & Collectibles, 182
Boating (boat rentals), 130
Books, recommended, 18
Bookstores, 186
Botanical Gardens
  Niagara Parks, 126
  Royal, 215
The Breeze Martini Bar, 200
Brick City, 119, 122
Brock, Sir Isaac, statue of, 12–13
Brockamour Manor, 138
Brock University, 202
Bruce Trail, 29, 34, 65, 126, 133, 135, 171
Buffalo Niagara International Airport, 222, 223
Burgoyne Woods, 127
Business hours, 228
Bus tours, 136–137
Bus travel, 223, 226–227
Butler's Barracks, 108, 138
Butterfly Conservatory, 102–103

C

Café Etc., 200
Calendar of events, 25–27
Canada Day, 27
Canada geese, 126
Canada One Factory Outlets, 179–180
The Canada Store, 190
Canadian National Institute for the Blind (CNIB), 230
Canadian Warplane Heritage Museum, 213–214
Canal Days Marine Heritage Festival, 27, 209
Candy Safari, 141
Capolongo, Bruno, 217
Car travel, 154, 224–226
Casino Niagara, 202

Casinos, 118, 202–203
Cave of the Winds, 105
  original, 106
Cave Spring Cellars, 155
Cecile's Home and Gift Shop, 190
Centre for the Arts, 194, 197
Chapters, 186
Château des Charmes, 156–157
Chez Fromage, 219
CHIC by Jansen, 191
Children, families with, 231
  best activities for, 6–7
  sights and attractions, 121–124
Chippawa Battlefield Park, 106
Chocolate, 110
Chocolates and sweets, 187–188
Cinemas, 202
Clifton Hill, 118
Climate, 24–25
Club Mardi Gras, 200
Club Rendezvous, 200
Club Rialto, 197
Colaneri Estate Winery, 23, 168–169
Coles, 186
Comair/Delta Connection, 222
Comedy club, 197
Conservation areas, 135–136
Continental, 222
Cooking classes, 85
CopaCabana's Brazilian Steak House, 197
The Copper Leaf, 190
Cosmic Coaster, 119
The Courthouse, 142
The Court House Theatre, 194
Cows, 187
Credit cards, 235
Creek Shores wineries, 149
Cross-country skiing, 130–131
The Crossing, 115
Crush on Niagara, 152
Cultural preservation, 12–13
Currency, 234
Customs regulations, 229–230

D

Dan Aykroyd wines, 167
Dance clubs and lounges, 197–198
Daniel Lenko Estate Winery, 162
Daredevil stunts, 120
DeCou House, 209
Dee Building, 141
Delta, 222
Department stores, 188
Dining, 20–21, 69–96, 154. *See also* Restaurant Index
  best, 4–5, 69–70
  by cuisine, 94–96
  falls-view, 77
  Fonthill, 92
  Hamilton, 216
  high tea, 81
  Niagara Falls, 70–78

Accommodations

Restaurants

NOTES